fushigi yûgi™

The Mysterious Play
VOL. 5: RIVAL

Story & Art By
YUU WATASE

FUSHIGI YÛGI
THE MYSTERIOUS PLAY
VOL. 5: RIVAL
SHÔJO EDITION

This volume contains the FUSHIGI YÛGI installments from Animerica Extra Vol. 3, No. 11 through Vol. 4, No. 5, in their entirety.

STORY AND ART BY YUU WATASE

English Adaptation/Yuji Oniki
Translation Assist/Kaori Kawakubo Inoue
Touch-up Art & Lettering/Andy Ristaino
Design/Hidemi Sahara
First Edition Editor/William Flanagan
Shôjo Edition Editor/Yuki Takagaki

Managing Editor/Megan Bates
Editorial Director/Elizabeth Kawasaki
Editor in Chief/Alvin Lu
Sr. Director of Acquisitions/Rika Inouye
Sr. VP of Marketing/Liza Coppola
Exec. VP of Sales & Marketing/John Easum
Publisher/Hyoe Narita

Printed in Canada

Published by VIZ Media, LLC
P.O. Box 77010
San Francisco, CA 94107

Shôjo Edition
10 9 8 7 6 5 4 3
First printing, December 2004
Second printing, April 2005
Third printing, August 2006
First English edition published September 2001

GRAPHIC
NOVEL
F
vol. 5

VIZ
MEDIA™

www.viz.com
store.viz.com

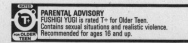

CONTENTS

STORY THUS FAR

Fifteen-year-old Miaka and her best friend Yui are physically drawn into the world of a strange book—*THE UNIVERSE OF THE FOUR GODS*. Miaka is offered the role of the lead character, the Priestess of the god Suzaku, and is charged with gathering the seven Celestial Warriors of Suzaku who will help her save the nation of Hong-Nan, and in the process grant her any wish she wants. She has already found six warriors: Tamahome, Hotohori, Nuriko, Chichiri, Tasuki and Mitsukake.

Yui's fate is much crueler than Miaka's. Upon entering the book, Yui suffers rape and manipulation, which drive her to attempt suicide. Now, Yui has become the Priestess of the god Seiryu, the enemy of Suzaku and Miaka.

Miaka's true love, Tamahome, willingly becomes Yui's prisoner to avert a war between Qu-Dong and the weaker Hong-Nan. Meanwhile, Miaka sets off on a journey with Hotohori and Nuriko to find the other Celestial Warriors, and now, only Chiriko remains to be found before the warriors can rescue Tamahome. But even if they find the seventh warrior, will vengeful Yui let Tamahome go?

THE UNIVERSE OF THE FOUR GODS is based on ancient Chinese legend, but Japanese pronunciation of Chinese names differs slightly from their Chinese equivalents. Here is a short glossary of the Japanese pronunciation of the Chinese names in this graphic novel:

CHINESE	JAPANESE	PERSON OR PLACE	MEANING
Hong-Nan	Kônan	Southern Kingdom	Crimson South
Qu-Dong	Kutô	Eastern Kingdom	Gathered East
Changhung	Chôkô	A Northern Town	Expansive Place
Zhong-Rong	Chûei	Second Son	Loyalty & Honor
Chun-Jing	Shunkei	Third Son	Spring & Respect
Yu-Lun	Gyokuran	Eldest Daughter	Jewel & Orchid
Jie-Lian	Yuiren	Youngest Daughter	Connection & Lotus
Diedu	Kodoku	A Potion	Seduction Potion

No da: An emphatic. A verbal exclamation point placed at the end of a sentence or phrase.

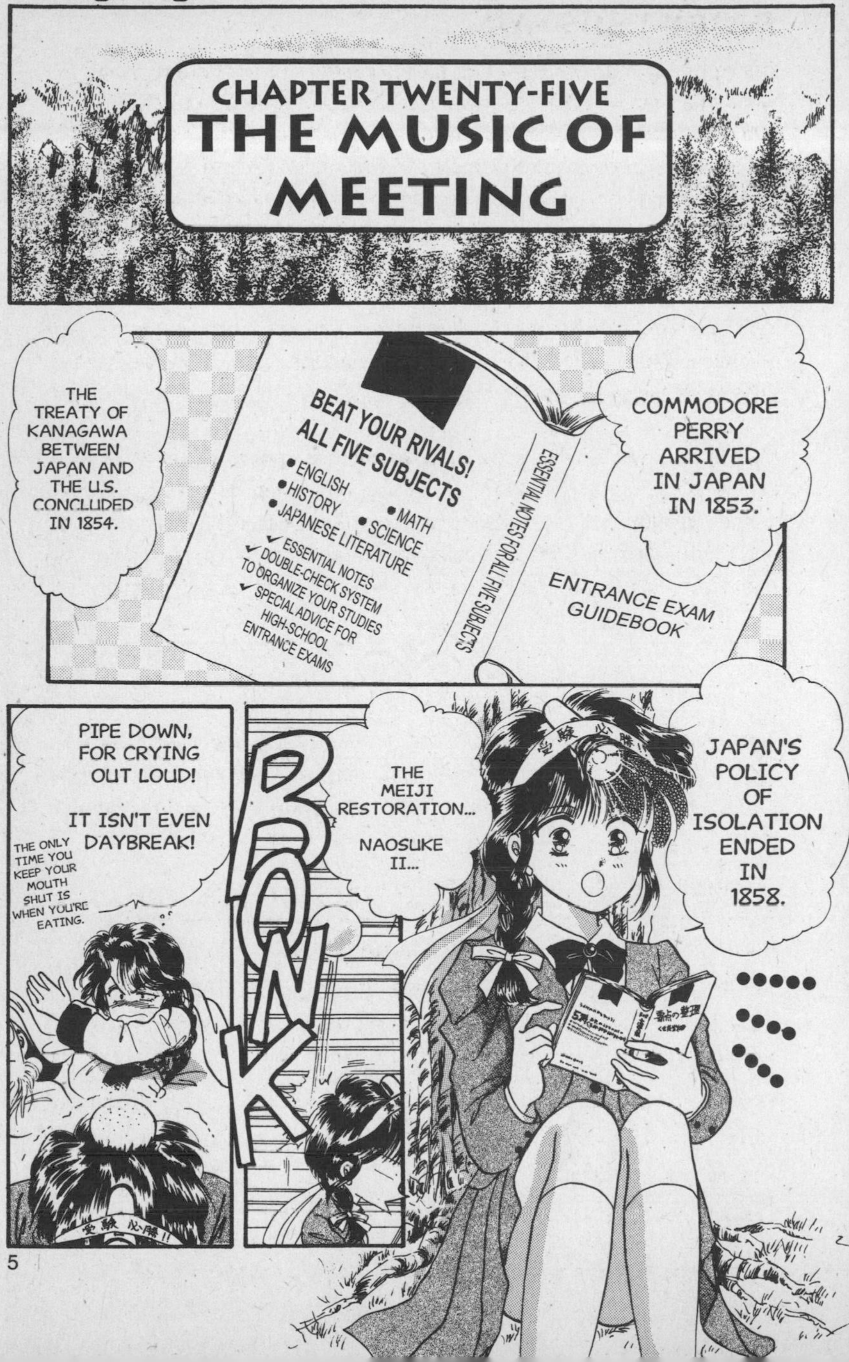
CHAPTER TWENTY-FIVE
THE MUSIC OF MEETING
COMMODORE PERRY ARRIVED IN JAPAN IN 1853.
THE TREATY OF KANAGAWA BETWEEN JAPAN AND THE U.S. CONCLUDED IN 1854.
ENTRANCE EXAM GUIDEBOOK
ESSENTIAL NOTES FOR ALL FIVE SUBJECTS
BEAT YOUR RIVALS! ALL FIVE SUBJECTS
• ENGLISH • MATH
• HISTORY • SCIENCE
• JAPANESE LITERATURE
✔ ESSENTIAL NOTES
✔ DOUBLE-CHECK SYSTEM TO ORGANIZE YOUR STUDIES
✔ SPECIAL ADVICE FOR HIGH-SCHOOL ENTRANCE EXAMS
JAPAN'S POLICY OF ISOLATION ENDED IN 1858.
THE MEIJI RESTORATION... NAOSUKE II...
.....
....
....
BONK
PIPE DOWN, FOR CRYING OUT LOUD!
IT ISN'T EVEN DAYBREAK!
THE ONLY TIME YOU KEEP YOUR MOUTH SHUT IS WHEN YOU'RE EATING.

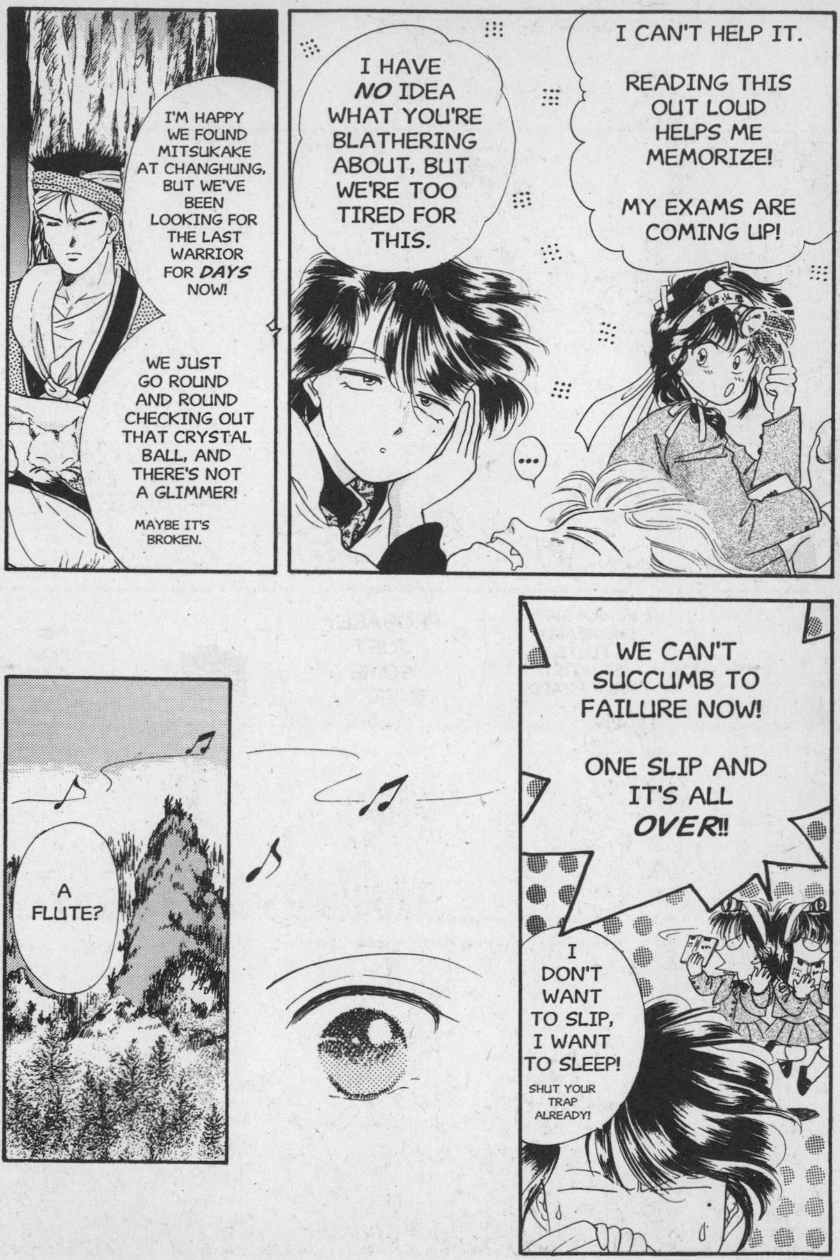
I CAN'T HELP IT.
READING THIS OUT LOUD HELPS ME MEMORIZE!
MY EXAMS ARE COMING UP!
I HAVE NO IDEA WHAT YOU'RE BLATHERING ABOUT, BUT WE'RE TOO TIRED FOR THIS.
...
I'M HAPPY WE FOUND MITSUKAKE AT CHANGHUNG, BUT WE'VE BEEN LOOKING FOR THE LAST WARRIOR FOR DAYS NOW!
WE JUST GO ROUND AND ROUND CHECKING OUT THAT CRYSTAL BALL, AND THERE'S NOT A GLIMMER!
MAYBE IT'S BROKEN.
WE CAN'T SUCCUMB TO FAILURE NOW!
ONE SLIP AND IT'S ALL OVER!!
I DON'T WANT TO SLIP, I WANT TO SLEEP!
SHUT YOUR TRAP ALREADY!
A FLUTE?

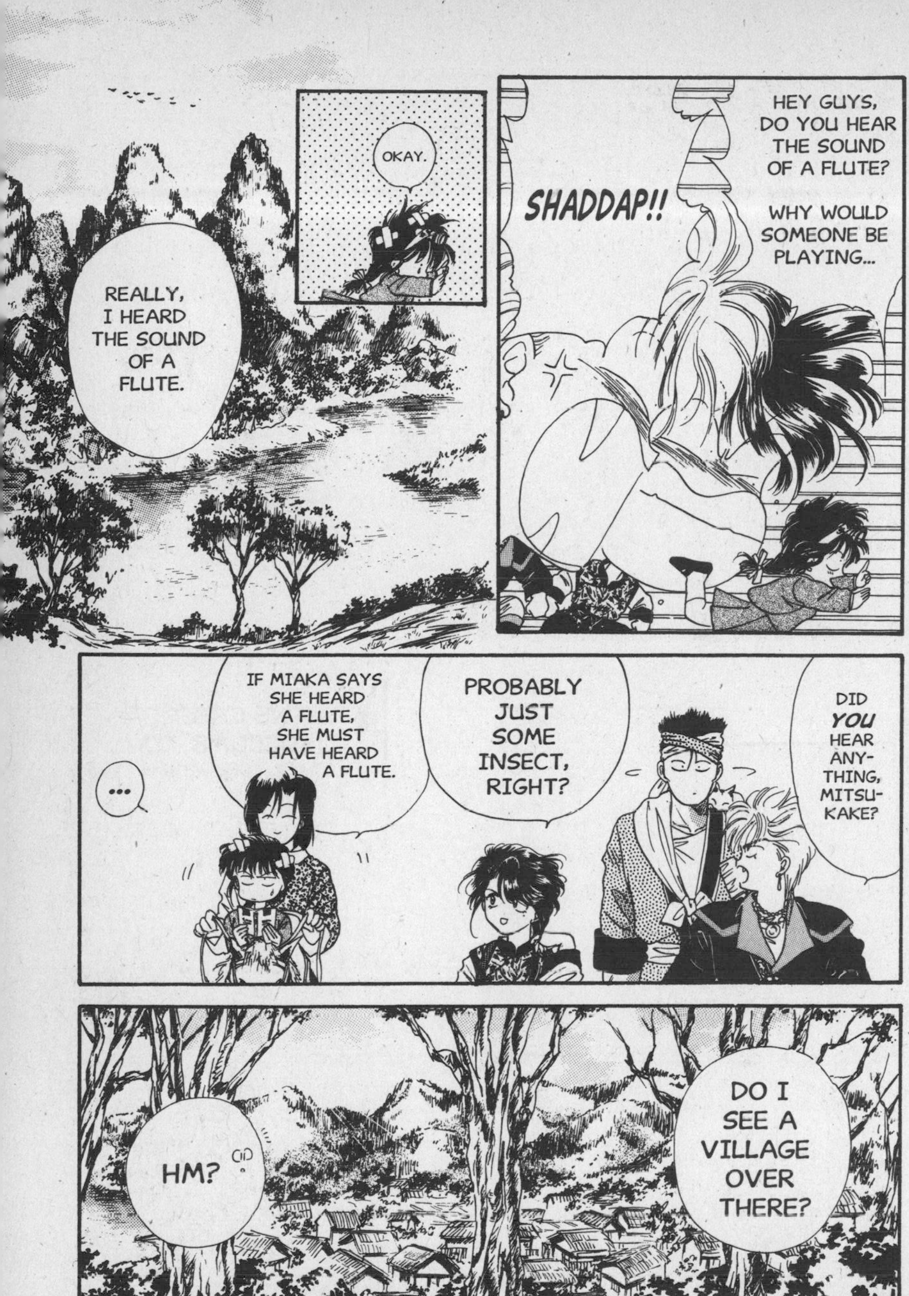
HEY GUYS, DO YOU HEAR THE SOUND OF A FLUTE?
WHY WOULD SOMEONE BE PLAYING...
SHADDAP!!
OKAY.
REALLY, I HEARD THE SOUND OF A FLUTE.
DID *YOU* HEAR ANY-THING, MITSU-KAKE?
PROBABLY JUST SOME INSECT, RIGHT?
IF MIAKA SAYS SHE HEARD A FLUTE, SHE MUST HAVE HEARD A FLUTE.
...
DO I SEE A VILLAGE OVER THERE?
HM?

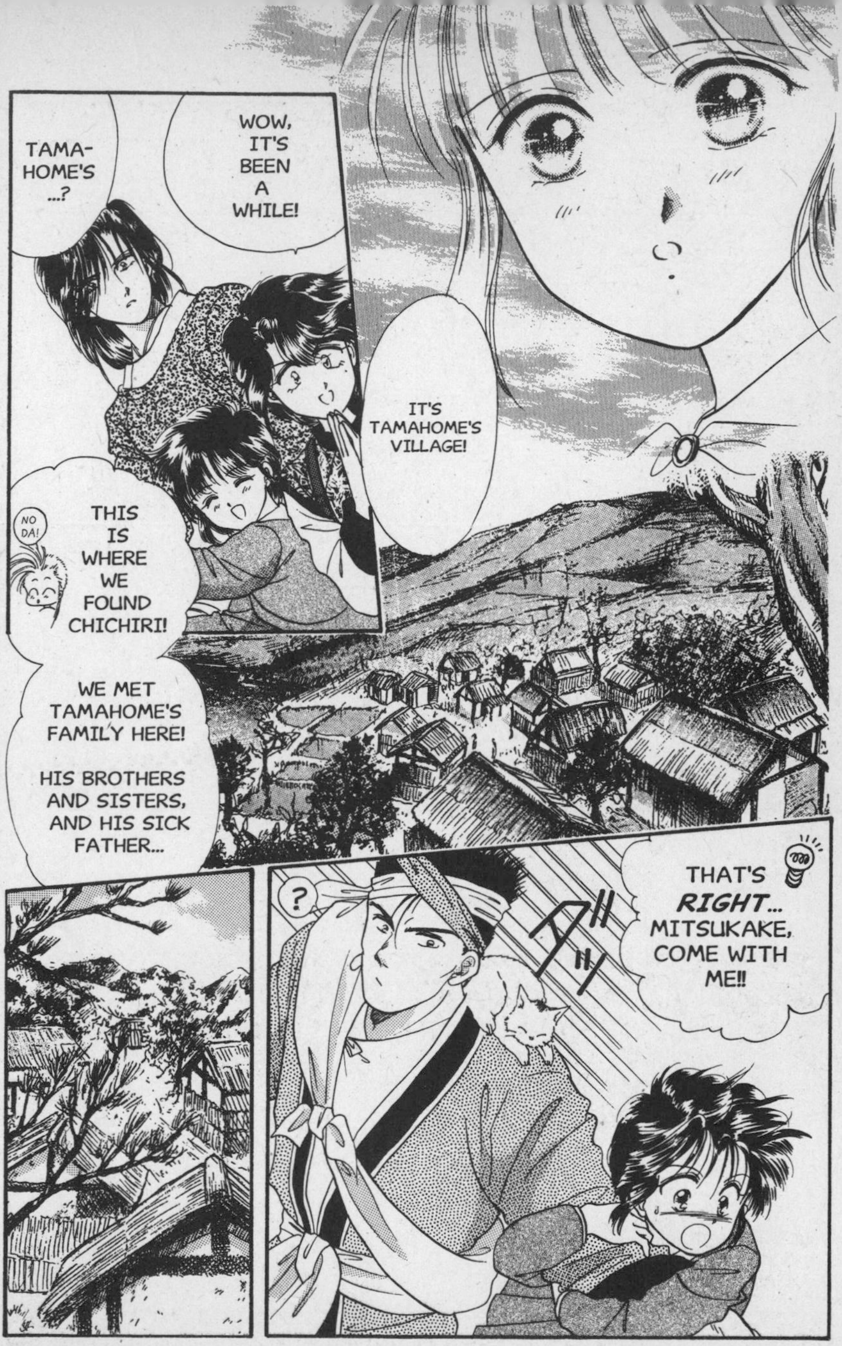
IT'S TAMAHOME'S VILLAGE!
WOW, IT'S BEEN A WHILE!
TAMA-HOME'S ...?
THIS IS WHERE WE FOUND CHICHIRI!
NO DA!
WE MET TAMAHOME'S FAMILY HERE!
HIS BROTHERS AND SISTERS, AND HIS SICK FATHER...
?
THAT'S ***RIGHT***... MITSUKAKE, COME WITH ME!!

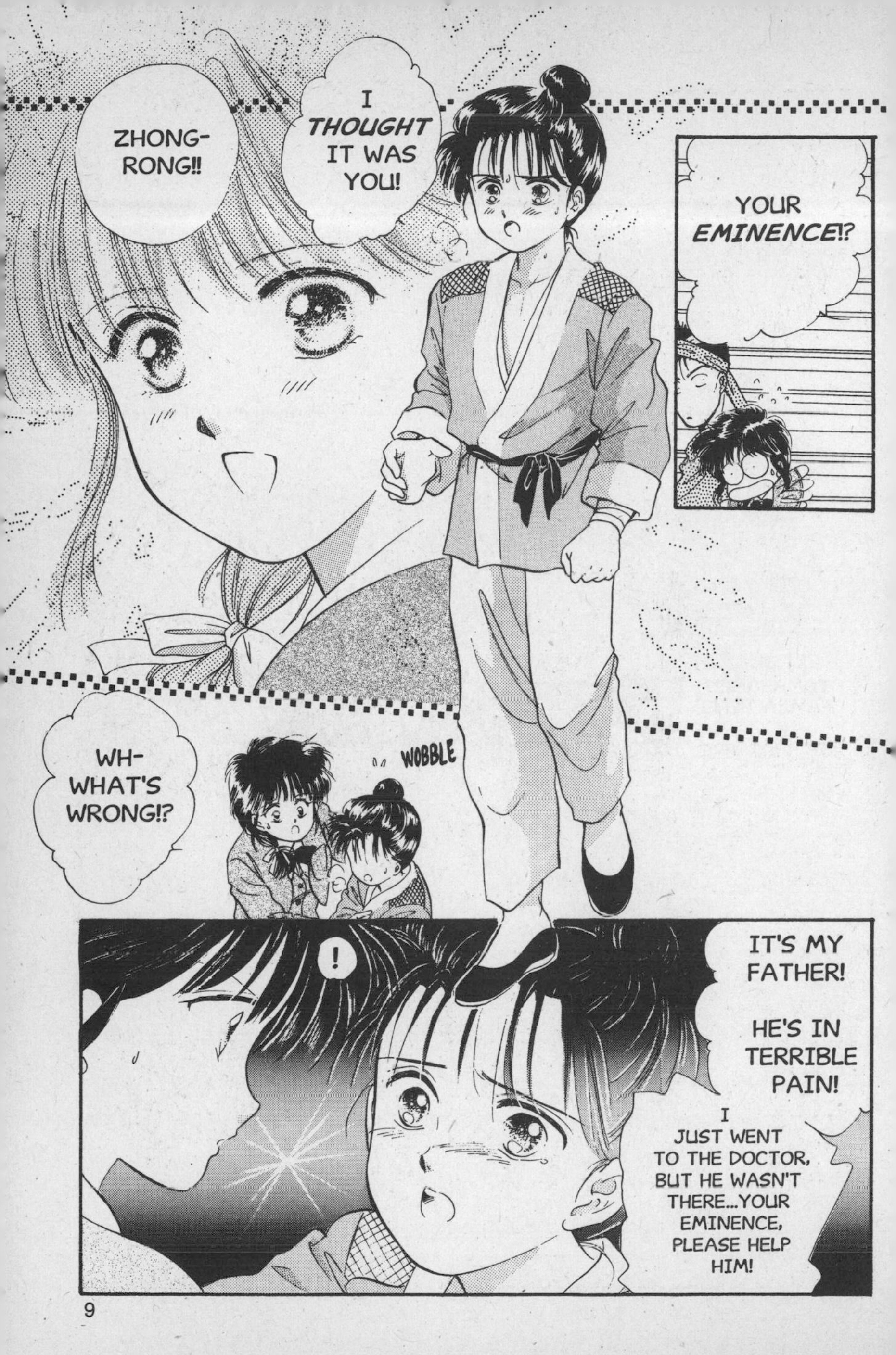
YOUR *EMINENCE*!?
I *THOUGHT* IT WAS YOU!
ZHONG-RONG!!
WOBBLE
WH- WHAT'S WRONG!?
!
IT'S MY FATHER!
HE'S IN TERRIBLE PAIN!
I JUST WENT TO THE DOCTOR, BUT HE WASN'T THERE...YOUR EMINENCE, PLEASE HELP HIM!

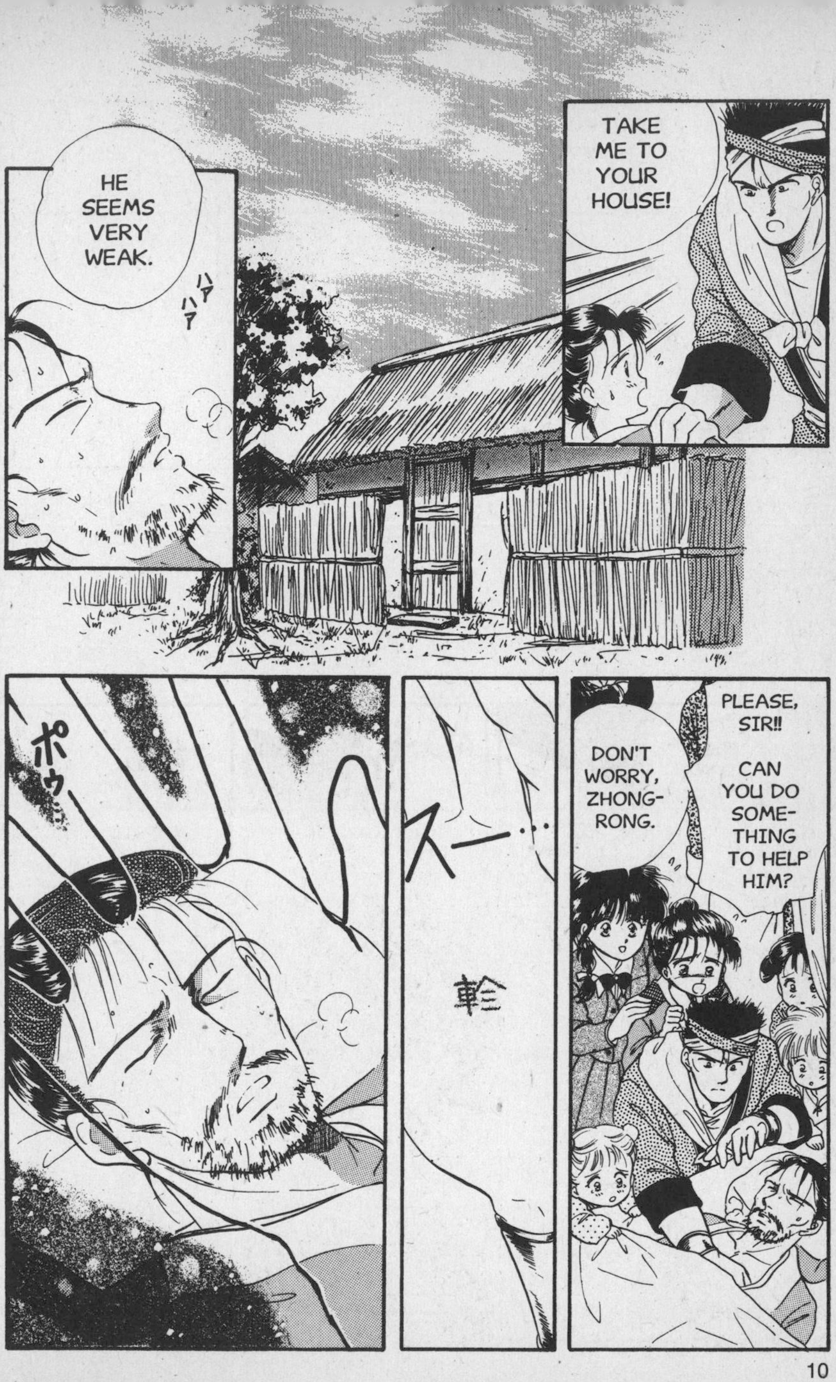
TAKE ME TO YOUR HOUSE!
HE SEEMS VERY WEAK.
ハァハァ
PLEASE, SIR!!
CAN YOU DO SOMETHING TO HELP HIM?
DON'T WORRY, ZHONG-RONG.
スー…
ポウッ

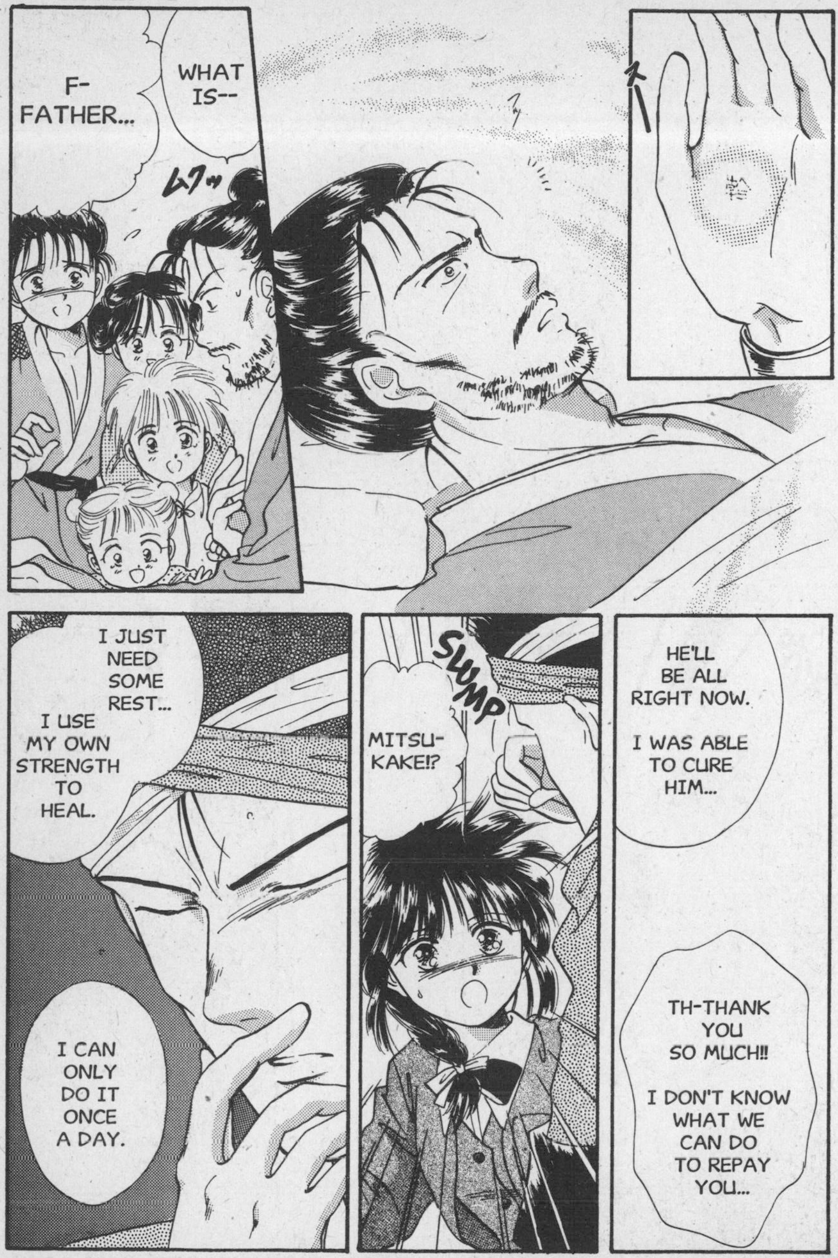
WHAT IS--
F-FATHER...
ムクッ
HE'LL BE ALL RIGHT NOW.
I WAS ABLE TO CURE HIM...
TH-THANK YOU SO MUCH!!
I DON'T KNOW WHAT WE CAN DO TO REPAY YOU...
SLUMP
MITSU-KAKE!?
I JUST NEED SOME REST...
I USE MY OWN STRENGTH TO HEAL.
I CAN ONLY DO IT ONCE A DAY.

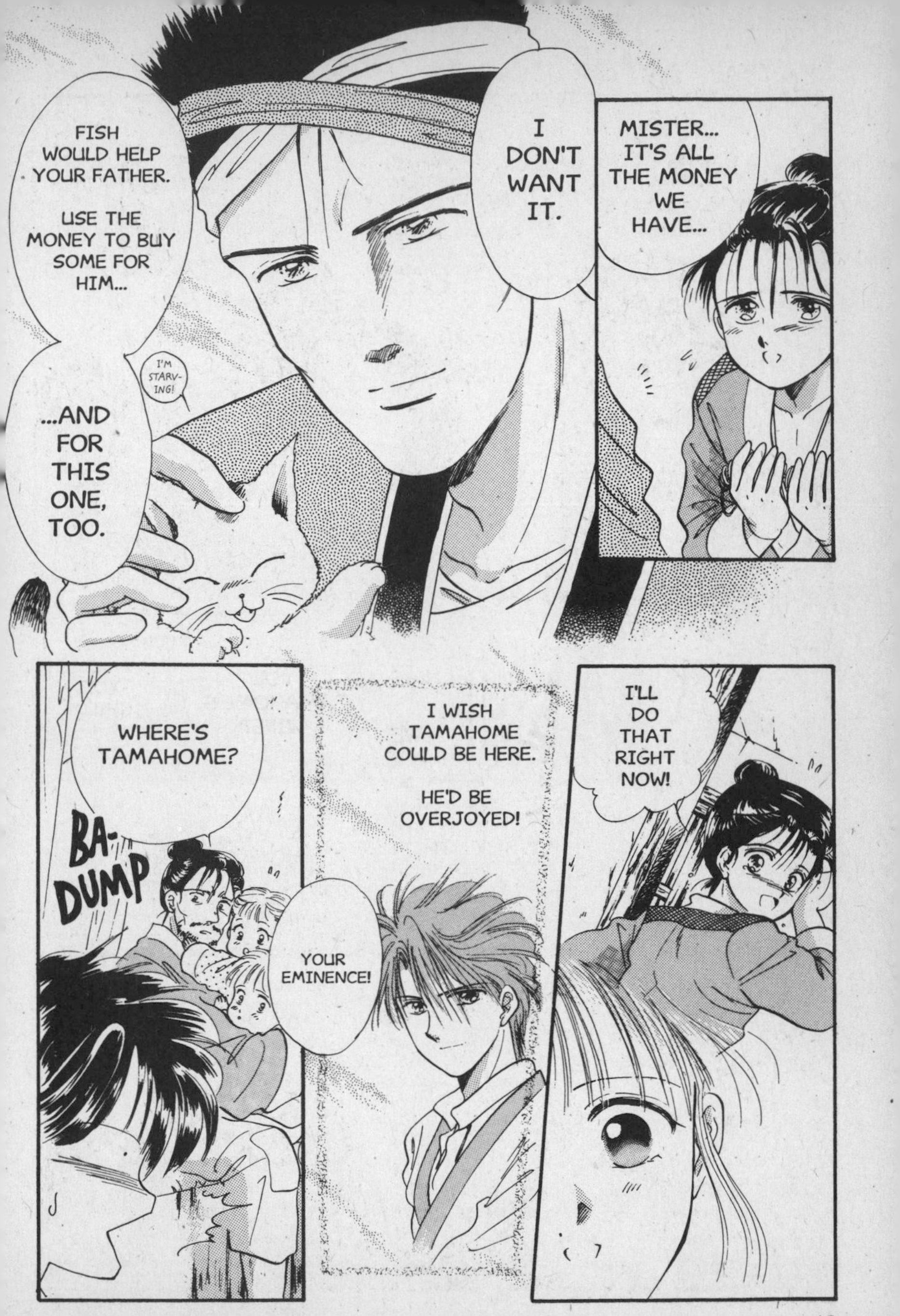
MISTER... IT'S ALL THE MONEY WE HAVE...
I DON'T WANT IT.
FISH WOULD HELP YOUR FATHER.
USE THE MONEY TO BUY SOME FOR HIM...
...AND FOR THIS ONE, TOO.
I'M STARVING!
I'LL DO THAT RIGHT NOW!
I WISH TAMAHOME COULD BE HERE.
HE'D BE OVERJOYED!
YOUR EMINENCE!
WHERE'S TAMAHOME?
BA-DUMP

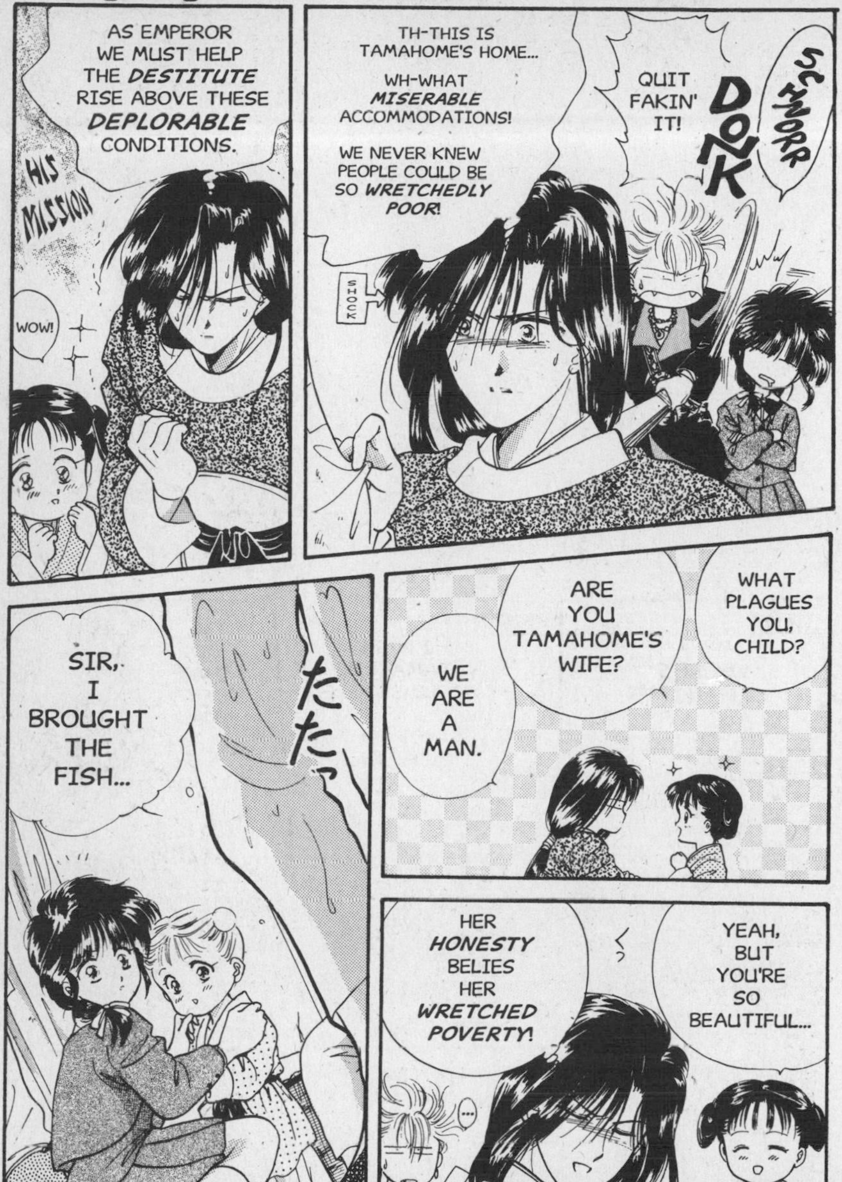
TH-THIS IS TAMAHOME'S HOME...
WH-WHAT *MISERABLE* ACCOMMODATIONS!
WE NEVER KNEW PEOPLE COULD BE SO *WRETCHEDLY POOR*!
QUIT FAKIN' IT!
SCHWORR
DONK
SHOCK
AS EMPEROR WE MUST HELP THE *DESTITUTE* RISE ABOVE THESE *DEPLORABLE* CONDITIONS.
HIS MISSION
WOW!
WHAT PLAGUES YOU, CHILD?
ARE YOU TAMAHOME'S WIFE?
WE ARE A MAN.
YEAH, BUT YOU'RE SO BEAUTIFUL...
くっ
HER *HONESTY* BELIES HER *WRETCHED POVERTY*!
...
SIR, I BROUGHT THE FISH...
たたっ

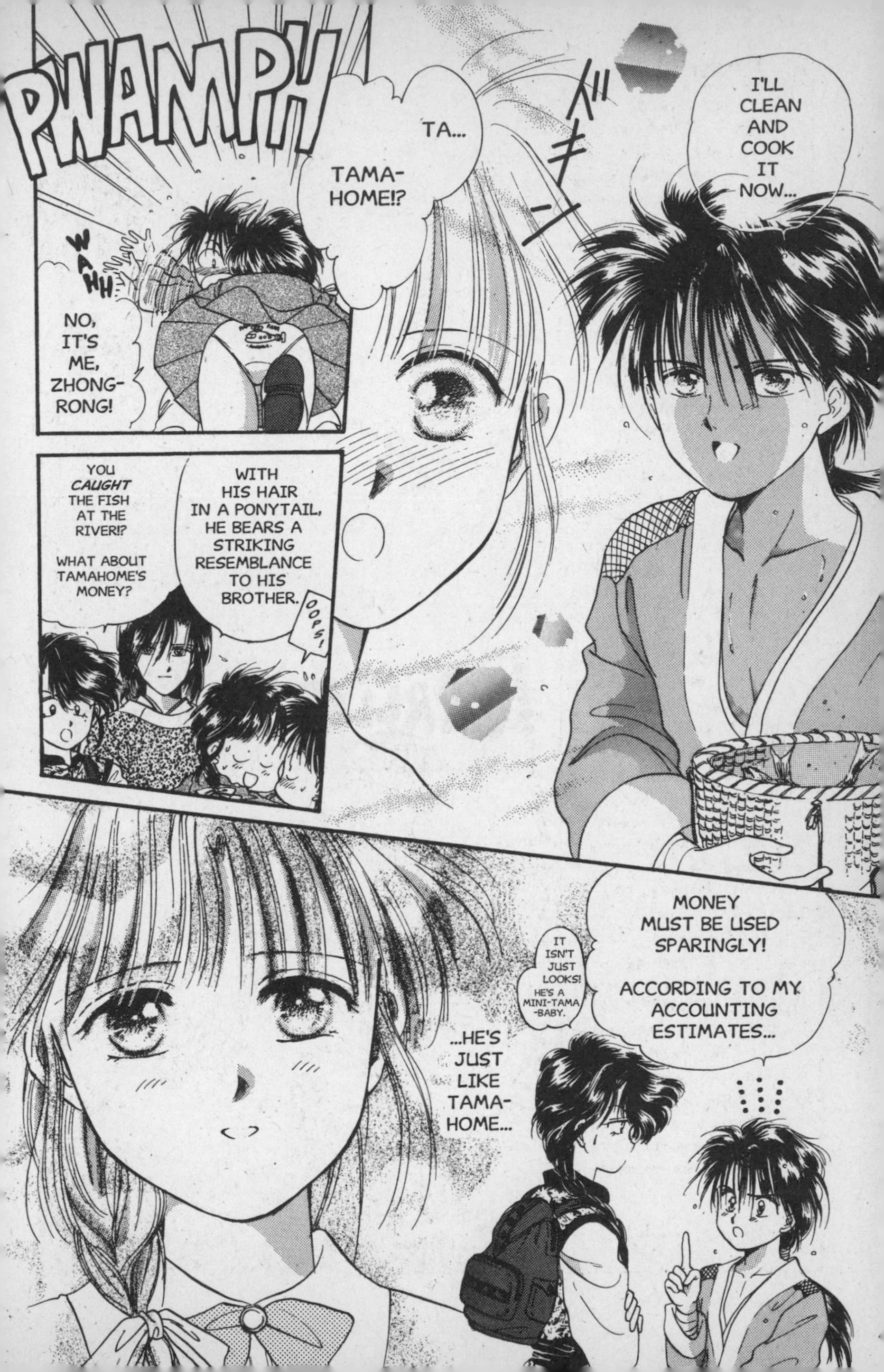

I'LL CLEAN AND COOK IT NOW...
TA...
TAMA-HOME!?
PWAMPH
WAHH
NO, IT'S ME, ZHONG-RONG!
WITH HIS HAIR IN A PONYTAIL, HE BEARS A STRIKING RESEMBLANCE TO HIS BROTHER.
YOU *CAUGHT* THE FISH AT THE RIVER!?
WHAT ABOUT TAMAHOME'S MONEY?
OOPS!
MONEY MUST BE USED SPARINGLY!
ACCORDING TO MY ACCOUNTING ESTIMATES...
IT ISN'T JUST LOOKS! HE'S A MINI-TAMA-BABY.
...HE'S JUST LIKE TAMA-HOME...

Rival

Hi, it's me Yū. I'm watching "The Game City" on TV right now. In other words, it's one in the morning. I love this show because they introduce a lot of games! I want to play the Turbo version of Street Fighter II. During my visit back home last year for New Year's, I went to the game center and completely revived my enthusiasm for games!! So I bought a Super Famicom unit (a little late I know), and borrowed Street Fighter II from my cousin ♂ and totally got into it. But the Street Fighter II at the game center is Turbo and more moves, so it's more fun. By the way, the only character I can play is Chun Lee. (sob sob) I'm sure that anyone not familiar with the game doesn't have a clue as to what I'm talking about. ♪ So for your sake, I'll just talk about my visit back home. I think. But you know, I love having a game console. "The Game City" was still broadcasting the commercial for Street Fighter II (which I mentioned in one of my earlier chat sections) so I just had to tape it. (They're not showing it anymore, though). I didn't know that the person playing Chun Lee in that commercial was the "Kiss Me" Miki Nagano. She did a total image overhaul! Now then—In December 1992, I went back home. There I met up with several friends, but I took my work with me, so I wasn't able to relax at all.

SIGH — 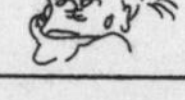

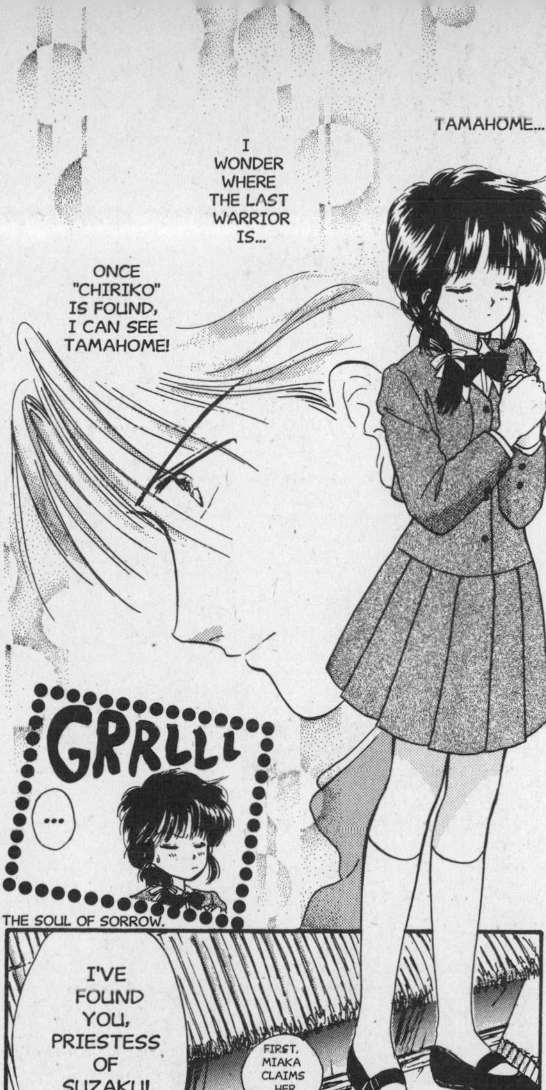
TAMAHOME...
I WONDER WHERE THE LAST WARRIOR IS...
ONCE "CHIRIKO" IS FOUND, I CAN SEE TAMAHOME!
GRRLLL
...
THE SOUL OF SORROW.
I'VE FOUND YOU, PRIESTESS OF SUZAKU!
FIRST, MIAKA CLAIMS HER FISH!
I'M COMING! ♪

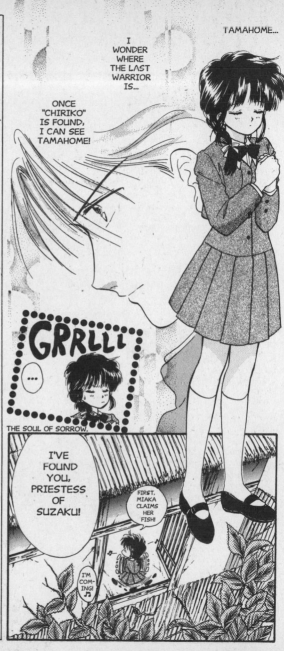

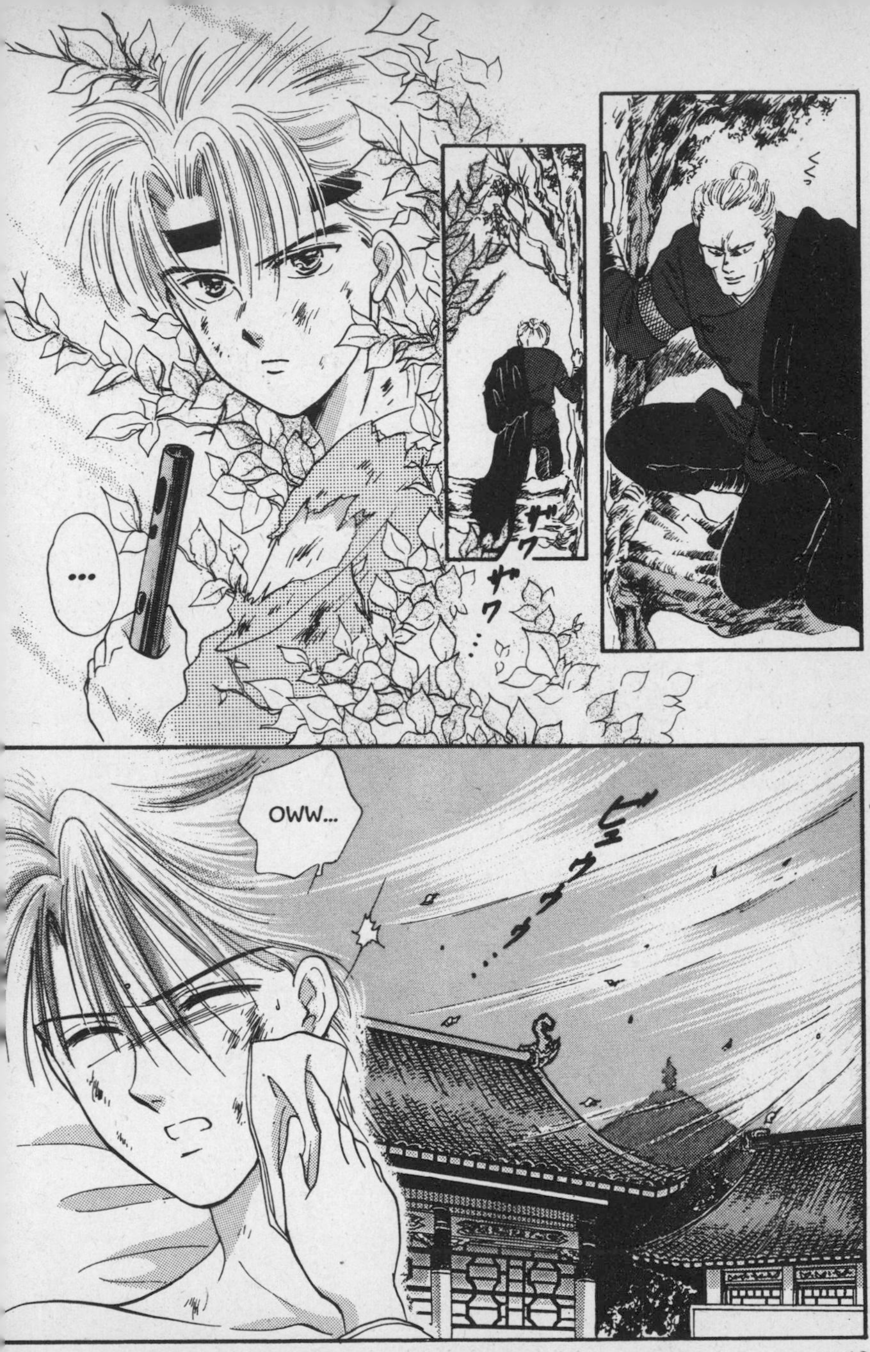
ザワ
ザワ…
...
OWW...
ビュウウウ…

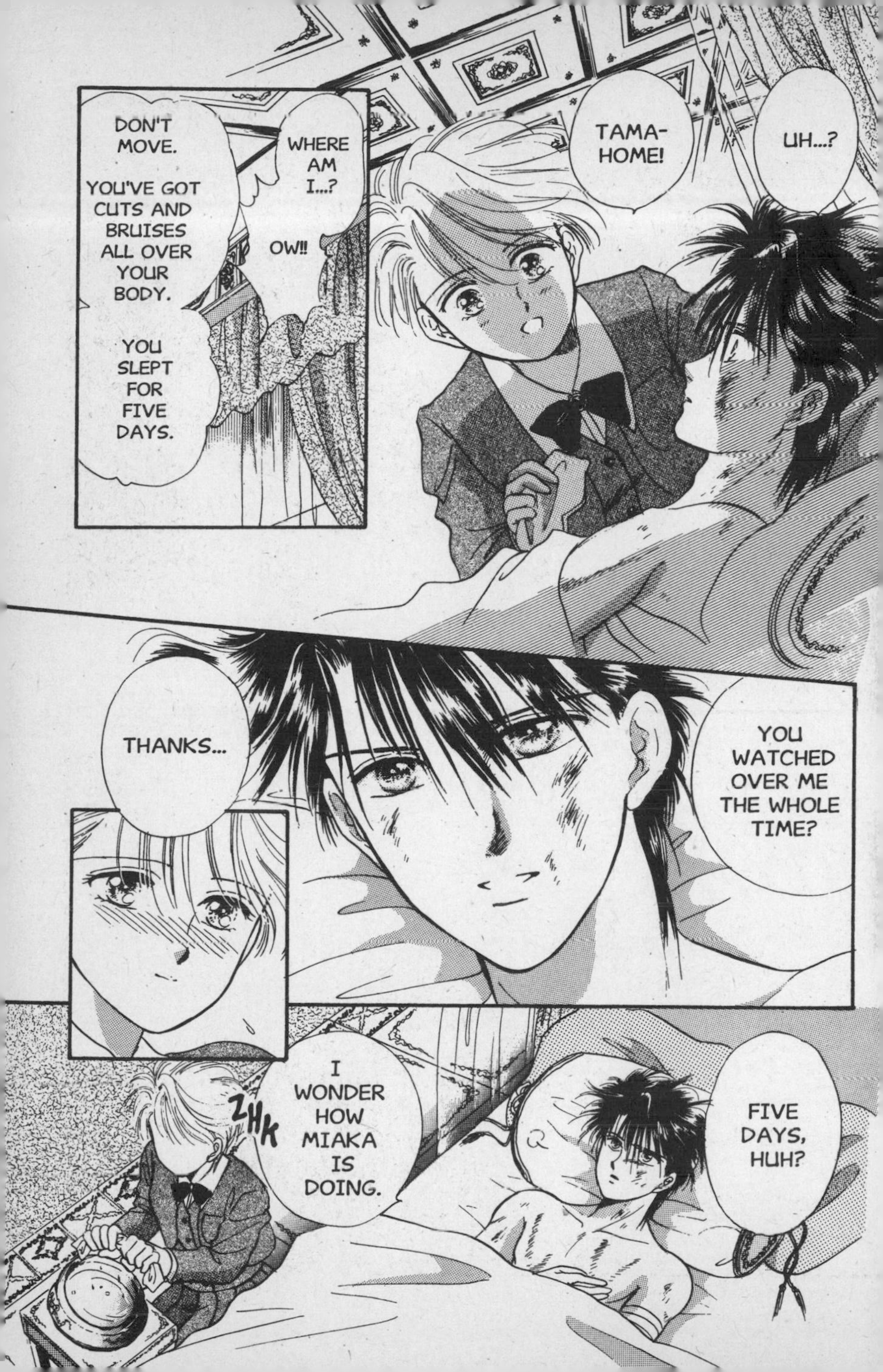
UH...?
TAMA-HOME!
WHERE AM I...?
OW!!
DON'T MOVE.
YOU'VE GOT CUTS AND BRUISES ALL OVER YOUR BODY.
YOU SLEPT FOR FIVE DAYS.
YOU WATCHED OVER ME THE WHOLE TIME?
THANKS...
FIVE DAYS, HUH?
I WONDER HOW MIAKA IS DOING.
ZHK

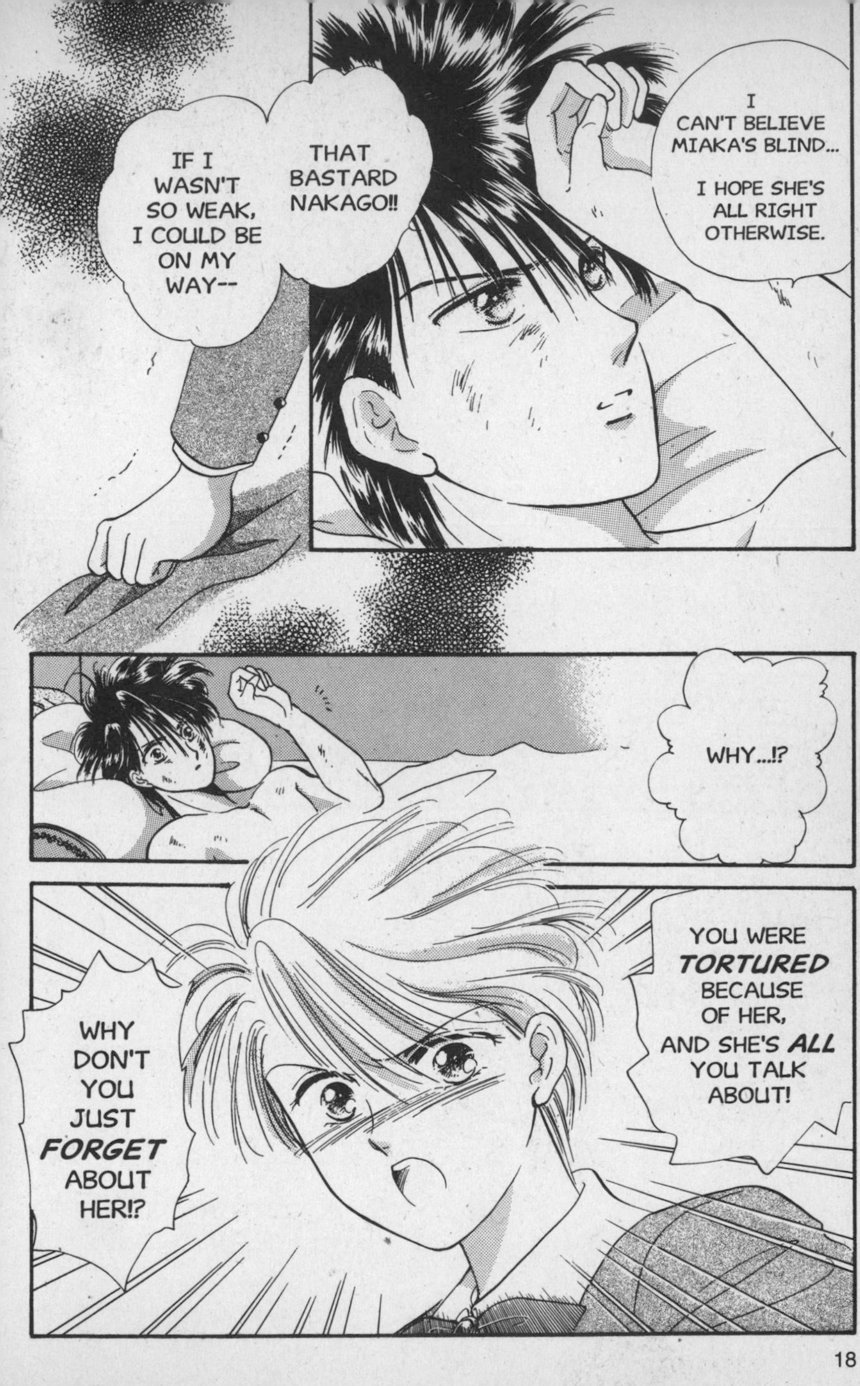
I CAN'T BELIEVE MIAKA'S BLIND...
I HOPE SHE'S ALL RIGHT OTHERWISE.
THAT BASTARD NAKAGO!!
IF I WASN'T SO WEAK, I COULD BE ON MY WAY--
WHY...!?
YOU WERE *TORTURED* BECAUSE OF HER, AND SHE'S *ALL* YOU TALK ABOUT!
WHY DON'T YOU JUST *FORGET* ABOUT HER!?

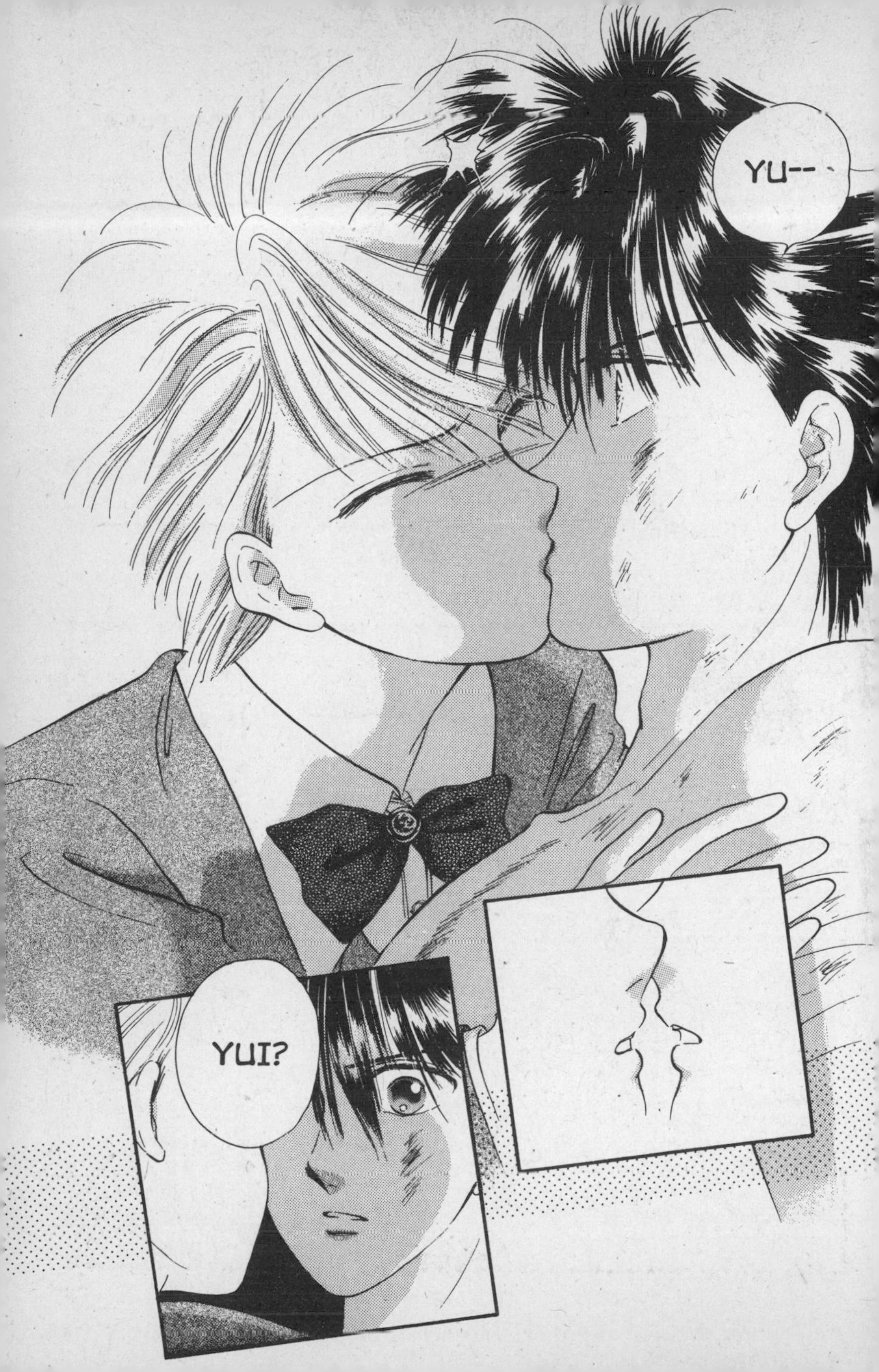
YU--
YUI?

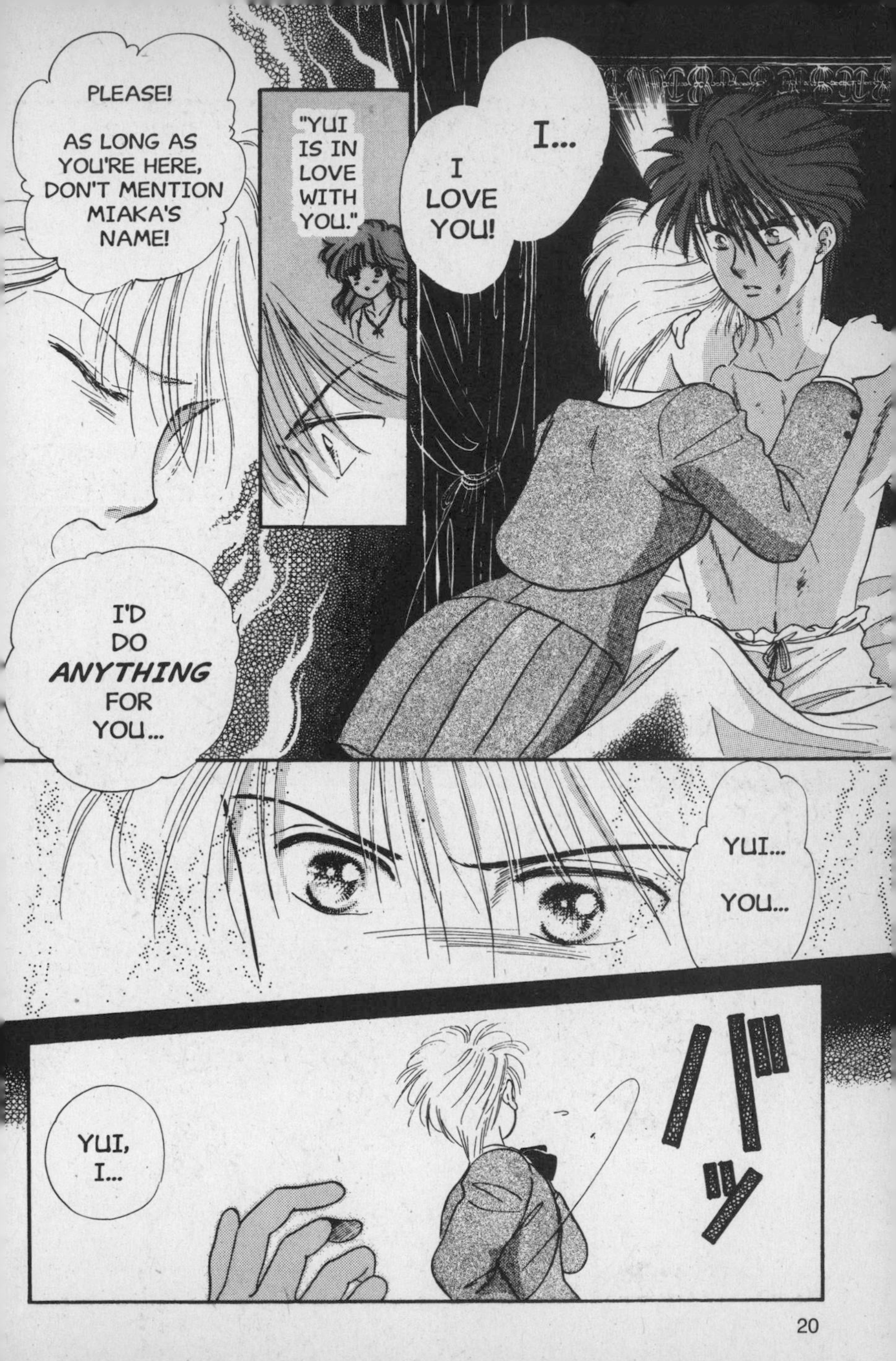
I...
I LOVE YOU!
"YUI IS IN LOVE WITH YOU."
PLEASE!
AS LONG AS YOU'RE HERE, DON'T MENTION MIAKA'S NAME!
I'D DO *ANYTHING* FOR YOU...
YUI...
YOU...
バッ
YUI, I...

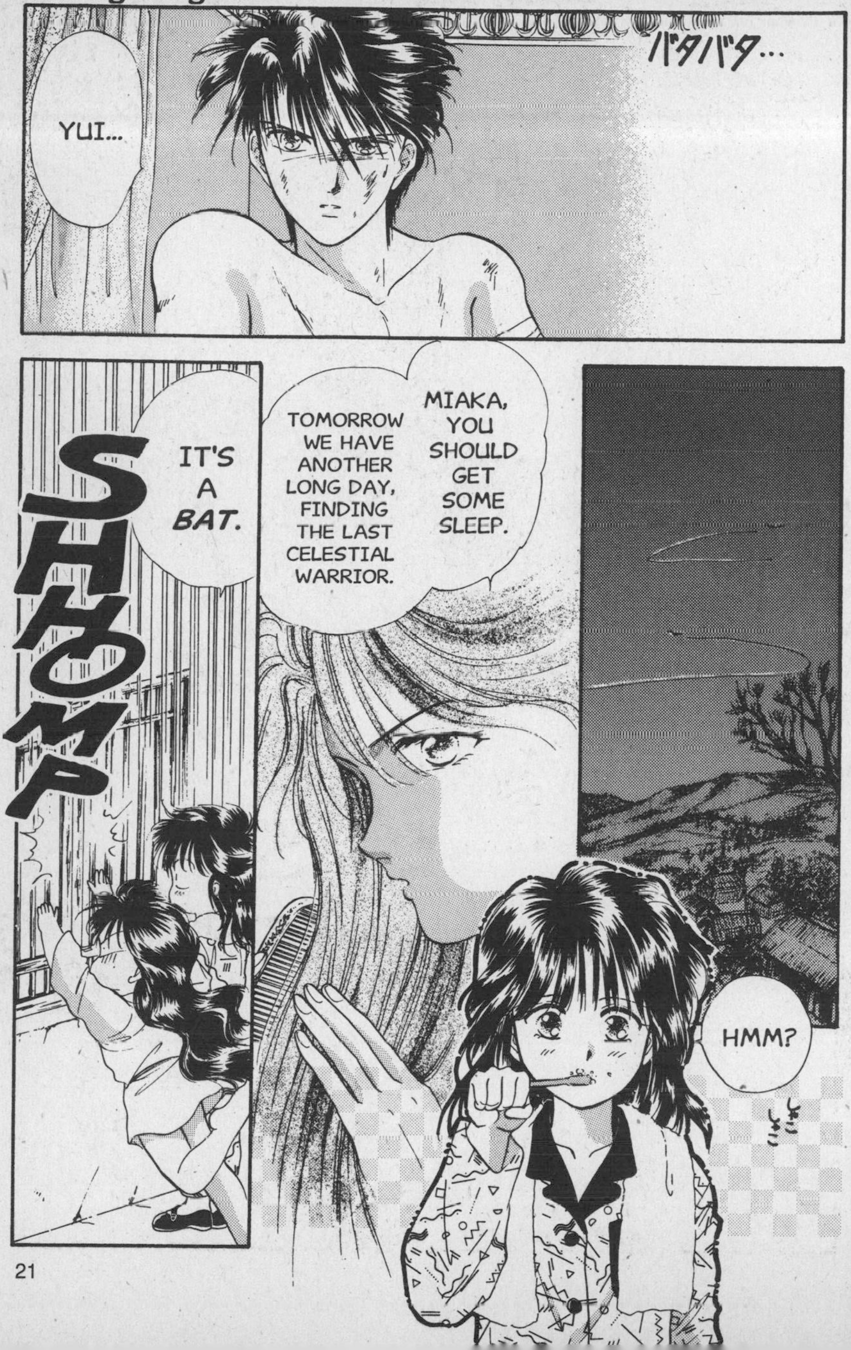
バタバタ…
YUI...
MIAKA, YOU SHOULD GET SOME SLEEP.
TOMORROW WE HAVE ANOTHER LONG DAY, FINDING THE LAST CELESTIAL WARRIOR.
HMM?
IT'S A *BAT.*
SHOMP

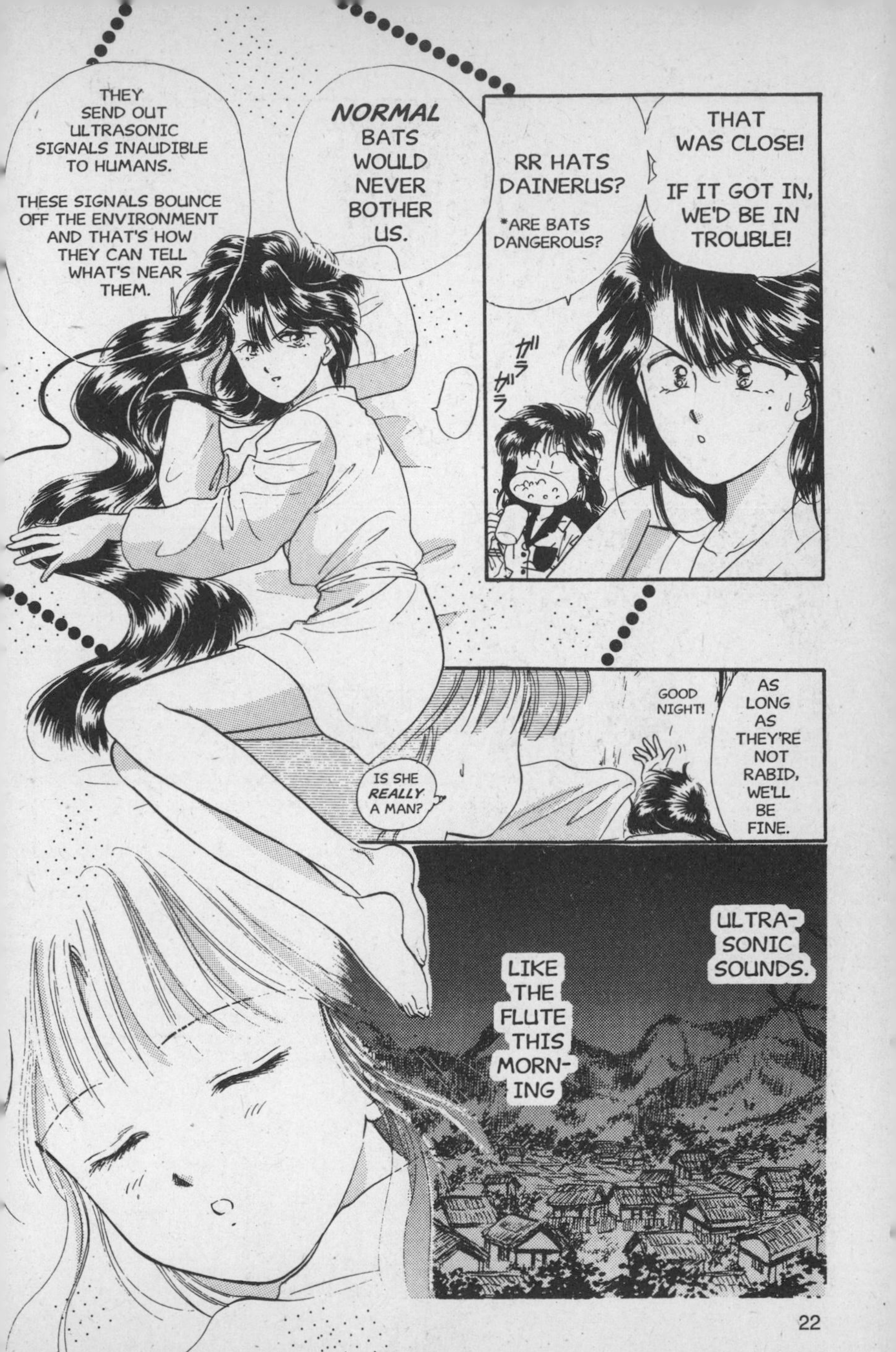
THAT WAS CLOSE!
IF IT GOT IN, WE'D BE IN TROUBLE!
RR HATS DAINERUS?
*ARE BATS DANGEROUS?
ガラ ガラ
NORMAL BATS WOULD NEVER BOTHER US.
THEY SEND OUT ULTRASONIC SIGNALS INAUDIBLE TO HUMANS.
THESE SIGNALS BOUNCE OFF THE ENVIRONMENT AND THAT'S HOW THEY CAN TELL WHAT'S NEAR THEM.
...
AS LONG AS THEY'RE NOT RABID, WE'LL BE FINE.
GOOD NIGHT!
IS SHE REALLY A MAN?
ULTRA-SONIC SOUNDS.
LIKE THE FLUTE THIS MORN-ING

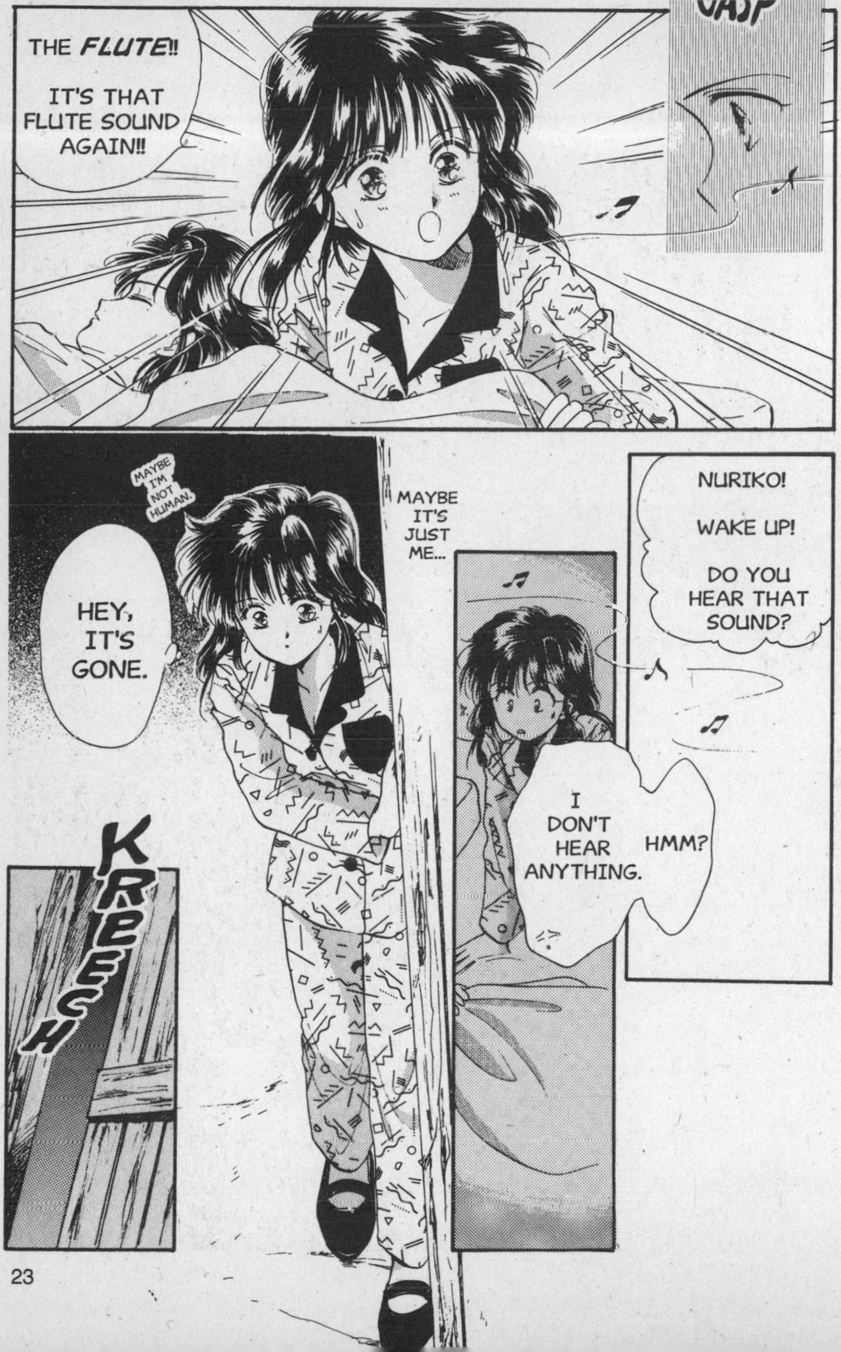
GASP
THE FLUTE!!
IT'S THAT FLUTE SOUND AGAIN!!
NURIKO!
WAKE UP!
DO YOU HEAR THAT SOUND?
HMM?
I DON'T HEAR ANYTHING.
MAYBE IT'S JUST ME...
MAYBE I'M NOT HUMAN.
HEY, IT'S GONE.
KREECH

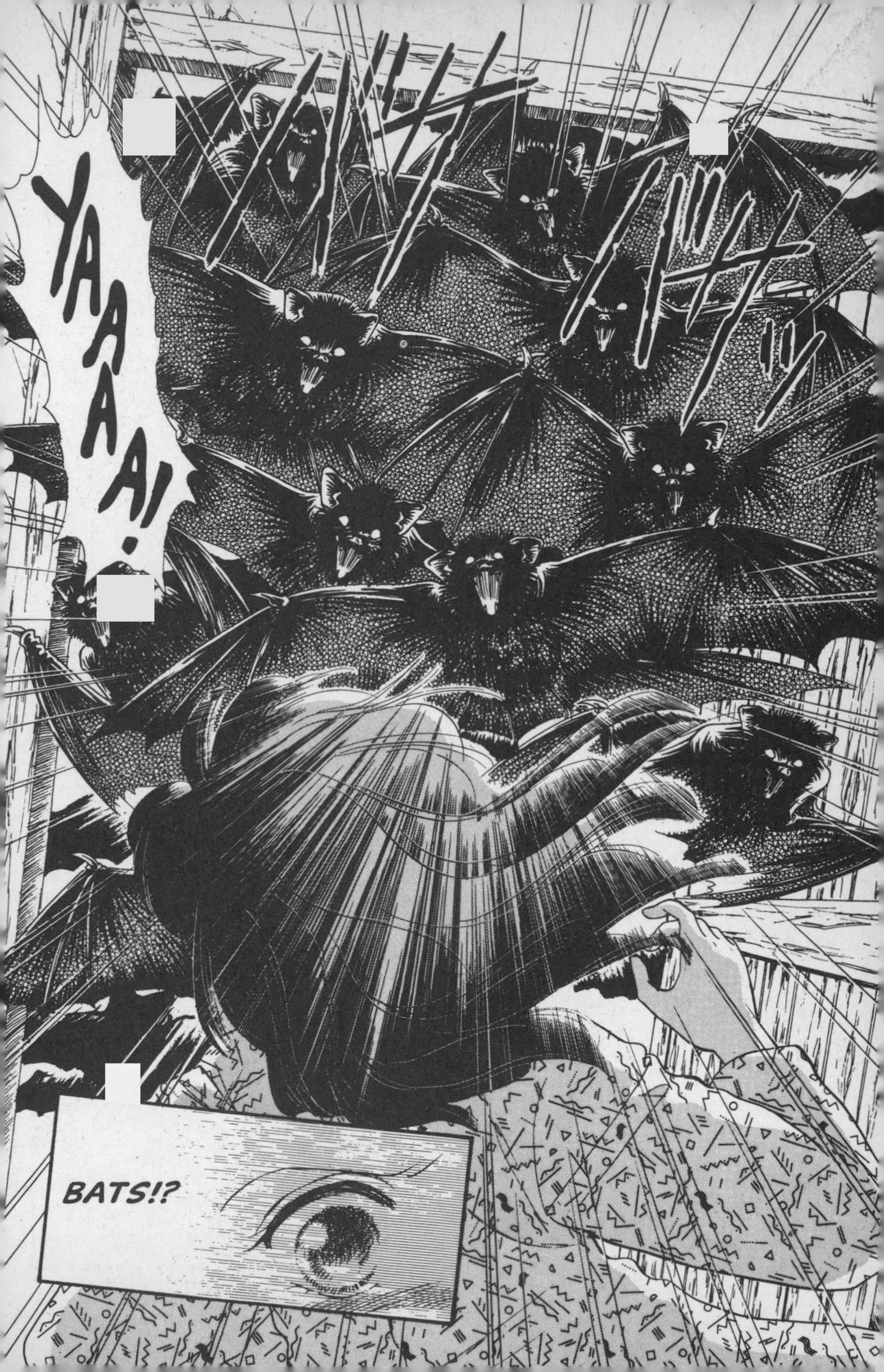
YAAAAA!!
BATS!?

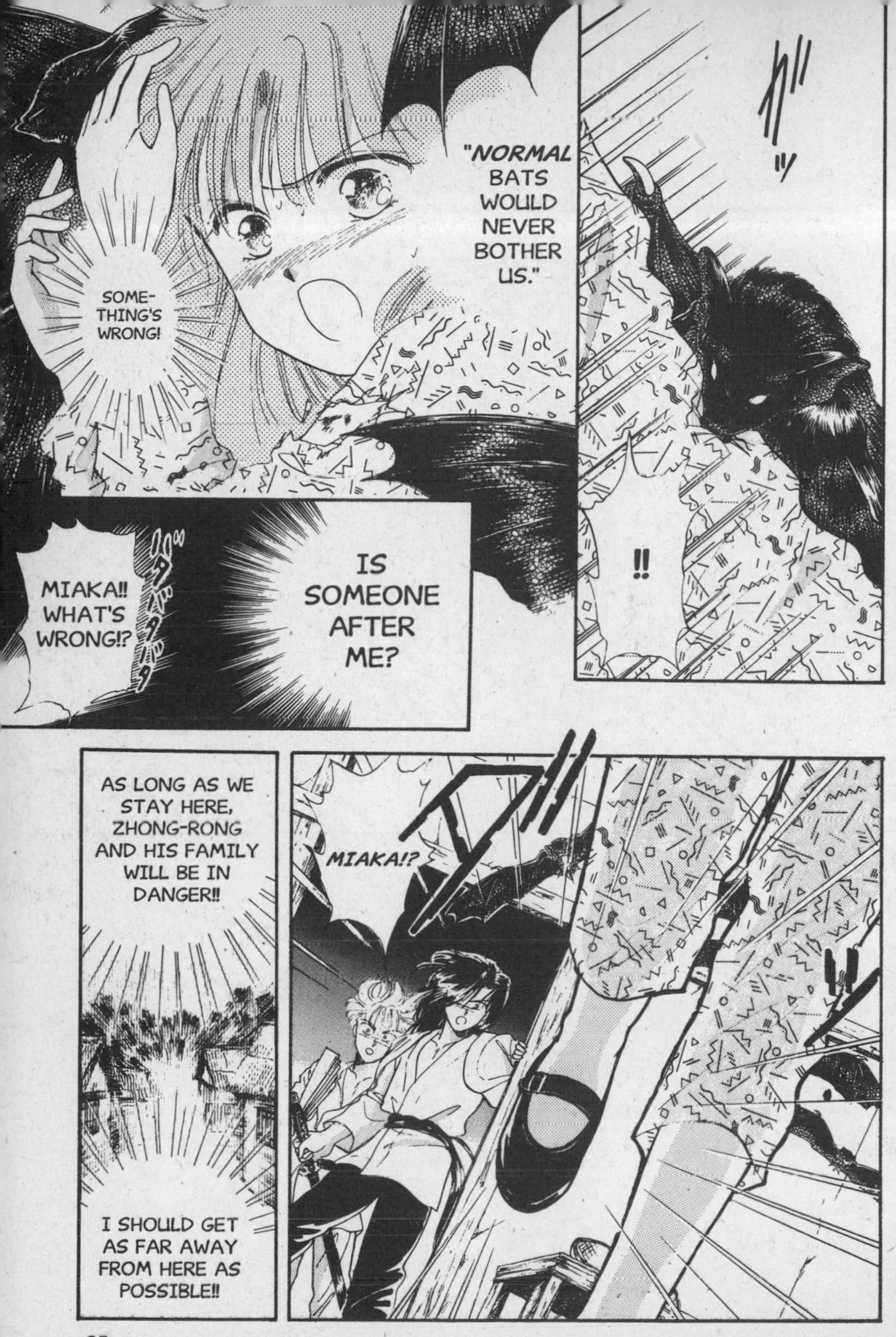
!!
"NORMAL BATS WOULD NEVER BOTHER US."
SOME-THING'S WRONG!
IS SOMEONE AFTER ME?
MIAKA!! WHAT'S WRONG!?
MIAKA!?
AS LONG AS WE STAY HERE, ZHONG-RONG AND HIS FAMILY WILL BE IN DANGER!!
I SHOULD GET AS FAR AWAY FROM HERE AS POSSIBLE!!

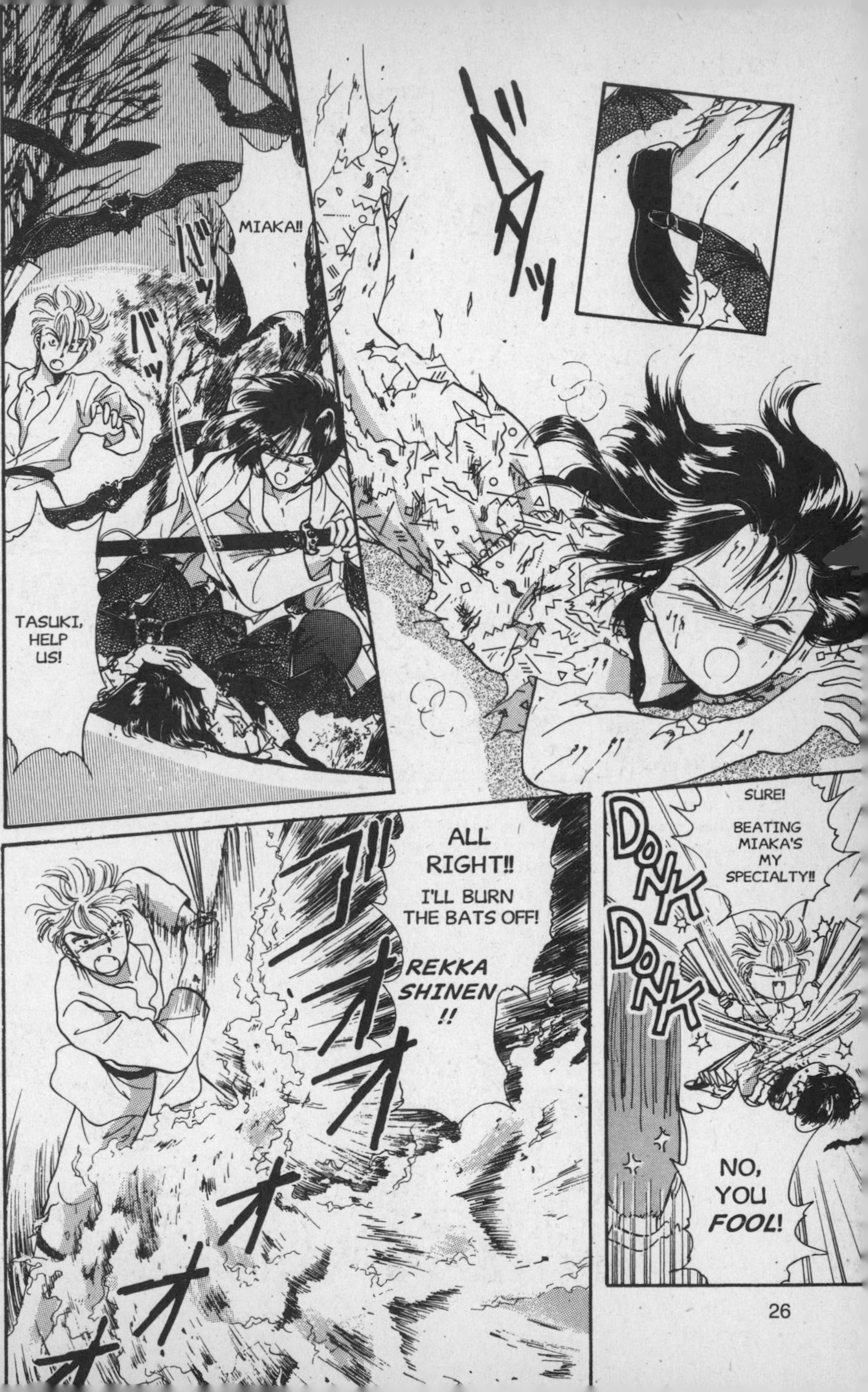
MIAKA!!
TASUKI, HELP US!
SURE!
BEATING MIAKA'S MY SPECIALTY!!
DONK DONK
NO, YOU FOOL!
ALL RIGHT!!
I'LL BURN THE BATS OFF!
REKKA SHINEN!!

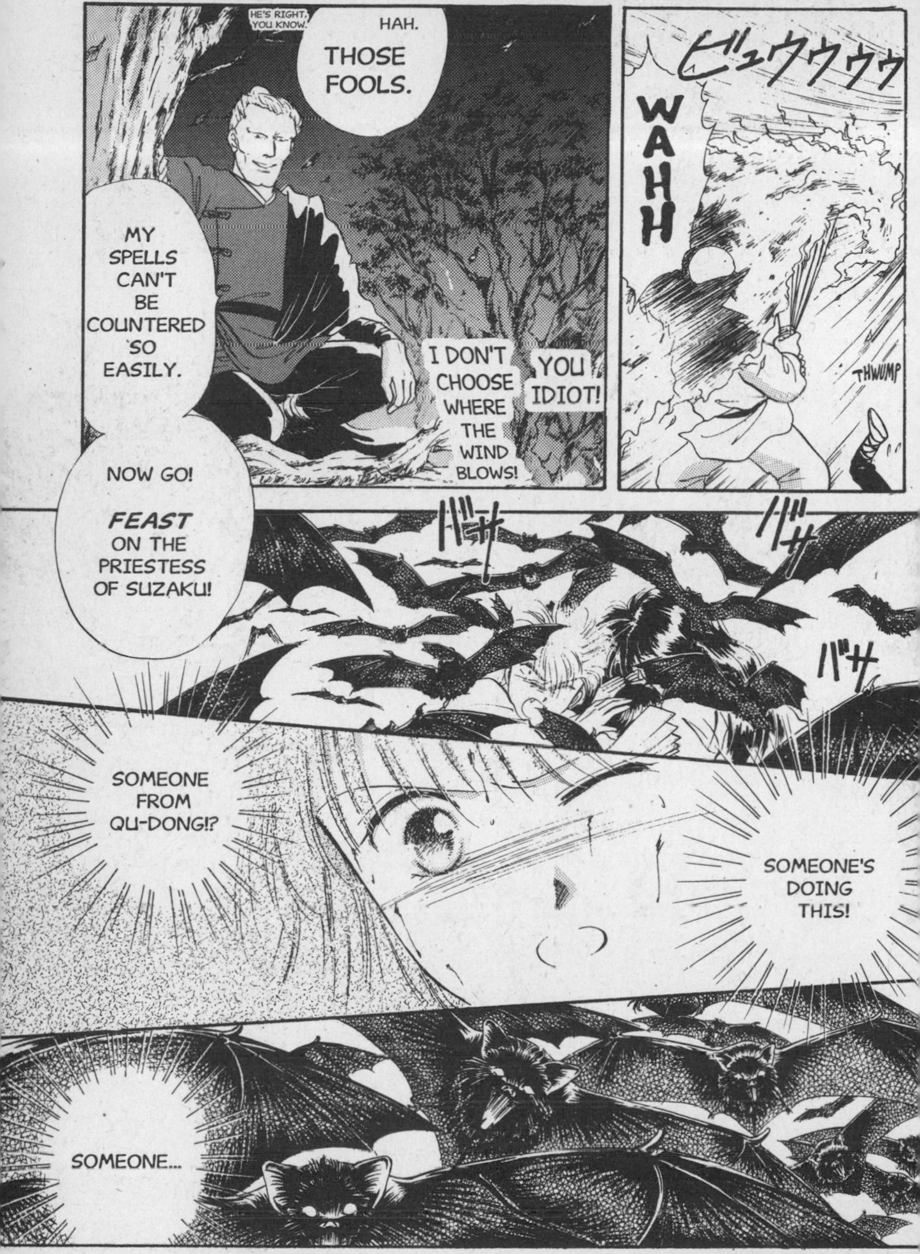
ビュウウウウ
WAHH
THWUMP
YOU IDIOT!
I DON'T CHOOSE WHERE THE WIND BLOWS!
HE'S RIGHT, YOU KNOW.
HAH. THOSE FOOLS.
MY SPELLS CAN'T BE COUNTERED SO EASILY.
NOW GO! FEAST ON THE PRIESTESS OF SUZAKU!
バサ
バサ
バサ
SOMEONE'S DOING THIS!
SOMEONE FROM QU-DONG!?
SOMEONE...

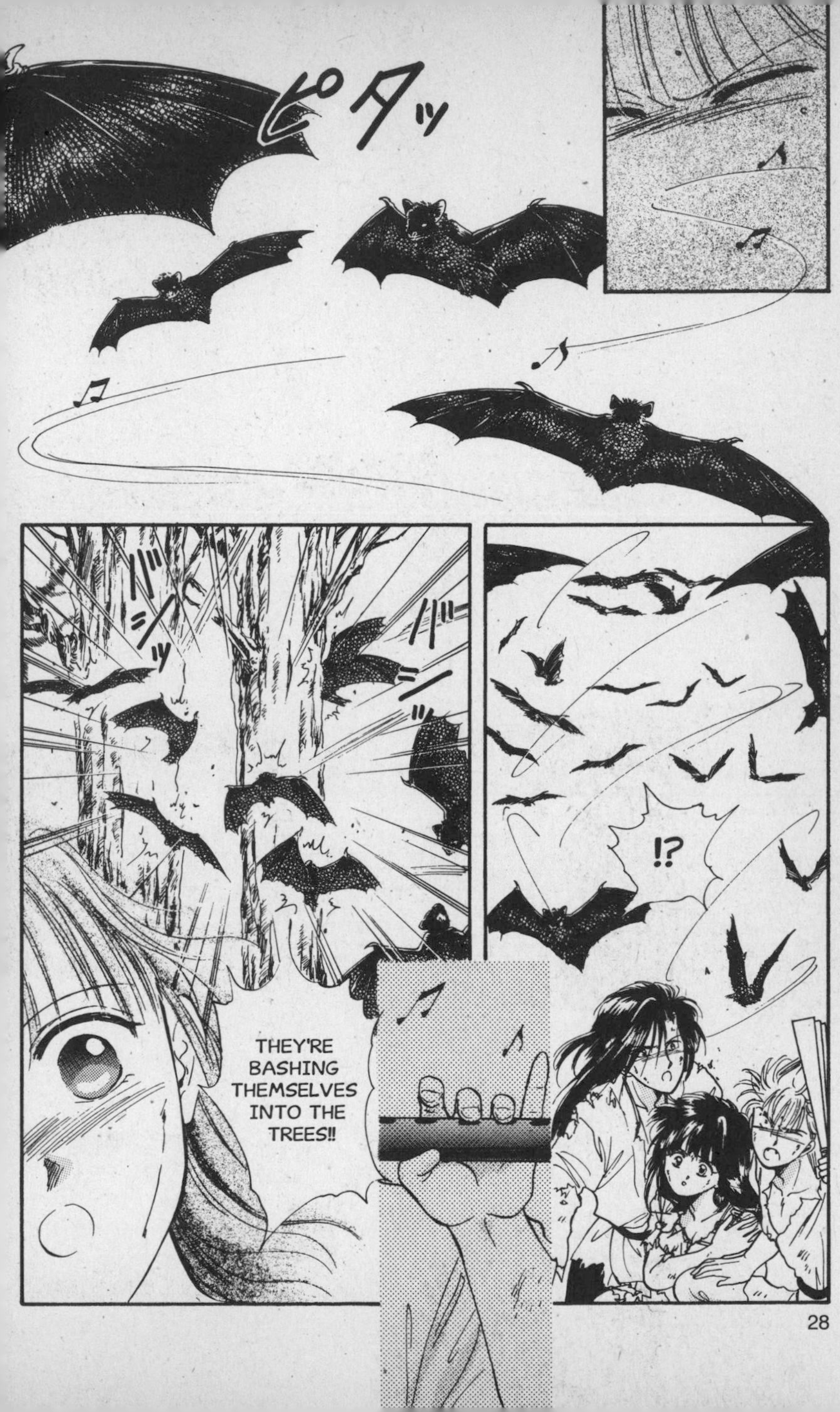
ピタッ
!?
THEY'RE BASHING THEMSELVES INTO THE TREES!!

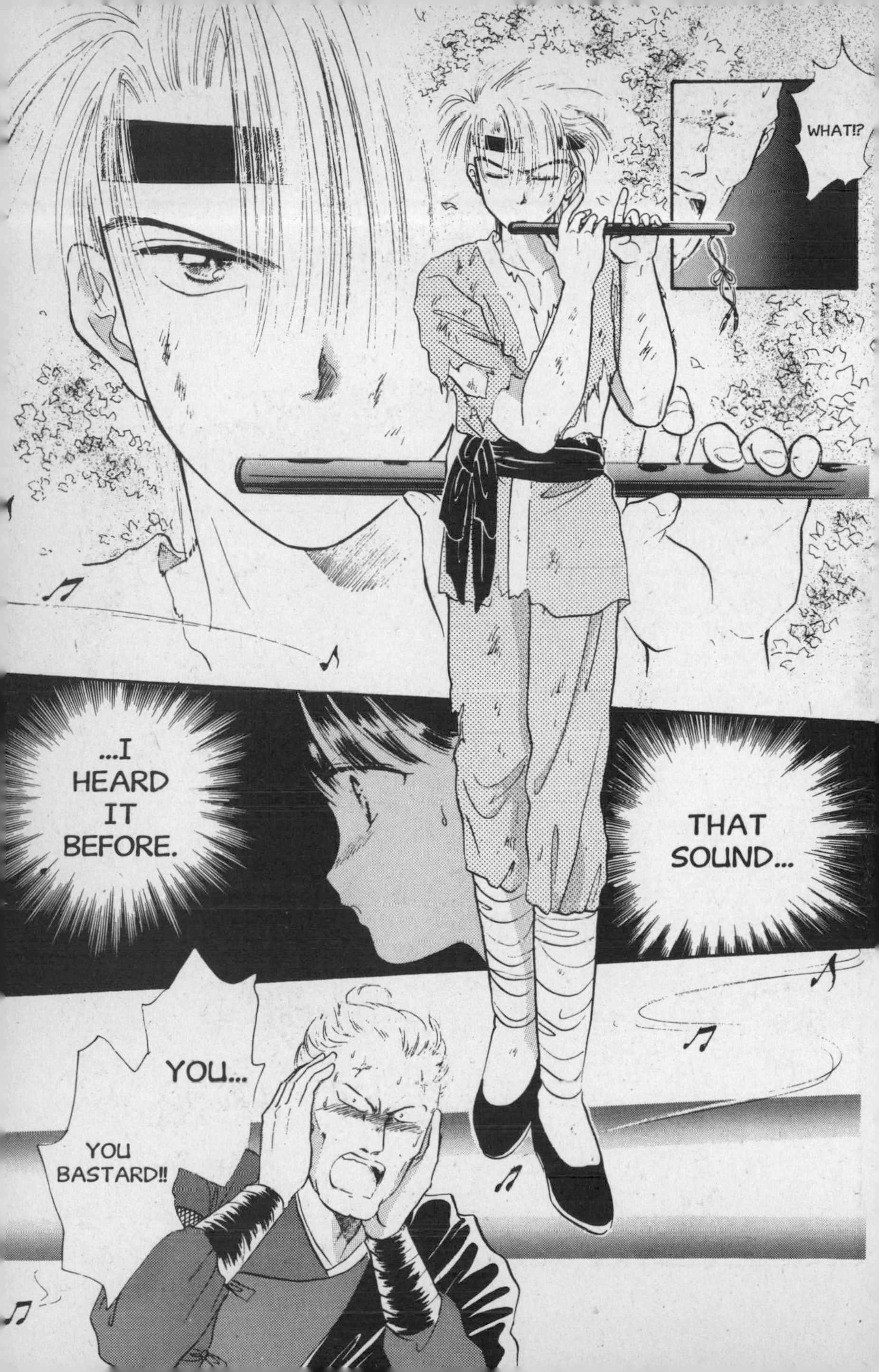
WHAT!?
THAT SOUND...
...I HEARD IT BEFORE.
YOU...
YOU BASTARD!!

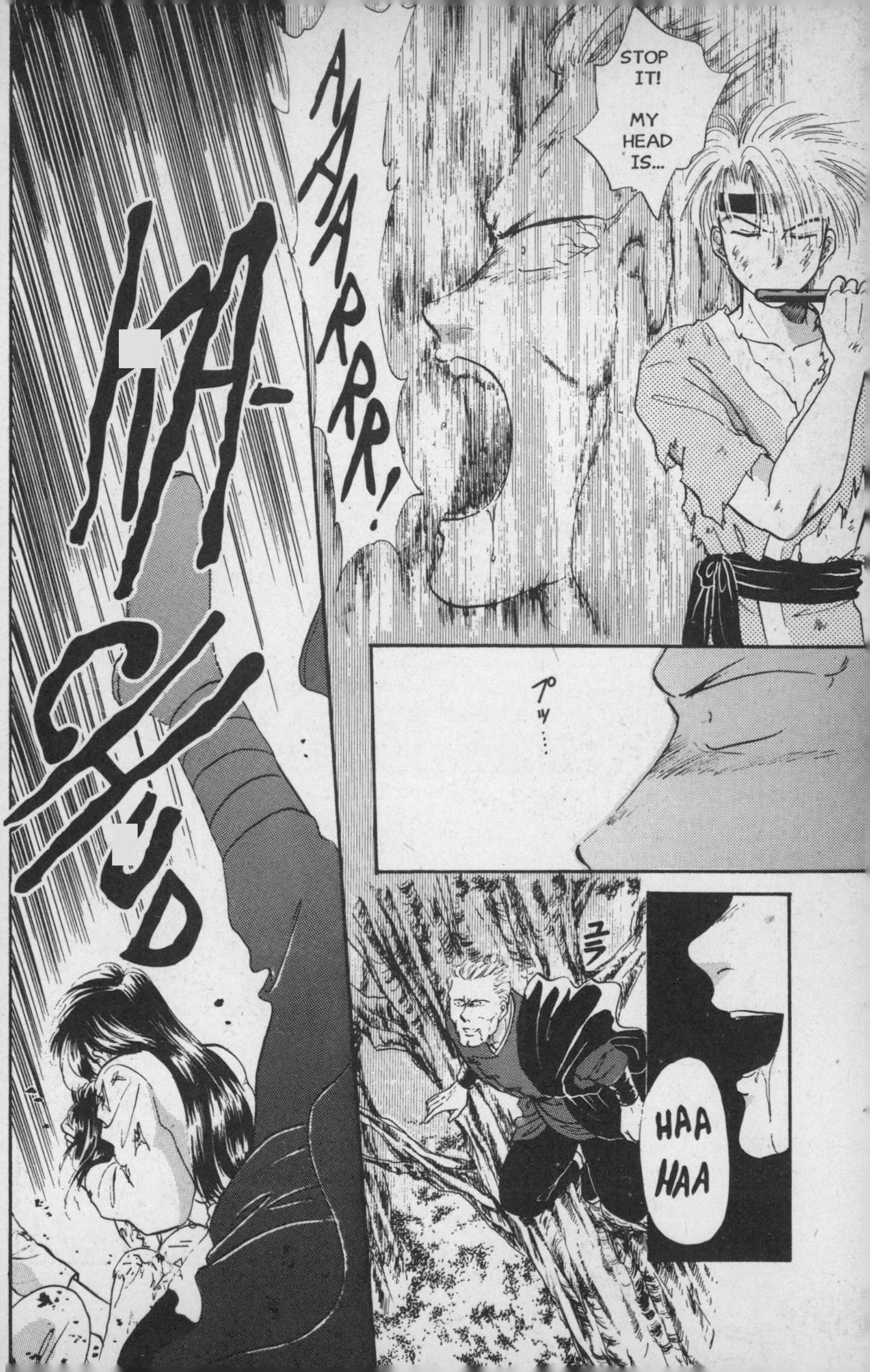

STOP IT!
MY HEAD IS...
AAARRR!
プッ…
HAA HAA
ユラ
THUD

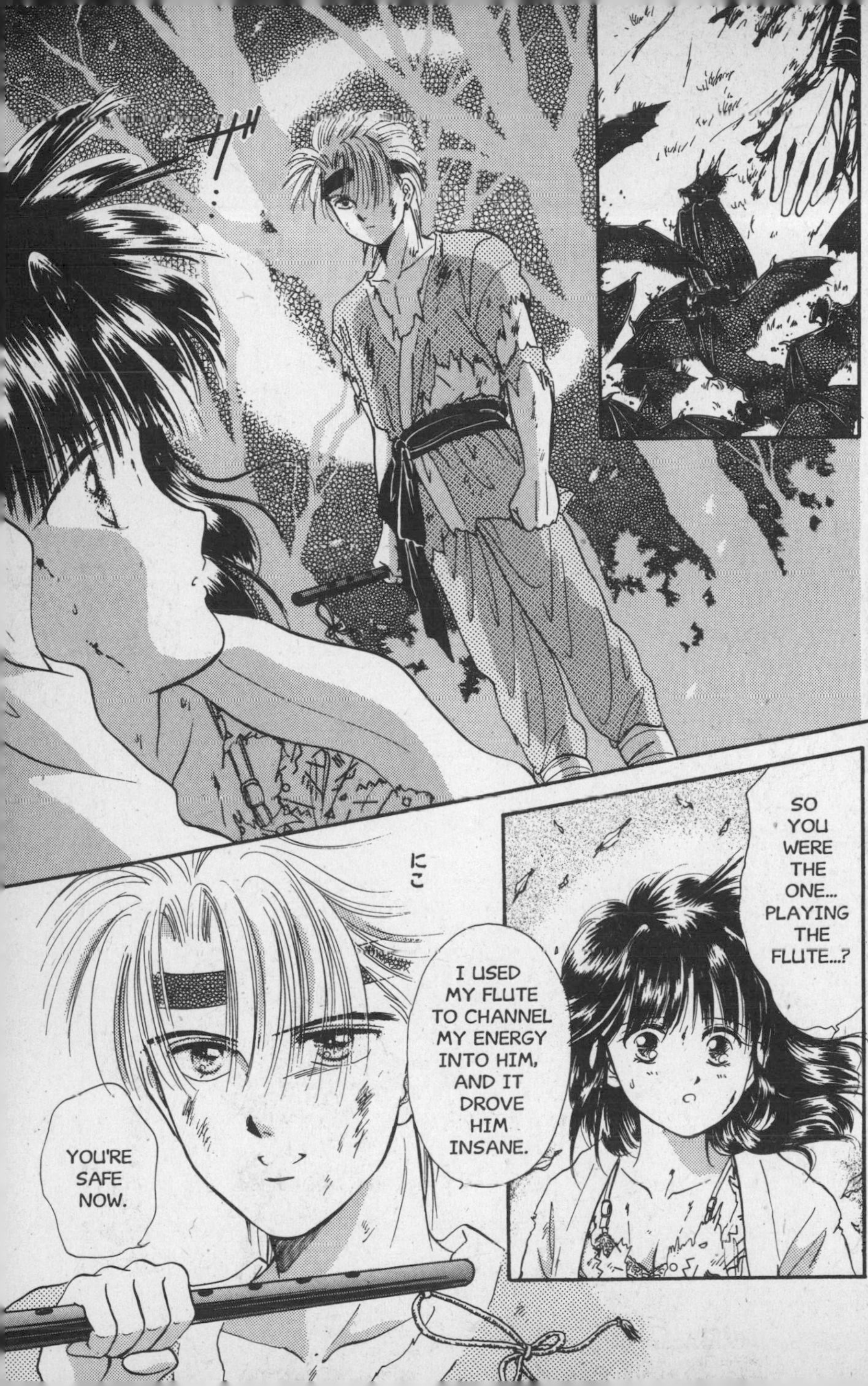
SO YOU WERE THE ONE... PLAYING THE FLUTE...?
にこ
I USED MY FLUTE TO CHANNEL MY ENERGY INTO HIM, AND IT DROVE HIM INSANE.
YOU'RE SAFE NOW.

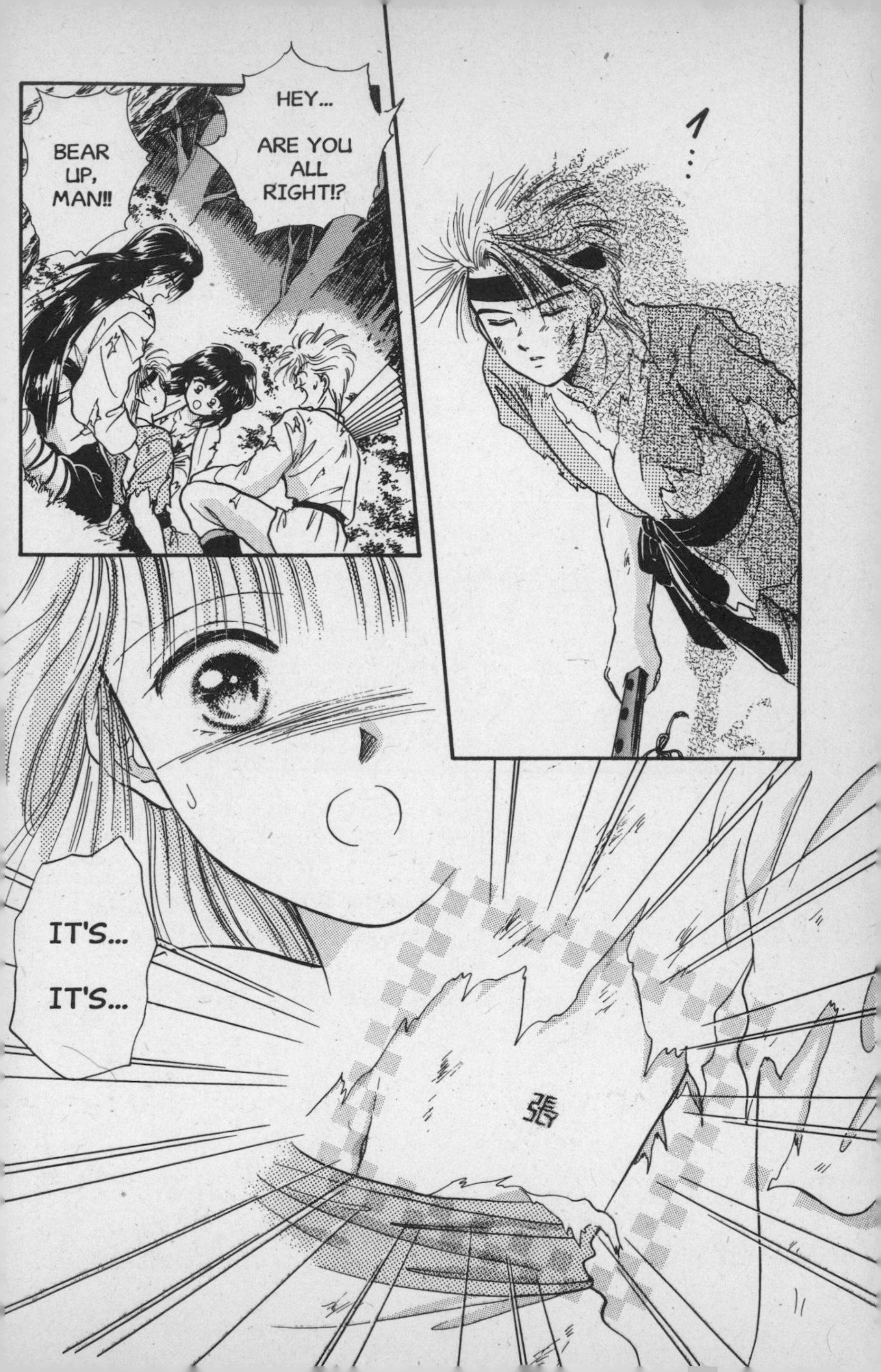
HEY...
ARE YOU ALL RIGHT!?
BEAR UP, MAN!!
IT'S...
IT'S...
張

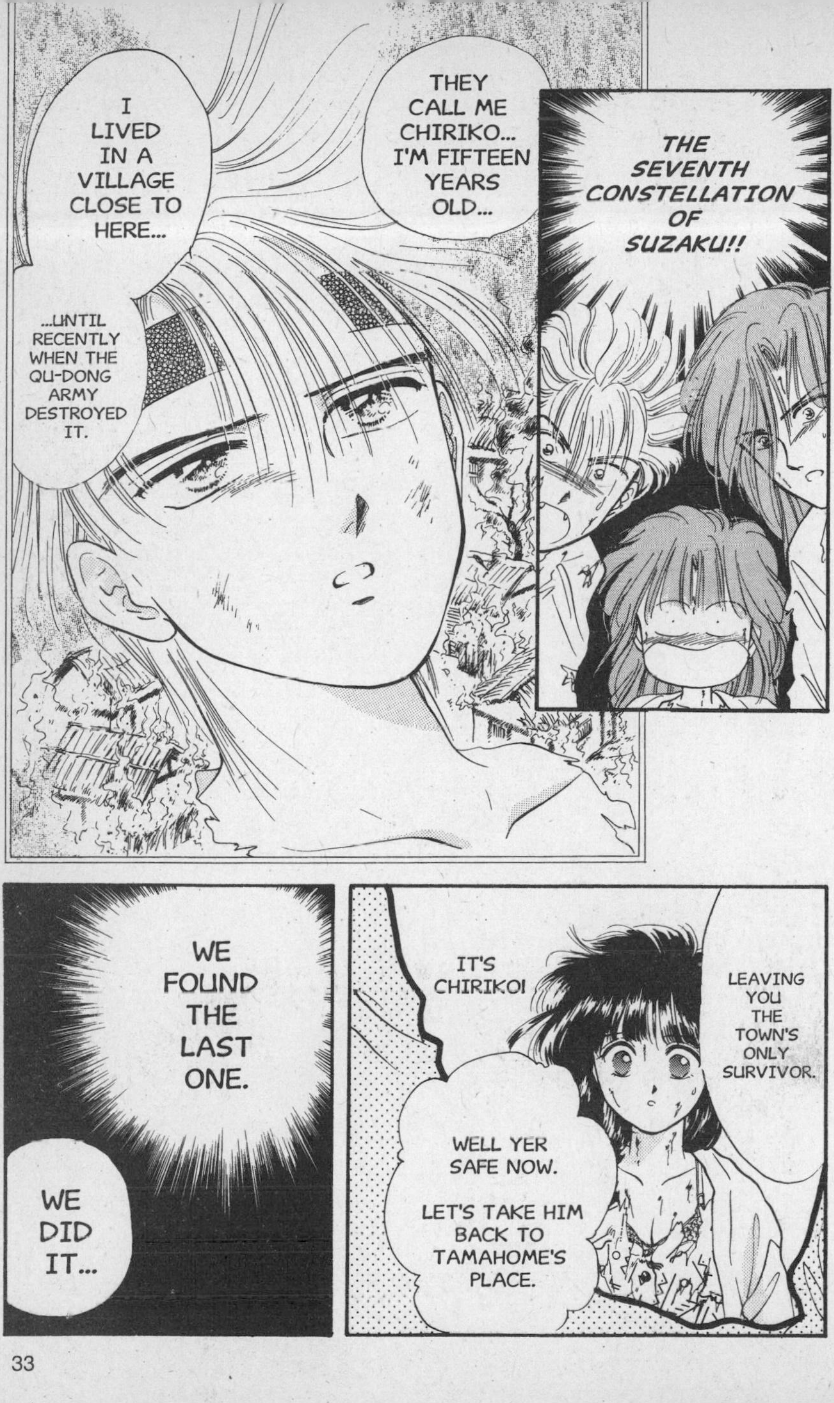
THEY CALL ME CHIRIKO... I'M FIFTEEN YEARS OLD...
THE SEVENTH CONSTELLATION OF SUZAKU!!
I LIVED IN A VILLAGE CLOSE TO HERE...
...UNTIL RECENTLY WHEN THE QU-DONG ARMY DESTROYED IT.
LEAVING YOU THE TOWN'S ONLY SURVIVOR.
IT'S CHIRIKO!
WELL YER SAFE NOW.
LET'S TAKE HIM BACK TO TAMAHOME'S PLACE.
WE FOUND THE LAST ONE.
WE DID IT...

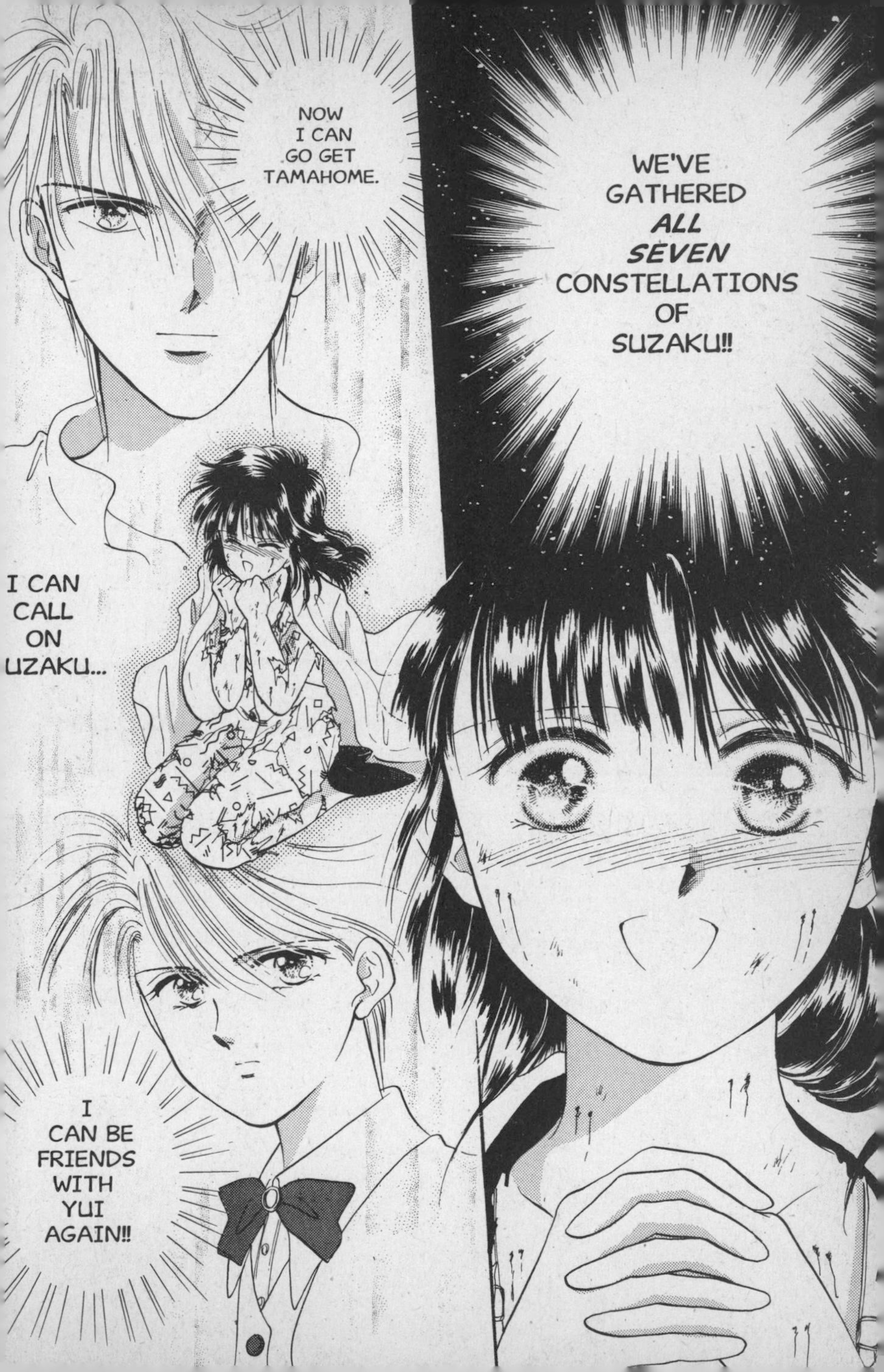
WE'VE GATHERED ALL SEVEN CONSTELLATIONS OF SUZAKU!!
NOW I CAN GO GET TAMAHOME.
I CAN CALL ON UZAKU...
I CAN BE FRIENDS WITH YUI AGAIN!!

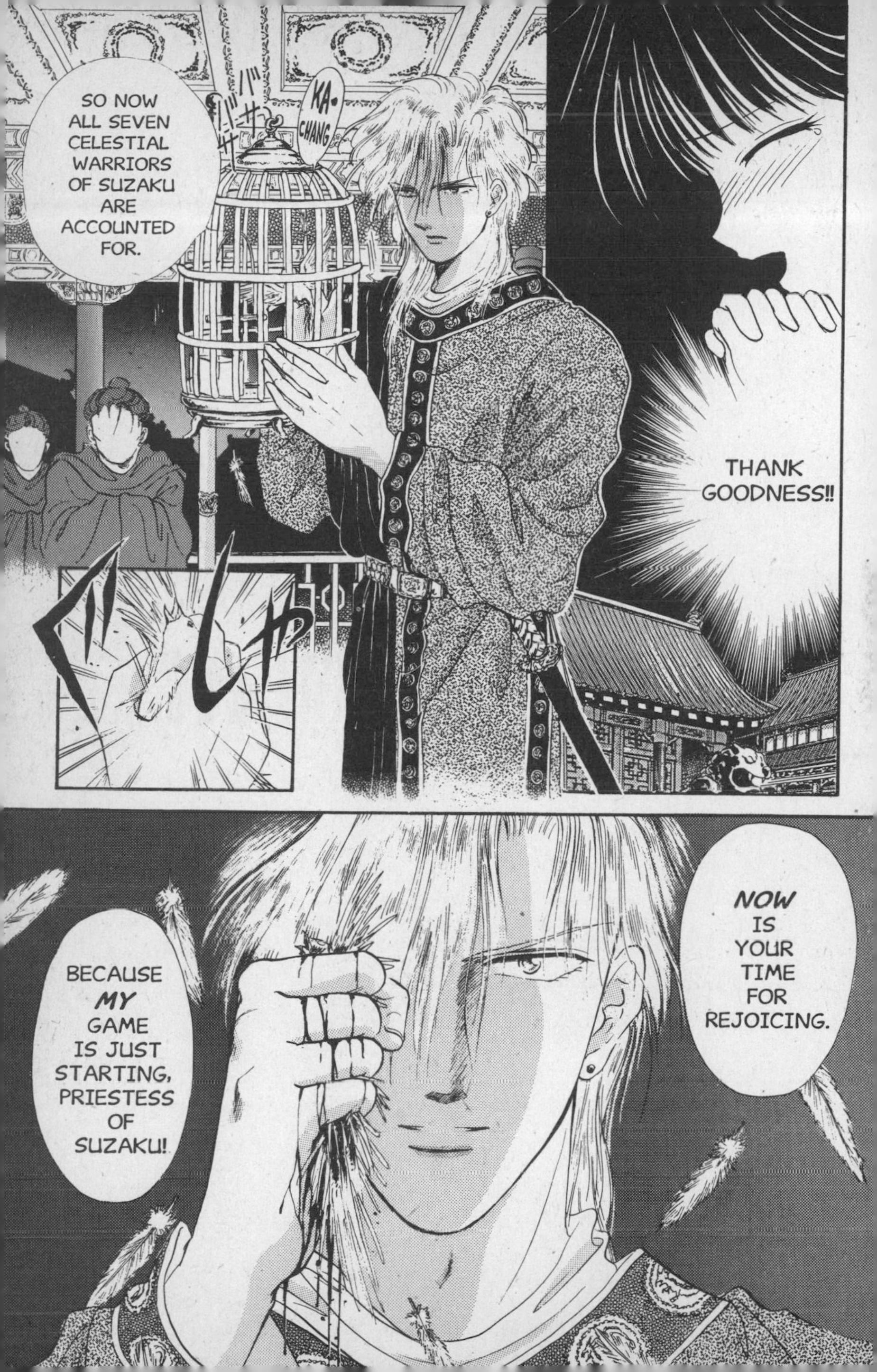
THANK GOODNESS!!
SO NOW ALL SEVEN CELESTIAL WARRIORS OF SUZAKU ARE ACCOUNTED FOR.
KA-CHANG
NOW IS YOUR TIME FOR REJOICING.
BECAUSE MY GAME IS JUST STARTING, PRIESTESS OF SUZAKU!

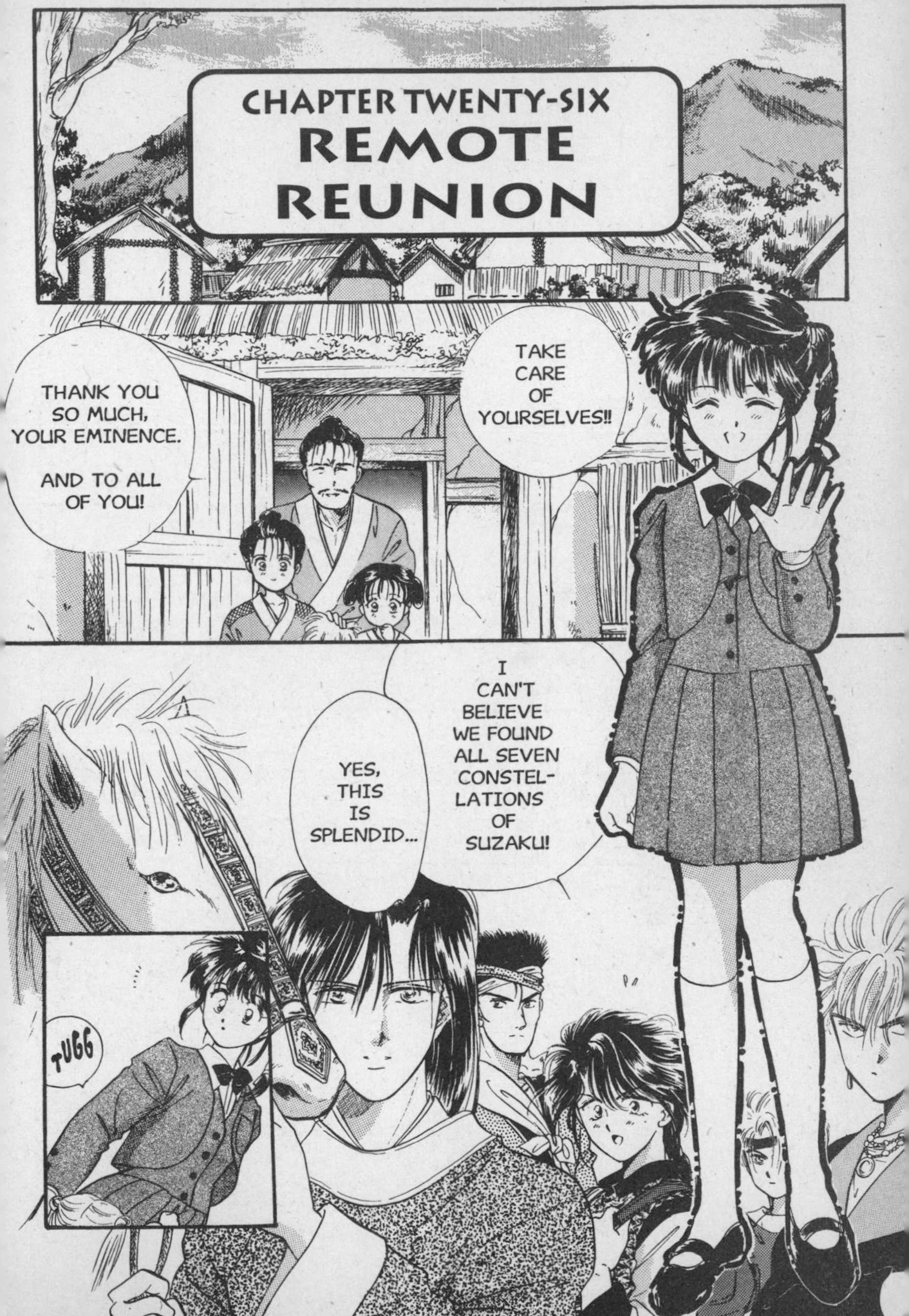
CHAPTER TWENTY-SIX
REMOTE REUNION
TAKE CARE OF YOURSELVES!!
THANK YOU SO MUCH, YOUR EMINENCE.
AND TO ALL OF YOU!
I CAN'T BELIEVE WE FOUND ALL SEVEN CONSTEL-LATIONS OF SUZAKU!
YES, THIS IS SPLENDID...
TUGG

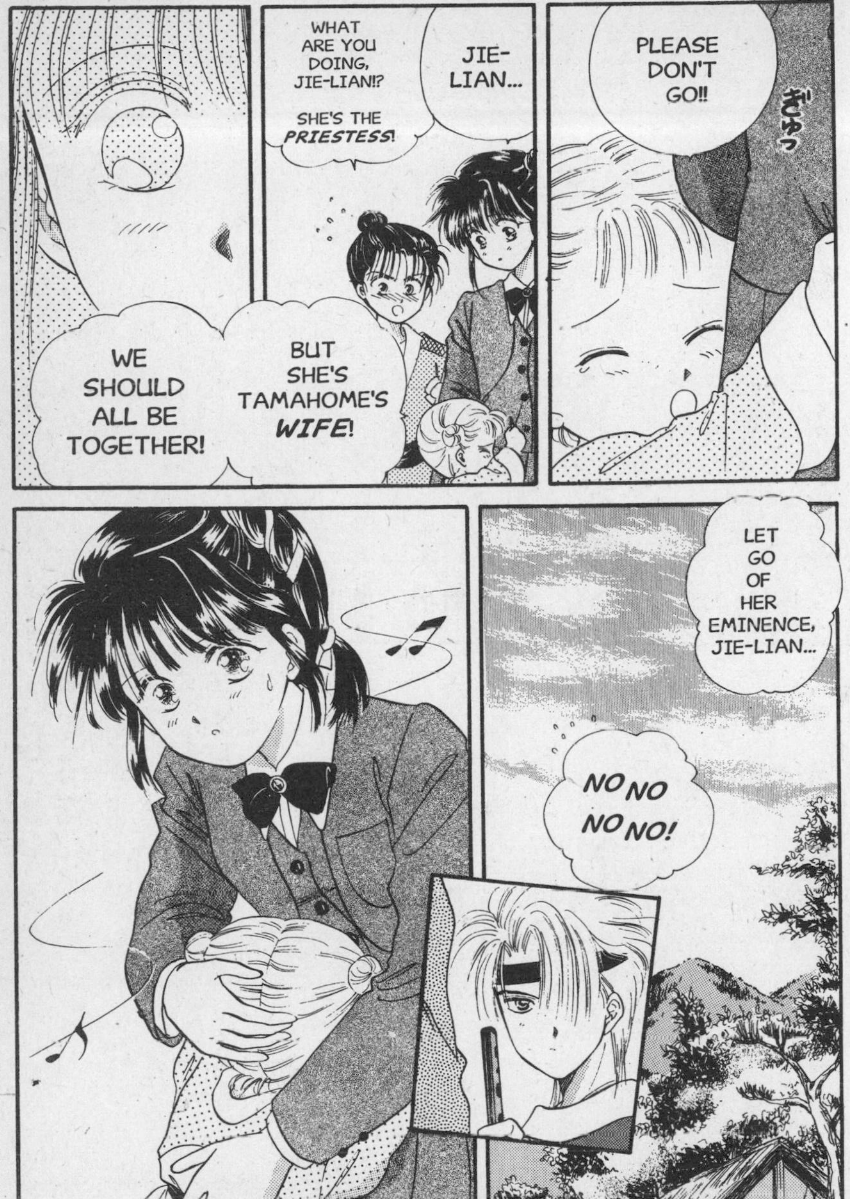
PLEASE DON'T GO!!
ぎゅっ
JIE-LIAN...
WHAT ARE YOU DOING, JIE-LIAN!?
SHE'S THE *PRIESTESS*!
BUT SHE'S TAMAHOME'S *WIFE*!
WE SHOULD ALL BE TOGETHER!
LET GO OF HER EMINENCE, JIE-LIAN...
NO NO NO NO!

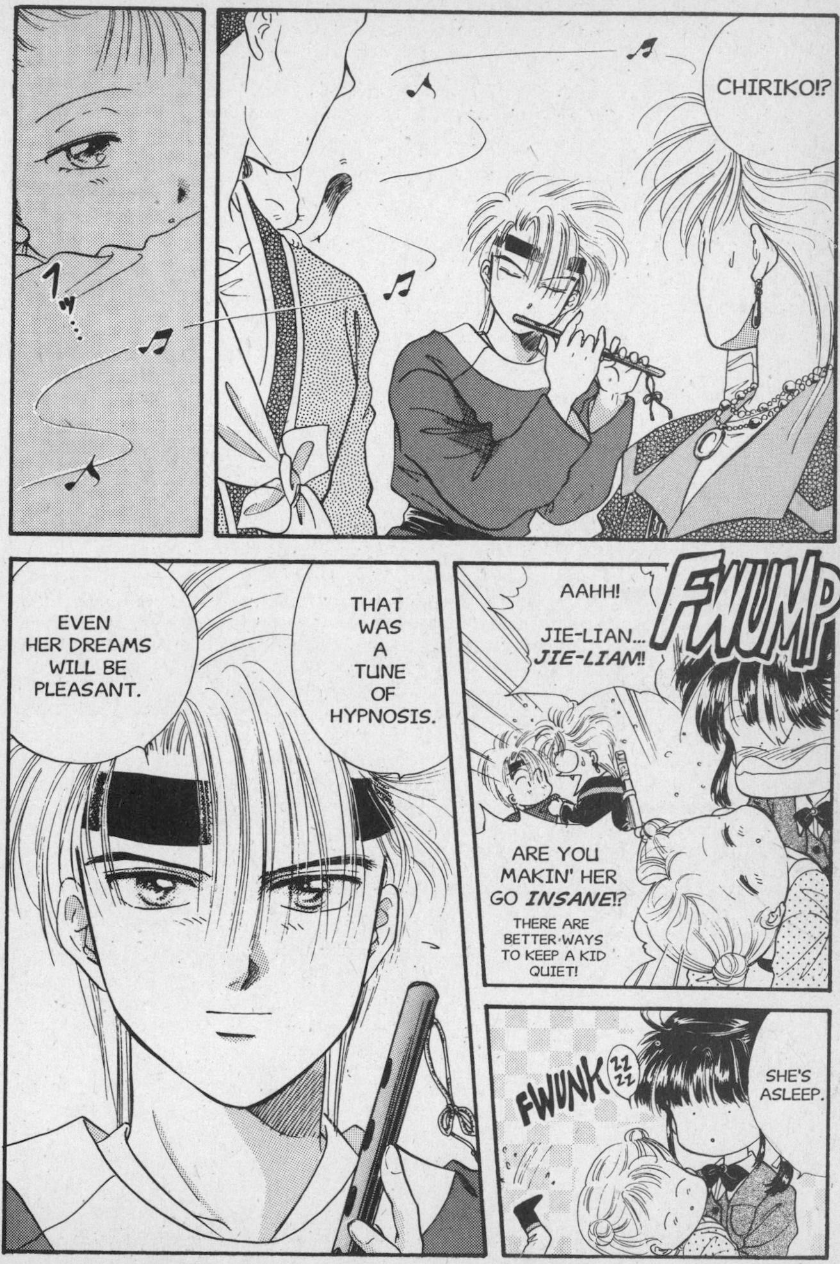
CHIRIKO!?
FWUMP
AAHH!
JIE-LIAN... *JIE-LIAM*!
ARE YOU MAKIN' HER GO *INSANE*!?
THERE ARE BETTER WAYS TO KEEP A KID QUIET!
SHE'S ASLEEP.
FWUNK
ZZZZ
THAT WAS A TUNE OF HYPNOSIS.
EVEN HER DREAMS WILL BE PLEASANT.

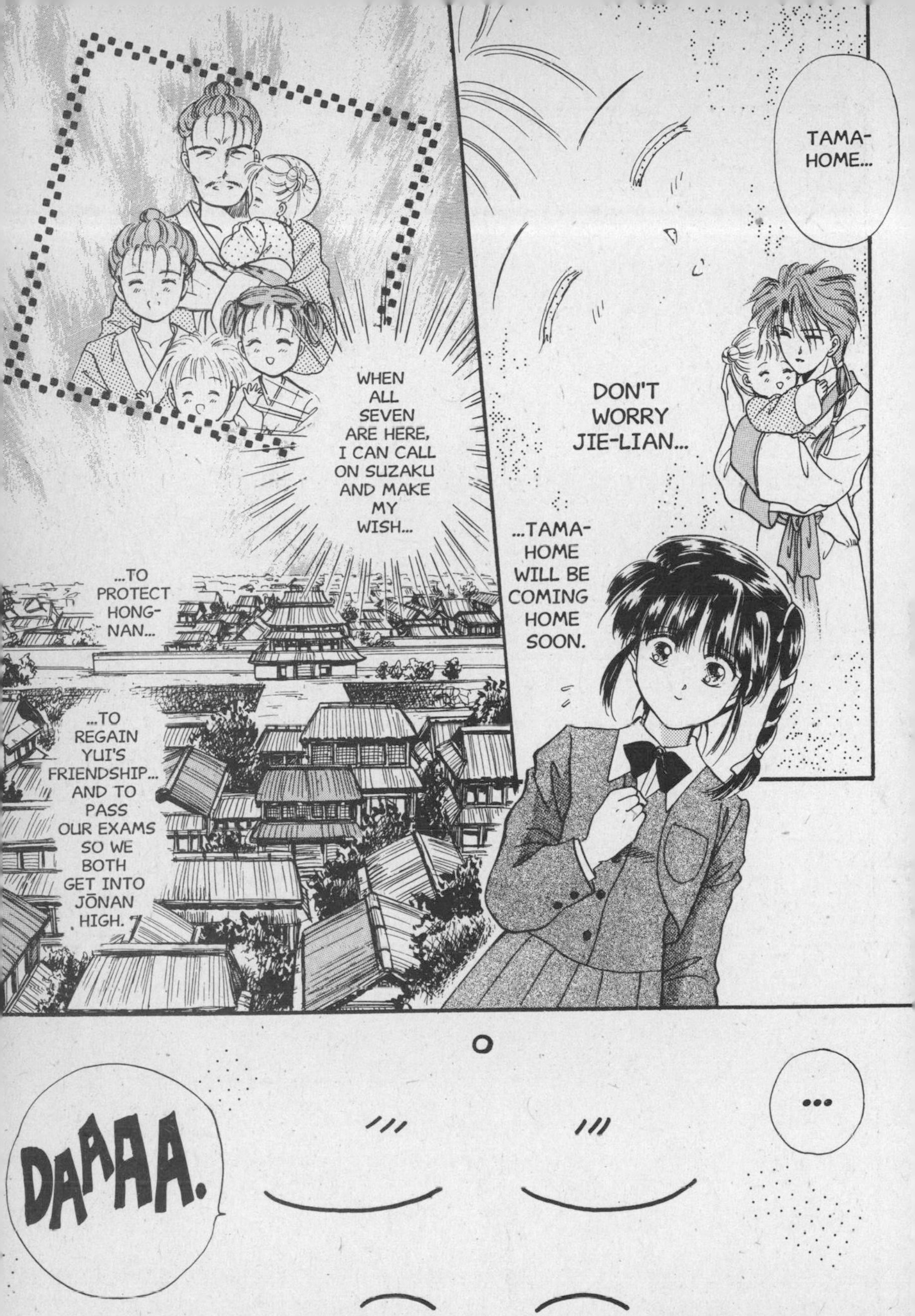
TAMA-HOME...
DON'T WORRY JIE-LIAN...
...TAMA-HOME WILL BE COMING HOME SOON.
WHEN ALL SEVEN ARE HERE, I CAN CALL ON SUZAKU AND MAKE MY WISH...
...TO PROTECT HONG-NAN...
...TO REGAIN YUI'S FRIENDSHIP... AND TO PASS OUR EXAMS SO WE BOTH GET INTO JŌNAN HIGH.
...
O
DAAAA.

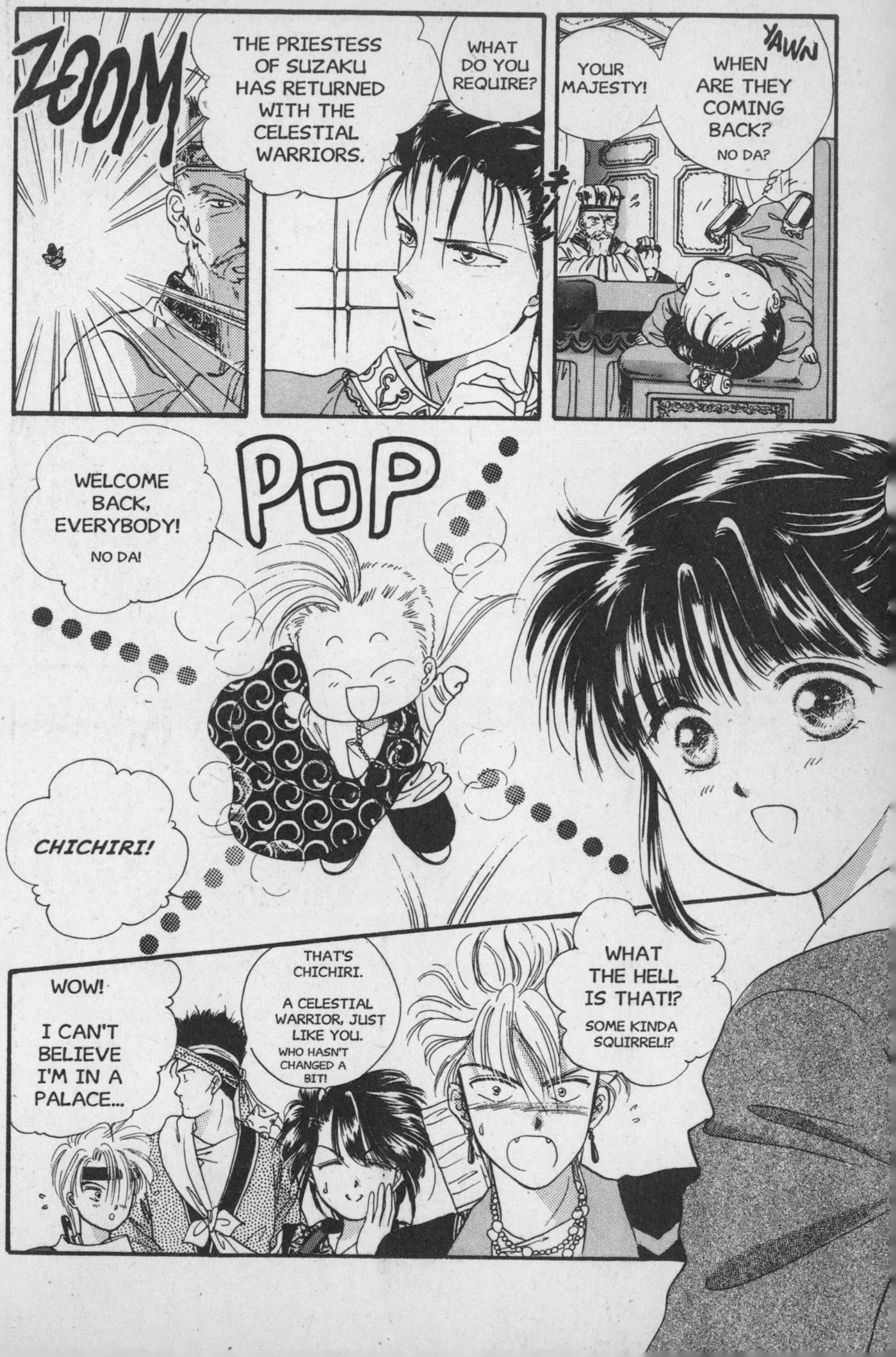
YAWN
WHEN ARE THEY COMING BACK?
NO DA?
YOUR MAJESTY!
WHAT DO YOU REQUIRE?
THE PRIESTESS OF SUZAKU HAS RETURNED WITH THE CELESTIAL WARRIORS.
ZOOM
POP
WELCOME BACK, EVERYBODY!
NO DA!
CHICHIRI!
WHAT THE HELL IS THAT!?
SOME KINDA SQUIRREL!?
THAT'S CHICHIRI.
A CELESTIAL WARRIOR, JUST LIKE YOU.
WHO HASN'T CHANGED A BIT!
WOW!
I CAN'T BELIEVE I'M IN A PALACE...

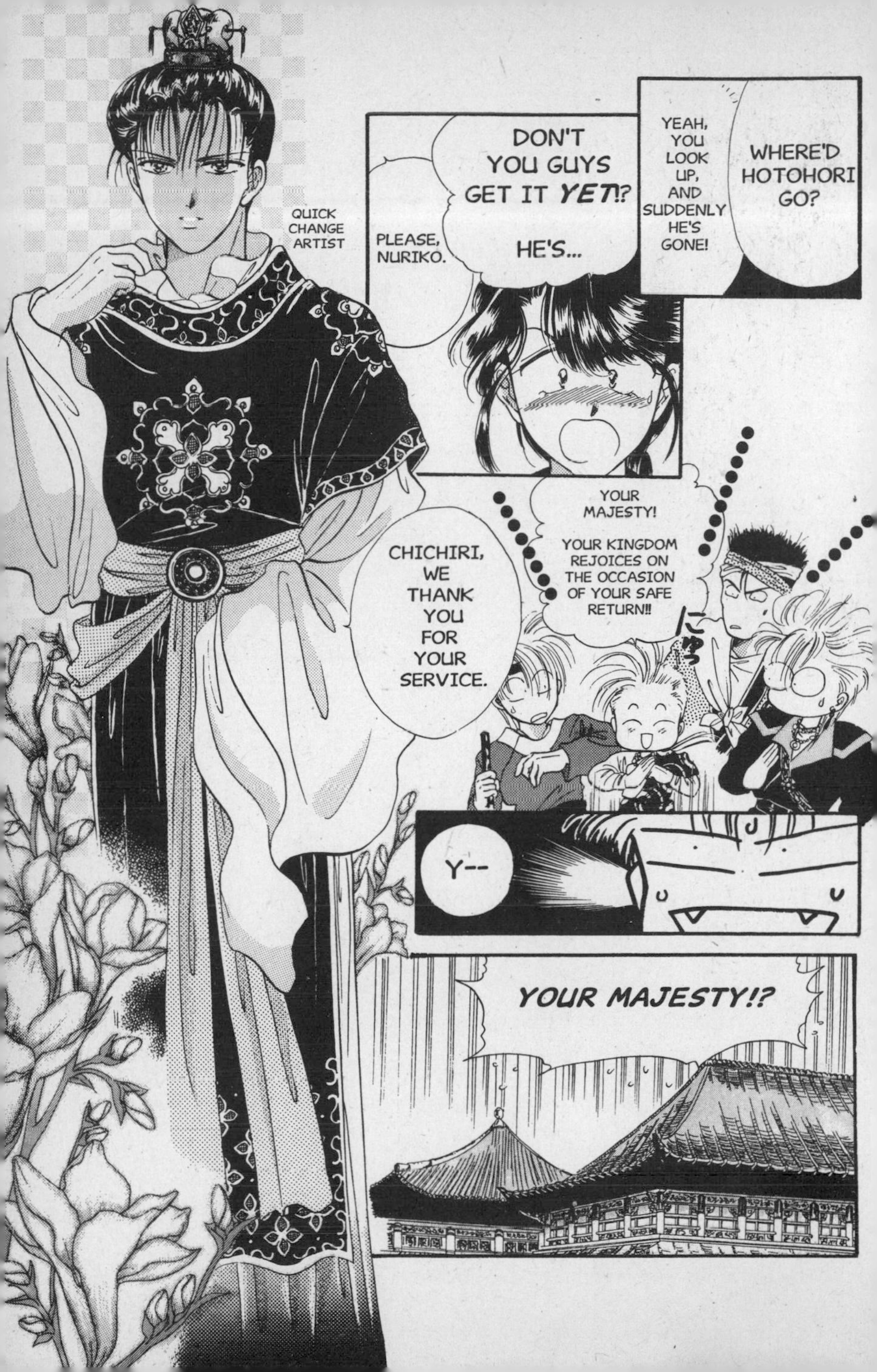
WHERE'D HOTOHORI GO?
YEAH, YOU LOOK UP, AND SUDDENLY HE'S GONE!
DON'T YOU GUYS GET IT *YET*!? HE'S...
PLEASE, NURIKO.
YOUR MAJESTY! YOUR KINGDOM REJOICES ON THE OCCASION OF YOUR SAFE RETURN!!
にゅっ
QUICK CHANGE ARTIST
CHICHIRI, WE THANK YOU FOR YOUR SERVICE.
Y--
YOUR MAJESTY!?

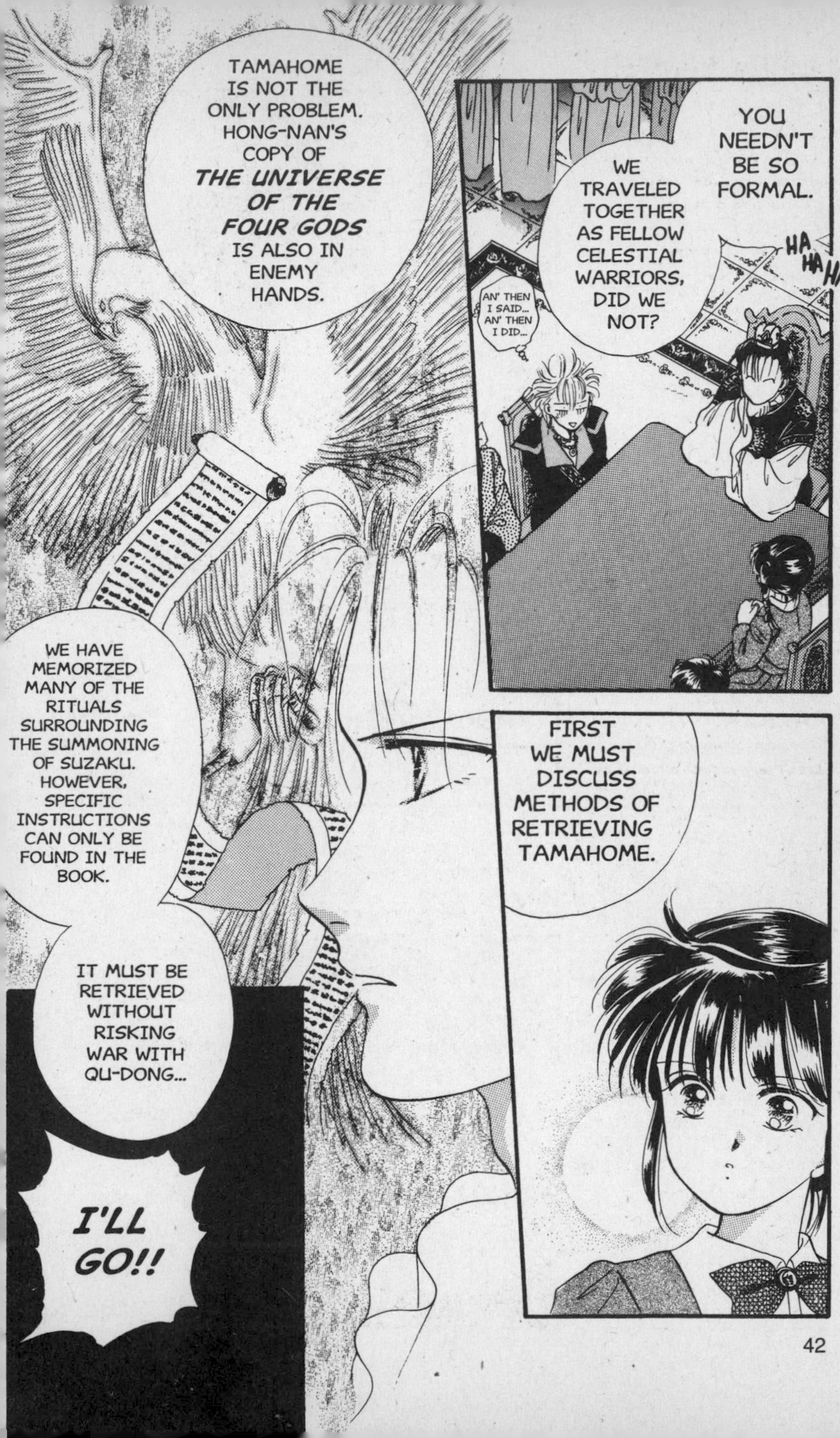
YOU NEEDN'T BE SO FORMAL.
HA HA HA
WE TRAVELED TOGETHER AS FELLOW CELESTIAL WARRIORS, DID WE NOT?
AN' THEN I SAID... AN' THEN I DID...
FIRST WE MUST DISCUSS METHODS OF RETRIEVING TAMAHOME.
TAMAHOME IS NOT THE ONLY PROBLEM. HONG-NAN'S COPY OF *THE UNIVERSE OF THE FOUR GODS* IS ALSO IN ENEMY HANDS.
WE HAVE MEMORIZED MANY OF THE RITUALS SURROUNDING THE SUMMONING OF SUZAKU. HOWEVER, SPECIFIC INSTRUCTIONS CAN ONLY BE FOUND IN THE BOOK.
IT MUST BE RETRIEVED WITHOUT RISKING WAR WITH QU-DONG...
I'LL GO!!

Since last year, I've been keeping an eye on "Ugo Ugo Rūga" (a live-action variety show), which is now becoming very popular. But in the Kansai region it isn't catching on at all.
That's right! The power of manga and anime in Kansai is outrageous!! I get dizzy over the onslaught of reruns! Modern kids have never seen this kind of great old anime!!
I'm in tears!!
Kansai rules. They've got "Anime Daisuki!" (We love Anime!) on TV. They play OAVs on TV! All my anime on video were dubbed from these programs.
The commercials are different, too. They don't run commercials like the ramen commercial "Suki ya nen!" ("I love it!" in Kansai dialect) in Tokyo!
It's been two and a half years since I moved. Just when I thought I was getting settled in, I'm realizing how great Osaka is. There are all my friends who I haven't seen in such a long time! (I saw some on my last visit, but I'm remembering all the ones I didn't have time to see!)
At the time, I got together with Y. (a young gentleman) and K. (a young lady -- I wonder if they're reading this), and we went to go see "Death Becomes Her," which was fun. The problem was when we went to the video arcade to kill some time. Y. walked right up to Street Fighter II and, using Ryu, cleared each stage all the way to the end!! That was the first time I saw Street Fighter II all the way through, but I soon wished I hadn't. Later, I watched K. play Terminator II, and it was fun, but Street Fighter II was still playing around in my head.
But even worse than that...
To be continued...

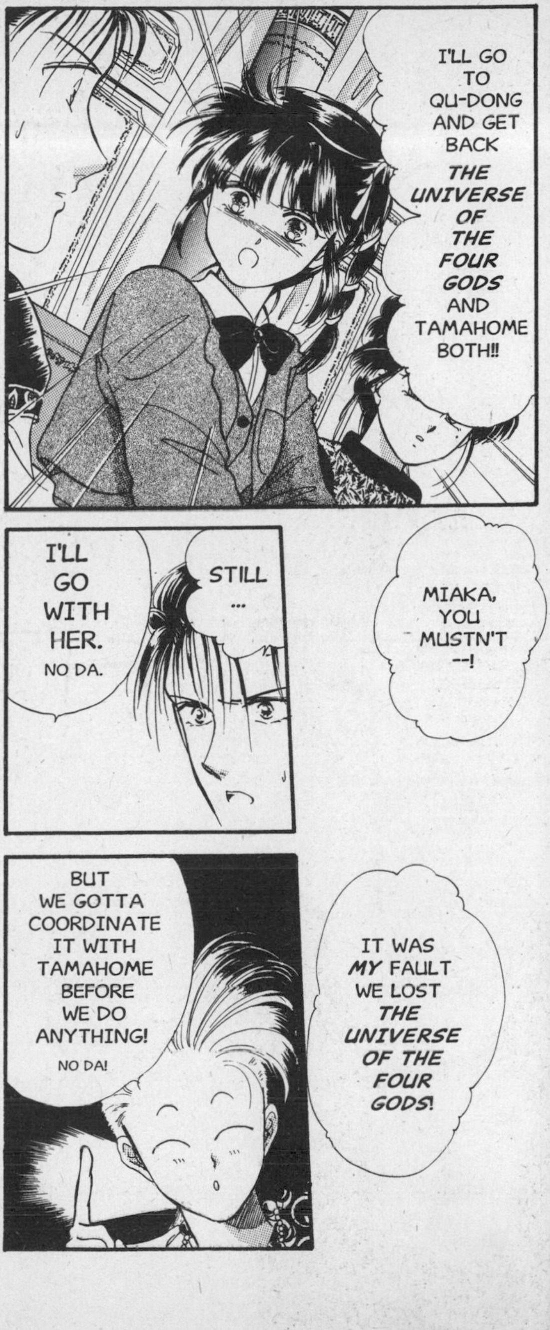
I'LL GO TO QU-DONG AND GET BACK *THE UNIVERSE OF THE FOUR GODS* AND TAMAHOME BOTH!!
MIAKA, YOU MUSTN'T --!
STILL ...
I'LL GO WITH HER. NO DA.
IT WAS *MY* FAULT WE LOST *THE UNIVERSE OF THE FOUR GODS*!
BUT WE GOTTA COORDINATE IT WITH TAMAHOME BEFORE WE DO ANYTHING! NO DA!

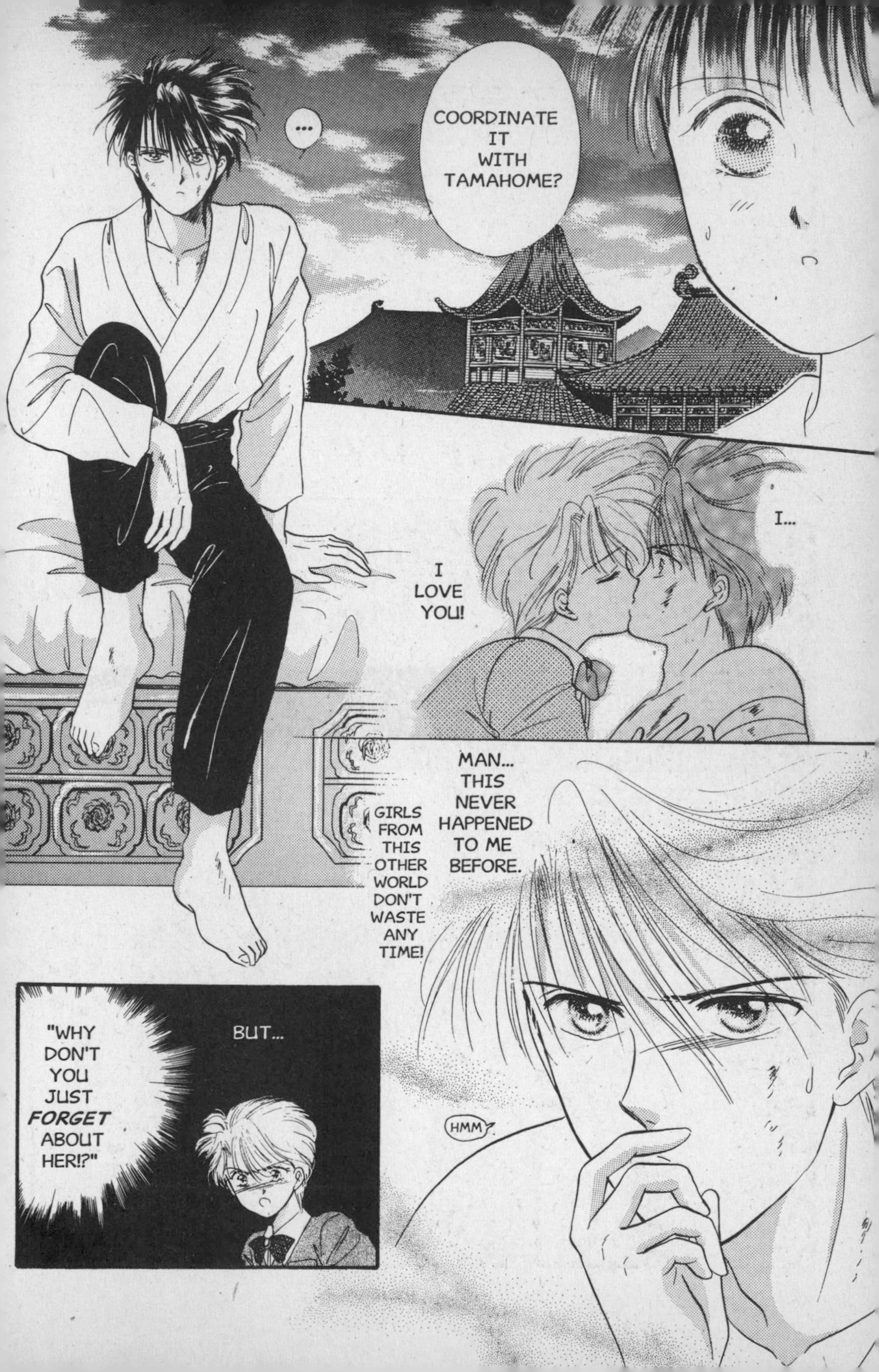
COORDINATE IT WITH TAMAHOME?
...
I...
I LOVE YOU!
MAN... THIS NEVER HAPPENED TO ME BEFORE.
GIRLS FROM THIS OTHER WORLD DON'T WASTE ANY TIME!
HMM
BUT...
"WHY DON'T YOU JUST FORGET ABOUT HER!?"

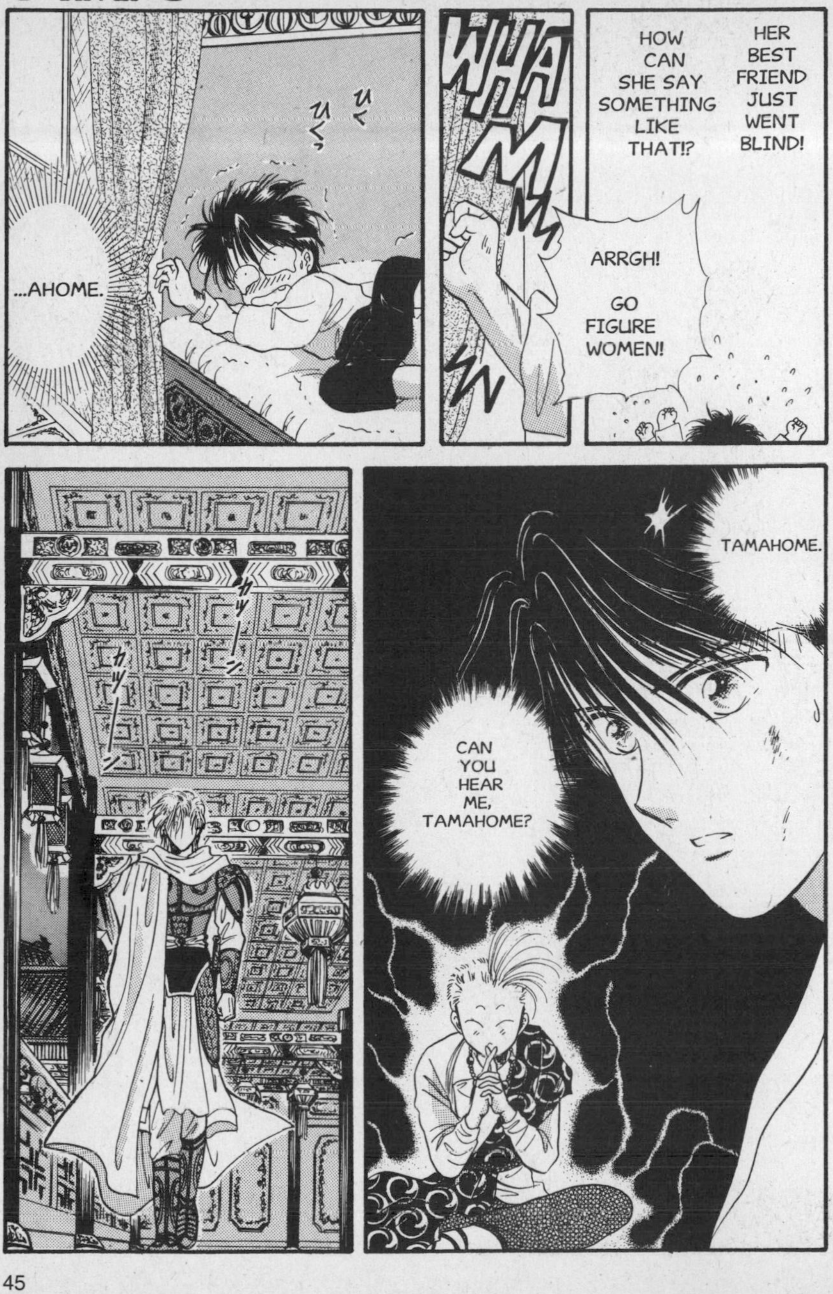
HER BEST FRIEND JUST WENT BLIND!
HOW CAN SHE SAY SOMETHING LIKE THAT!?
WHAMMM
ARRGH! GO FIGURE WOMEN!
ひく ひくっ
...AHOME.
TAMAHOME.
CAN YOU HEAR ME, TAMAHOME?
カツーン カツーン

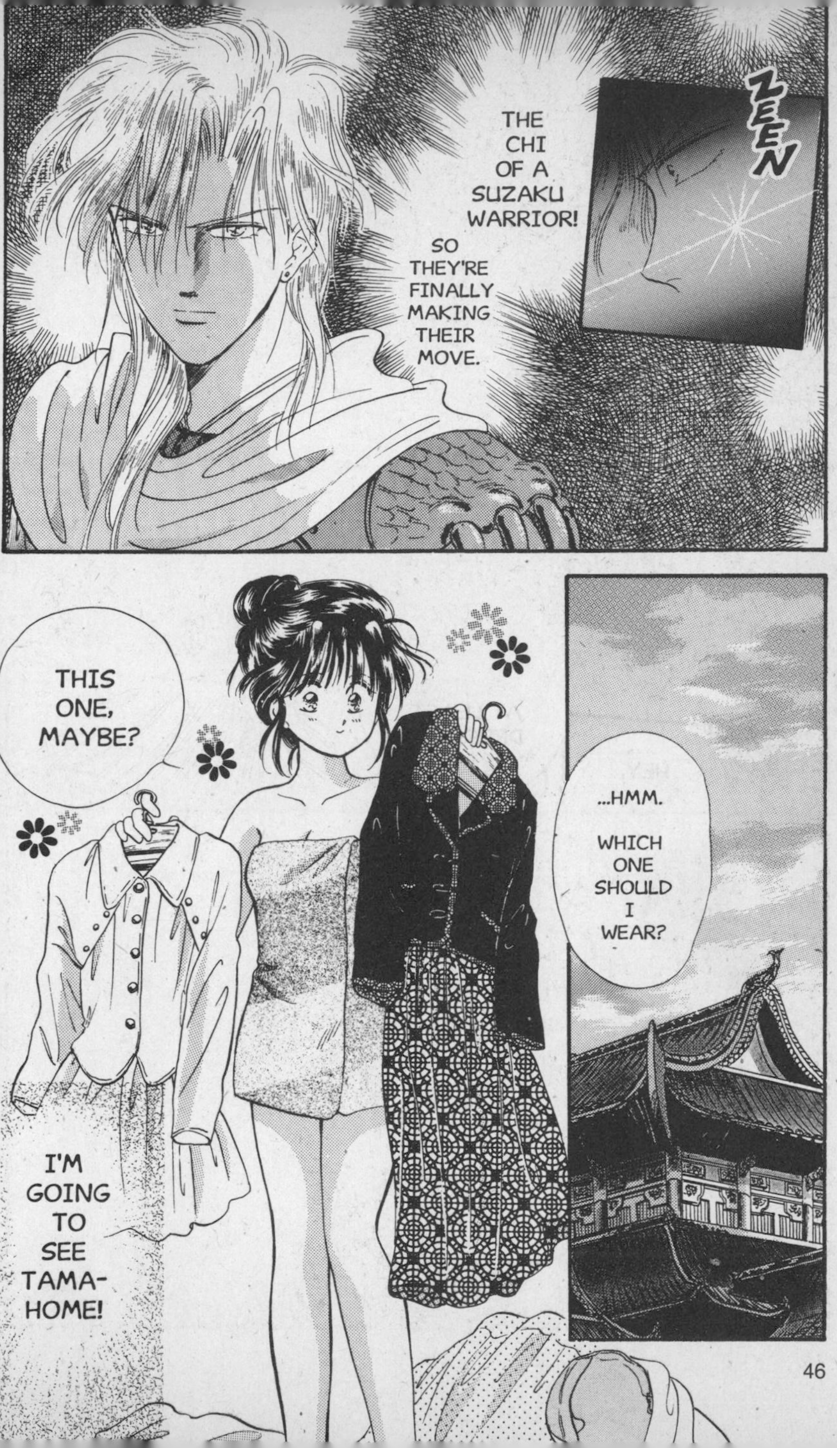
ZEEN
THE CHI OF A SUZAKU WARRIOR!
SO THEY'RE FINALLY MAKING THEIR MOVE.
...HMM. WHICH ONE SHOULD I WEAR?
THIS ONE, MAYBE?
I'M GOING TO SEE TAMA-HOME!

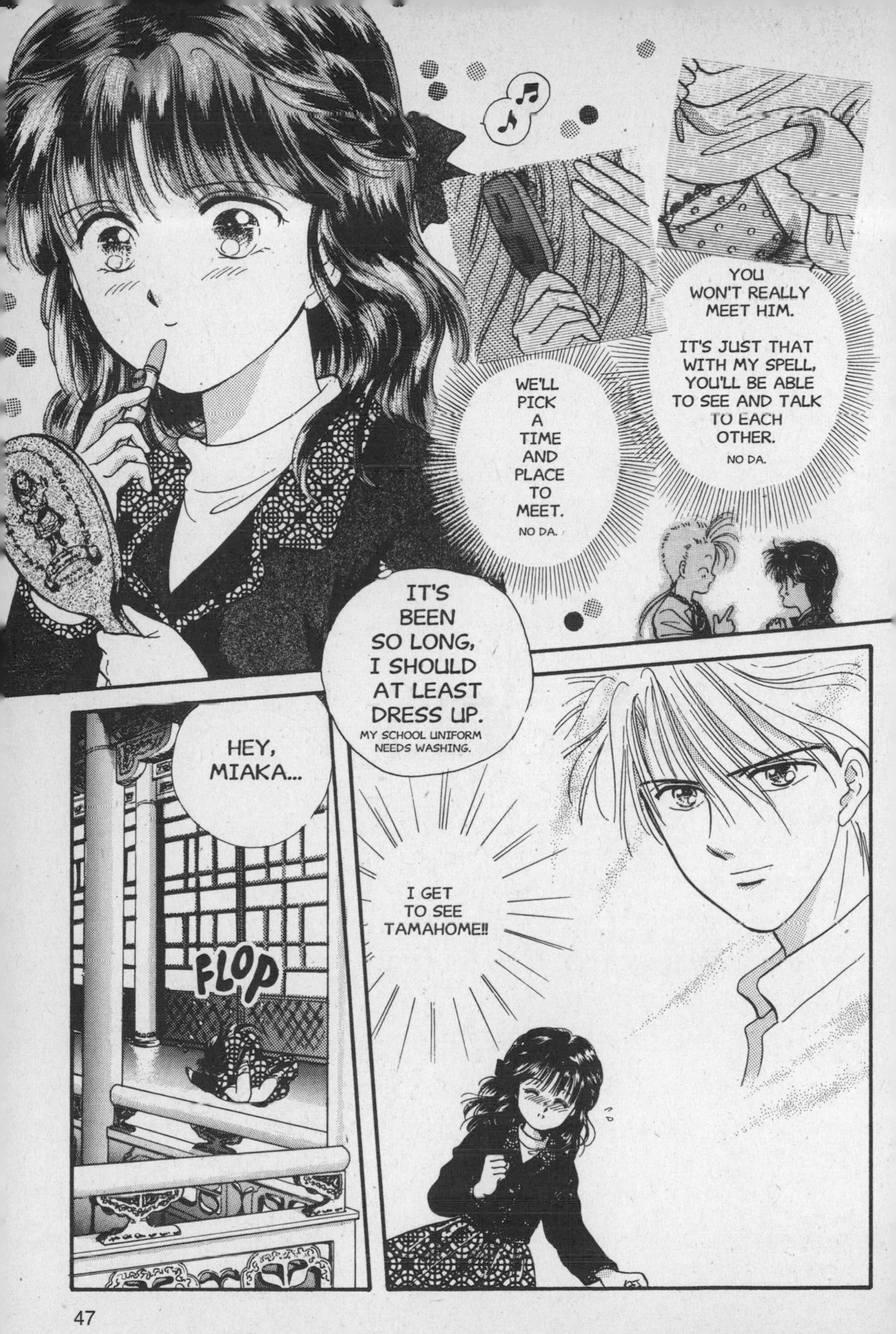
YOU WON'T REALLY MEET HIM.
IT'S JUST THAT WITH MY SPELL, YOU'LL BE ABLE TO SEE AND TALK TO EACH OTHER.
NO DA.
WE'LL PICK A TIME AND PLACE TO MEET.
NO DA.
IT'S BEEN SO LONG, I SHOULD AT LEAST DRESS UP.
MY SCHOOL UNIFORM NEEDS WASHING.
I GET TO SEE TAMAHOME!!
HEY, MIAKA...
FLOP

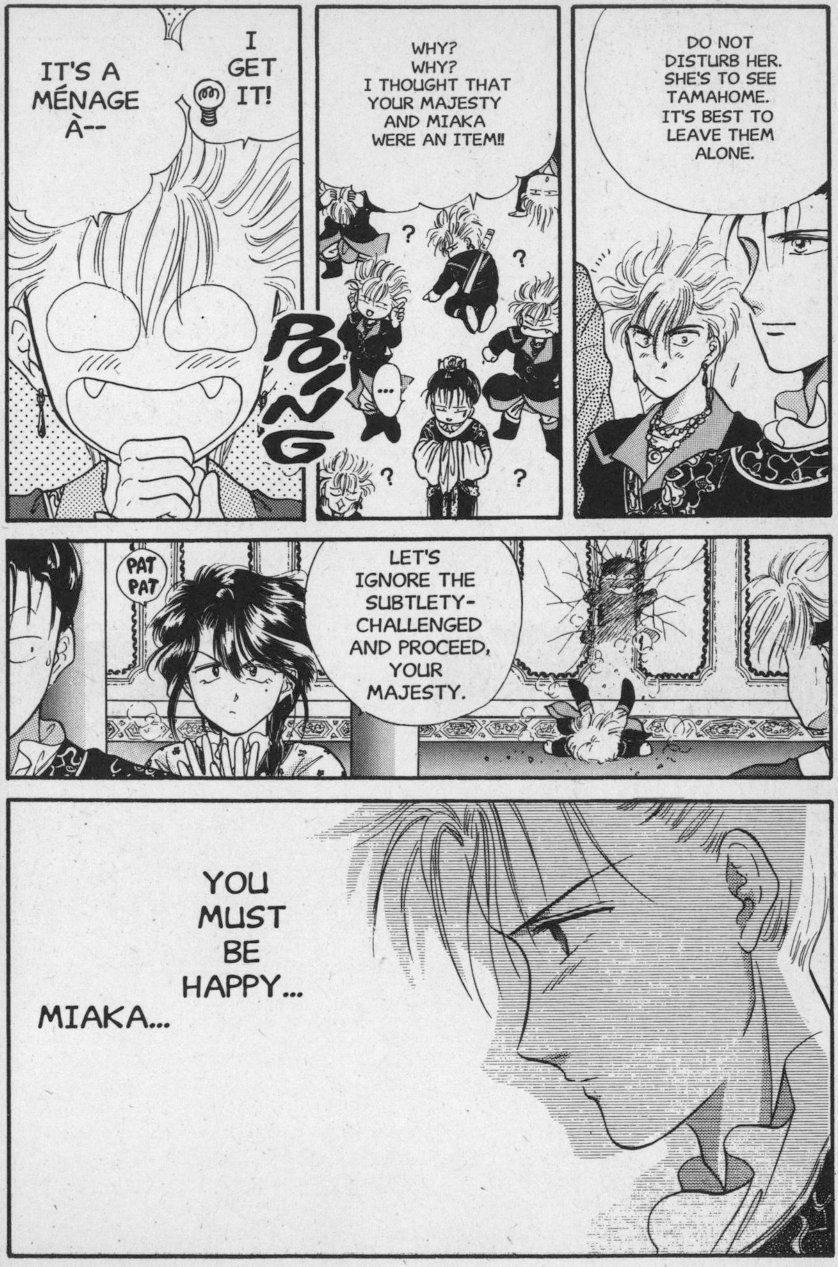
DO NOT DISTURB HER. SHE'S TO SEE TAMAHOME. IT'S BEST TO LEAVE THEM ALONE.
WHY? WHY? I THOUGHT THAT YOUR MAJESTY AND MIAKA WERE AN ITEM!!
POING
...
I GET IT!
IT'S A MÉNAGE À--
LET'S IGNORE THE SUBTLETY-CHALLENGED AND PROCEED, YOUR MAJESTY.
PAT PAT
YOU MUST BE HAPPY...
MIAKA...

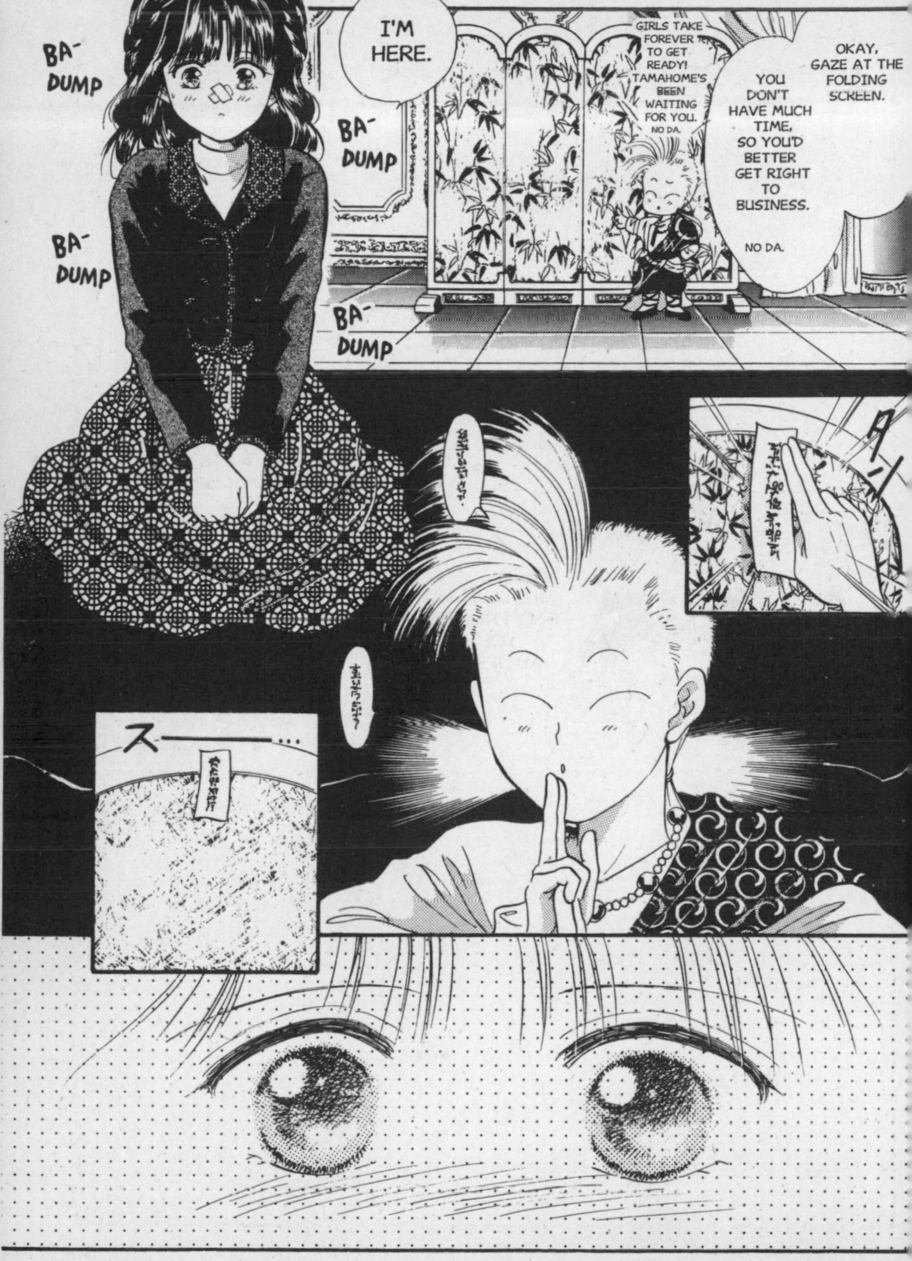
OKAY, GAZE AT THE FOLDING SCREEN.
YOU DON'T HAVE MUCH TIME, SO YOU'D BETTER GET RIGHT TO BUSINESS.
NO DA.
GIRLS TAKE FOREVER TO GET READY! TAMAHOME'S BEEN WAITING FOR YOU. NO DA.
I'M HERE.
BA-DUMP
BA-DUMP
BA-DUMP
BA-DUMP
スー…

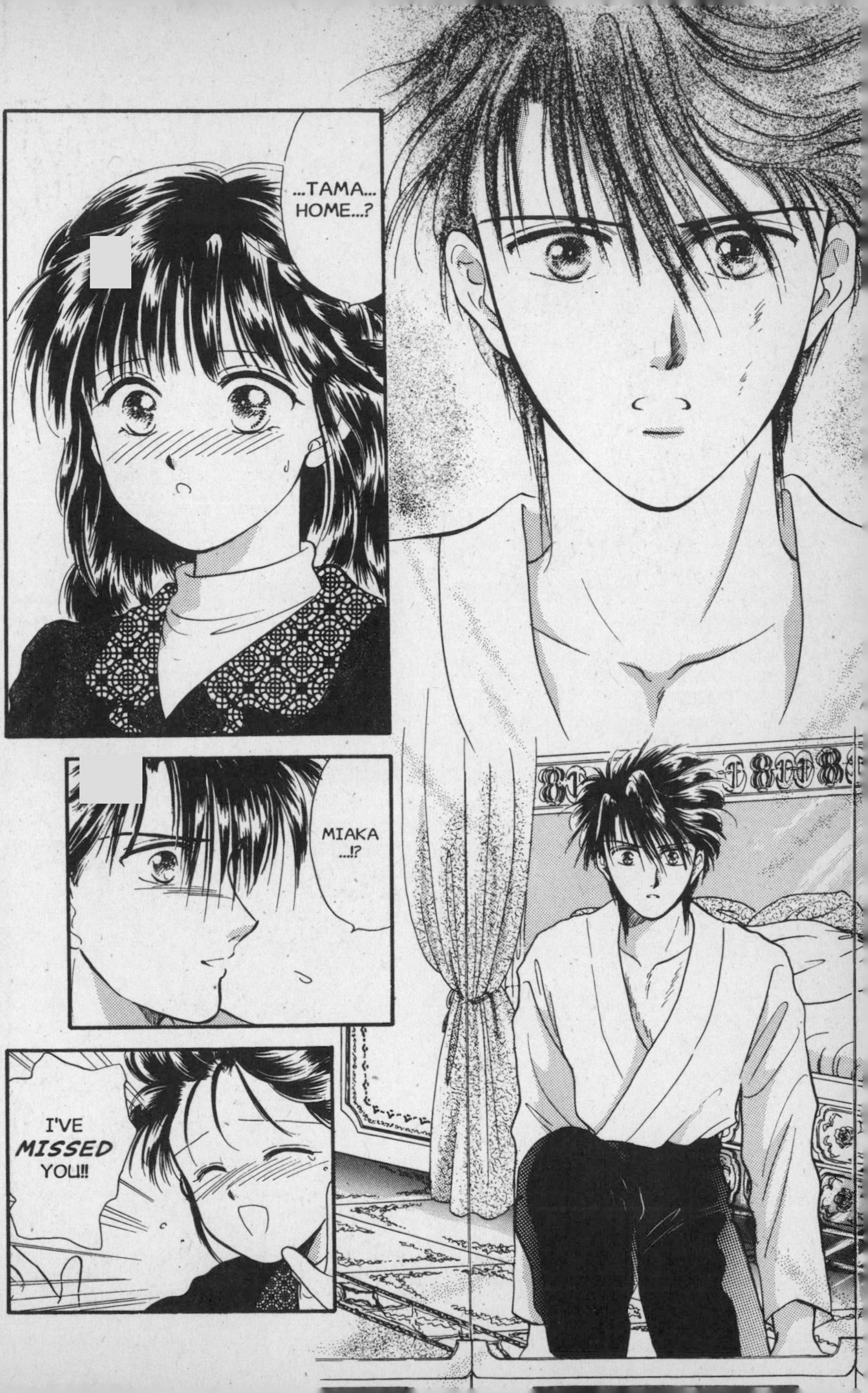
...TAMA... HOME...?
MIAKA ...!?
I'VE MISSED YOU!!

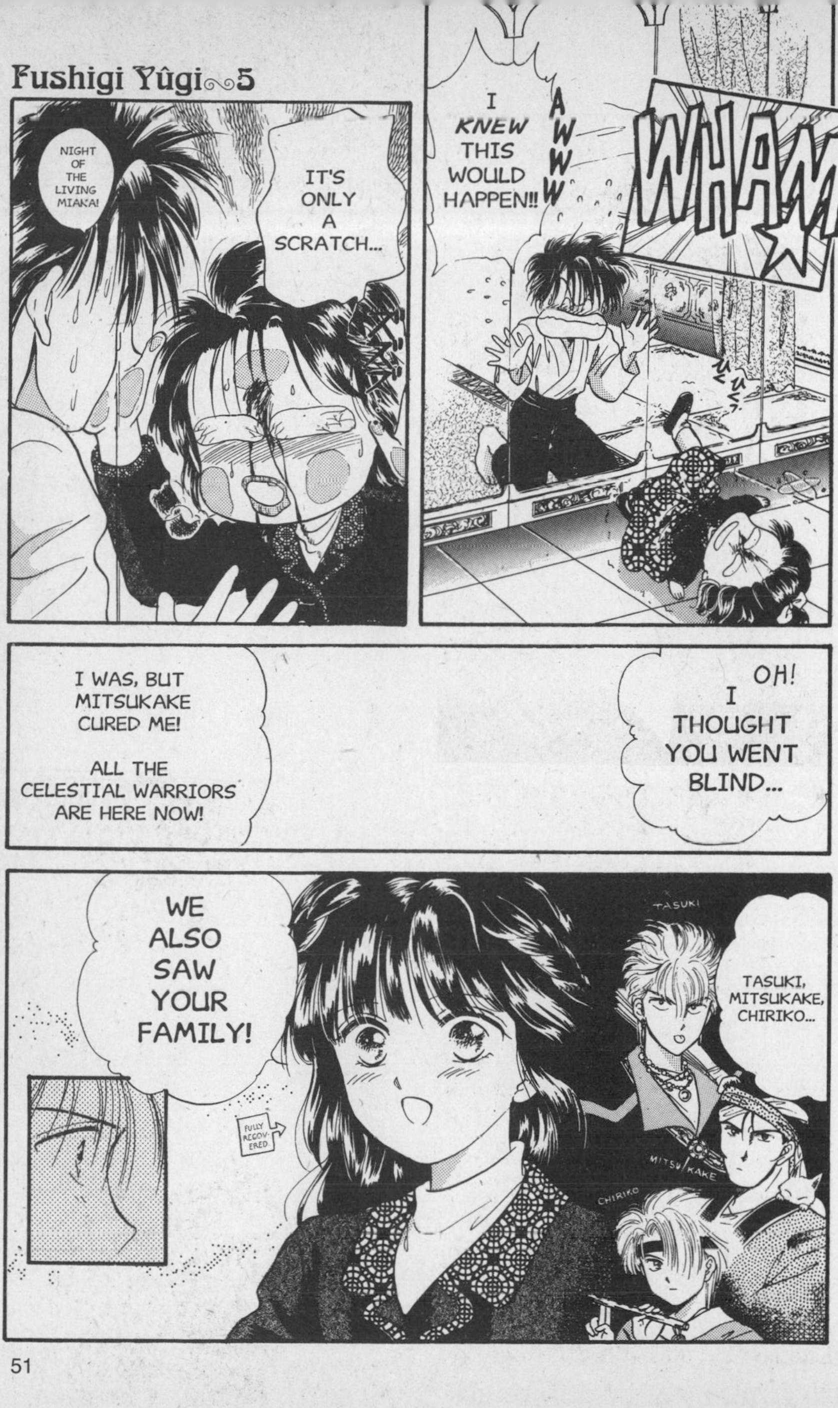
WHAM
AWWWW
I KNEW THIS WOULD HAPPEN!!
IT'S ONLY A SCRATCH...
NIGHT OF THE LIVING MIAKA!
OH! I THOUGHT YOU WENT BLIND...
I WAS, BUT MITSUKAKE CURED ME!
ALL THE CELESTIAL WARRIORS ARE HERE NOW!
TASUKI, MITSUKAKE, CHIRIKO...
TASUKI
MITSUKAKE
CHIRIKO
WE ALSO SAW YOUR FAMILY!
FULLY RECOVERED

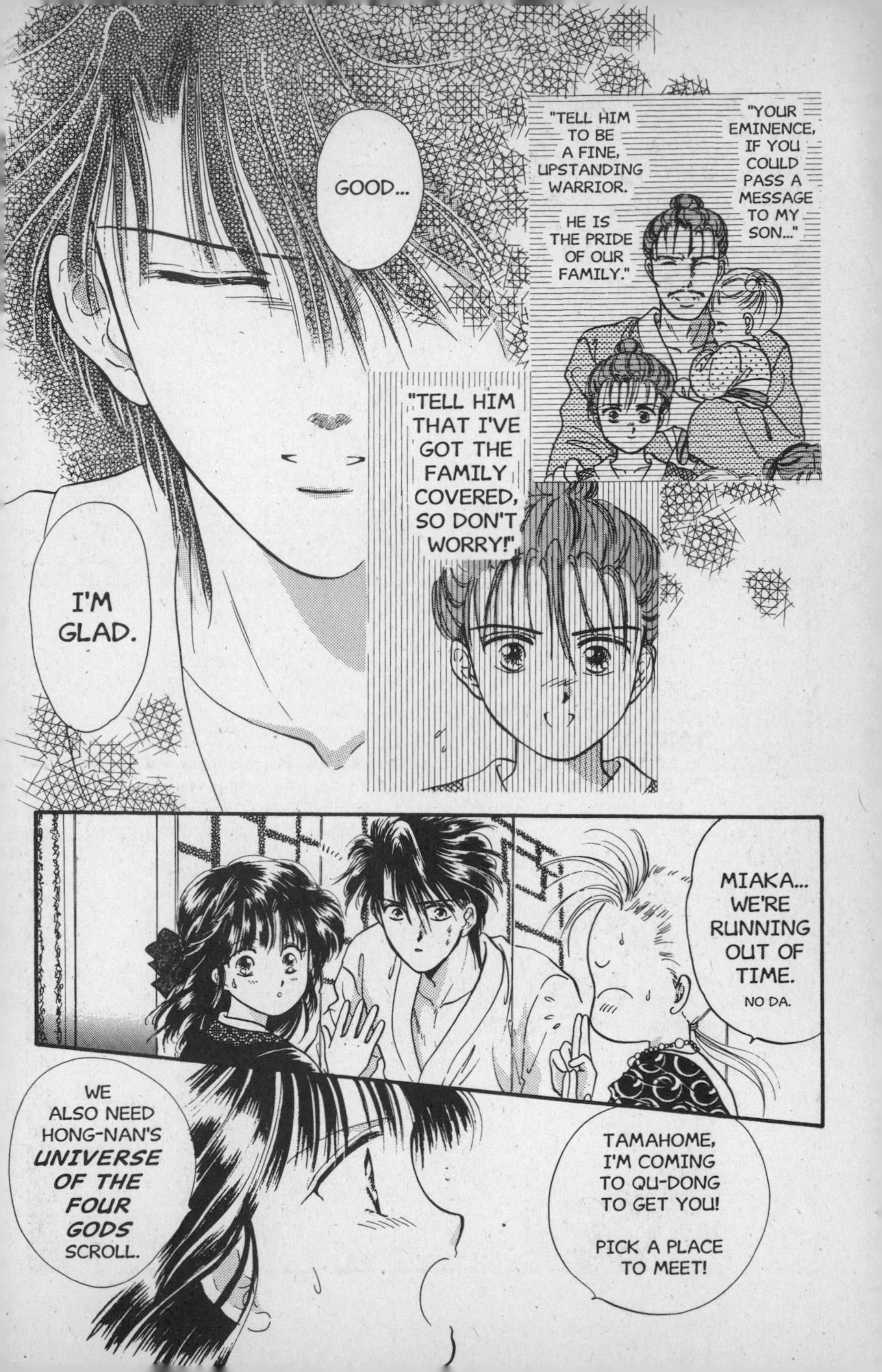
"YOUR EMINENCE, IF YOU COULD PASS A MESSAGE TO MY SON..."
"TELL HIM TO BE A FINE, UPSTANDING WARRIOR.
HE IS THE PRIDE OF OUR FAMILY."
"TELL HIM THAT I'VE GOT THE FAMILY COVERED, SO DON'T WORRY!"
GOOD...
I'M GLAD.
MIAKA... WE'RE RUNNING OUT OF TIME. NO DA.
TAMAHOME, I'M COMING TO QU-DONG TO GET YOU!
PICK A PLACE TO MEET!
WE ALSO NEED HONG-NAN'S *UNIVERSE OF THE FOUR GODS* SCROLL.

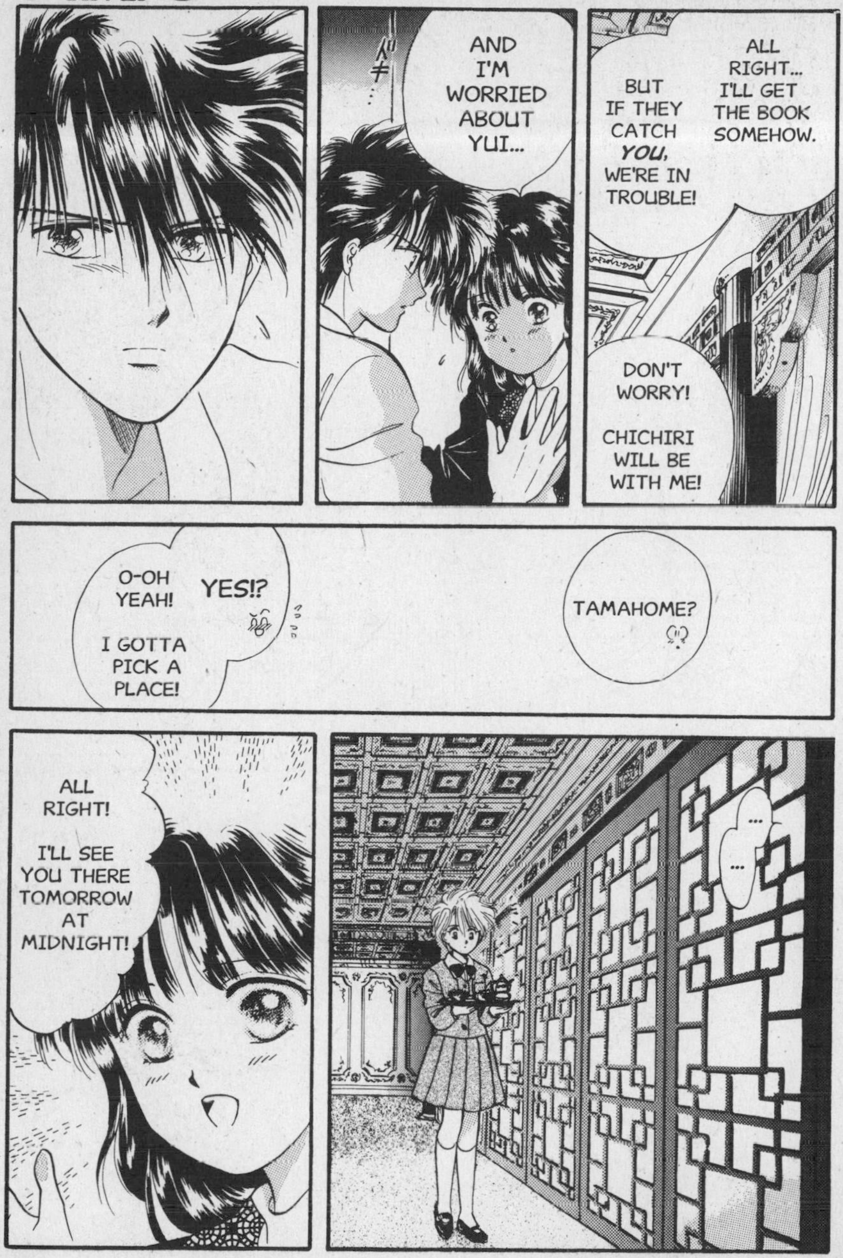
ALL RIGHT... I'LL GET THE BOOK SOMEHOW.
BUT IF THEY CATCH *YOU*, WE'RE IN TROUBLE!
DON'T WORRY!
CHICHIRI WILL BE WITH ME!
AND I'M WORRIED ABOUT YUI...
TAMAHOME?
YES!?
O-OH YEAH!
I GOTTA PICK A PLACE!
...
...
ALL RIGHT!
I'LL SEE YOU THERE TOMORROW AT MIDNIGHT!

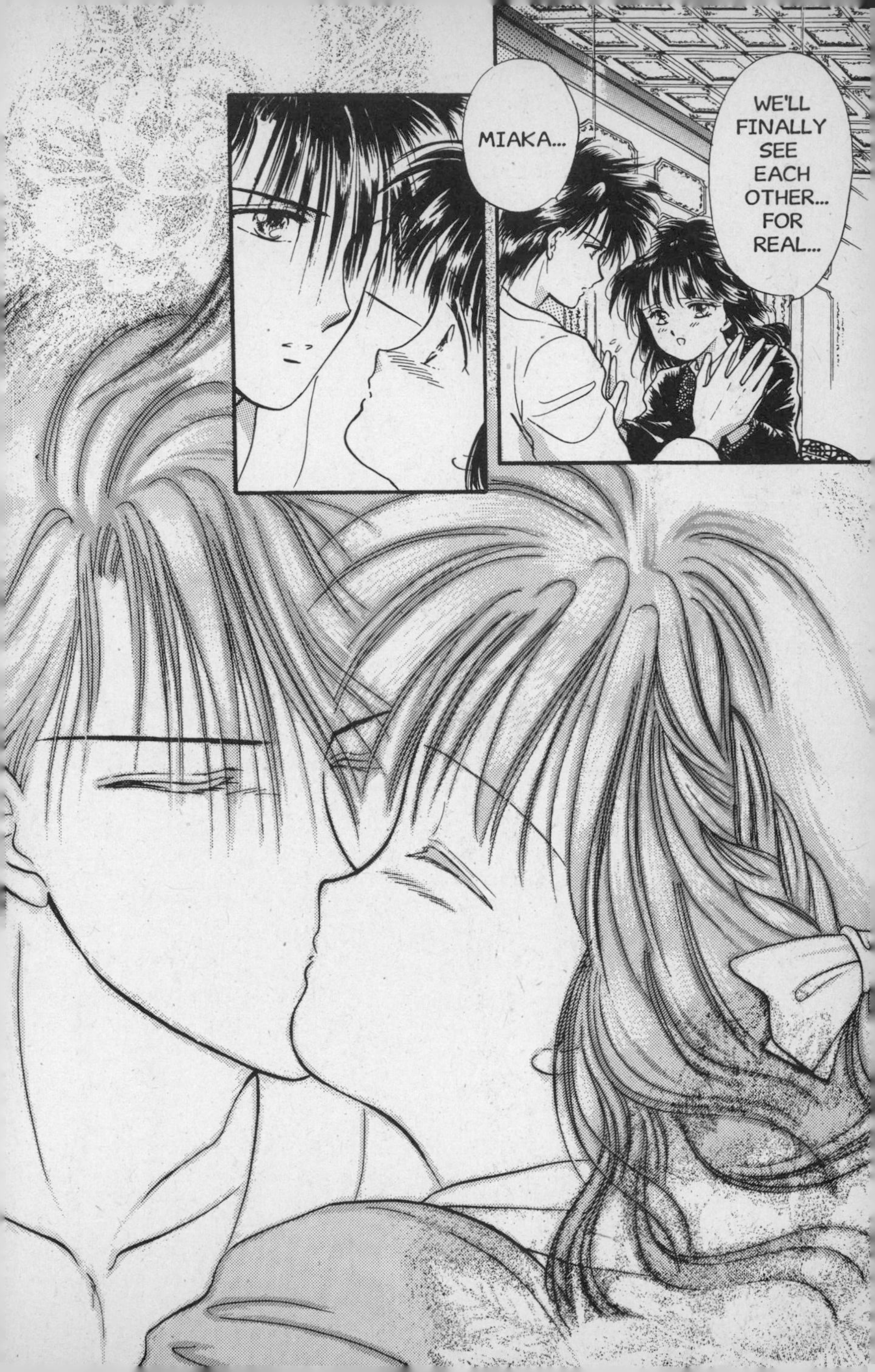
WE'LL FINALLY SEE EACH OTHER... FOR REAL...
MIAKA...

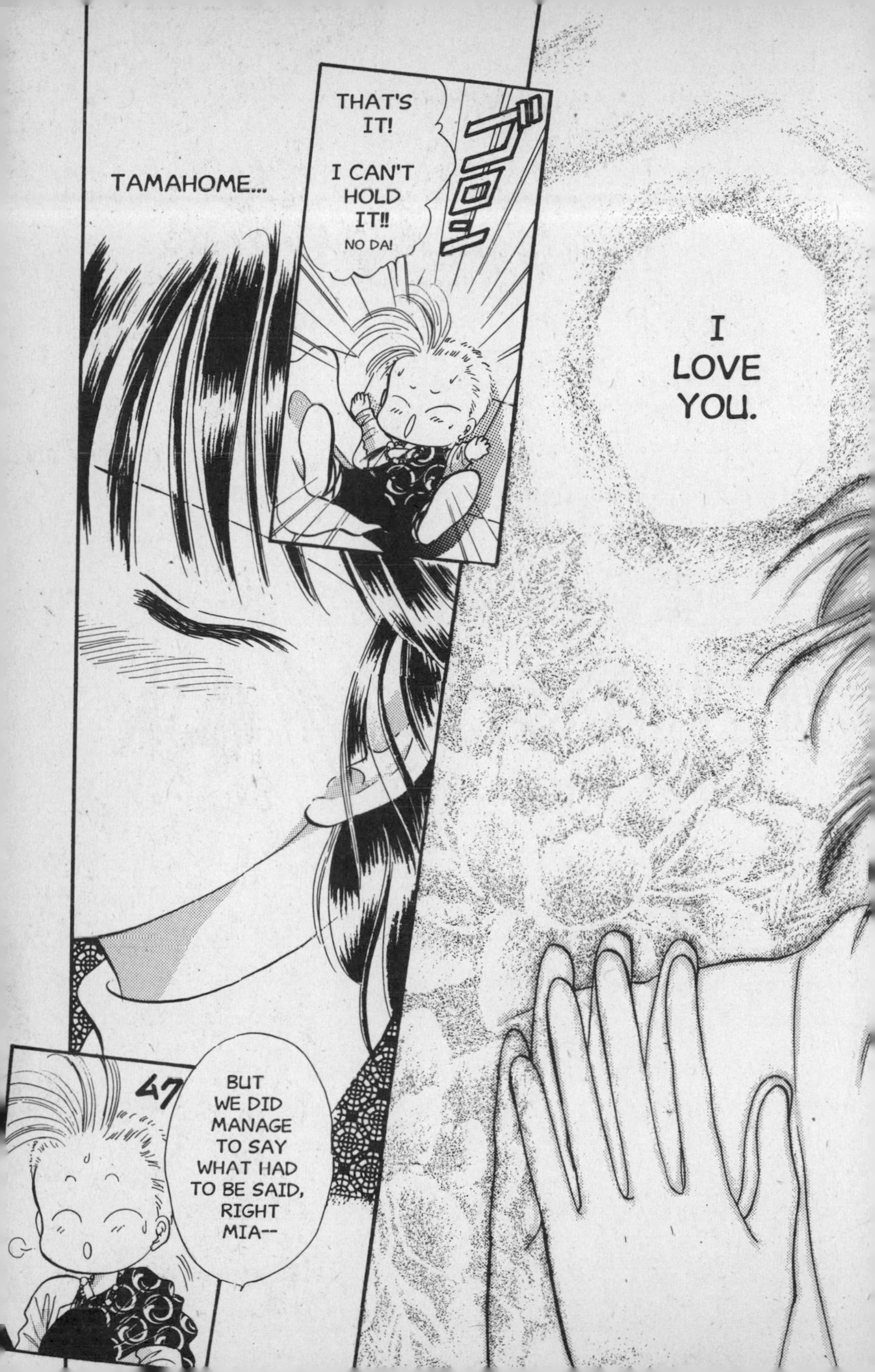
TAMAHOME...
I LOVE YOU.
THAT'S IT!
I CAN'T HOLD IT!!
NO DA!
BUT WE DID MANAGE TO SAY WHAT HAD TO BE SAID, RIGHT MIA--

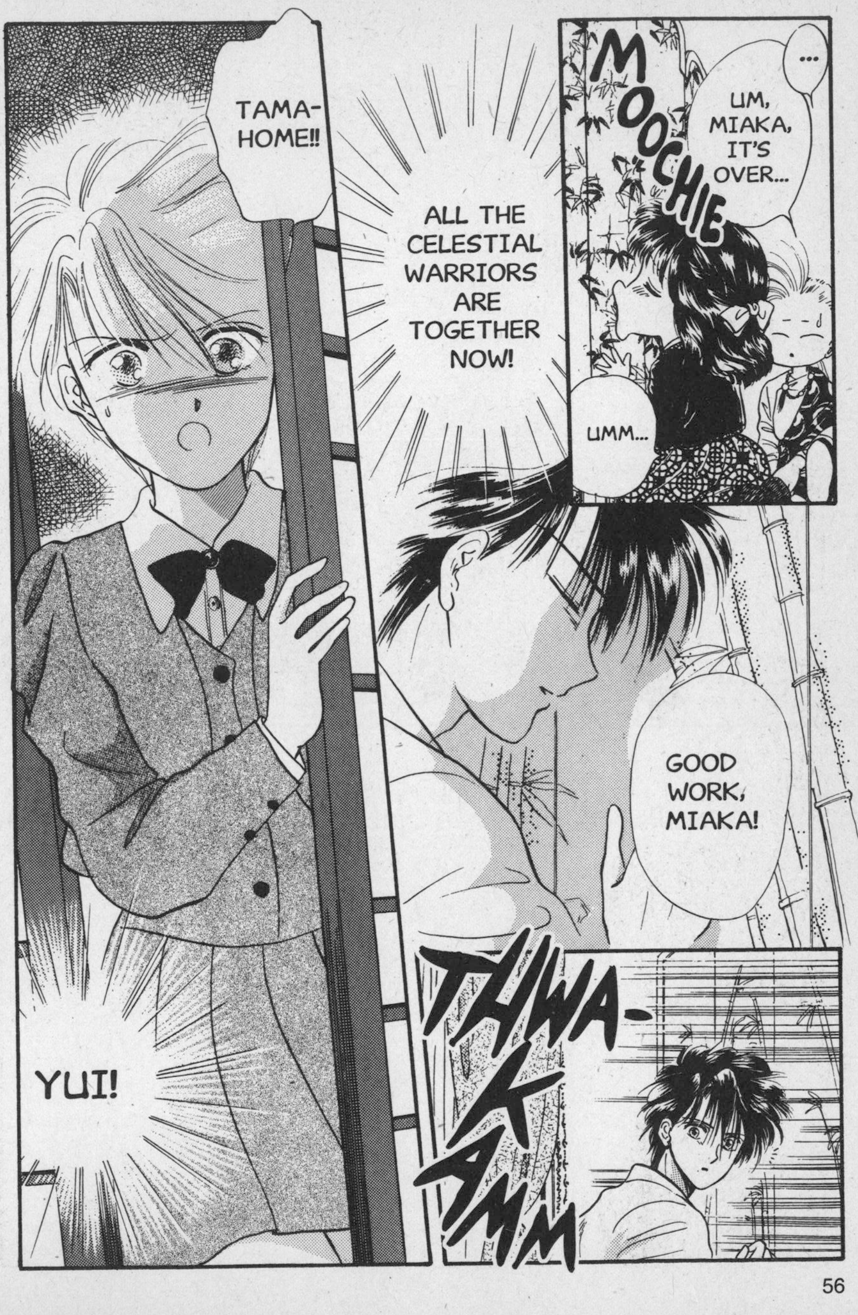
...
UM, MIAKA, IT'S OVER...
MOOCHIE
UMM...
ALL THE CELESTIAL WARRIORS ARE TOGETHER NOW!
GOOD WORK, MIAKA!
THWA-K-AMM
TAMA-HOME!!
YUI!

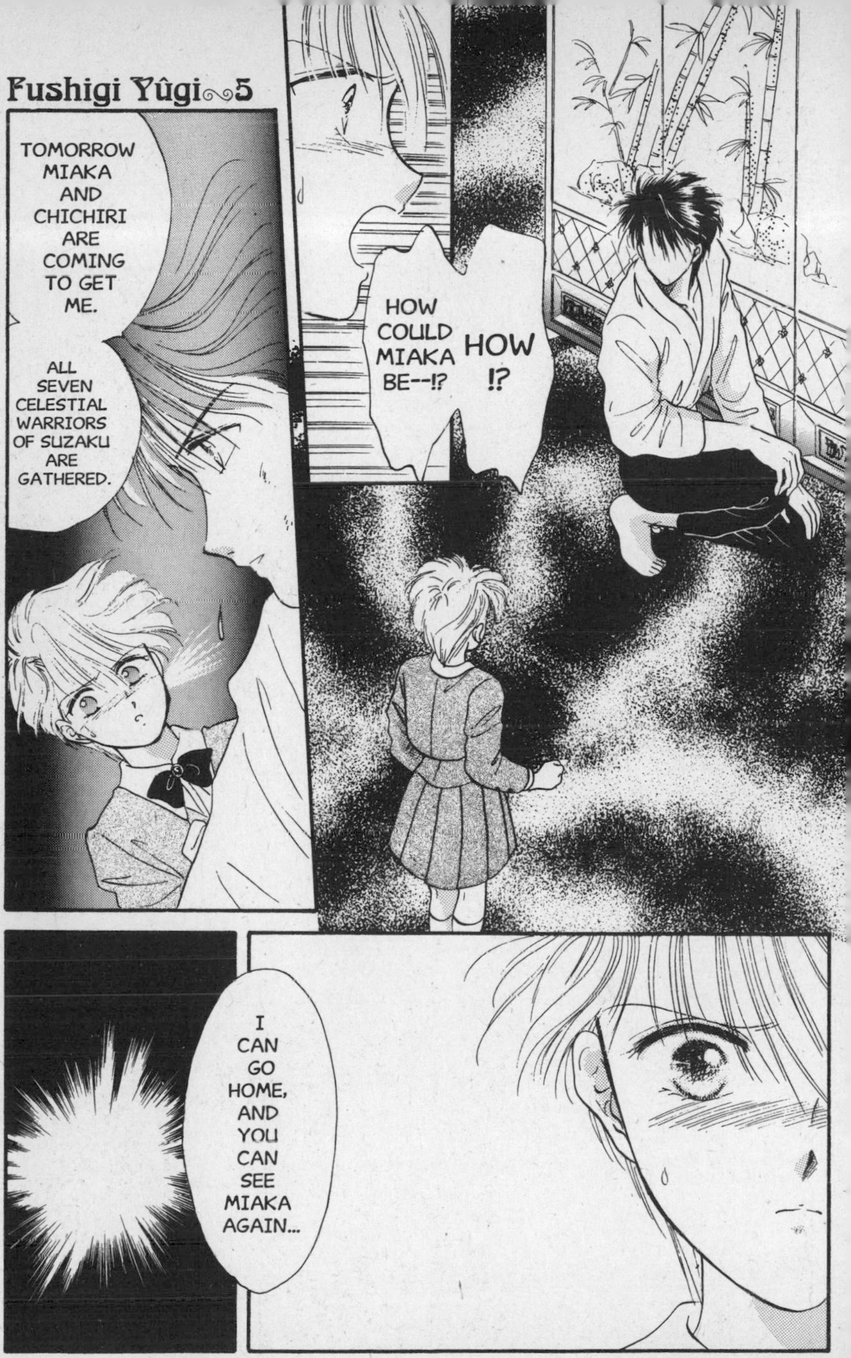
HOW COULD MIAKA BE--!?
HOW !?
TOMORROW MIAKA AND CHICHIRI ARE COMING TO GET ME.
ALL SEVEN CELESTIAL WARRIORS OF SUZAKU ARE GATHERED.
I CAN GO HOME, AND YOU CAN SEE MIAKA AGAIN...

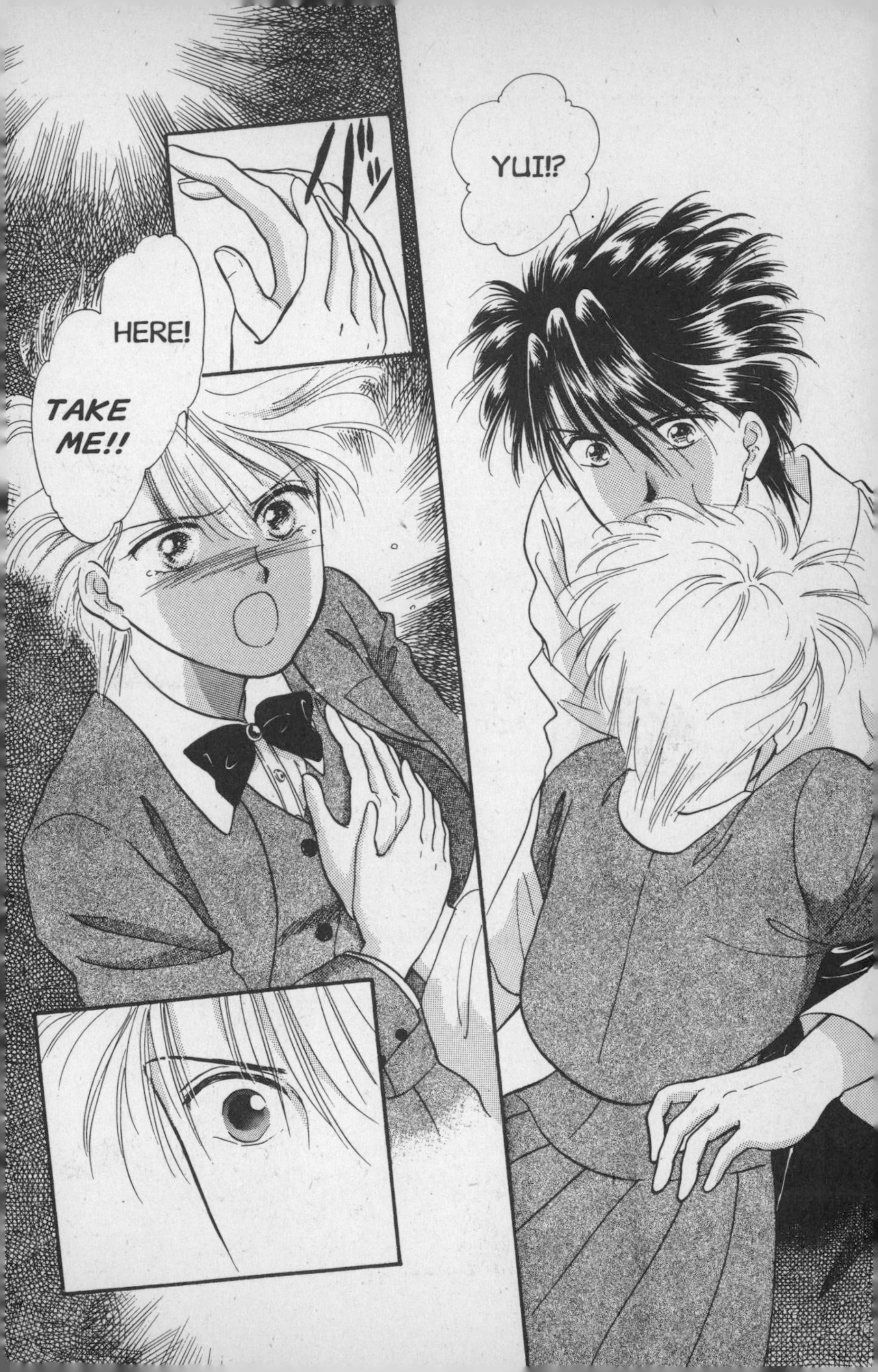
YUI!?
HERE!
TAKE ME!!

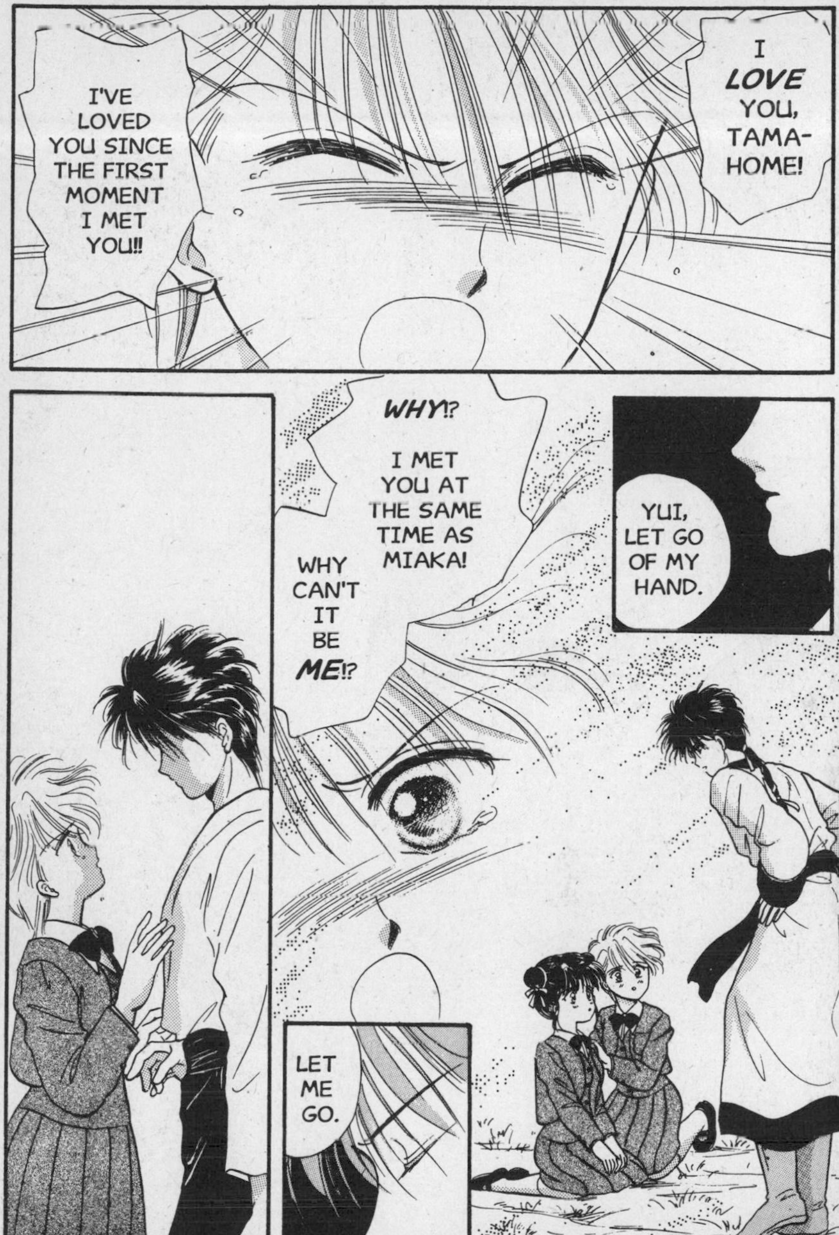
I LOVE YOU, TAMA-HOME!
I'VE LOVED YOU SINCE THE FIRST MOMENT I MET YOU!!
YUI, LET GO OF MY HAND.
WHY!?
I MET YOU AT THE SAME TIME AS MIAKA!
WHY CAN'T IT BE ME!?
LET ME GO.

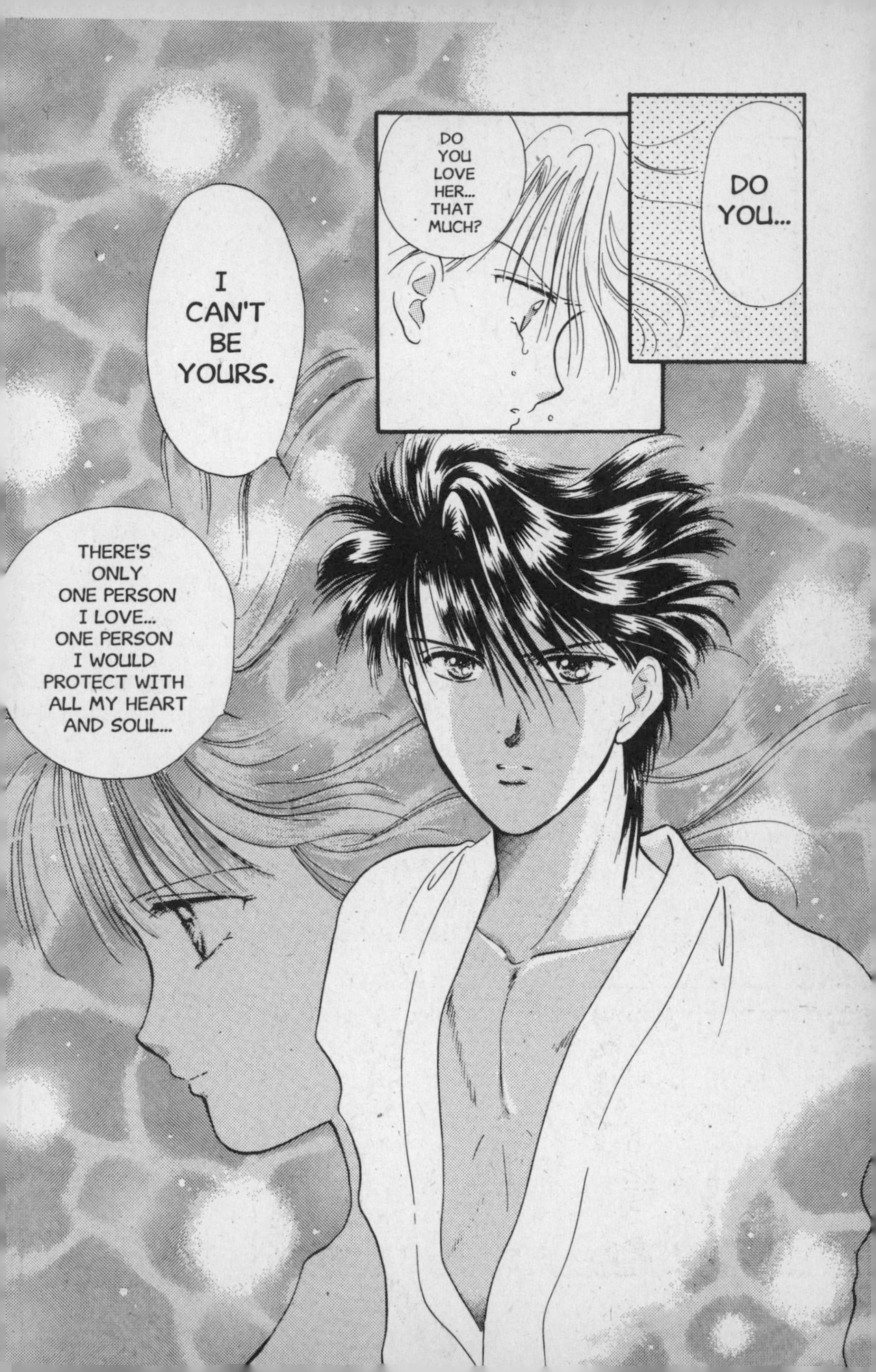
DO YOU...
DO YOU LOVE HER... THAT MUCH?
I CAN'T BE YOURS.
THERE'S ONLY ONE PERSON I LOVE... ONE PERSON I WOULD PROTECT WITH ALL MY HEART AND SOUL...

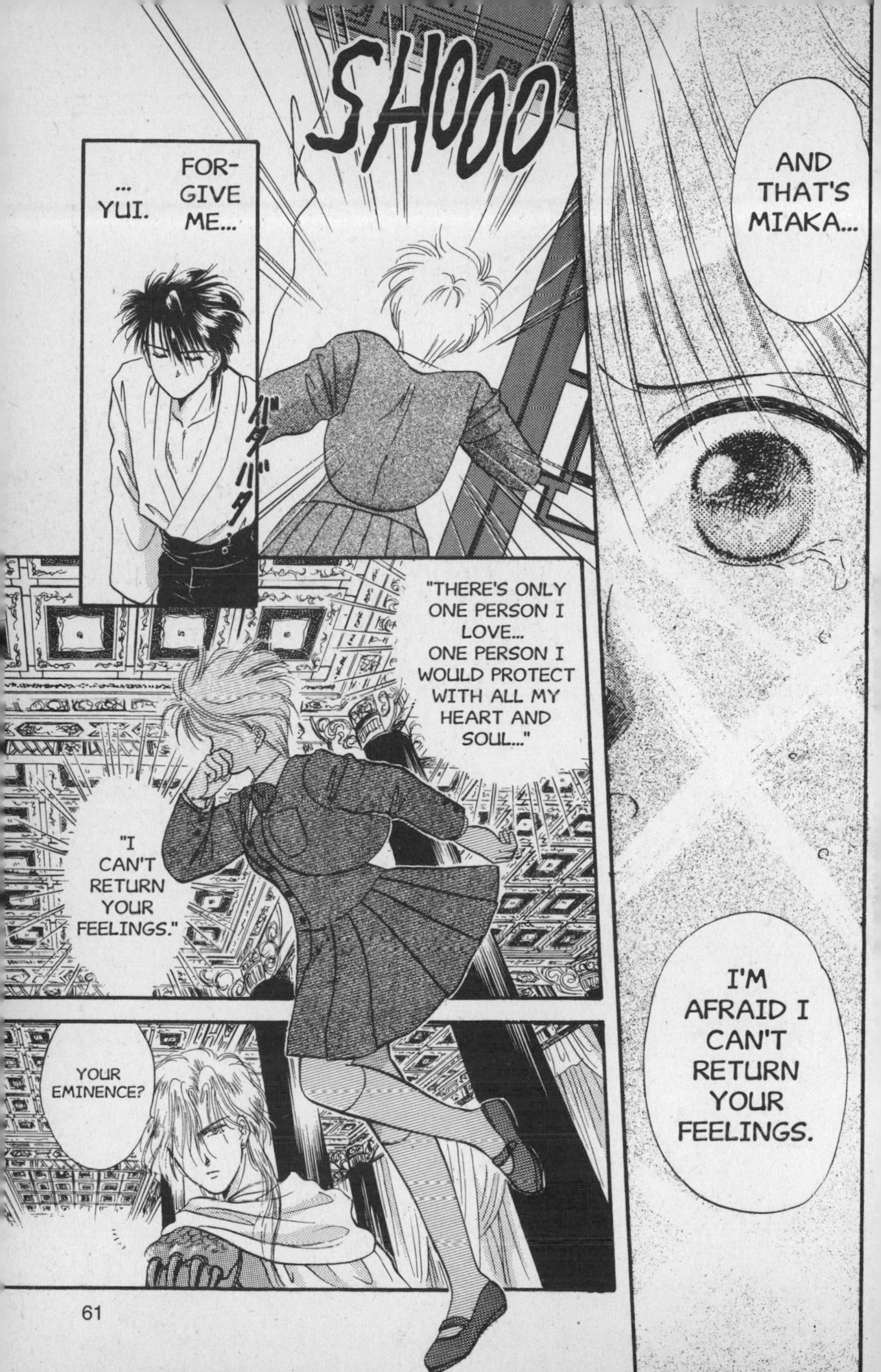
AND THAT'S MIAKA...
I'M AFRAID I CAN'T RETURN YOUR FEELINGS.
SHOOO
FOR-GIVE ME...
... YUI.
"THERE'S ONLY ONE PERSON I LOVE... ONE PERSON I WOULD PROTECT WITH ALL MY HEART AND SOUL..."
"I CAN'T RETURN YOUR FEELINGS."
YOUR EMINENCE?

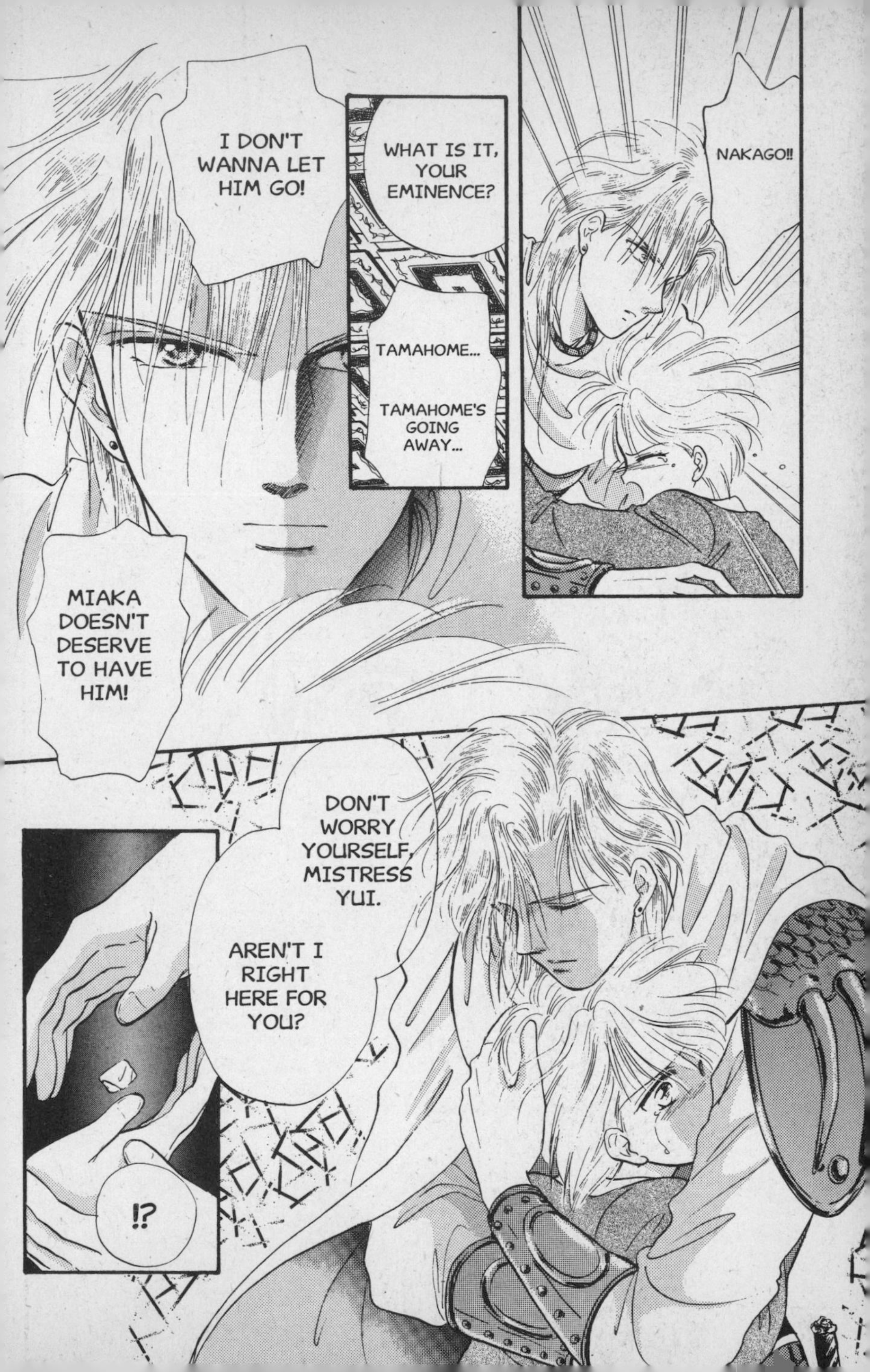
NAKAGO!!
WHAT IS IT, YOUR EMINENCE?
TAMAHOME...
TAMAHOME'S GOING AWAY...
I DON'T WANNA LET HIM GO!
MIAKA DOESN'T DESERVE TO HAVE HIM!
DON'T WORRY YOURSELF, MISTRESS YUI.
AREN'T I RIGHT HERE FOR YOU?
!?

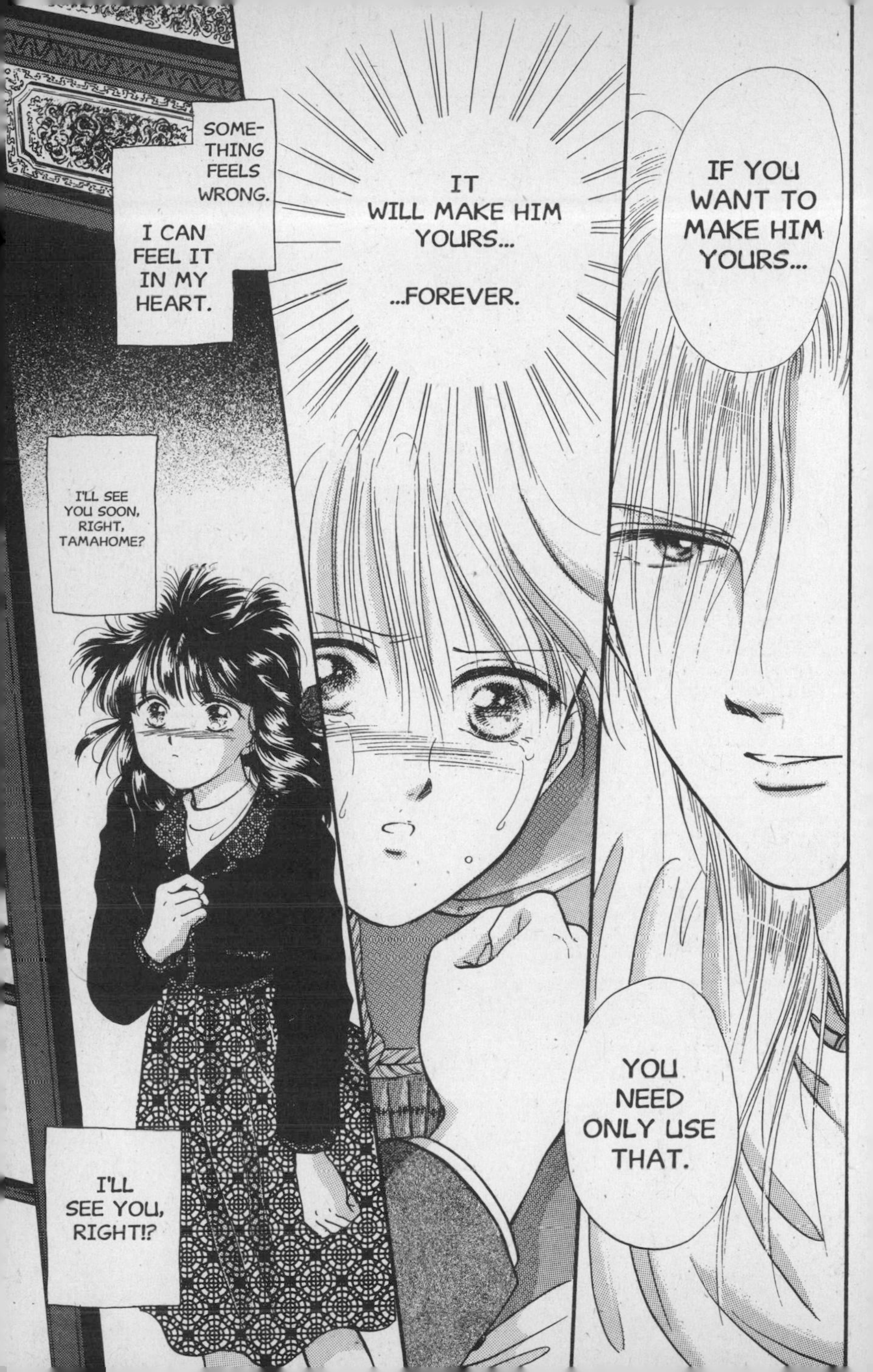
IF YOU WANT TO MAKE HIM YOURS...
YOU NEED ONLY USE THAT.
IT WILL MAKE HIM YOURS...
...FOREVER.
SOME-THING FEELS WRONG.
I CAN FEEL IT IN MY HEART.
I'LL SEE YOU SOON, RIGHT, TAMAHOME?
I'LL SEE YOU, RIGHT!?

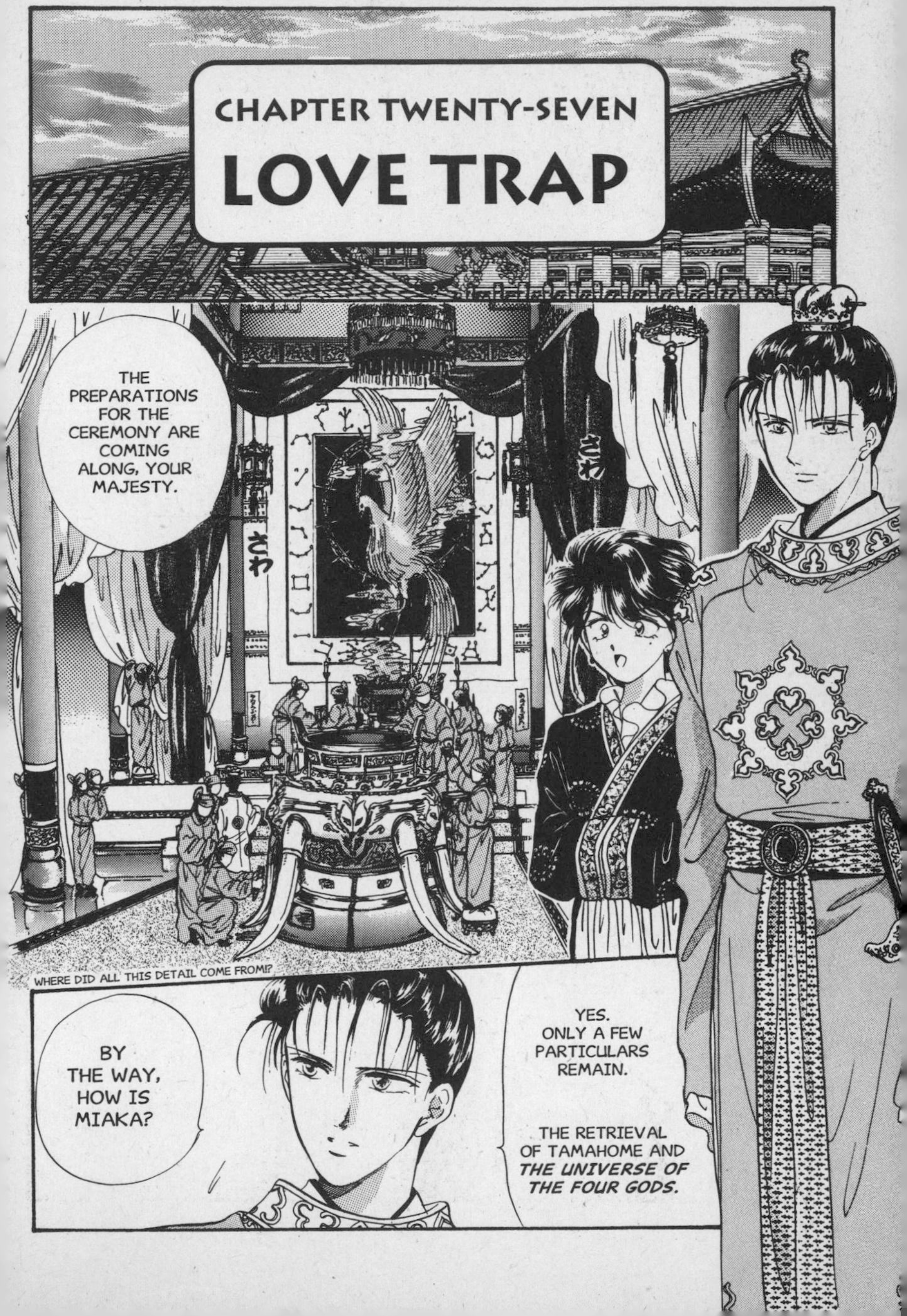
CHAPTER TWENTY-SEVEN
LOVE TRAP
THE PREPARATIONS FOR THE CEREMONY ARE COMING ALONG, YOUR MAJESTY.
さわ
さわ
WHERE DID ALL THIS DETAIL COME FROM!?
YES. ONLY A FEW PARTICULARS REMAIN.
THE RETRIEVAL OF TAMAHOME AND *THE UNIVERSE OF THE FOUR GODS.*
BY THE WAY, HOW IS MIAKA?

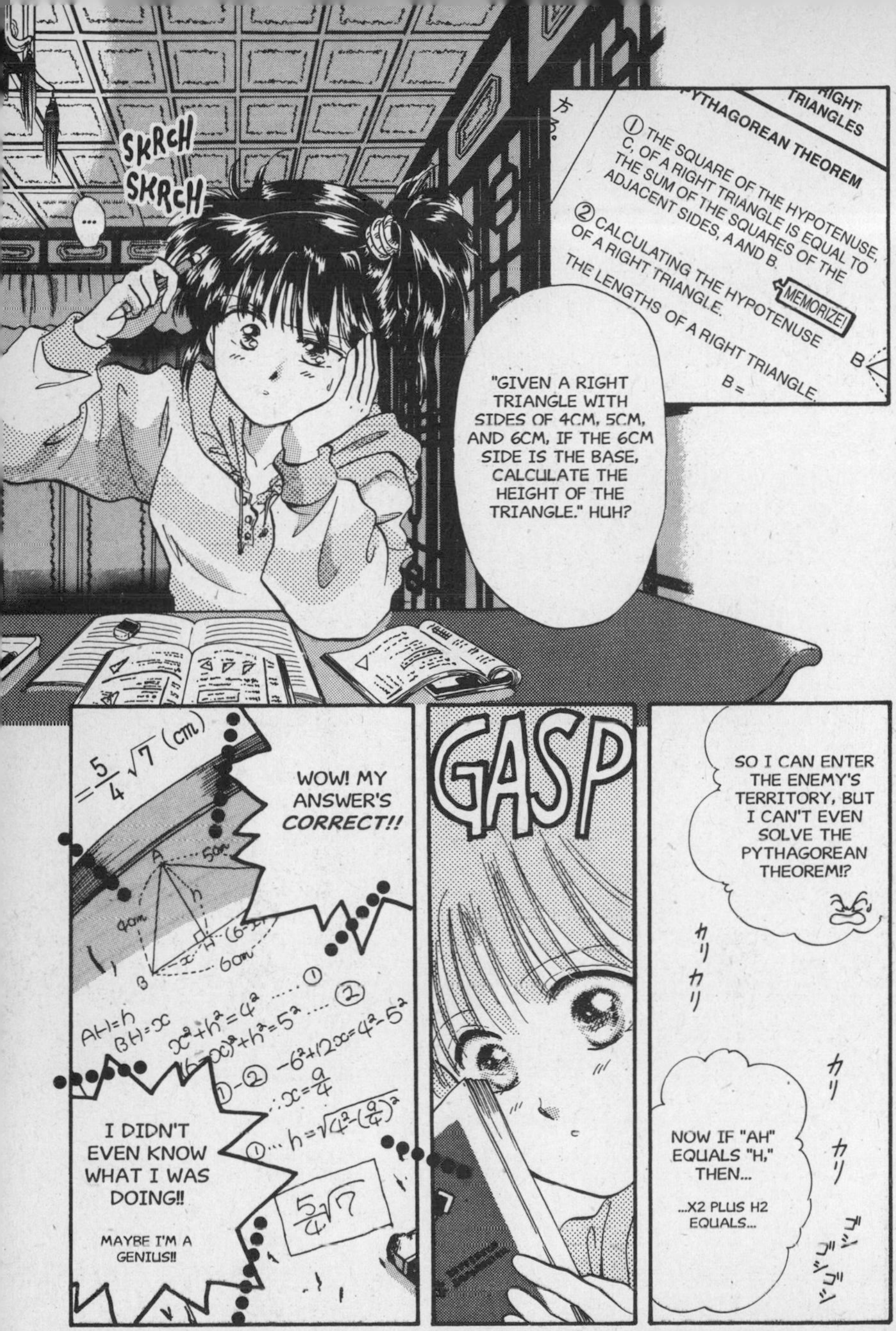
RIGHT TRIANGLES
PYTHAGOREAN THEOREM
① THE SQUARE OF THE HYPOTENUSE, C, OF A RIGHT TRIANGLE IS EQUAL TO THE SUM OF THE SQUARES OF THE ADJACENT SIDES, A AND B.
MEMORIZE!
② CALCULATING THE HYPOTENUSE OF A RIGHT TRIANGLE.
THE LENGTHS OF A RIGHT TRIANGLE.
B =
"GIVEN A RIGHT TRIANGLE WITH SIDES OF 4CM, 5CM, AND 6CM, IF THE 6CM SIDE IS THE BASE, CALCULATE THE HEIGHT OF THE TRIANGLE." HUH?
SKRCH SKRCH
...
SO I CAN ENTER THE ENEMY'S TERRITORY, BUT I CAN'T EVEN SOLVE THE PYTHAGOREAN THEOREM!?
カリカリ
NOW IF "AH" EQUALS "H," THEN...
...X2 PLUS H2 EQUALS...
カリ カリ
ゴシゴシ
GASP
= 5/4 √7 (cm)
WOW! MY ANSWER'S *CORRECT!!*
I DIDN'T EVEN KNOW WHAT I WAS DOING!!
MAYBE I'M A GENIUS!!

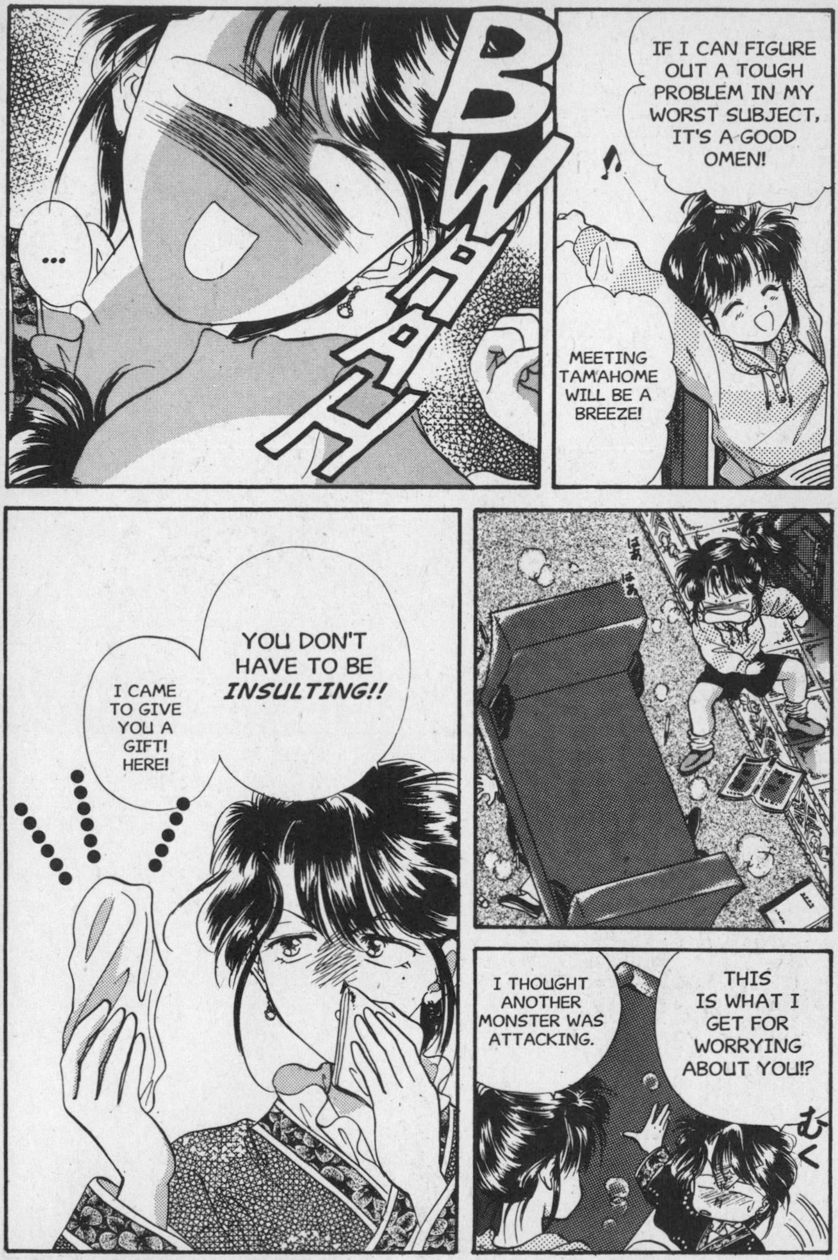
IF I CAN FIGURE OUT A TOUGH PROBLEM IN MY WORST SUBJECT, IT'S A GOOD OMEN!
MEETING TAMAHOME WILL BE A BREEZE!
BWHAAH
...
はあ はあ
THIS IS WHAT I GET FOR WORRYING ABOUT YOU!?
I THOUGHT ANOTHER MONSTER WAS ATTACKING.
むく
YOU DON'T HAVE TO BE *INSULTING!!*
I CAME TO GIVE YOU A GIFT! HERE!

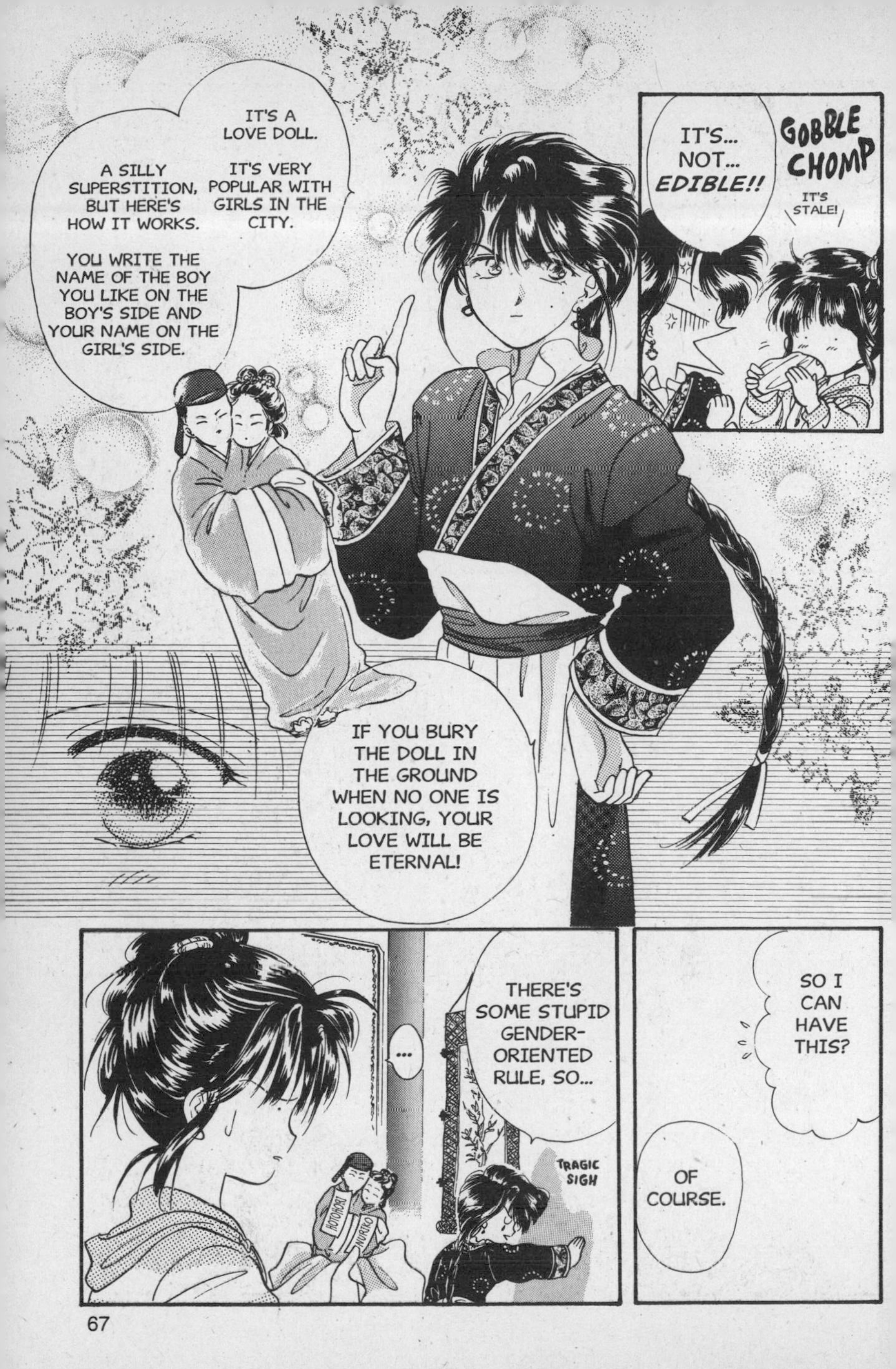
GOBBLE CHOMP
IT'S STALE!
IT'S... NOT... *EDIBLE!!*
IT'S A LOVE DOLL.
IT'S VERY POPULAR WITH GIRLS IN THE CITY.
A SILLY SUPERSTITION, BUT HERE'S HOW IT WORKS.
YOU WRITE THE NAME OF THE BOY YOU LIKE ON THE BOY'S SIDE AND YOUR NAME ON THE GIRL'S SIDE.
IF YOU BURY THE DOLL IN THE GROUND WHEN NO ONE IS LOOKING, YOUR LOVE WILL BE ETERNAL!
SO I CAN HAVE THIS?
OF COURSE.
THERE'S SOME STUPID GENDER-ORIENTED RULE, SO...
TRAGIC SIGH
...
HOTOHORI
NURIKO

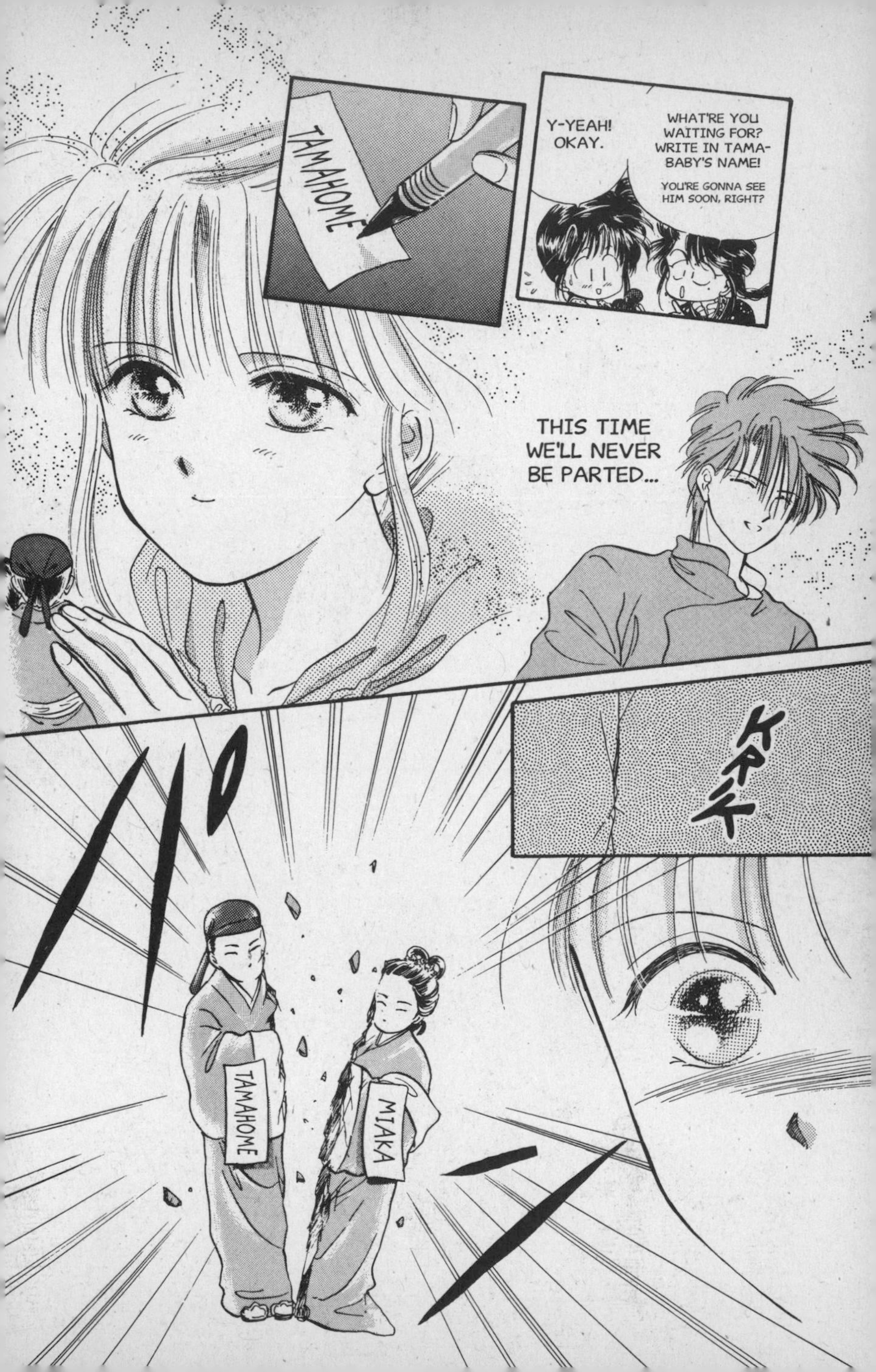
WHAT'RE YOU WAITING FOR? WRITE IN TAMA-BABY'S NAME!
YOU'RE GONNA SEE HIM SOON, RIGHT?
Y-YEAH! OKAY.
TAMAHOME
THIS TIME WE'LL NEVER BE PARTED...
TAMAHOME
MIAKA

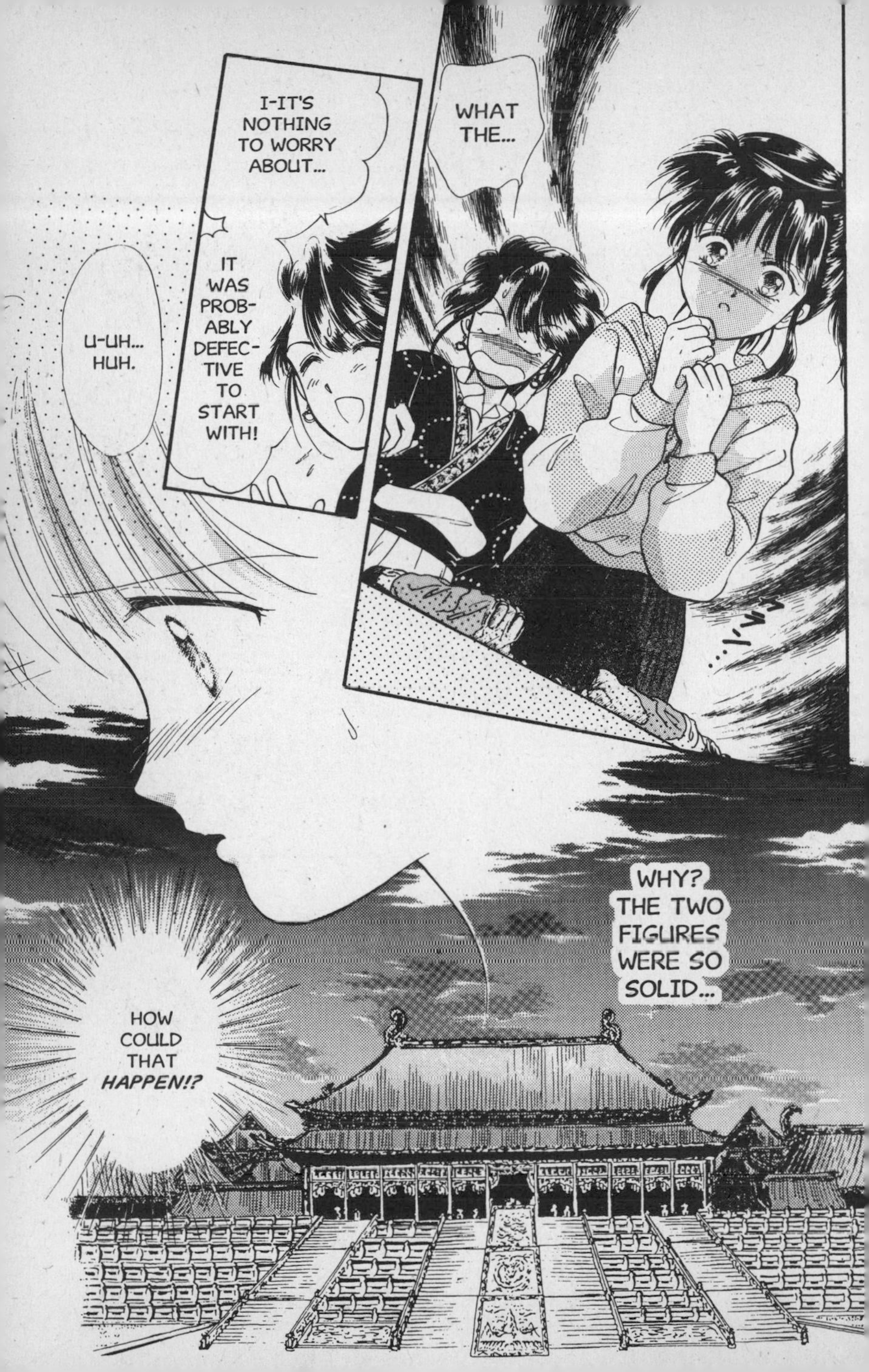
WHAT THE...
I-IT'S NOTHING TO WORRY ABOUT...
IT WAS PROBABLY DEFECTIVE TO START WITH!
U-UH... HUH.
WHY? THE TWO FIGURES WERE SO SOLID...
HOW COULD THAT *HAPPEN!?*

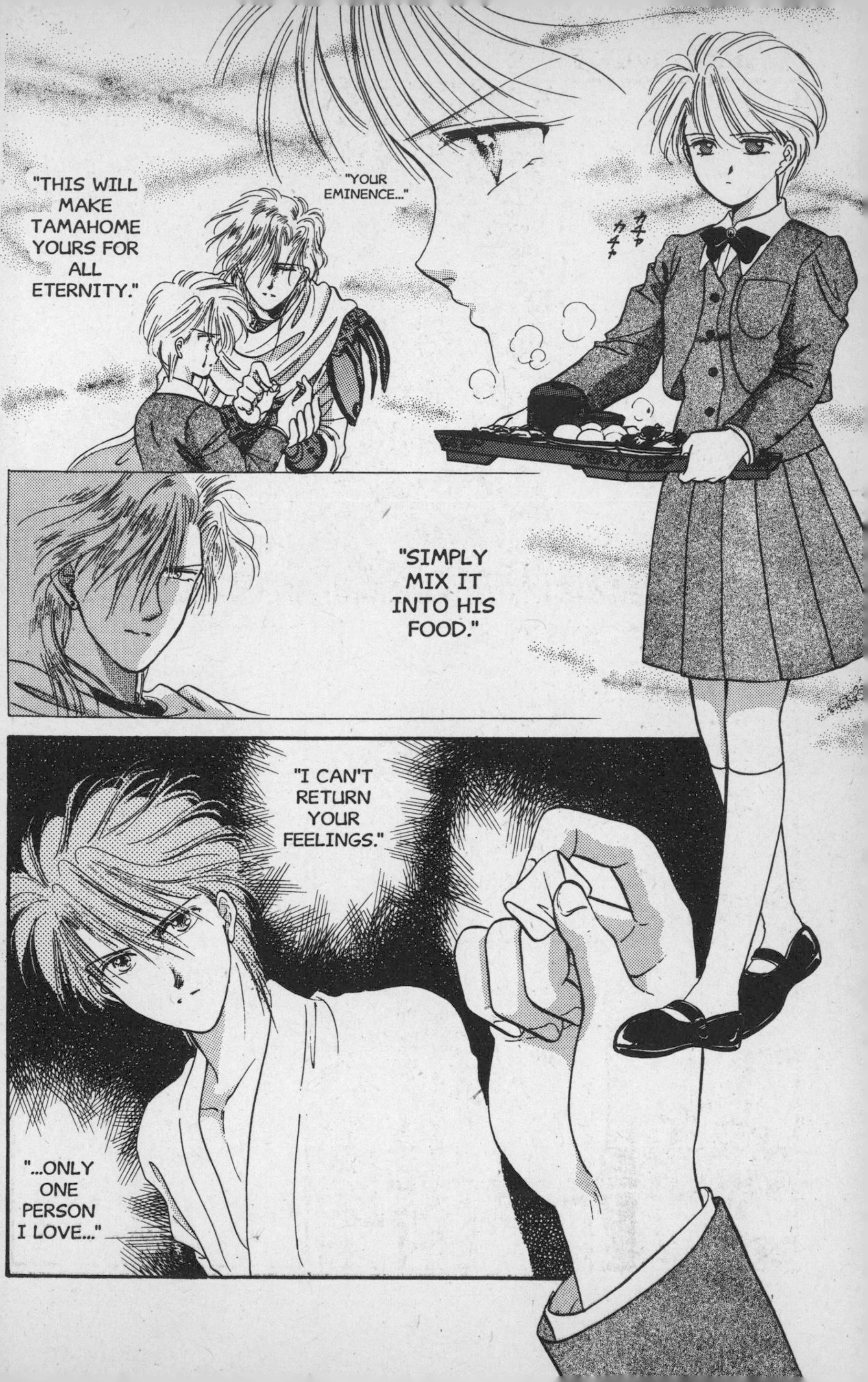
カチャ カチャ
"YOUR EMINENCE..."
"THIS WILL MAKE TAMAHOME YOURS FOR ALL ETERNITY."
"SIMPLY MIX IT INTO HIS FOOD."
"I CAN'T RETURN YOUR FEELINGS."
"...ONLY ONE PERSON I LOVE..."

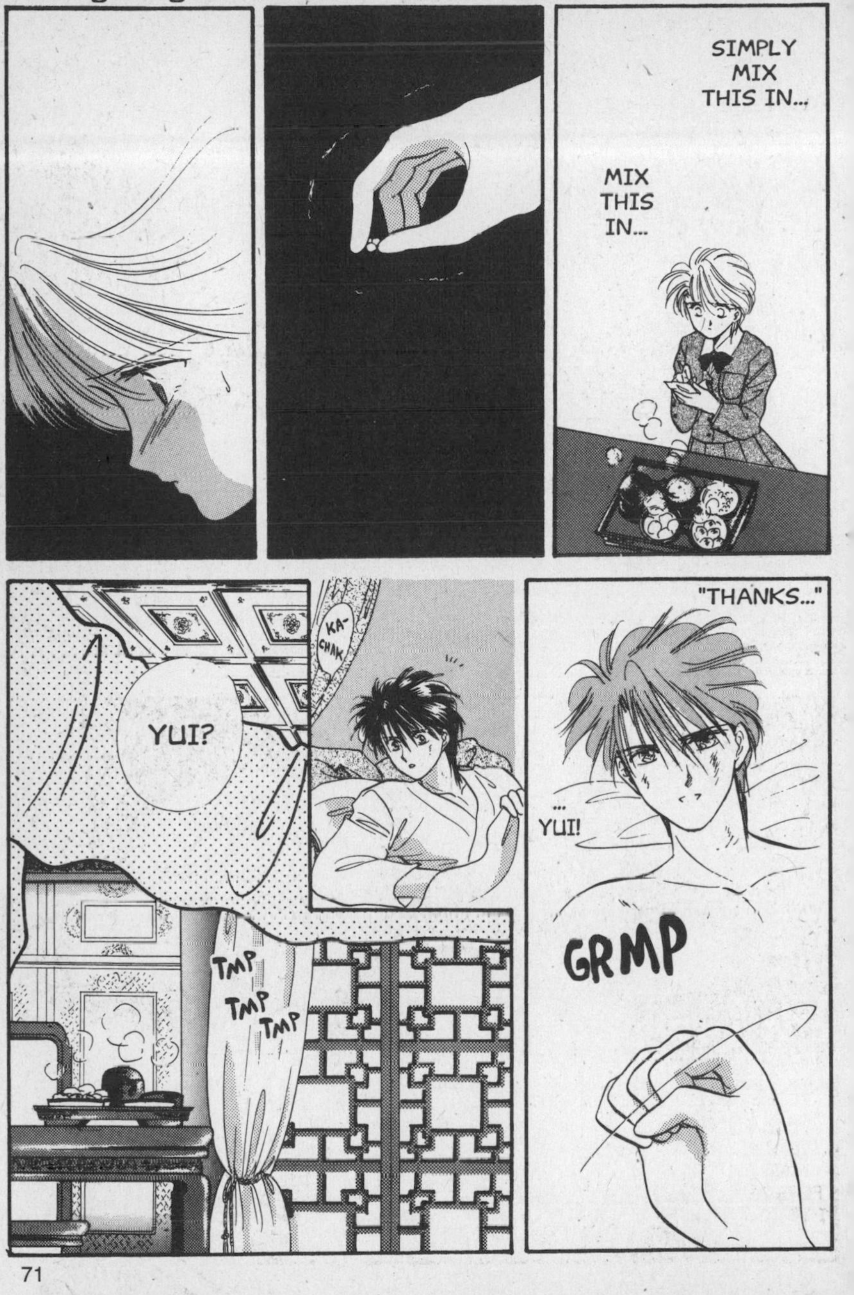
SIMPLY MIX THIS IN...
MIX THIS IN...
"THANKS..."
...YUI!
GRMP
KA-CHAK
YUI?
TMP TMP TMP

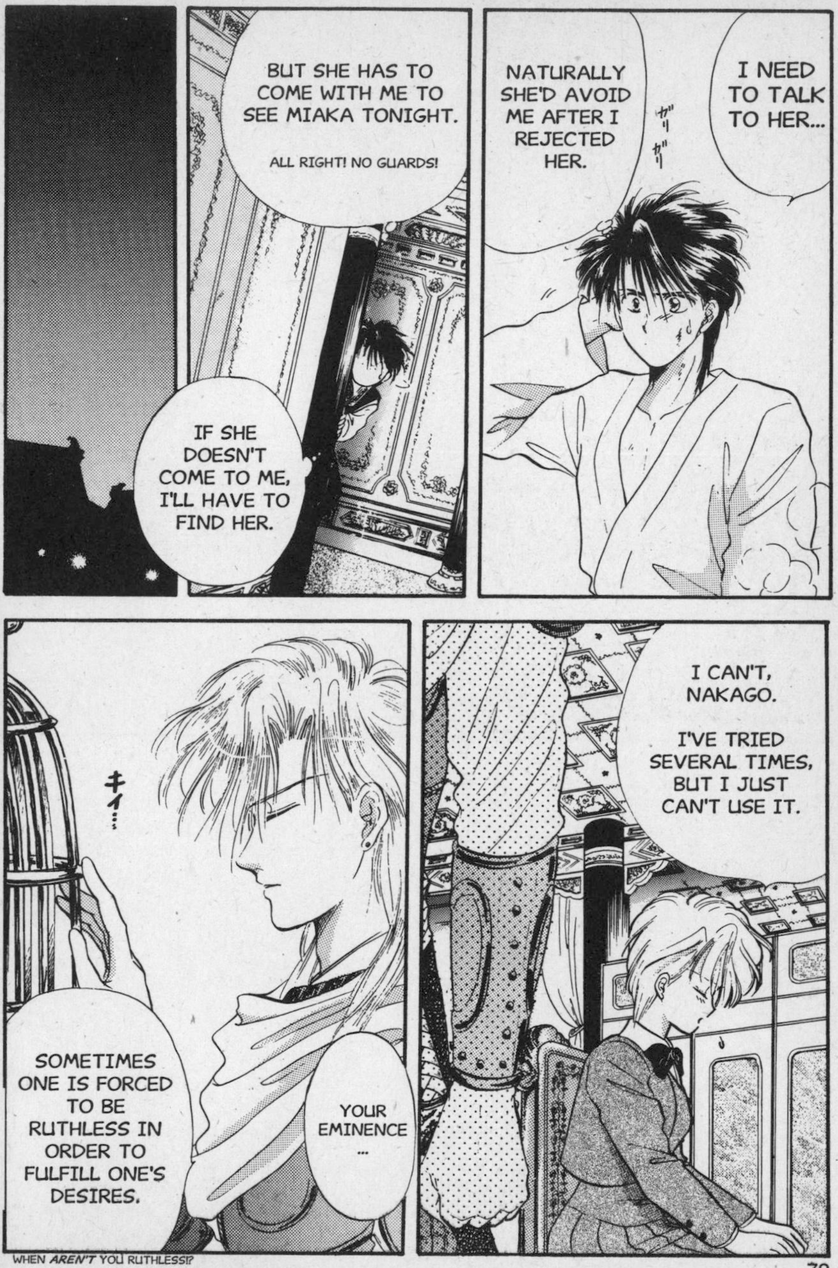
I NEED TO TALK TO HER...
ガリ ガリ
NATURALLY SHE'D AVOID ME AFTER I REJECTED HER.
BUT SHE HAS TO COME WITH ME TO SEE MIAKA TONIGHT.
ALL RIGHT! NO GUARDS!
IF SHE DOESN'T COME TO ME, I'LL HAVE TO FIND HER.
I CAN'T, NAKAGO.
I'VE TRIED SEVERAL TIMES, BUT I JUST CAN'T USE IT.
キイ…
YOUR EMINENCE ...
SOMETIMES ONE IS FORCED TO BE RUTHLESS IN ORDER TO FULFILL ONE'S DESIRES.

WHEN *AREN'T* YOU RUTHLESS!?

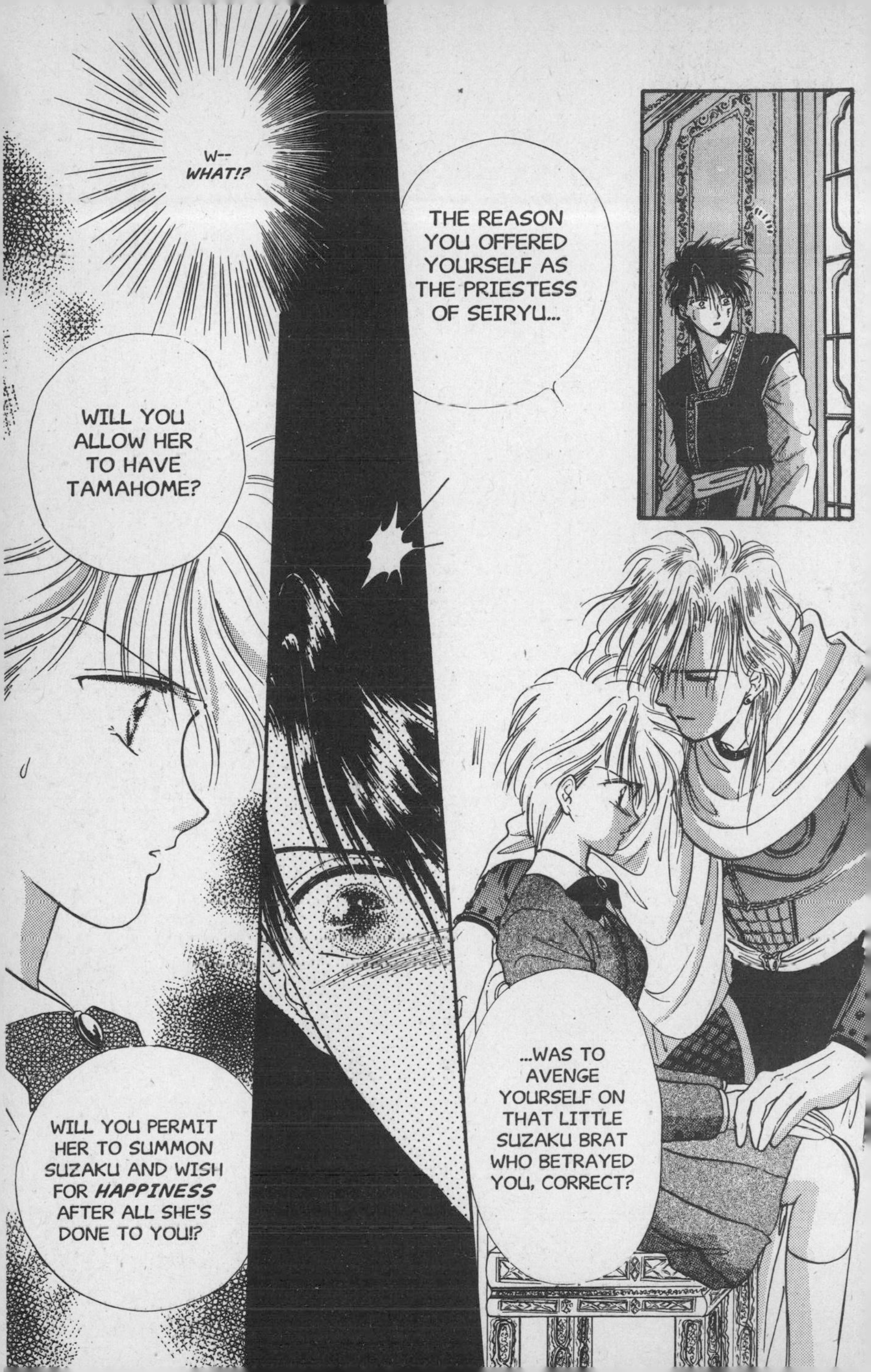
THE REASON YOU OFFERED YOURSELF AS THE PRIESTESS OF SEIRYU...
...WAS TO AVENGE YOURSELF ON THAT LITTLE SUZAKU BRAT WHO BETRAYED YOU, CORRECT?
W-- *WHAT!?*
WILL YOU ALLOW HER TO HAVE TAMAHOME?
WILL YOU PERMIT HER TO SUMMON SUZAKU AND WISH FOR *HAPPINESS* AFTER ALL SHE'S DONE TO YOU!?

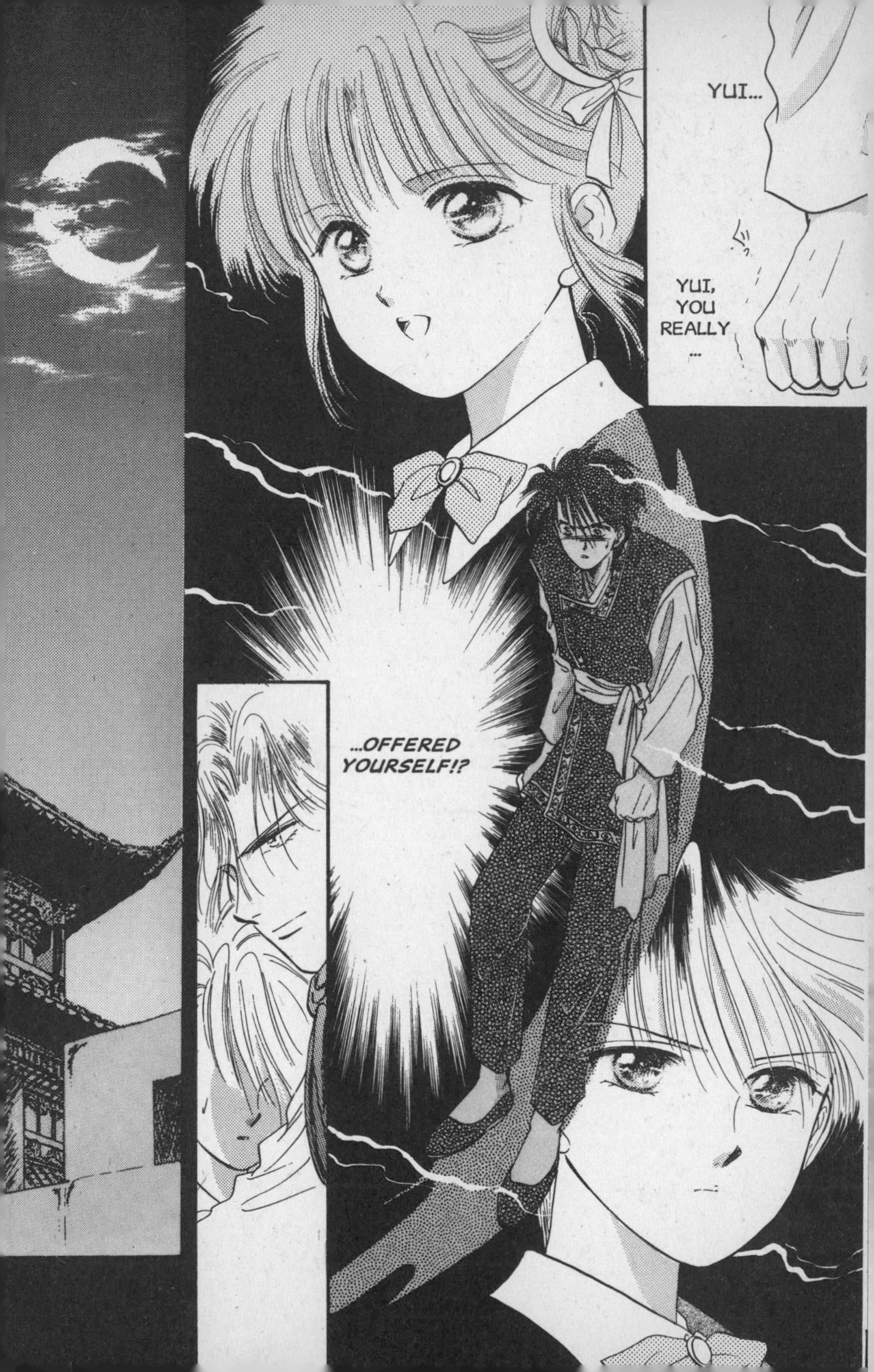
YUI...
YUI, YOU REALLY ...
...OFFERED YOURSELF!?

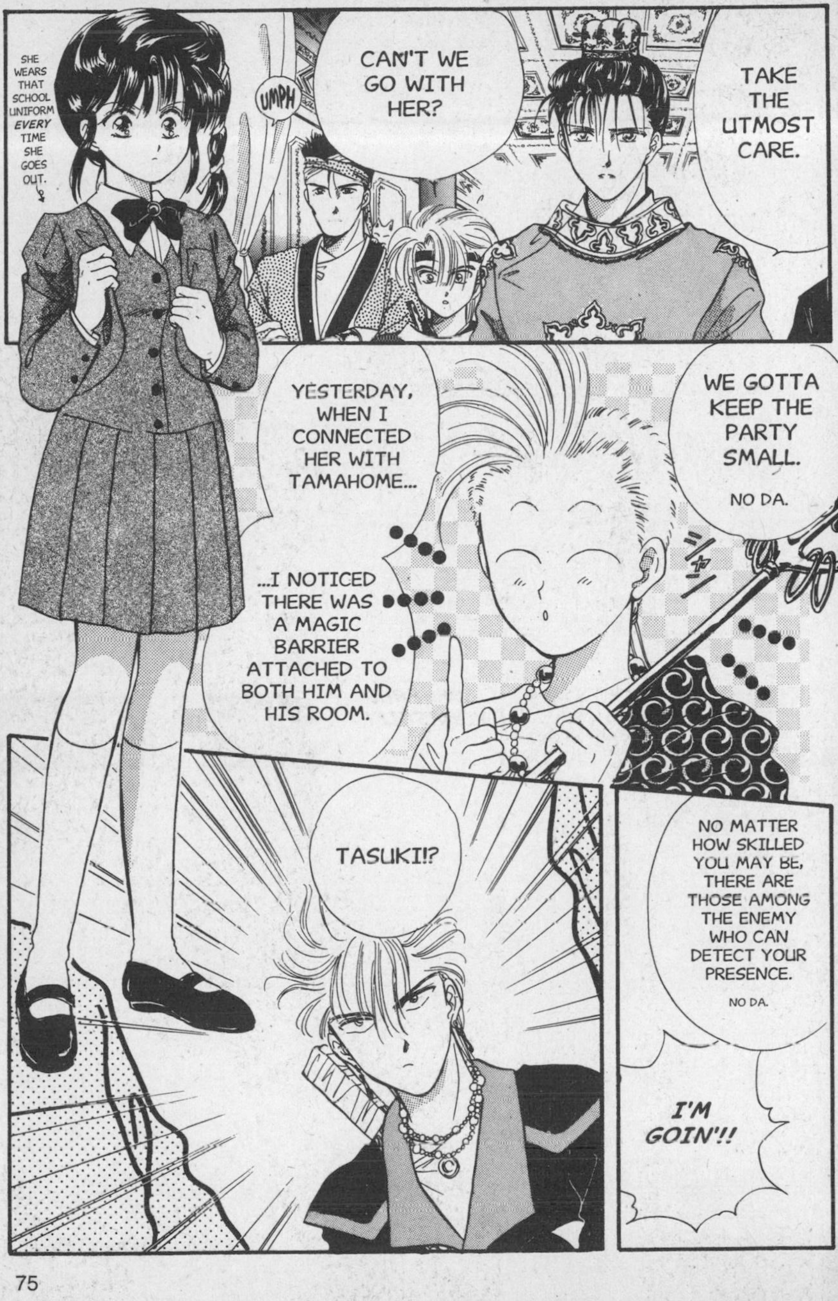
TAKE THE UTMOST CARE.
CAN'T WE GO WITH HER?
UMPH
SHE WEARS THAT SCHOOL UNIFORM *EVERY* TIME SHE GOES OUT.
WE GOTTA KEEP THE PARTY SMALL.
NO DA.
YESTERDAY, WHEN I CONNECTED HER WITH TAMAHOME...
...I NOTICED THERE WAS A MAGIC BARRIER ATTACHED TO BOTH HIM AND HIS ROOM.
NO MATTER HOW SKILLED YOU MAY BE, THERE ARE THOSE AMONG THE ENEMY WHO CAN DETECT YOUR PRESENCE.
NO DA.
I'M GOIN'!!
TASUKI!?

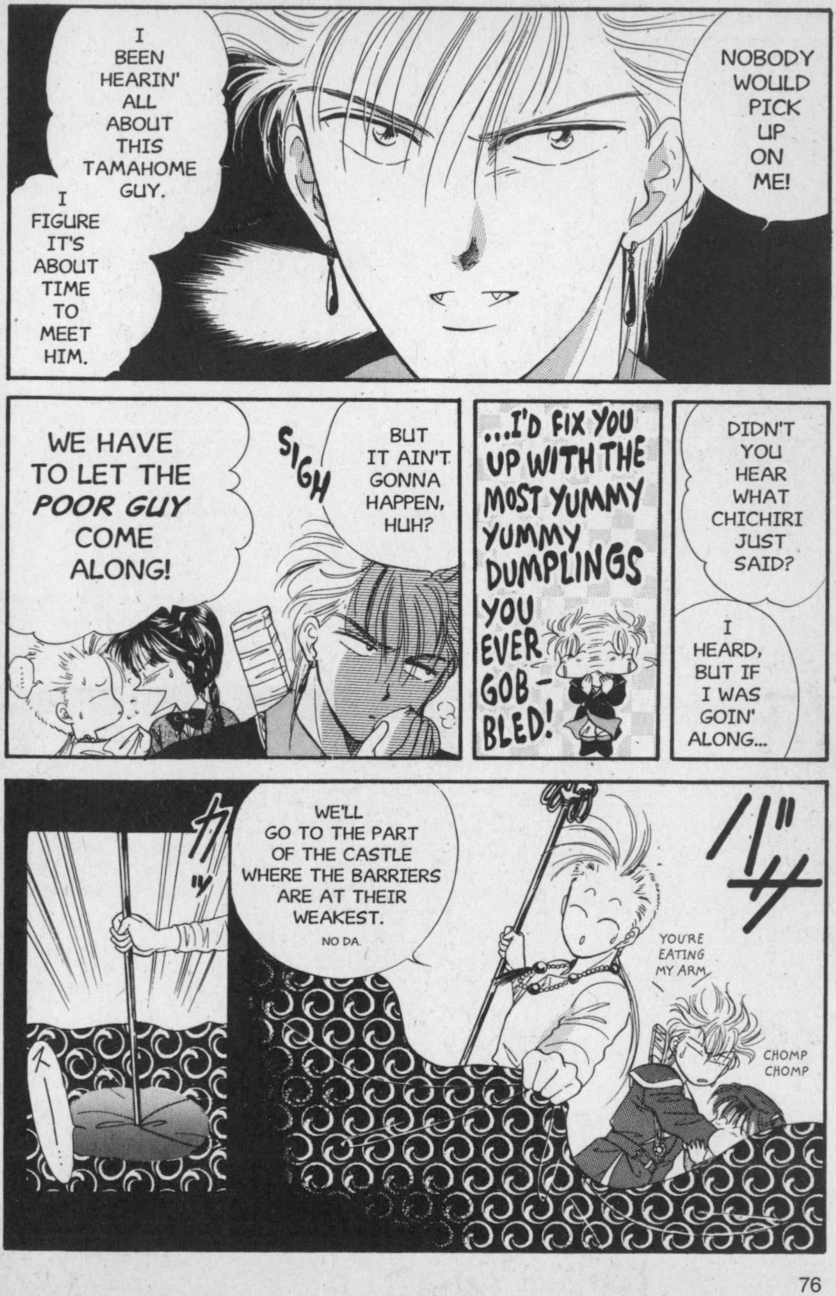
NOBODY WOULD PICK UP ON ME!
I BEEN HEARIN' ALL ABOUT THIS TAMAHOME GUY.
I FIGURE IT'S ABOUT TIME TO MEET HIM.
DIDN'T YOU HEAR WHAT CHICHIRI JUST SAID?
I HEARD, BUT IF I WAS GOIN' ALONG...
...I'D FIX YOU UP WITH THE MOST YUMMY YUMMY DUMPLINGS YOU EVER GOBBLED!
BUT IT AIN'T GONNA HAPPEN, HUH?
SIGH
WE HAVE TO LET THE *POOR GUY* COME ALONG!
...
バッ
YOU'RE EATING MY ARM
CHOMP CHOMP
WE'LL GO TO THE PART OF THE CASTLE WHERE THE BARRIERS ARE AT THEIR WEAKEST.
NO DA.
カッ
ス…

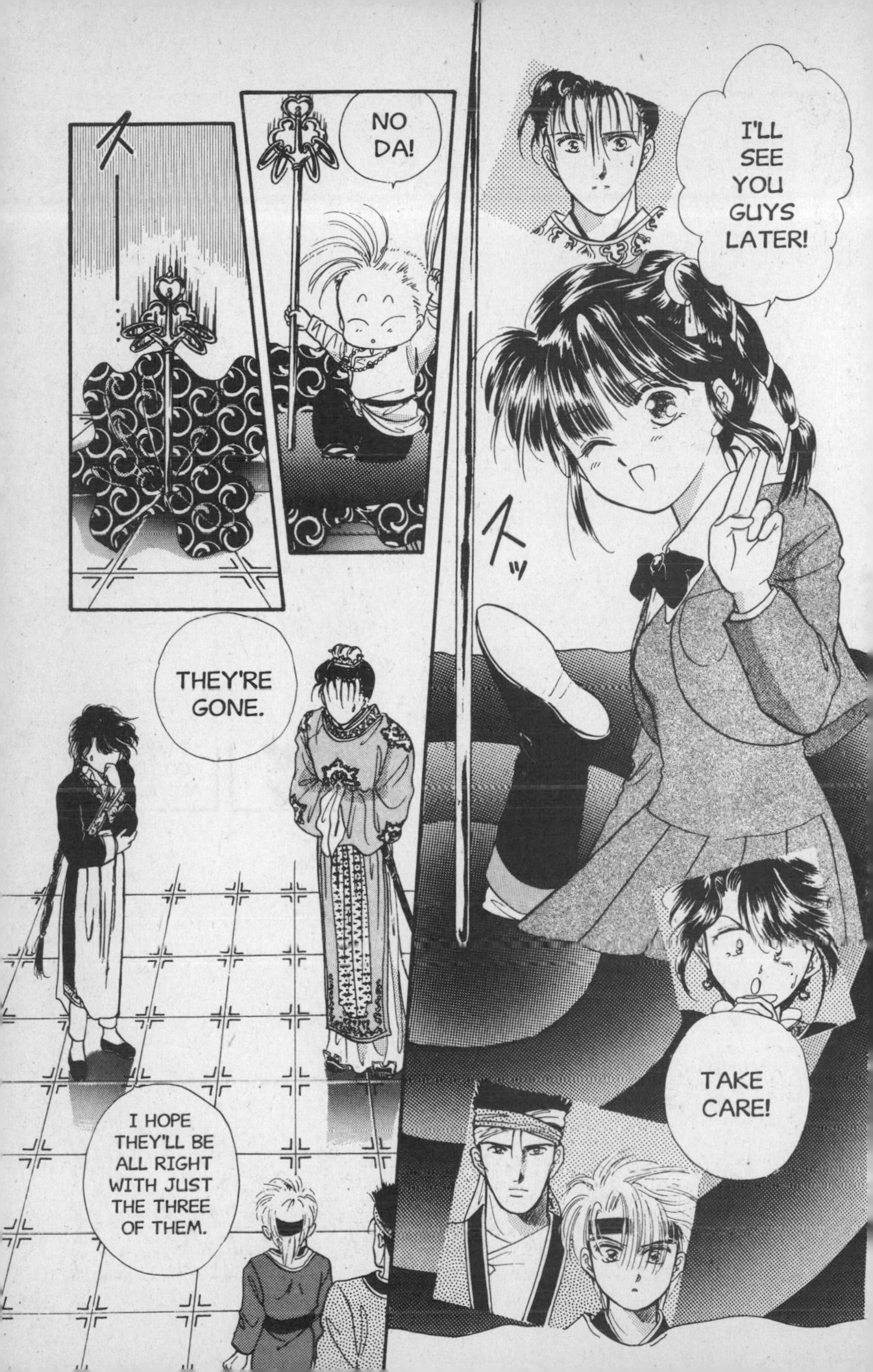
I'LL SEE YOU GUYS LATER!
スッ
TAKE CARE!
NO DA!
ス—
THEY'RE GONE.
I HOPE THEY'LL BE ALL RIGHT WITH JUST THE THREE OF THEM.

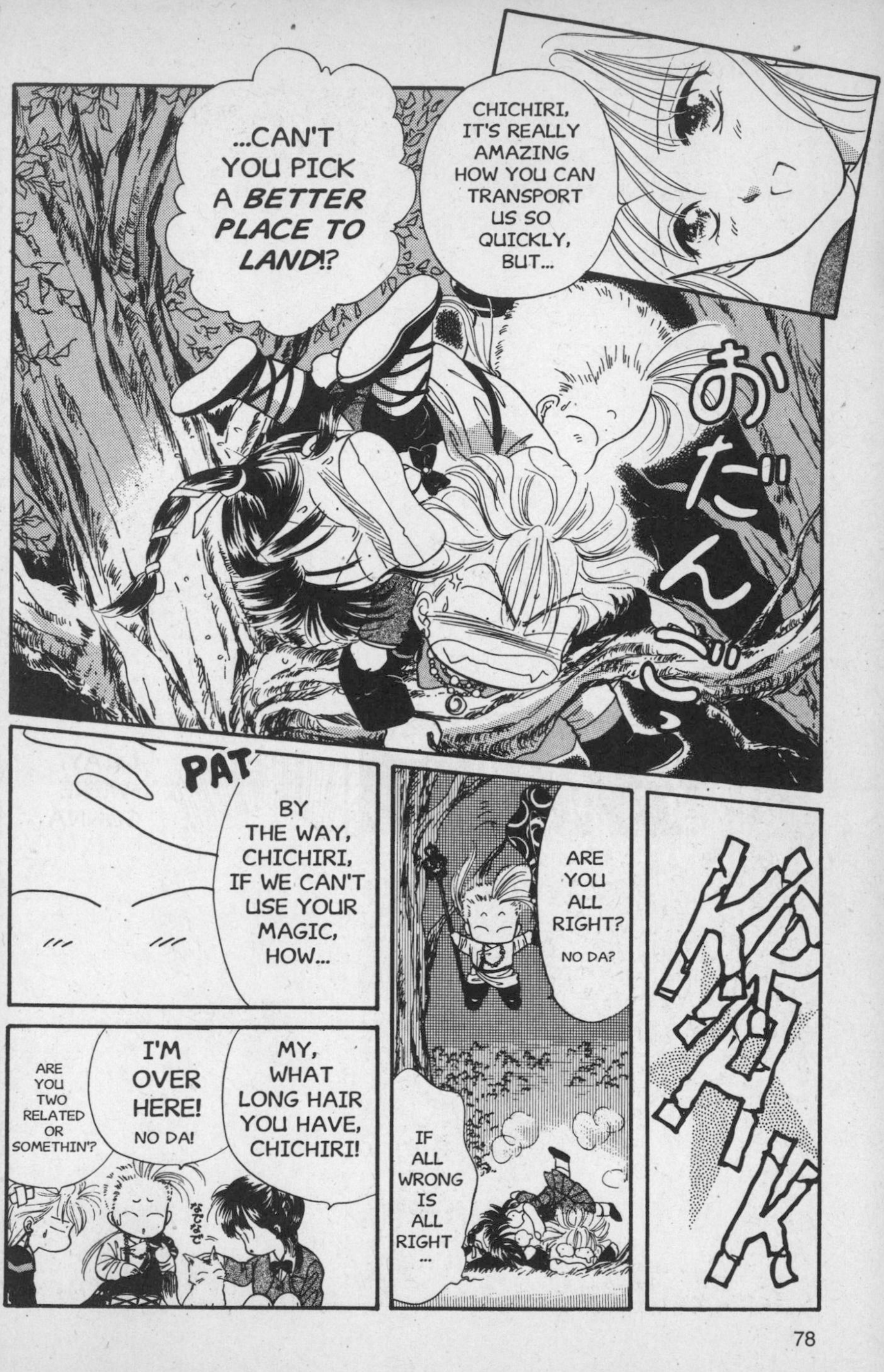
CHICHIRI, IT'S REALLY AMAZING HOW YOU CAN TRANSPORT US SO QUICKLY, BUT...
...CAN'T YOU PICK A *BETTER PLACE TO LAND!?*
おだんご
ARE YOU ALL RIGHT? NO DA?
IF ALL WRONG IS ALL RIGHT...
PAT
BY THE WAY, CHICHIRI, IF WE CAN'T USE YOUR MAGIC, HOW...
MY, WHAT LONG HAIR YOU HAVE, CHICHIRI!
なでなで
I'M OVER HERE! NO DA!
ARE YOU TWO RELATED OR SOMETHIN'?

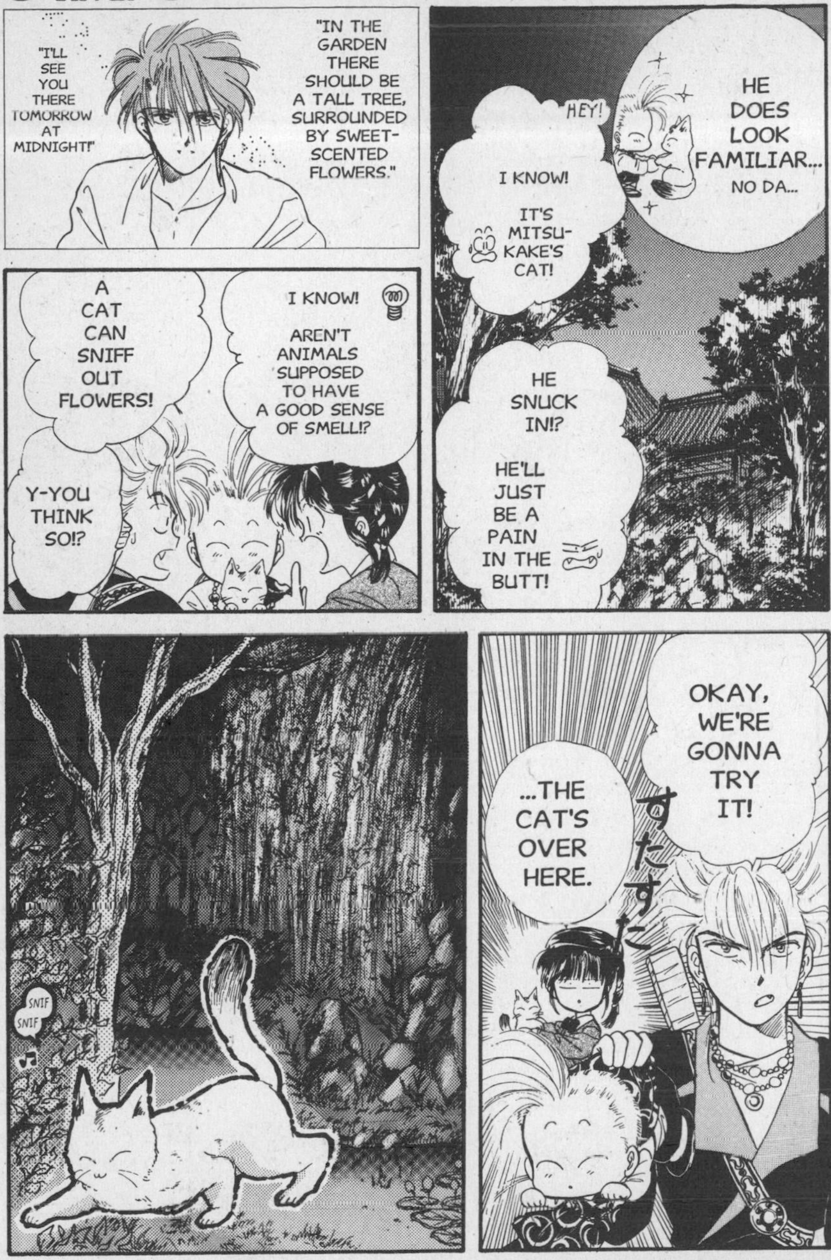
HEY!
HE DOES LOOK FAMILIAR... NO DA...
I KNOW! IT'S MITSU-KAKE'S CAT!
HE SNUCK IN!? HE'LL JUST BE A PAIN IN THE BUTT!
"IN THE GARDEN THERE SHOULD BE A TALL TREE, SURROUNDED BY SWEET-SCENTED FLOWERS."
"I'LL SEE YOU THERE TOMORROW AT MIDNIGHT!"
I KNOW! AREN'T ANIMALS SUPPOSED TO HAVE A GOOD SENSE OF SMELL!?
A CAT CAN SNIFF OUT FLOWERS!
Y-YOU THINK SO!?
OKAY, WE'RE GONNA TRY IT!
...THE CAT'S OVER HERE.
SNIF SNIF

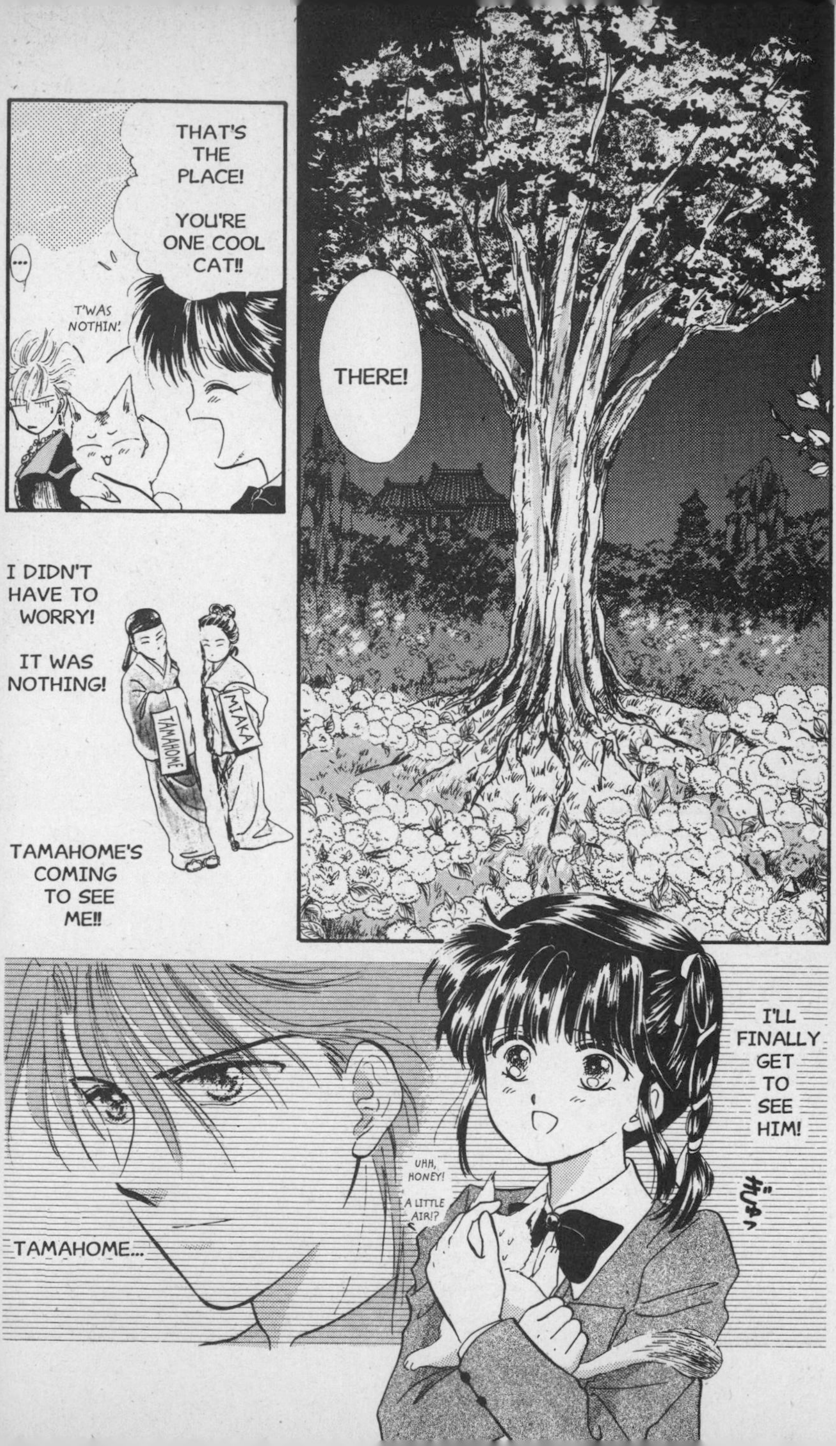
THERE!
THAT'S THE PLACE!
YOU'RE ONE COOL CAT!!
...
T'WAS NOTHIN'!
I DIDN'T HAVE TO WORRY!
IT WAS NOTHING!
TAMAHOME
MIAKA
TAMAHOME'S COMING TO SEE ME!!
I'LL FINALLY GET TO SEE HIM!
UHH, HONEY!
A LITTLE AIR!?
TAMAHOME...

"WILL YOU PERMIT HER TO SUMMON SUZAKU AND WISH FOR ***HAPPINESS*** AFTER ALL SHE'S DONE TO YOU!?"

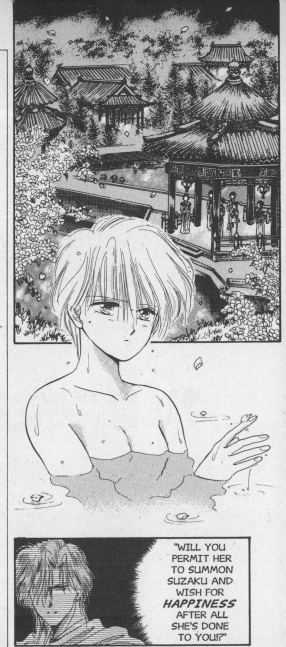

A couple of days later, I met my friends from my tech-school years. We didn't have anything better to do, so we sat around in cafes and looked for the local game centers. While one of my friends was snatching up dolls on the UFO catcher, Ms. A. and I played Street Fighter II on the super-size screen. I liked watching Ms. A. play almost more than watching the screen! I played the tough guy saying, "What the hell're you doin'!? You bastard--you kicked me!!" And she would say, "Oh, how awful! Stop it, please!" or "Gosh, you shouldn't give in to your violent urges like that!" Eventually we got tired of the game center, so we went to karaoke, even though one of our friends was pregnant. I lost my voice from all the yelling at the game center so I just sat and listened to everyone else sing. (What an idiot!) But actually, I had a cold! Despite all the loud noises in the room, the five-month-old fetus in my friend's tummy didn't wake up once! I had a great time tapping out the time on her stomach (but that's just me). I'm really looking forward to when the baby is born. I was thinking about how this newborn child would eventually read my manga, and I can brainwash it into being my mind-slave. (Those are the kind of stupid thoughts I have.) I was so happy to be back in Osaka, I ate at my favorite *okonomiyaki* place six times!! Yet I didn't eat any *takoyaki!* I don't know why. It'll have to be a mystery.
The *okonomiyaki* shop Ikkyu is so good, your jaw drops, and your taste buds do a quintuple flip, earning a perfect 10 from the judges!
The key to *okonomiyaki* is pork! You hear me? Pork! I don't like meat, but the pork flavor is crucial. Trust me on this.

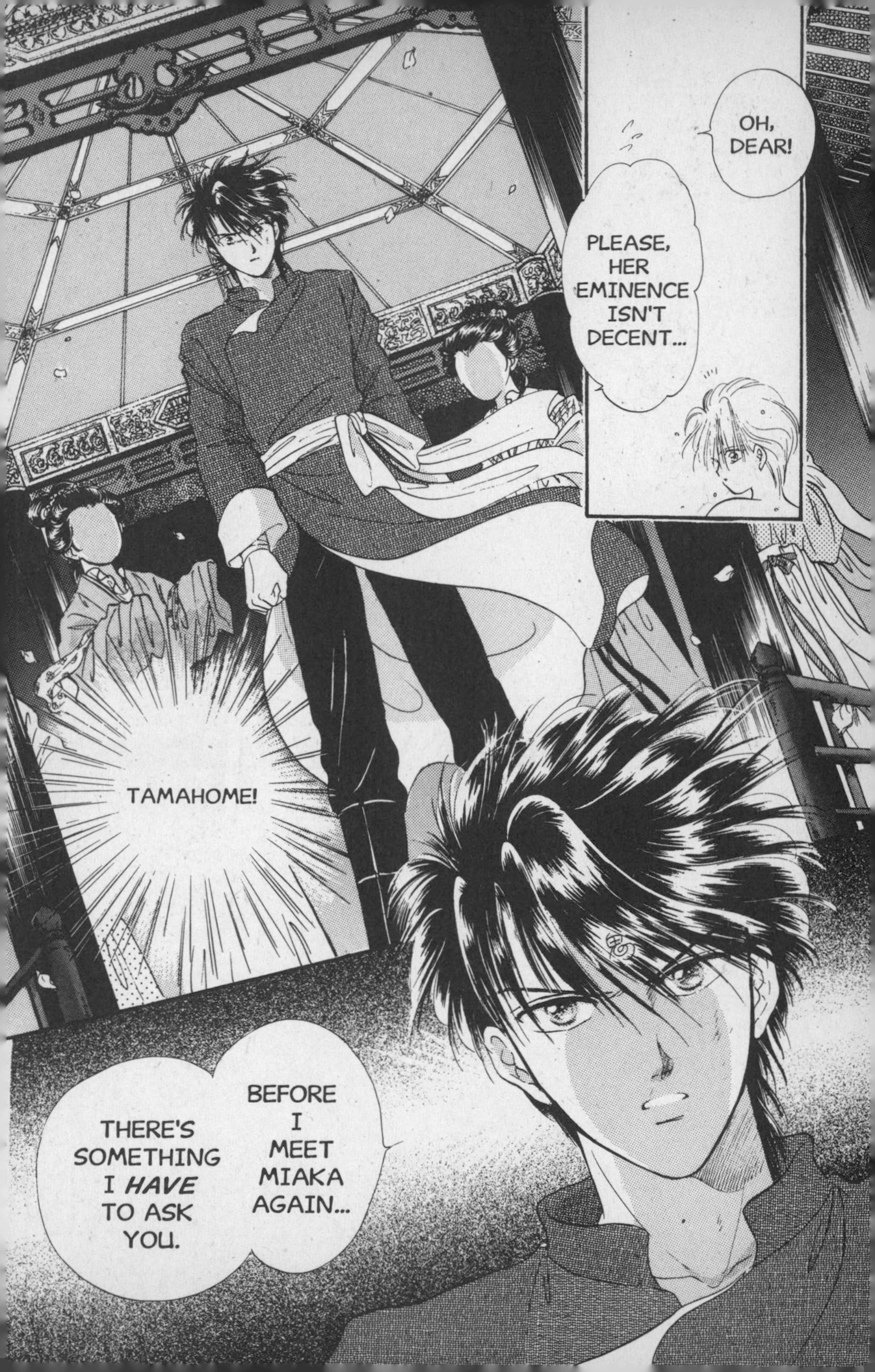
OH, DEAR!
PLEASE, HER EMINENCE ISN'T DECENT...
TAMAHOME!
BEFORE I MEET MIAKA AGAIN...
THERE'S SOMETHING I *HAVE* TO ASK YOU.

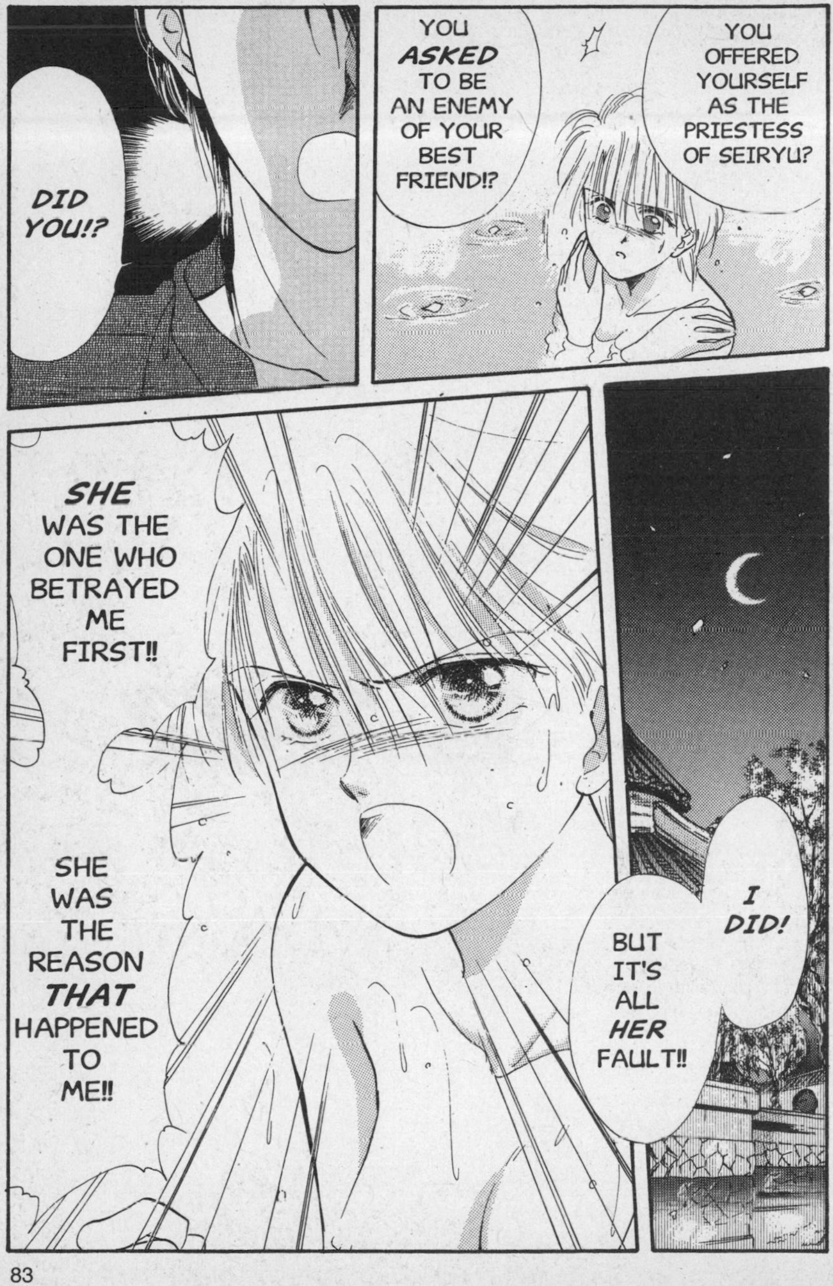
YOU OFFERED YOURSELF AS THE PRIESTESS OF SEIRYU?
YOU *ASKED* TO BE AN ENEMY OF YOUR BEST FRIEND!?
DID YOU!?
I DID!
BUT IT'S ALL *HER* FAULT!!
SHE WAS THE ONE WHO BETRAYED ME FIRST!!
SHE WAS THE REASON *THAT* HAPPENED TO ME!!

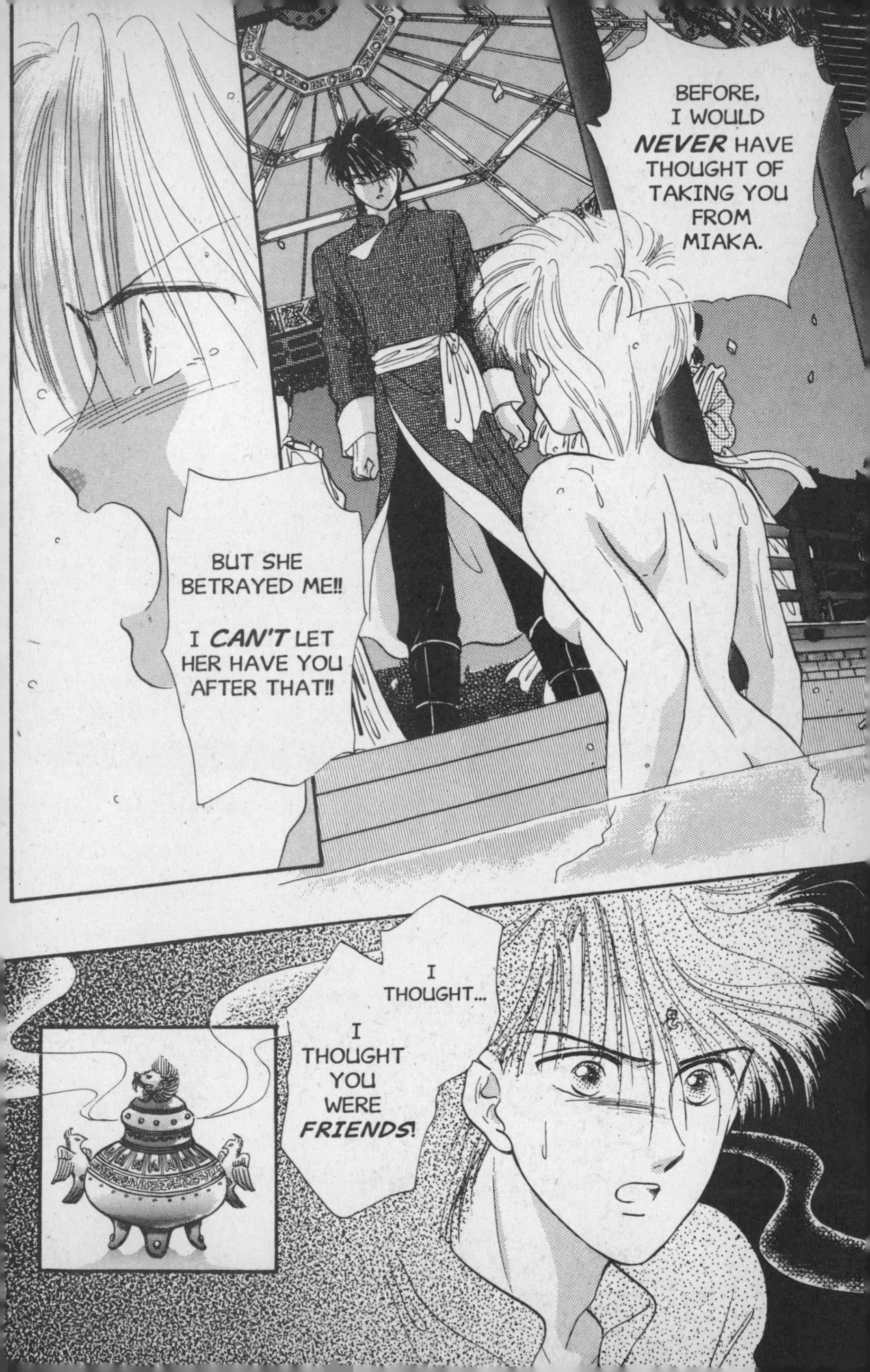
BEFORE, I WOULD NEVER HAVE THOUGHT OF TAKING YOU FROM MIAKA.
BUT SHE BETRAYED ME!!
I CAN'T LET HER HAVE YOU AFTER THAT!!
I THOUGHT...
I THOUGHT YOU WERE FRIENDS!

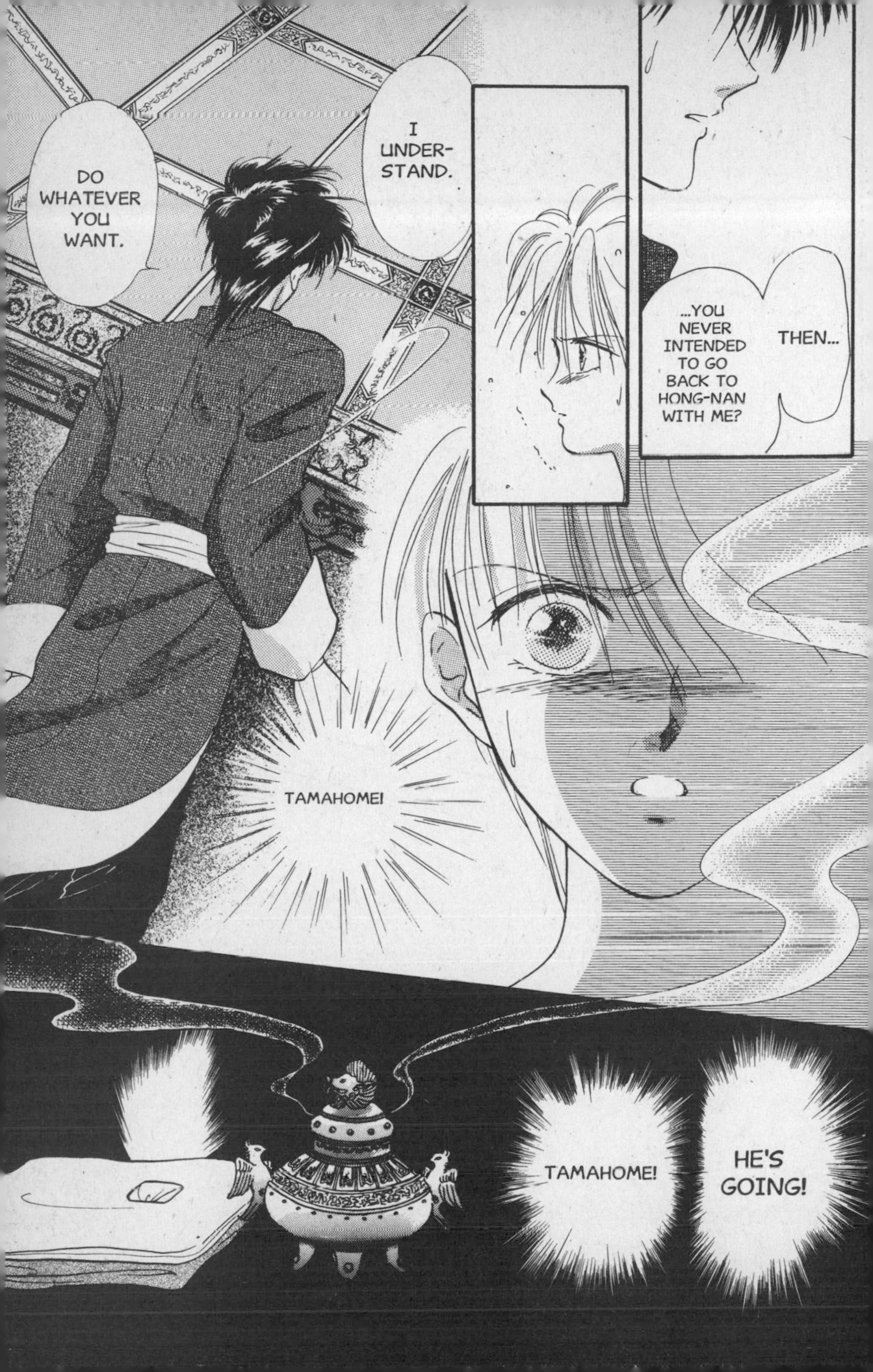
THEN...
...YOU NEVER INTENDED TO GO BACK TO HONG-NAN WITH ME?
I UNDER-STAND.
DO WHATEVER YOU WANT.
TAMAHOME!
HE'S GOING!
TAMAHOME!

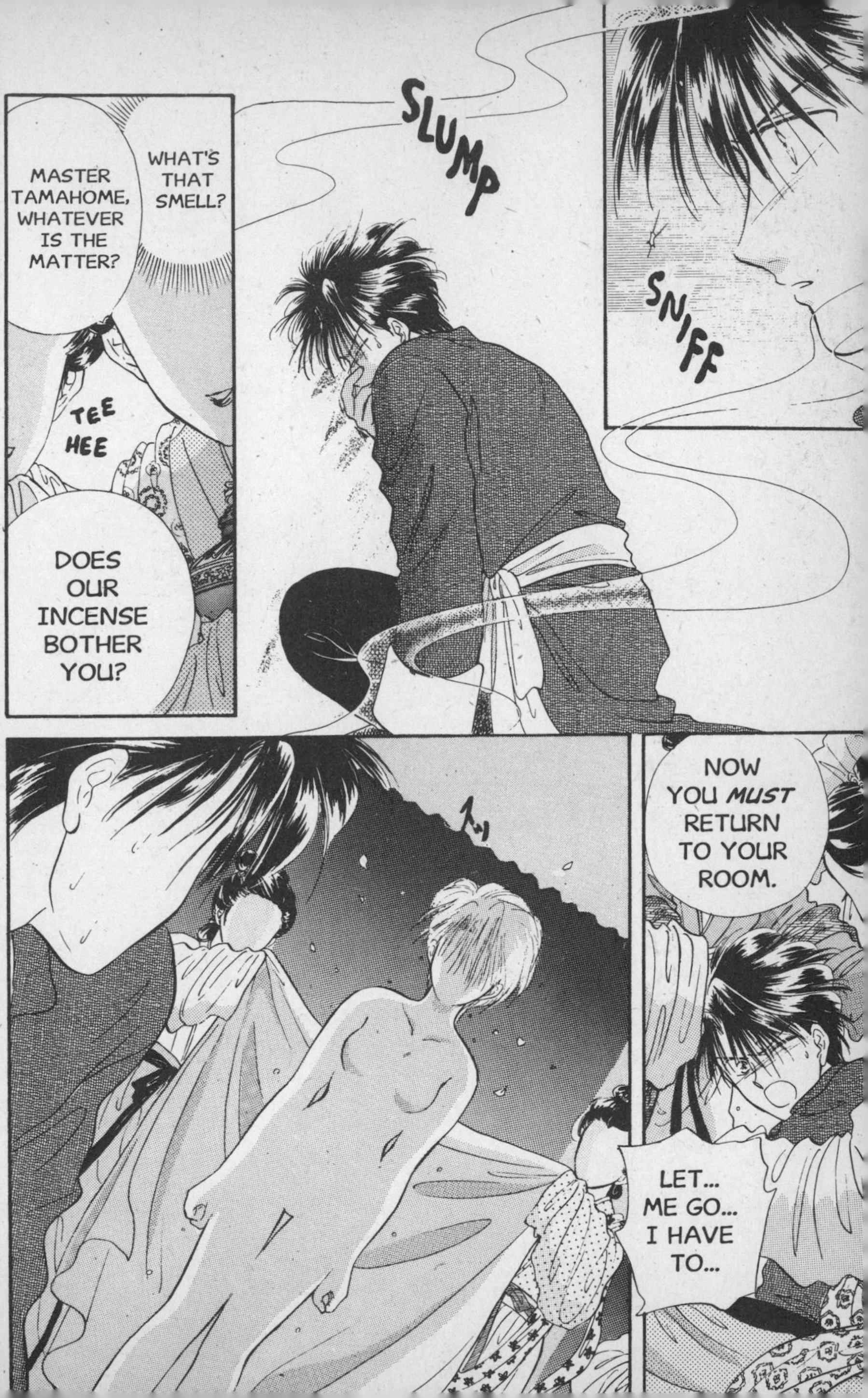
SNIFF
SLUMP
WHAT'S THAT SMELL?
MASTER TAMAHOME, WHATEVER IS THE MATTER?
TEE HEE
DOES OUR INCENSE BOTHER YOU?
NOW YOU *MUST* RETURN TO YOUR ROOM.
LET... ME GO... I HAVE TO...

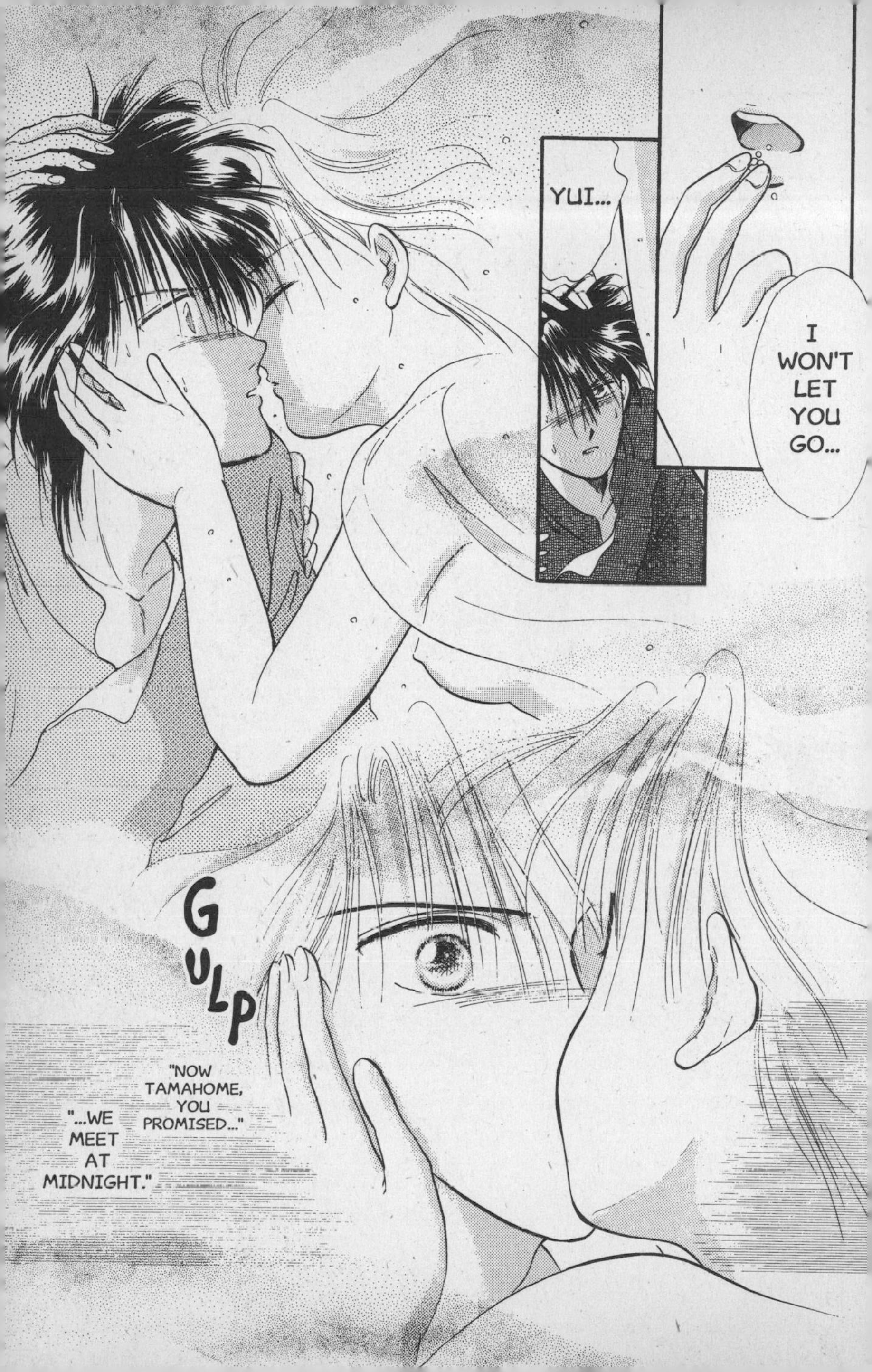
I WON'T LET YOU GO...
YUI...
GULP
"NOW TAMAHOME, YOU PROMISED..."
"...WE MEET AT MIDNIGHT."

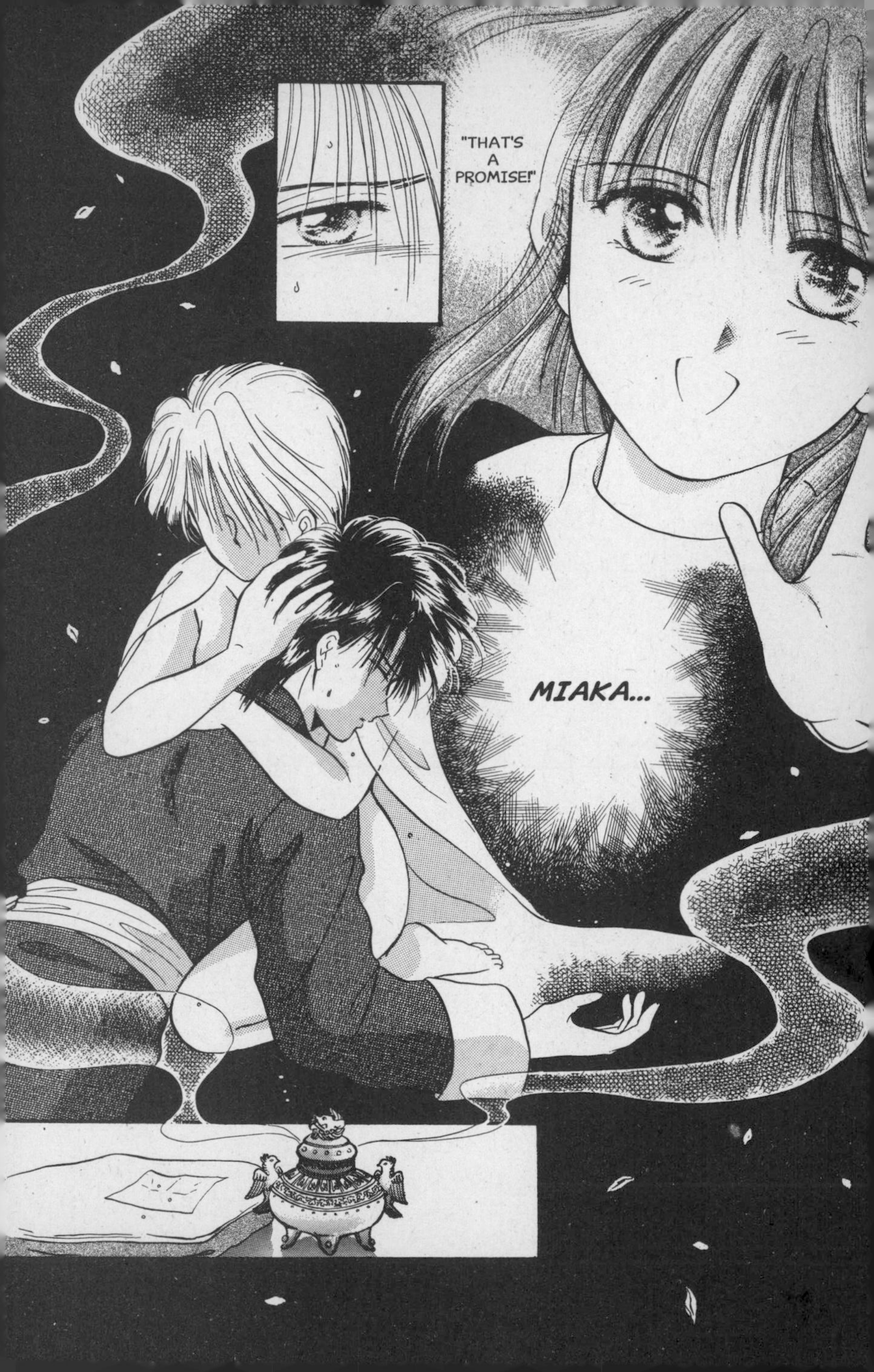
"THAT'S A PROMISE!"
MIAKA...

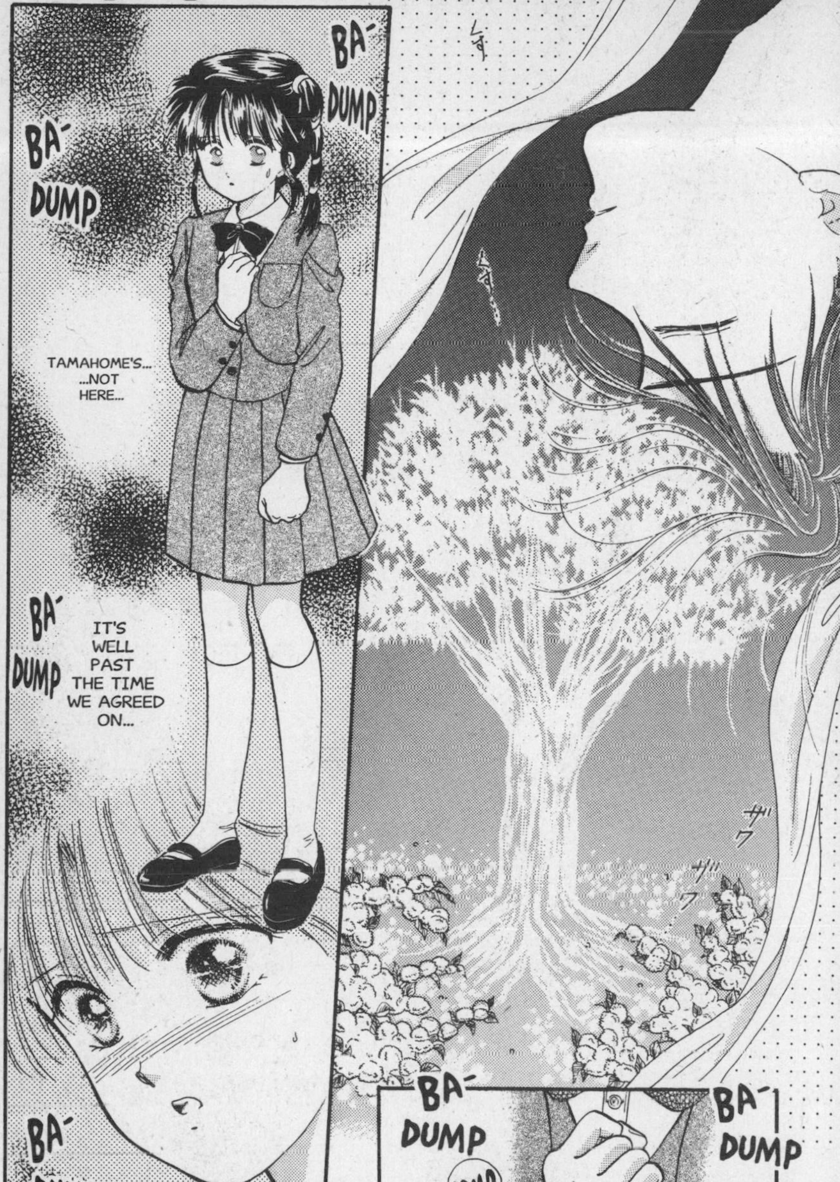
くす くす
ザワ ザワ
BA-DUMP
BA-DUMP
GRMP
BA-DUMP
BA-DUMP
TAMAHOME'S... ...NOT HERE...
BA-DUMP
IT'S WELL PAST THE TIME WE AGREED ON...
BA-DUMP

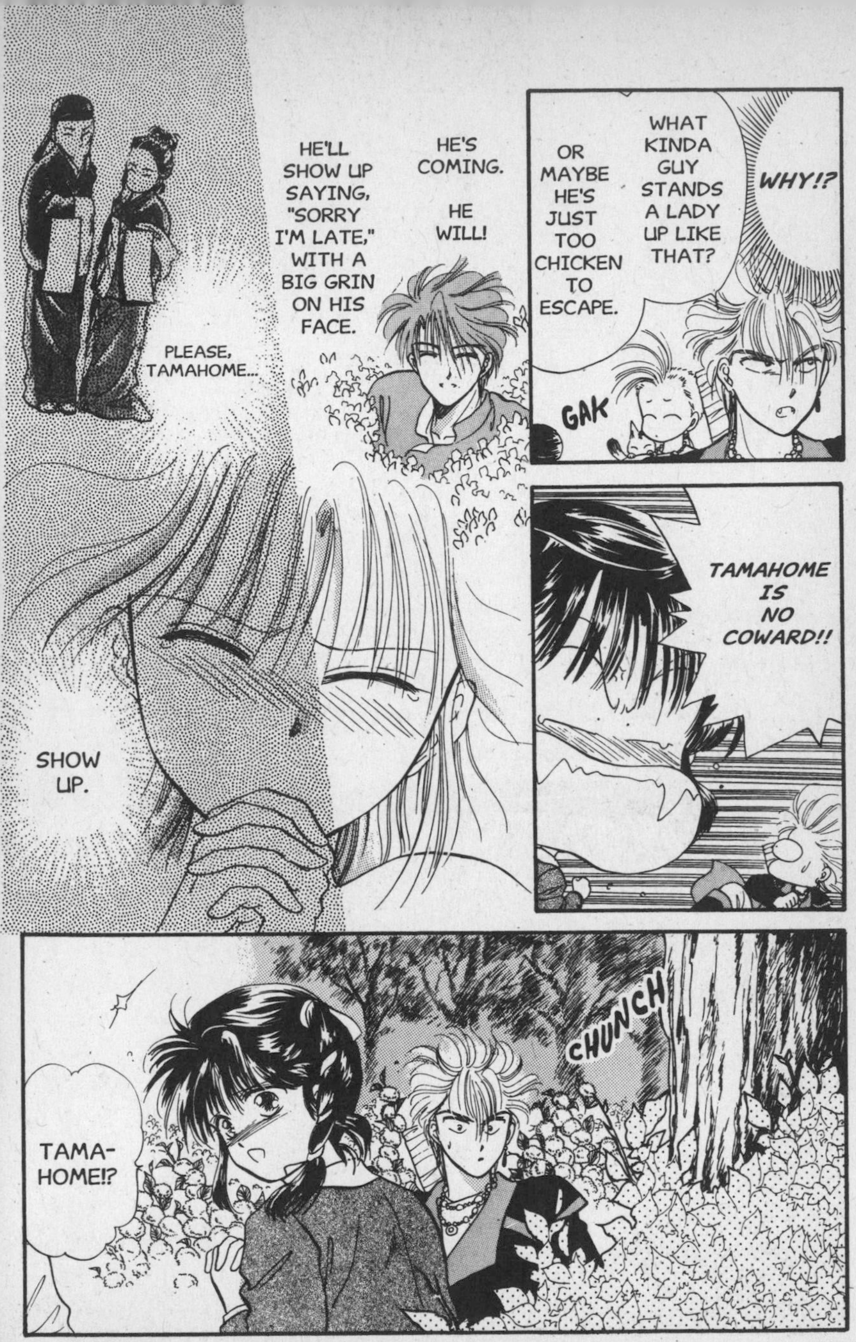
WHY!?
WHAT KINDA GUY STANDS A LADY UP LIKE THAT?
OR MAYBE HE'S JUST TOO CHICKEN TO ESCAPE.
GAK
TAMAHOME IS NO COWARD!!
HE'S COMING.
HE WILL!
HE'LL SHOW UP SAYING, "SORRY I'M LATE," WITH A BIG GRIN ON HIS FACE.
PLEASE, TAMAHOME...
SHOW UP.
CHUNCH
TAMA-HOME!?

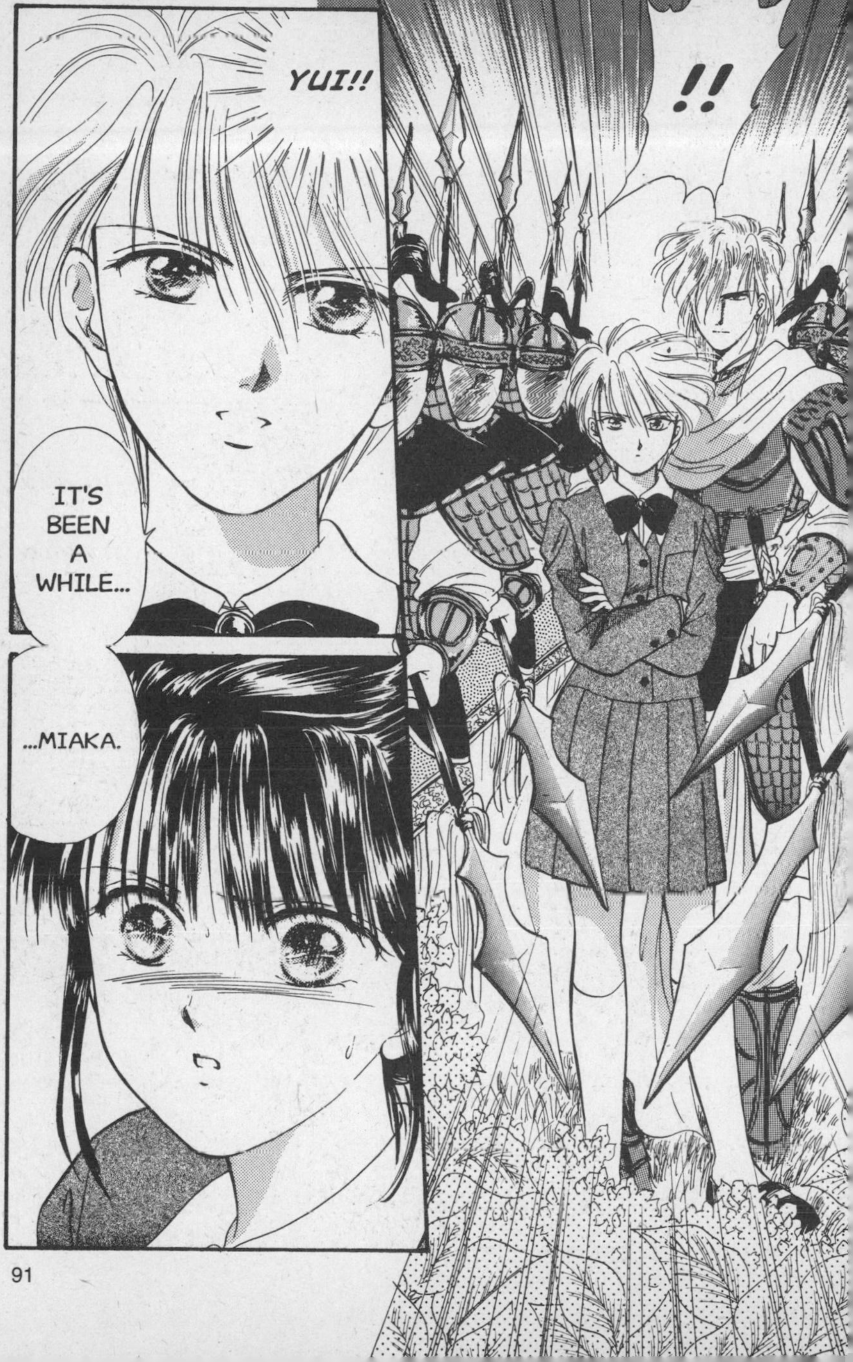
!!
YUI!!
IT'S BEEN A WHILE...
...MIAKA.

CHAPTER TWENTY-EIGHT
A PRELUDE TO LOVE

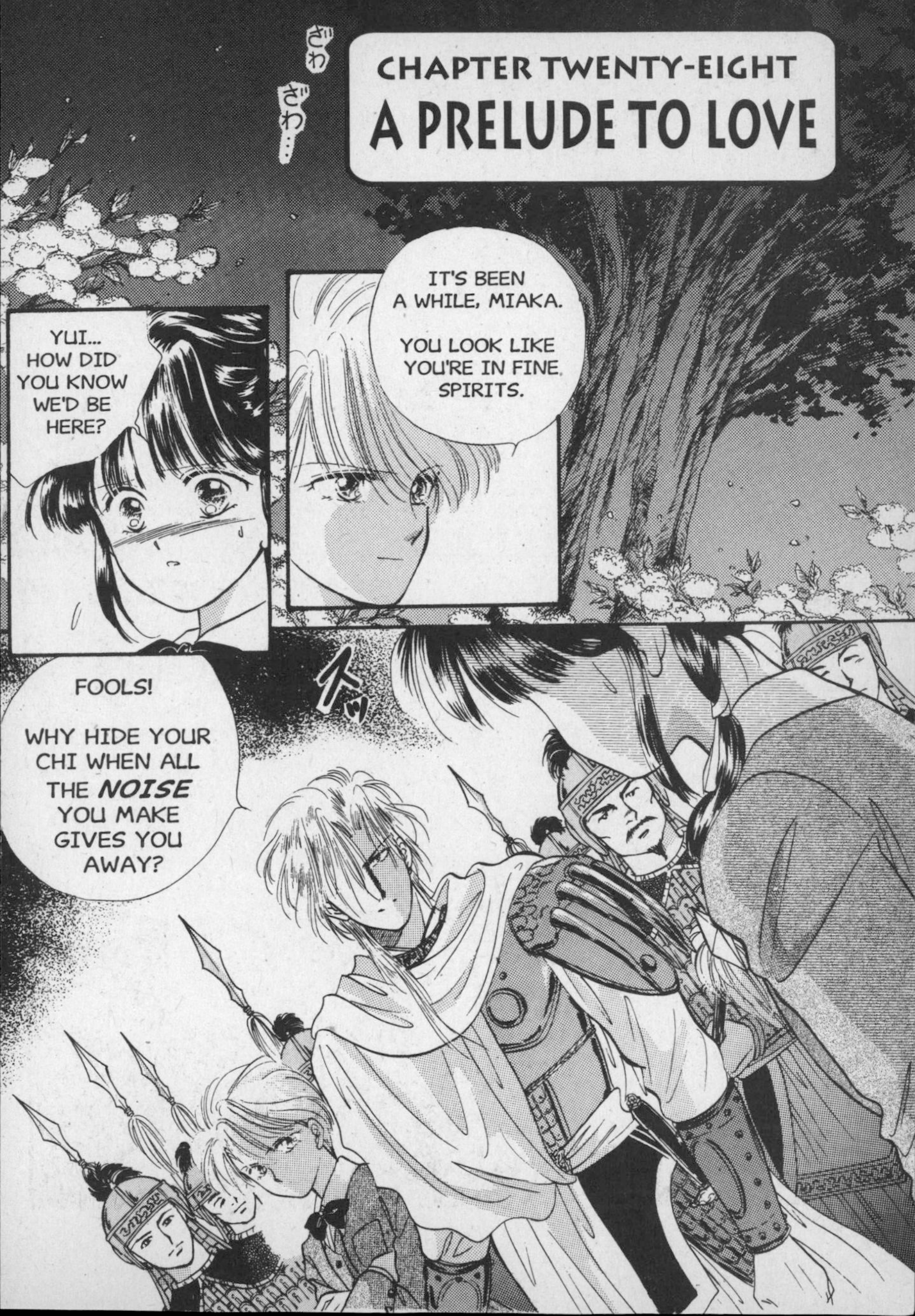
ざわ ざわ…
IT'S BEEN A WHILE, MIAKA.
YOU LOOK LIKE YOU'RE IN FINE SPIRITS.
YUI... HOW DID YOU KNOW WE'D BE HERE?
スッ
FOOLS!
WHY HIDE YOUR CHI WHEN ALL THE *NOISE* YOU MAKE GIVES YOU AWAY?

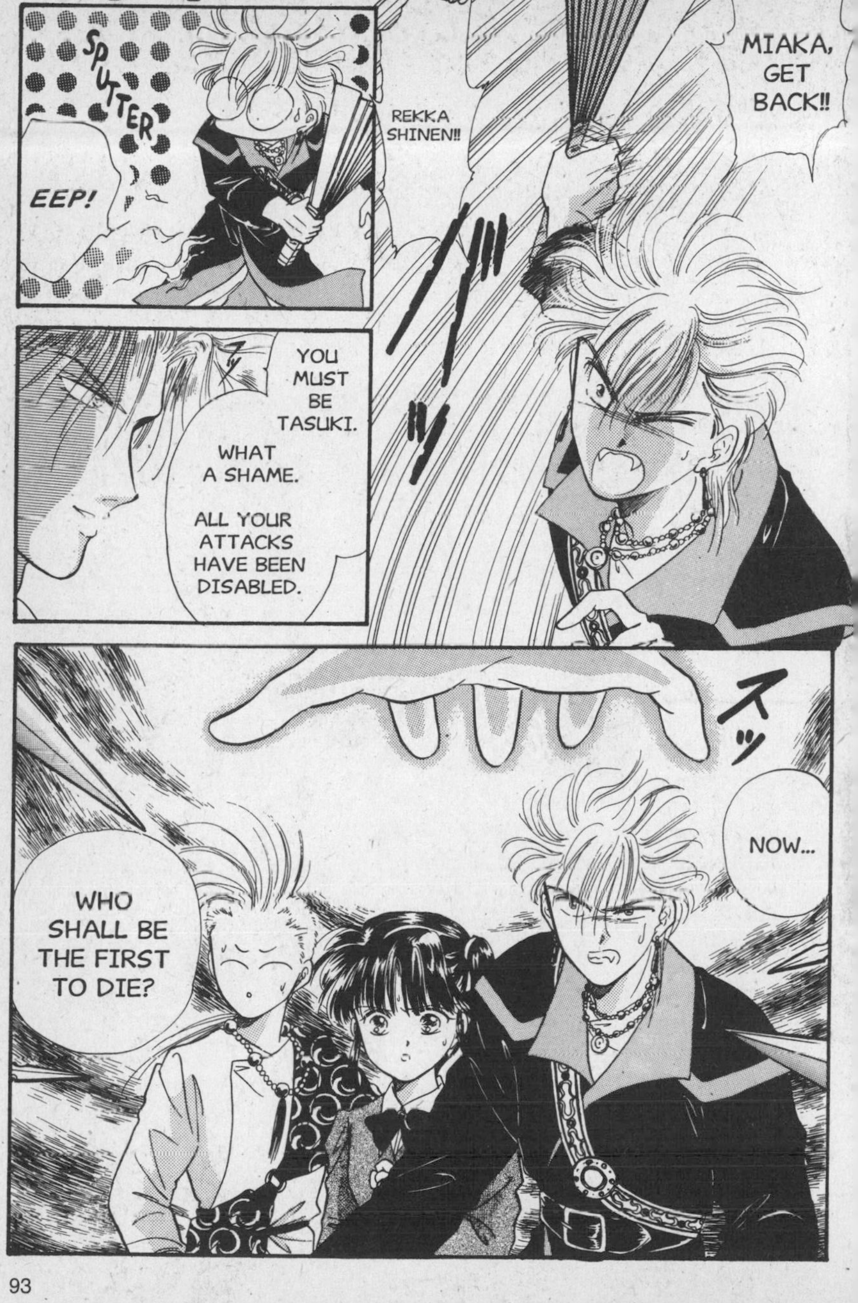
MIAKA, GET BACK!!
REKKA SHINEN!!
SPUTTER
EEP!
YOU MUST BE TASUKI.
WHAT A SHAME.
ALL YOUR ATTACKS HAVE BEEN DISABLED.
スッ
NOW...
WHO SHALL BE THE FIRST TO DIE?

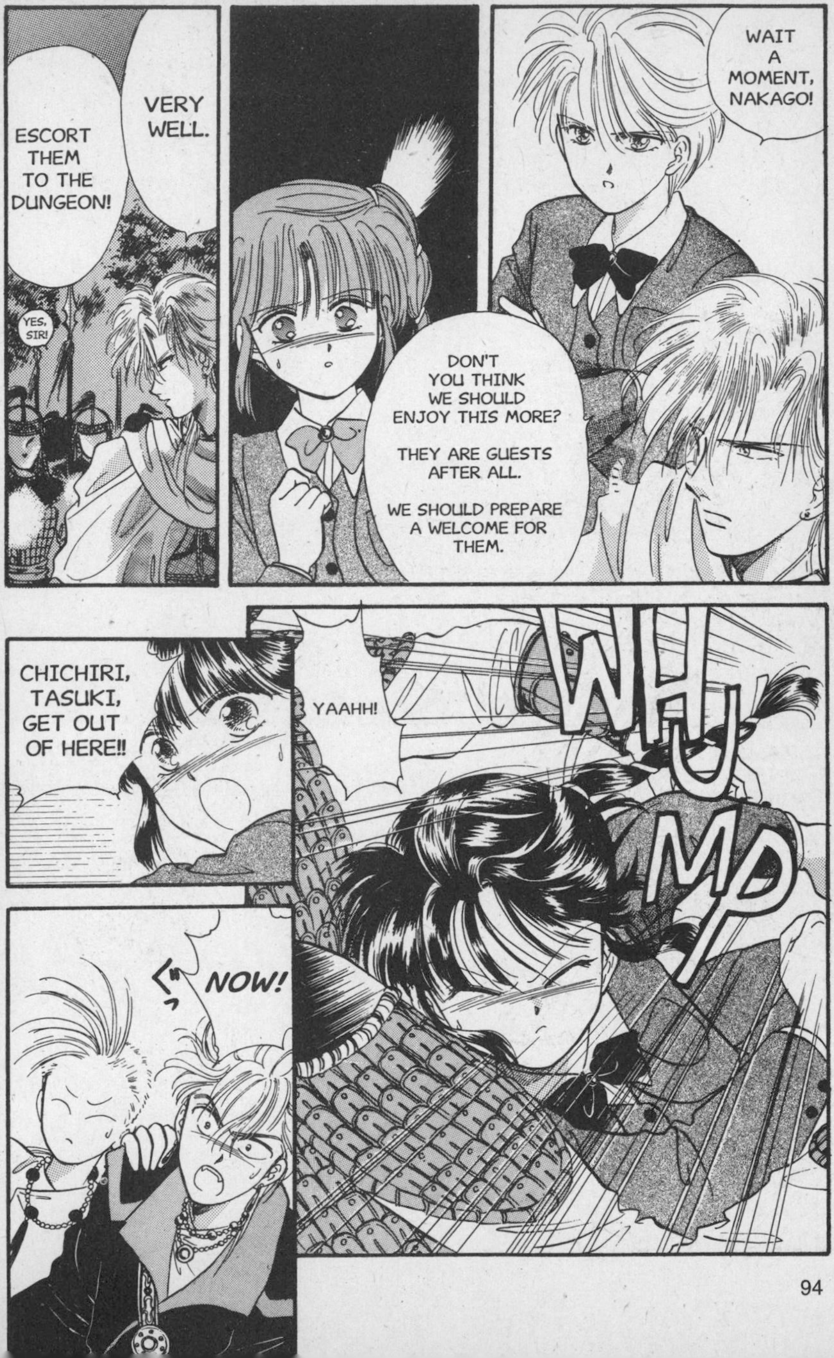
WAIT A MOMENT, NAKAGO!
DON'T YOU THINK WE SHOULD ENJOY THIS MORE?
THEY ARE GUESTS AFTER ALL.
WE SHOULD PREPARE A WELCOME FOR THEM.
VERY WELL.
ESCORT THEM TO THE DUNGEON!
YES, SIR!
WHUMP
YAAHH!
CHICHIRI, TASUKI, GET OUT OF HERE!!
NOW!

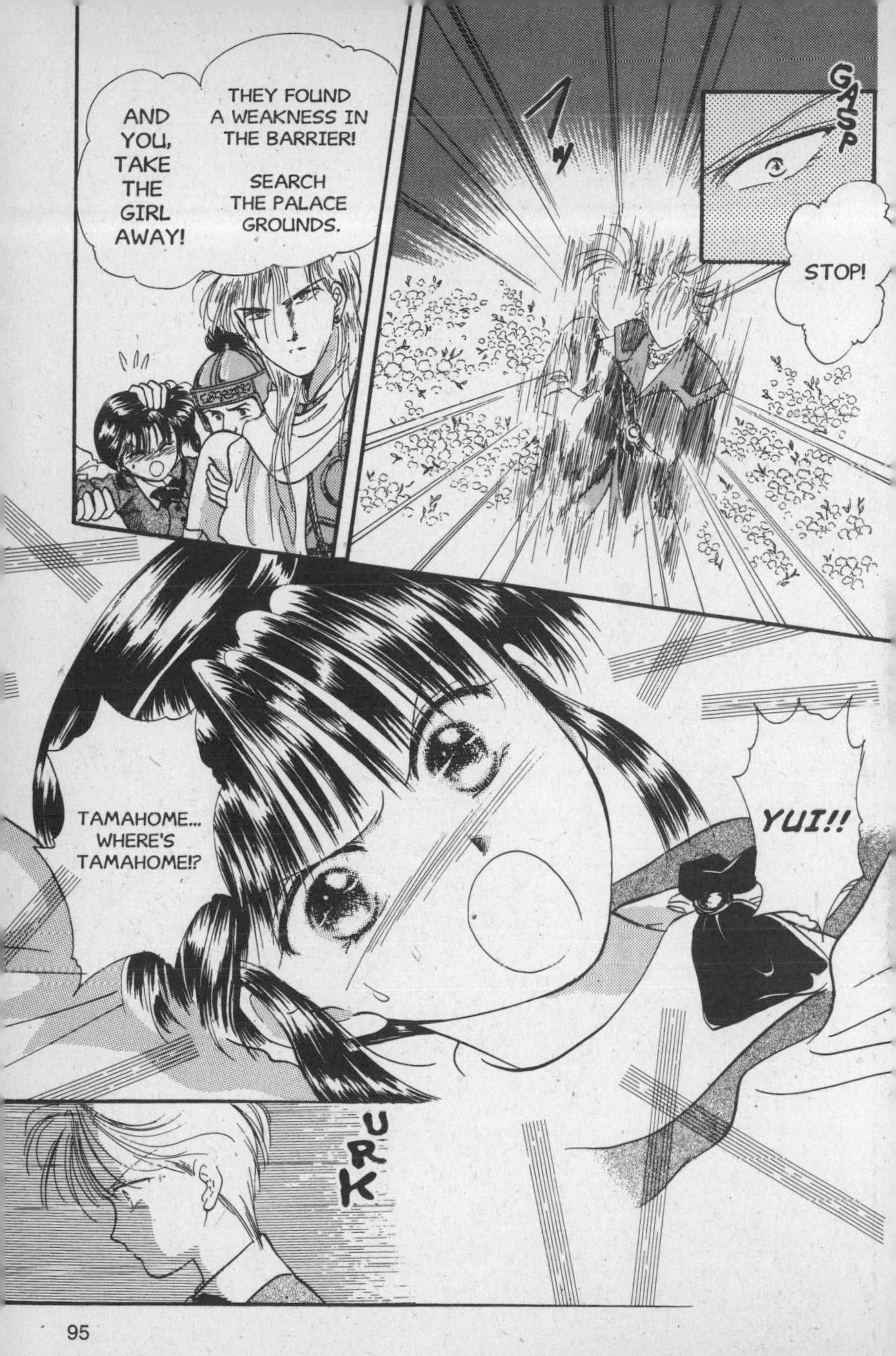
GASP
STOP!
THEY FOUND A WEAKNESS IN THE BARRIER!
SEARCH THE PALACE GROUNDS.
AND YOU, TAKE THE GIRL AWAY!
YUI!!
TAMAHOME... WHERE'S TAMAHOME!?
URK

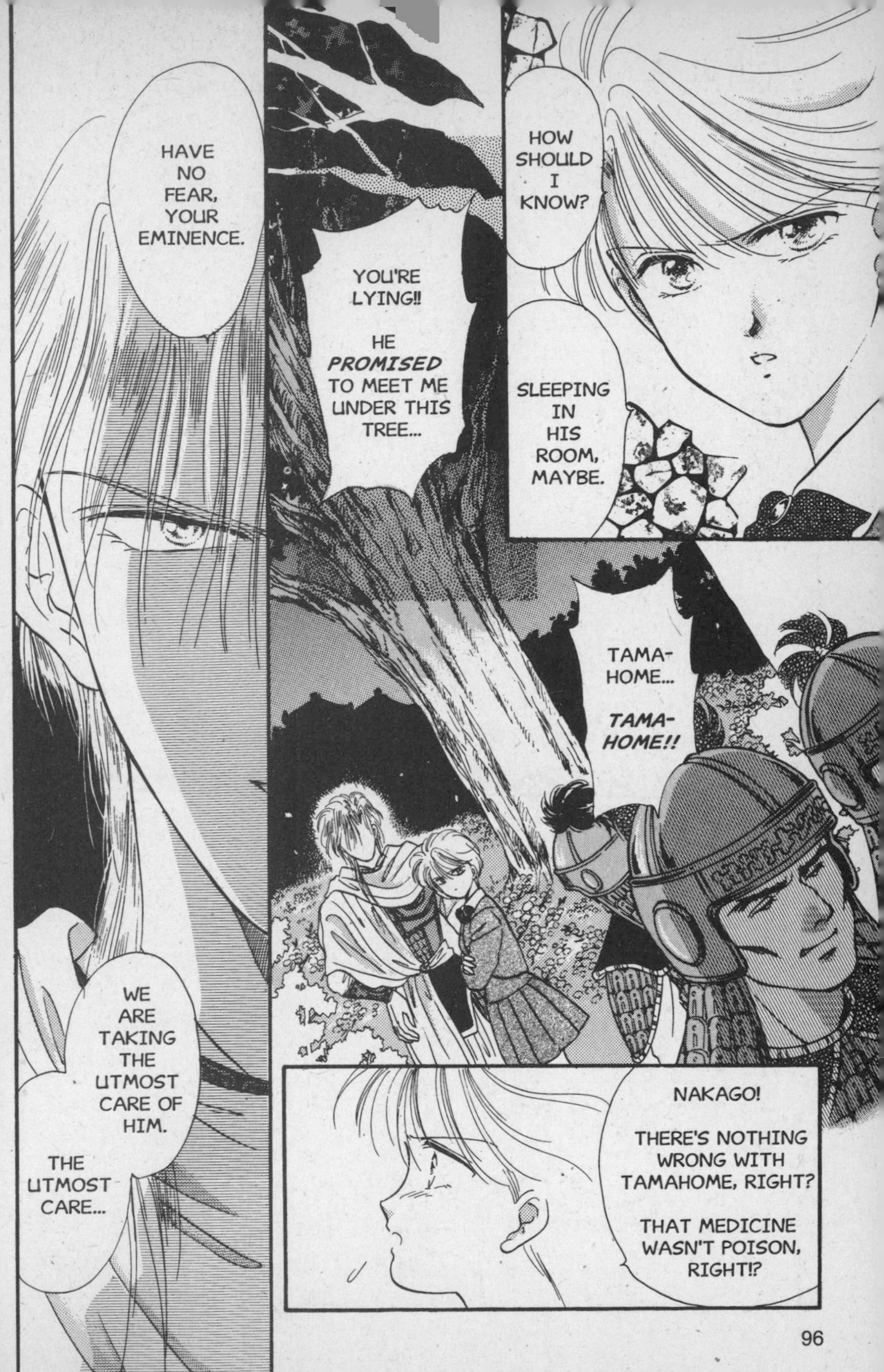
HOW SHOULD I KNOW?
SLEEPING IN HIS ROOM, MAYBE.
YOU'RE LYING!!
HE *PROMISED* TO MEET ME UNDER THIS TREE...
TAMA-HOME...
TAMA-HOME!!
NAKAGO!
THERE'S NOTHING WRONG WITH TAMAHOME, RIGHT?
THAT MEDICINE WASN'T POISON, RIGHT!?
HAVE NO FEAR, YOUR EMINENCE.
WE ARE TAKING THE UTMOST CARE OF HIM.
THE UTMOST CARE...

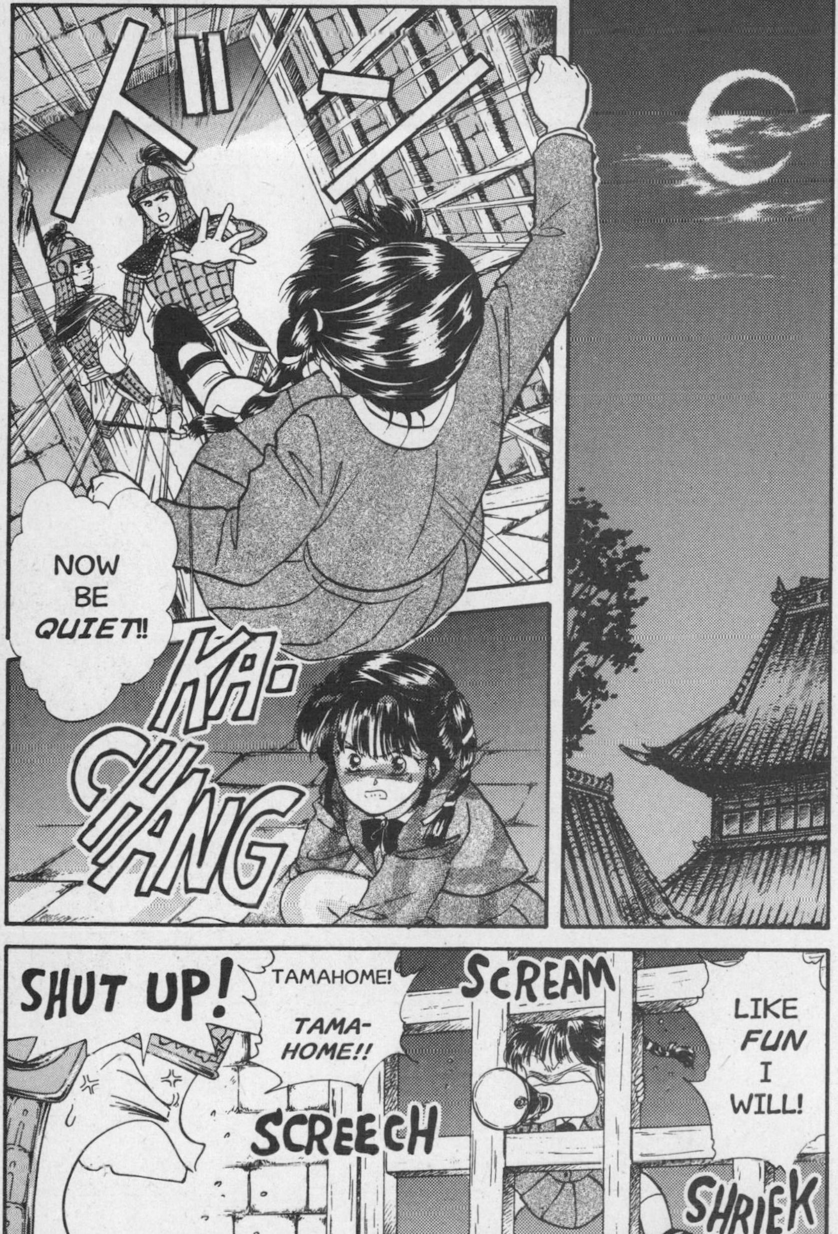
NOW BE QUIET!!
KA-CHANG
LIKE FUN I WILL!
SHRIEK
SCREAM
TAMAHOME!
TAMA-HOME!!
SCREECH
SHUT UP!

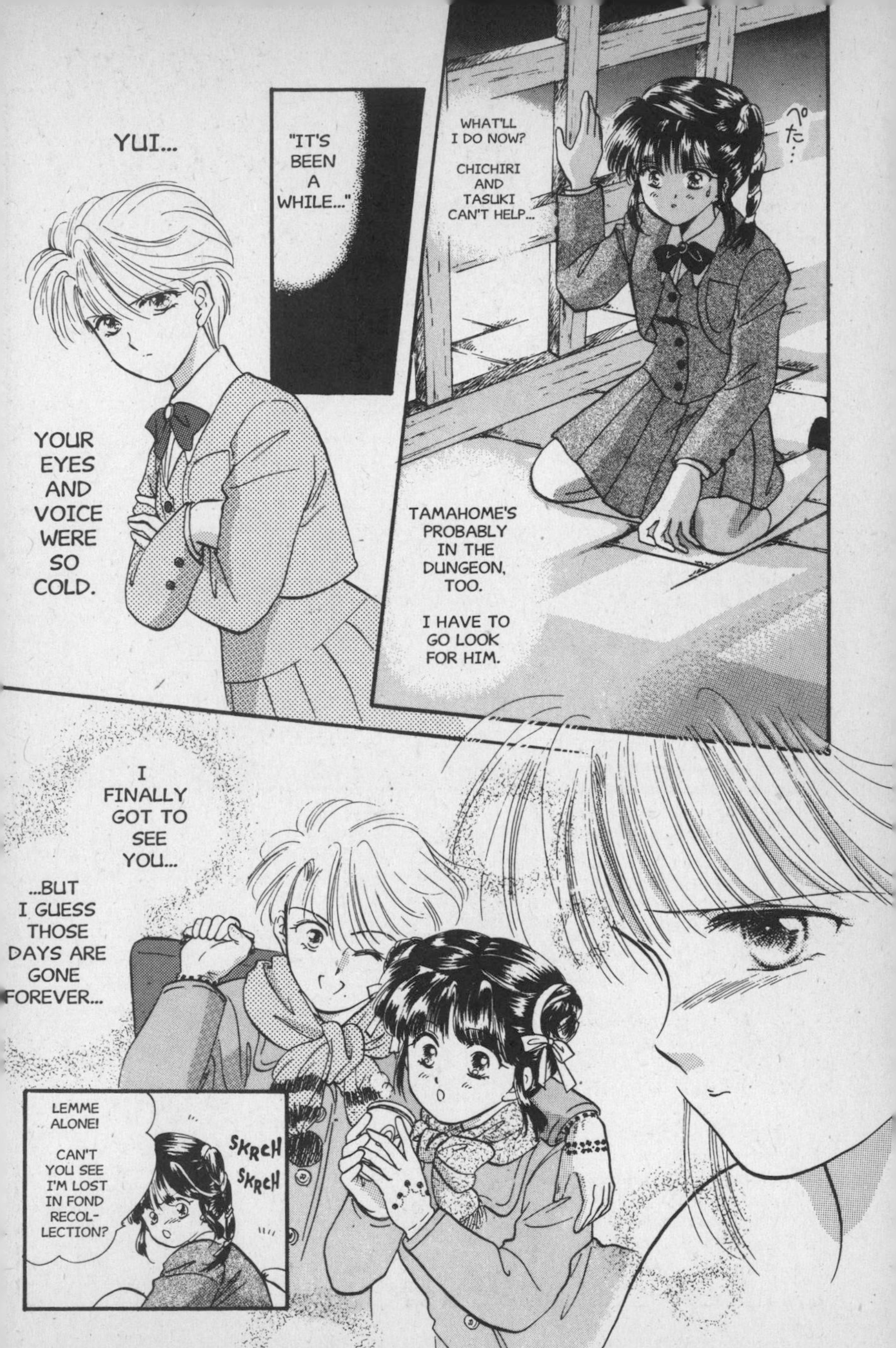
ぺた…
WHAT'LL I DO NOW?
CHICHIRI AND TASUKI CAN'T HELP...
TAMAHOME'S PROBABLY IN THE DUNGEON, TOO.
I HAVE TO GO LOOK FOR HIM.
"IT'S BEEN A WHILE..."
YUI...
YOUR EYES AND VOICE WERE SO COLD.
I FINALLY GOT TO SEE YOU...
...BUT I GUESS THOSE DAYS ARE GONE FOREVER...
SKRCH SKRCH
LEMME ALONE!
CAN'T YOU SEE I'M LOST IN FOND RECOL-LECTION?

BWAH
CHICHIRI...
YO!
HOW'S IT HANGIN'?
ガバッ
...YOU AGAIN.
OH, MISTER STUDLY GUARD...

Now... When I visit my home town, the distance is about a third of the length of the whole country. I usually take the bullet train, but this time I decided that I'd go ahead and fly. That was fine as far as it went. While I'd flown before, nobody else in my family had (mother and brother). I'm the type to leave details to other people, and this time it got all three of us in trouble. You know how you're supposed to check in at the gate 20 minutes early? Well, I completely forgot about that. We arrived at Haneda airport only 15 minutes before our departure time, so we were already late. But we just sat around in the waiting area, only to suddenly realize that there were only five minutes left! We totally panicked when we heard the flight announcement. On top of this, they stopped me at security because of my letter opener! You shouldn't do things you're not used to. I can't believe how stupid we were. I swear, we were acting like manga characters. In the end though, we did get on the flight with no problems. The flight was delayed, but it wasn't our fault!! The pilot was late or something like that! Please believe me! Don't say it's my fault! This is what happens when the whole family doesn't take responsibility! I wasn't planning on telling Dad about it, but I can't keep things to myself. I ended up telling him. And of course he made fun of us. Waaahh!

Well, failure is the mother of success, so our return trip was totally smooth. We arrived one hour early. Are we just...stupid, maybe? See if I care!

This year I'm going to China. Flying is a breeze!

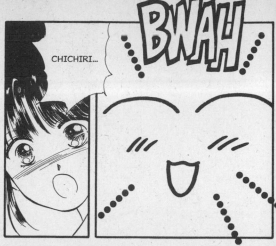

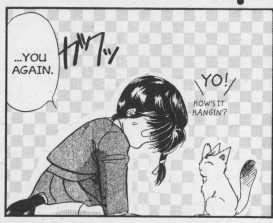

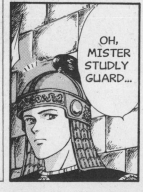

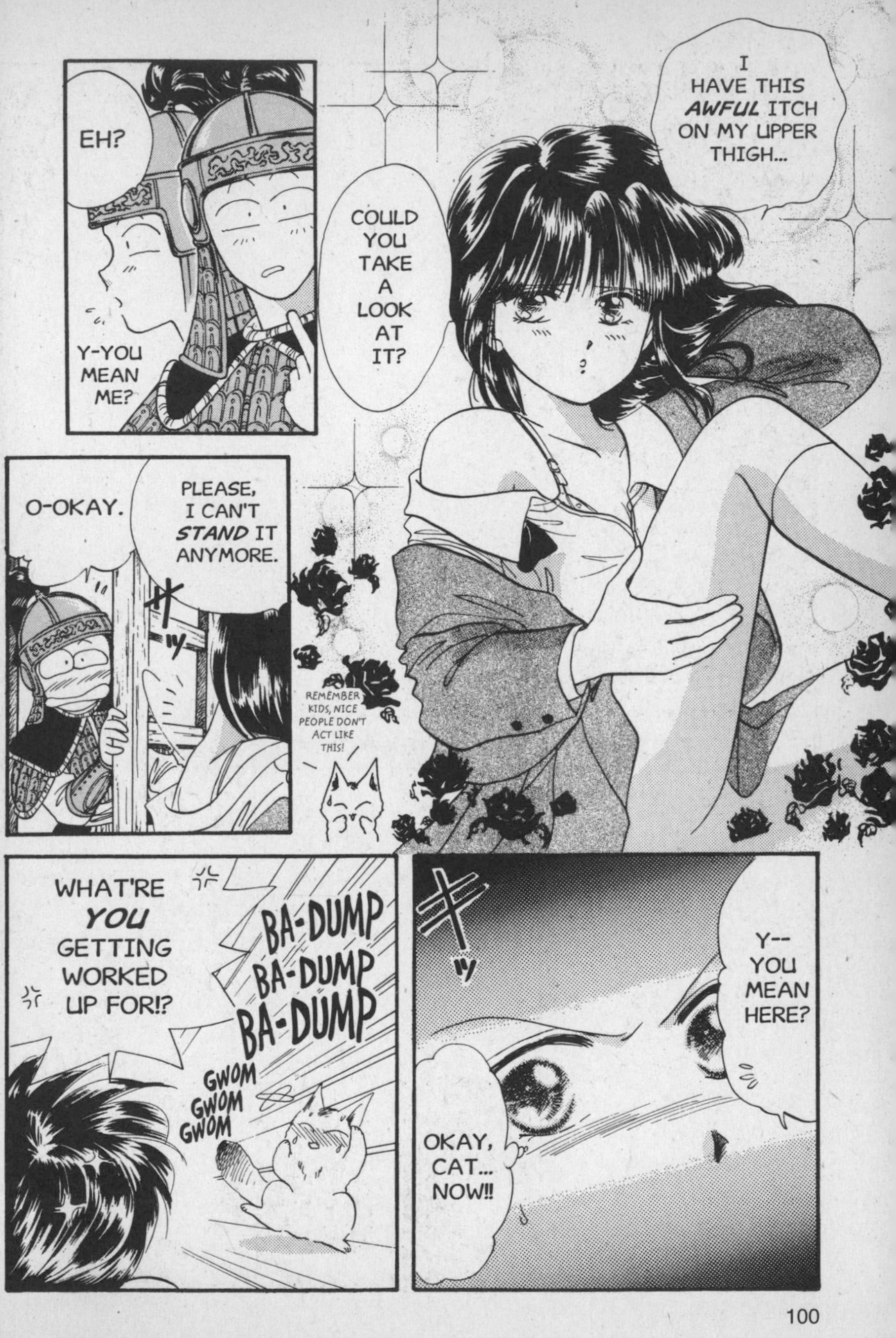
I HAVE THIS *AWFUL* ITCH ON MY UPPER THIGH...
COULD YOU TAKE A LOOK AT IT?
EH?
Y-YOU MEAN ME?
PLEASE, I CAN'T *STAND* IT ANYMORE.
O-OKAY.
REMEMBER KIDS, NICE PEOPLE DON'T ACT LIKE THIS!
Y-- YOU MEAN HERE?
OKAY, CAT... NOW!!
WHAT'RE *YOU* GETTING WORKED UP FOR!?
BA-DUMP
BA-DUMP
BA-DUMP
GWOM
GWOM
GWOM

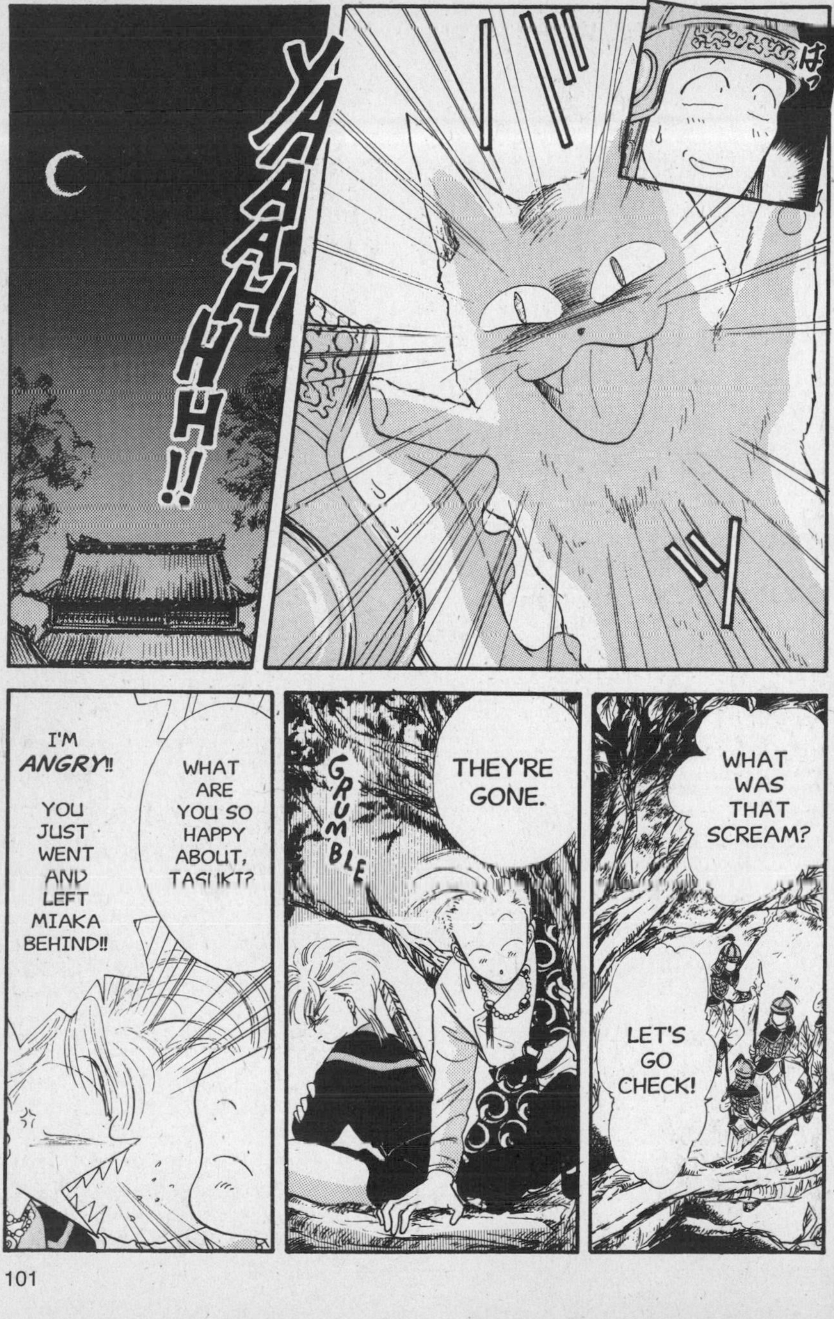
はっ
YAAAHHH!!
WHAT WAS THAT SCREAM?
LET'S GO CHECK!
THEY'RE GONE.
GRUMBLE
WHAT ARE YOU SO HAPPY ABOUT, TASUKI?
I'M *ANGRY*!!
YOU JUST WENT AND LEFT MIAKA BEHIND!!

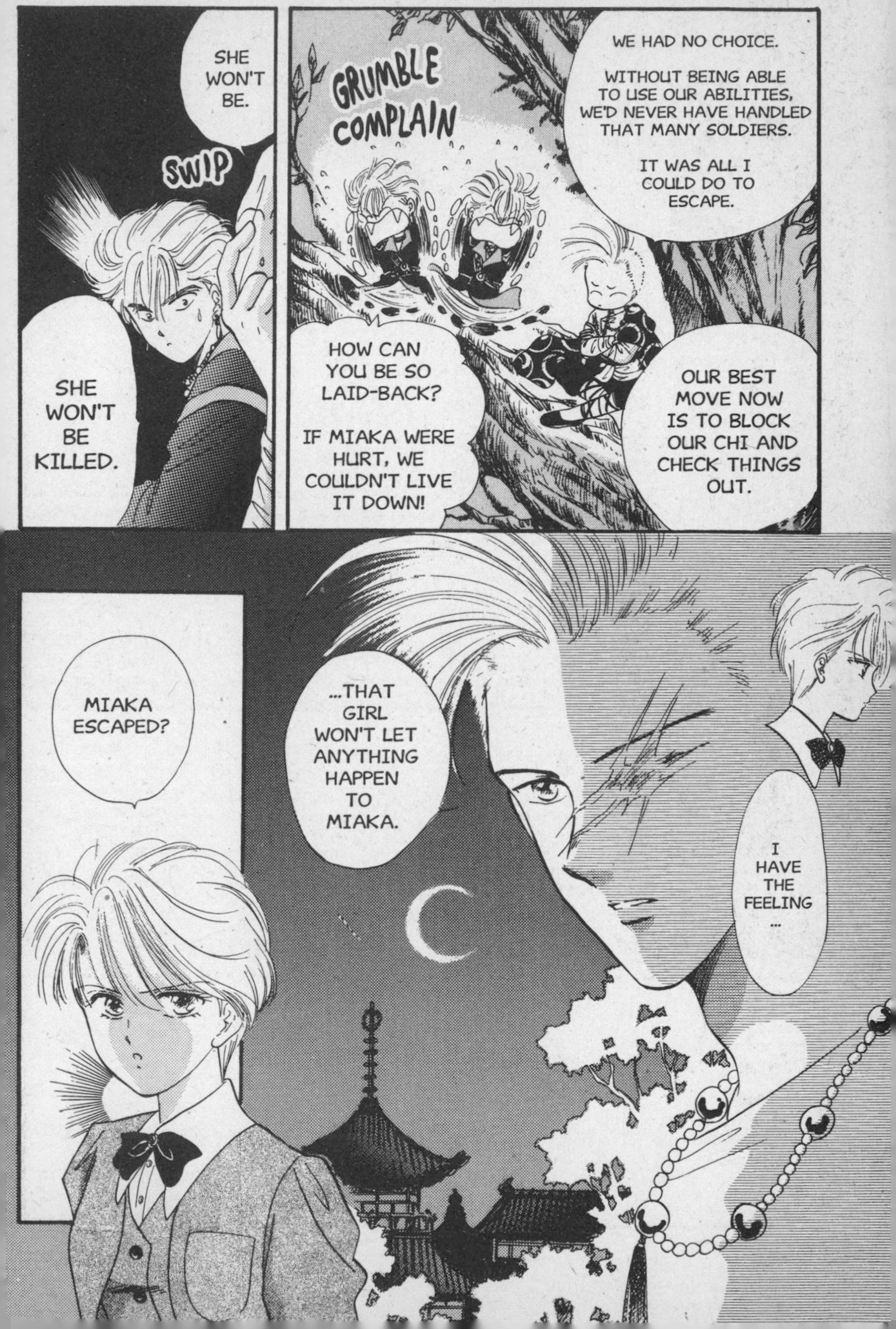
WE HAD NO CHOICE.
WITHOUT BEING ABLE TO USE OUR ABILITIES, WE'D NEVER HAVE HANDLED THAT MANY SOLDIERS.
IT WAS ALL I COULD DO TO ESCAPE.
GRUMBLE COMPLAIN
HOW CAN YOU BE SO LAID-BACK?
IF MIAKA WERE HURT, WE COULDN'T LIVE IT DOWN!
OUR BEST MOVE NOW IS TO BLOCK OUR CHI AND CHECK THINGS OUT.
SHE WON'T BE.
SWIP
SHE WON'T BE KILLED.
I HAVE THE FEELING ...
...THAT GIRL WON'T LET ANYTHING HAPPEN TO MIAKA.
MIAKA ESCAPED?

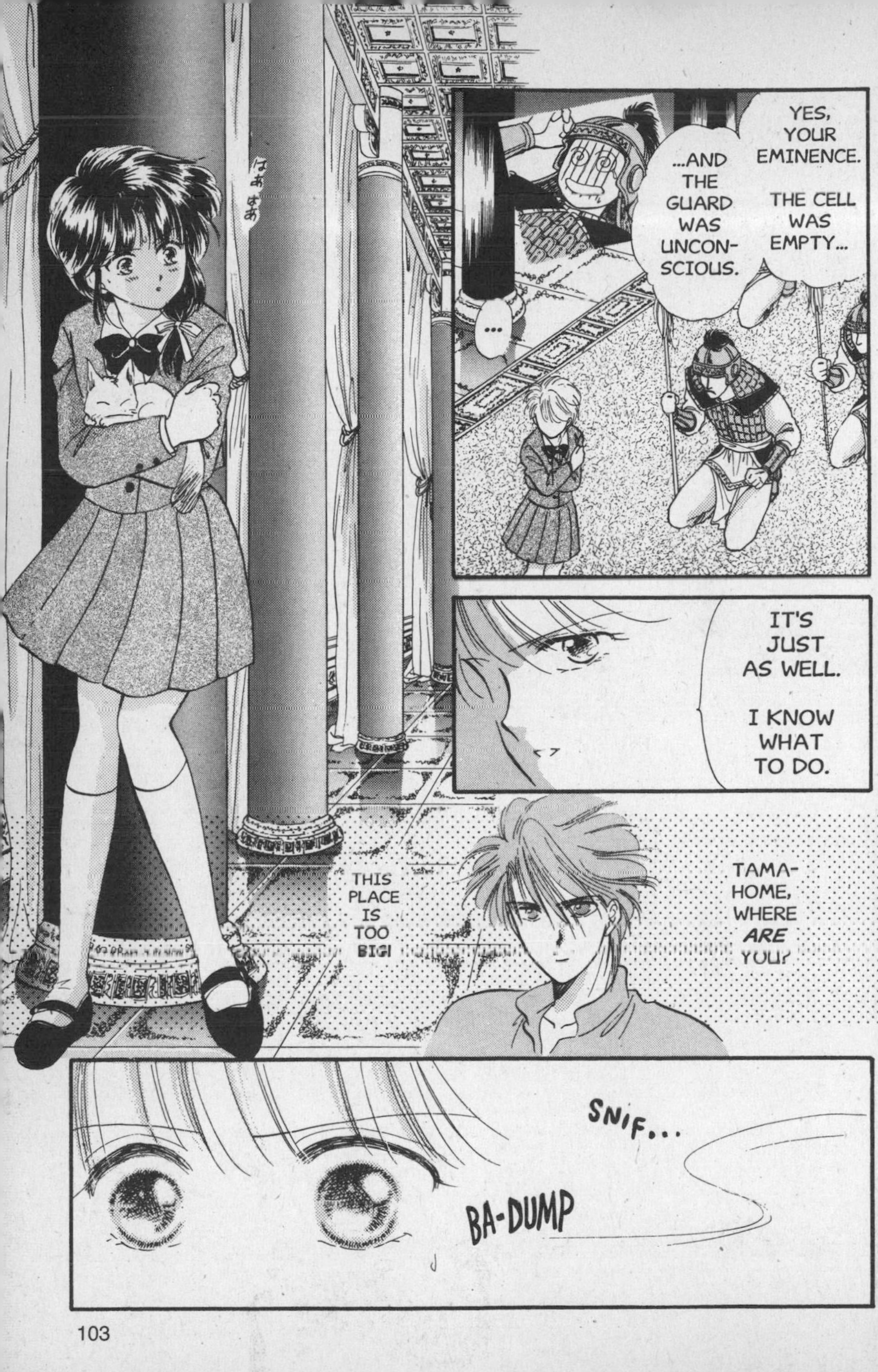
YES, YOUR EMINENCE. THE CELL WAS EMPTY...
...AND THE GUARD WAS UNCONSCIOUS.
...
IT'S JUST AS WELL.
I KNOW WHAT TO DO.
TAMAHOME, WHERE *ARE* YOU?
はぁ はぁ
THIS PLACE IS TOO BIG!
SNIF...
BA-DUMP

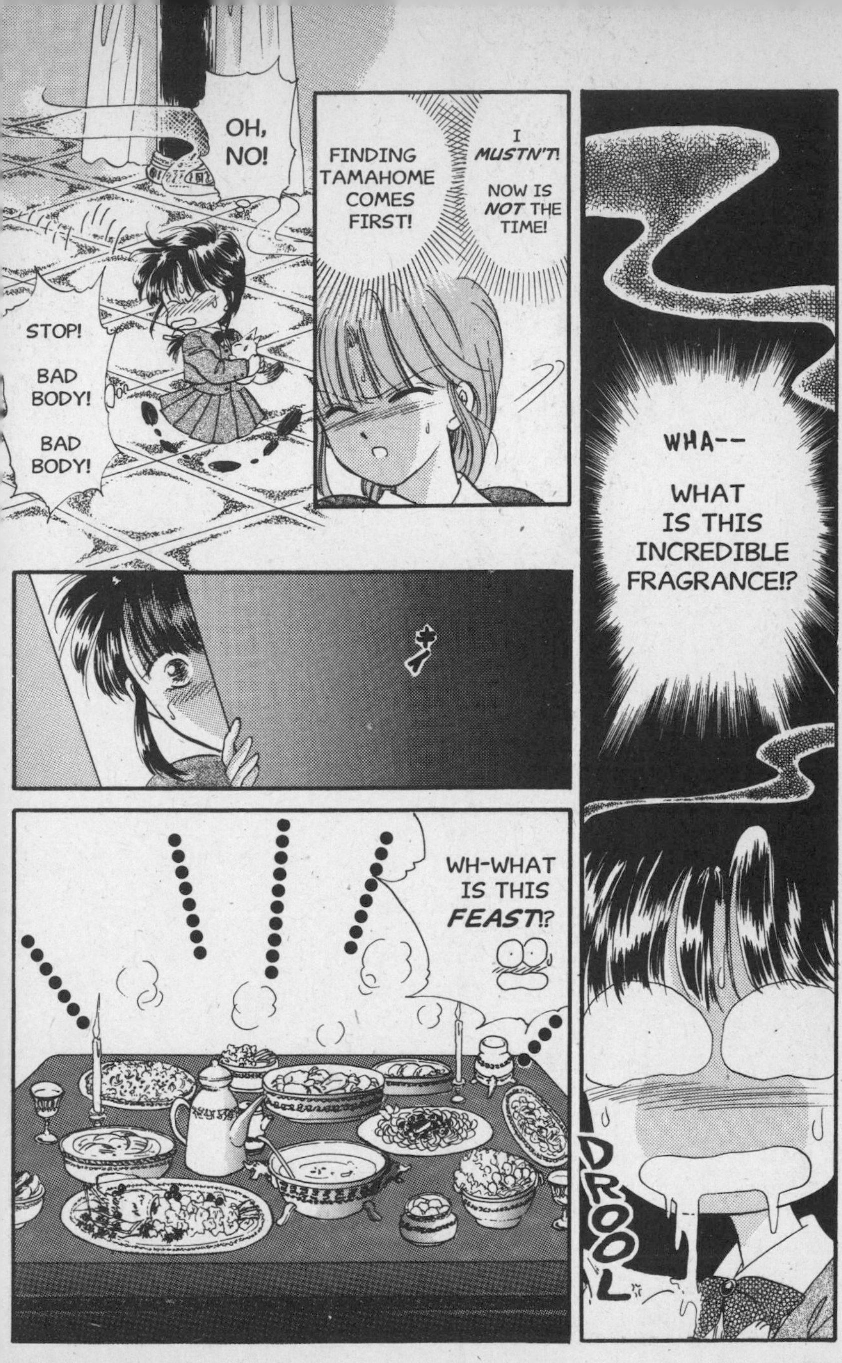
WHA--
WHAT IS THIS INCREDIBLE FRAGRANCE!?
DROOL
I MUSTN'T! NOW IS NOT THE TIME!
FINDING TAMAHOME COMES FIRST!
OH, NO!
STOP! BAD BODY! BAD BODY!
WH-WHAT IS THIS FEAST!?

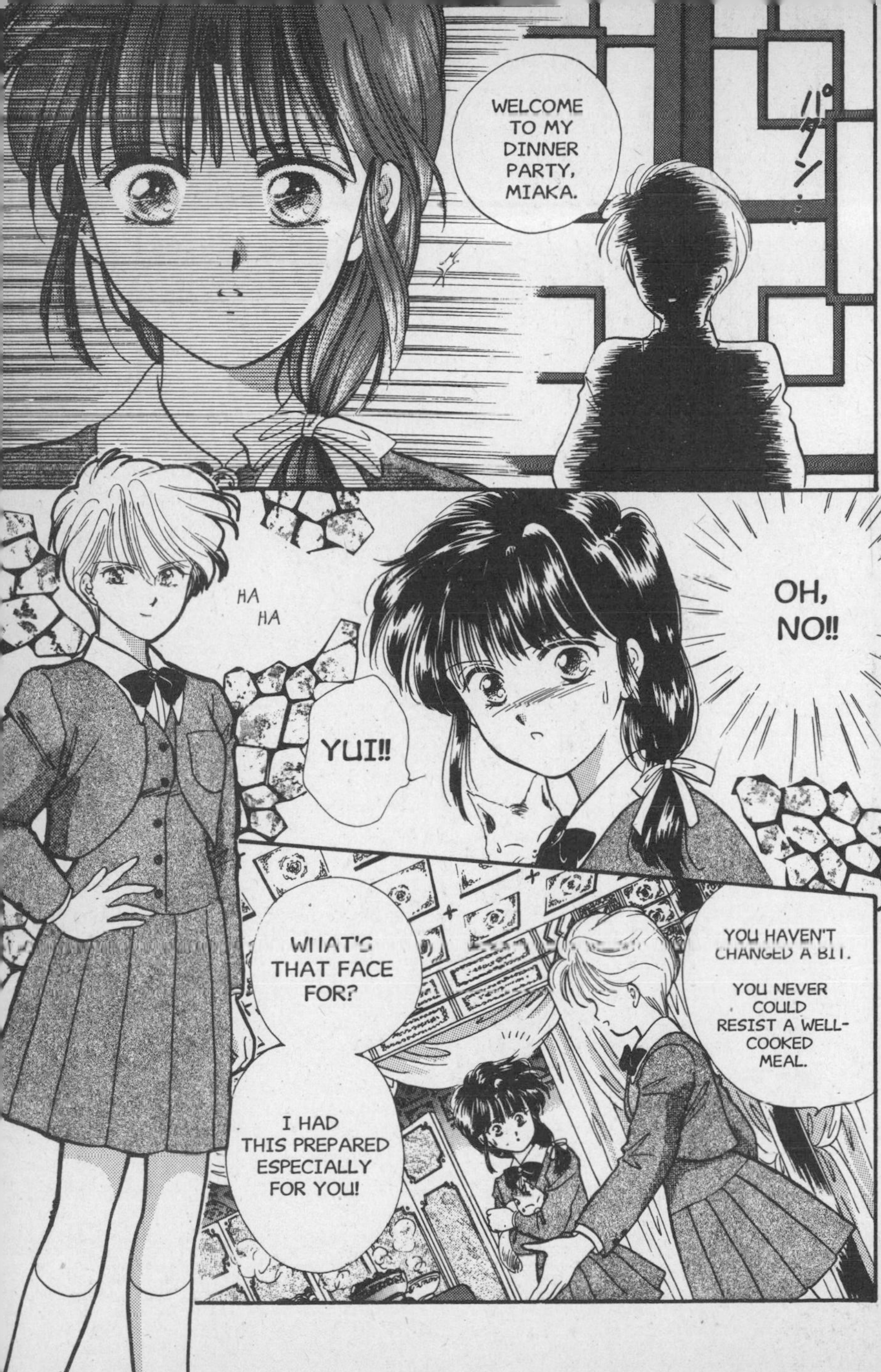
WELCOME TO MY DINNER PARTY, MIAKA.
パタン・・・
OH, NO!!
YUI!!
HA HA
YOU HAVEN'T CHANGED A BIT.
YOU NEVER COULD RESIST A WELL-COOKED MEAL.
WHAT'S THAT FACE FOR?
I HAD THIS PREPARED ESPECIALLY FOR YOU!

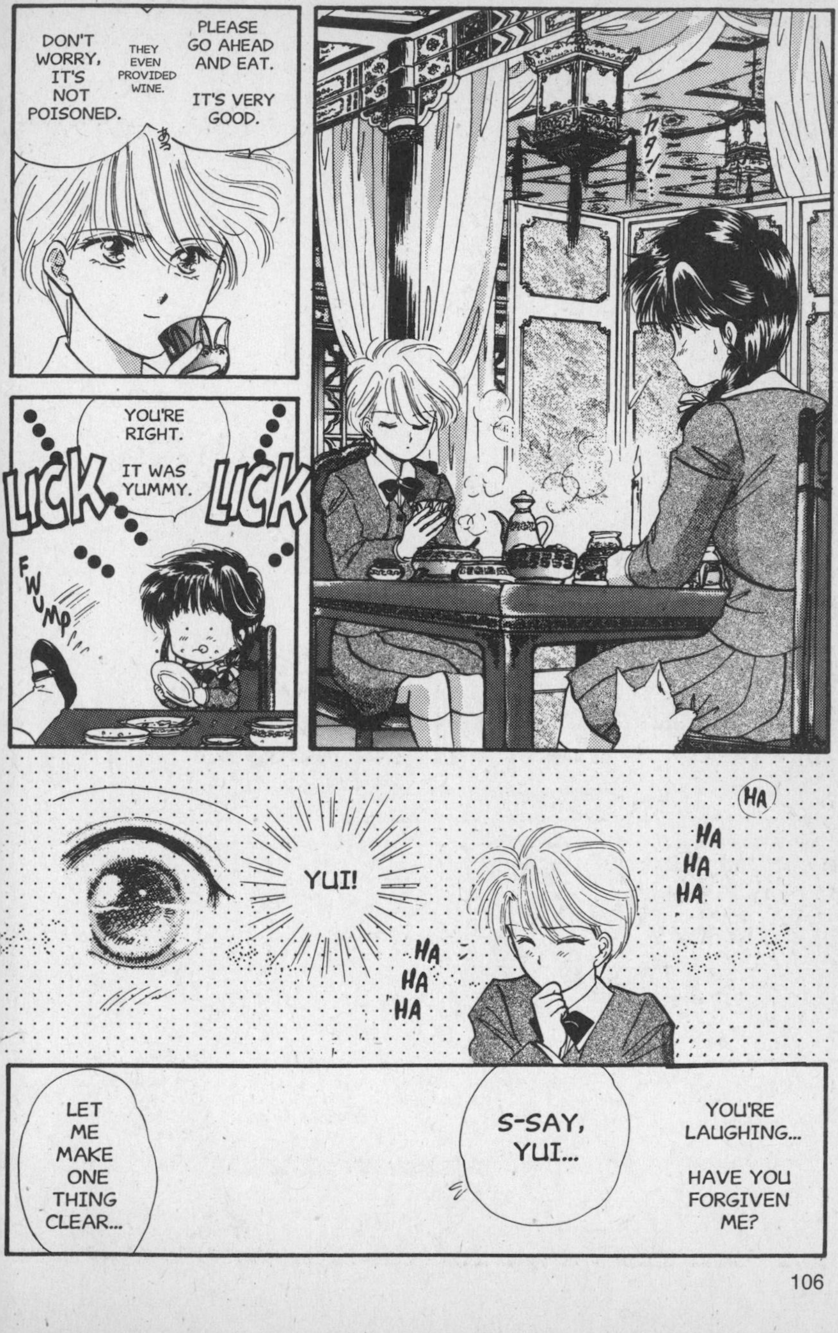
PLEASE GO AHEAD AND EAT.
IT'S VERY GOOD.
THEY EVEN PROVIDED WINE.
DON'T WORRY, IT'S NOT POISONED.
LICK
YOU'RE RIGHT.
IT WAS YUMMY.
LICK
FWUMP
HA
HA HA HA
YUI!
HA HA HA
YOU'RE LAUGHING...
HAVE YOU FORGIVEN ME?
S-SAY, YUI...
LET ME MAKE ONE THING CLEAR...

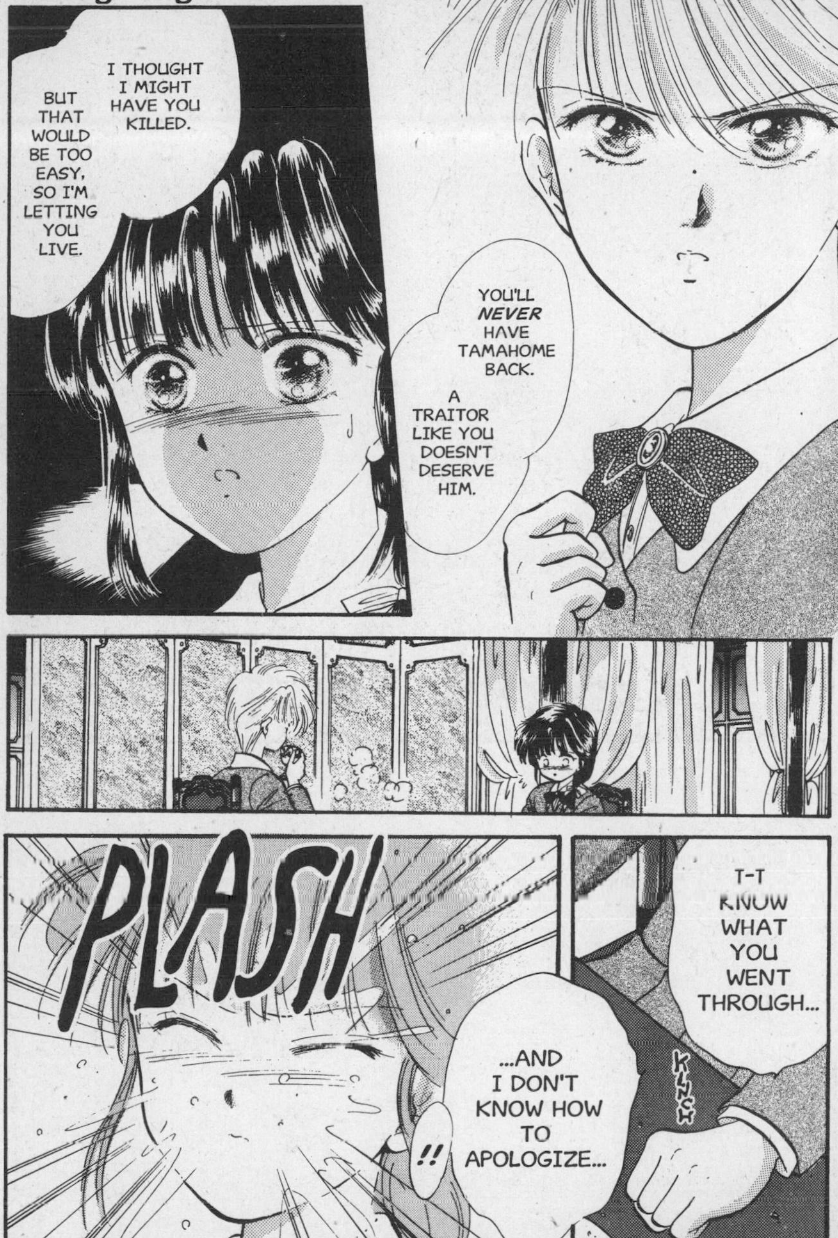
I THOUGHT I MIGHT HAVE YOU KILLED.
BUT THAT WOULD BE TOO EASY, SO I'M LETTING YOU LIVE.
YOU'LL *NEVER* HAVE TAMAHOME BACK.
A TRAITOR LIKE YOU DOESN'T DESERVE HIM.
I-I KNOW WHAT YOU WENT THROUGH...
...AND I DON'T KNOW HOW TO APOLOGIZE...
KLINCH
PLASH
!!

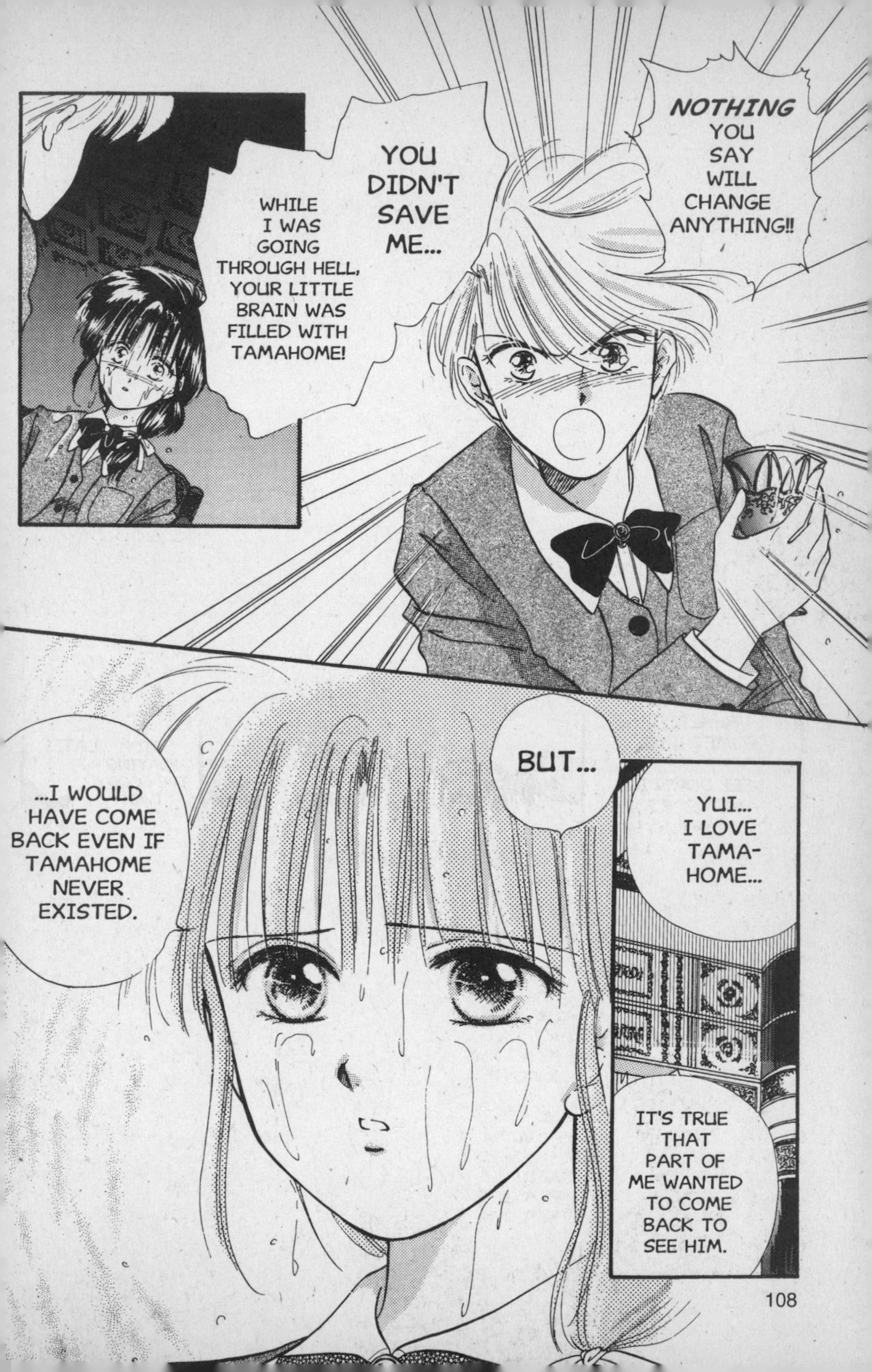
NOTHING YOU SAY WILL CHANGE ANYTHING!!
YOU DIDN'T SAVE ME...
WHILE I WAS GOING THROUGH HELL, YOUR LITTLE BRAIN WAS FILLED WITH TAMAHOME!
YUI... I LOVE TAMA-HOME...
IT'S TRUE THAT PART OF ME WANTED TO COME BACK TO SEE HIM.
BUT...
...I WOULD HAVE COME BACK EVEN IF TAMAHOME NEVER EXISTED.

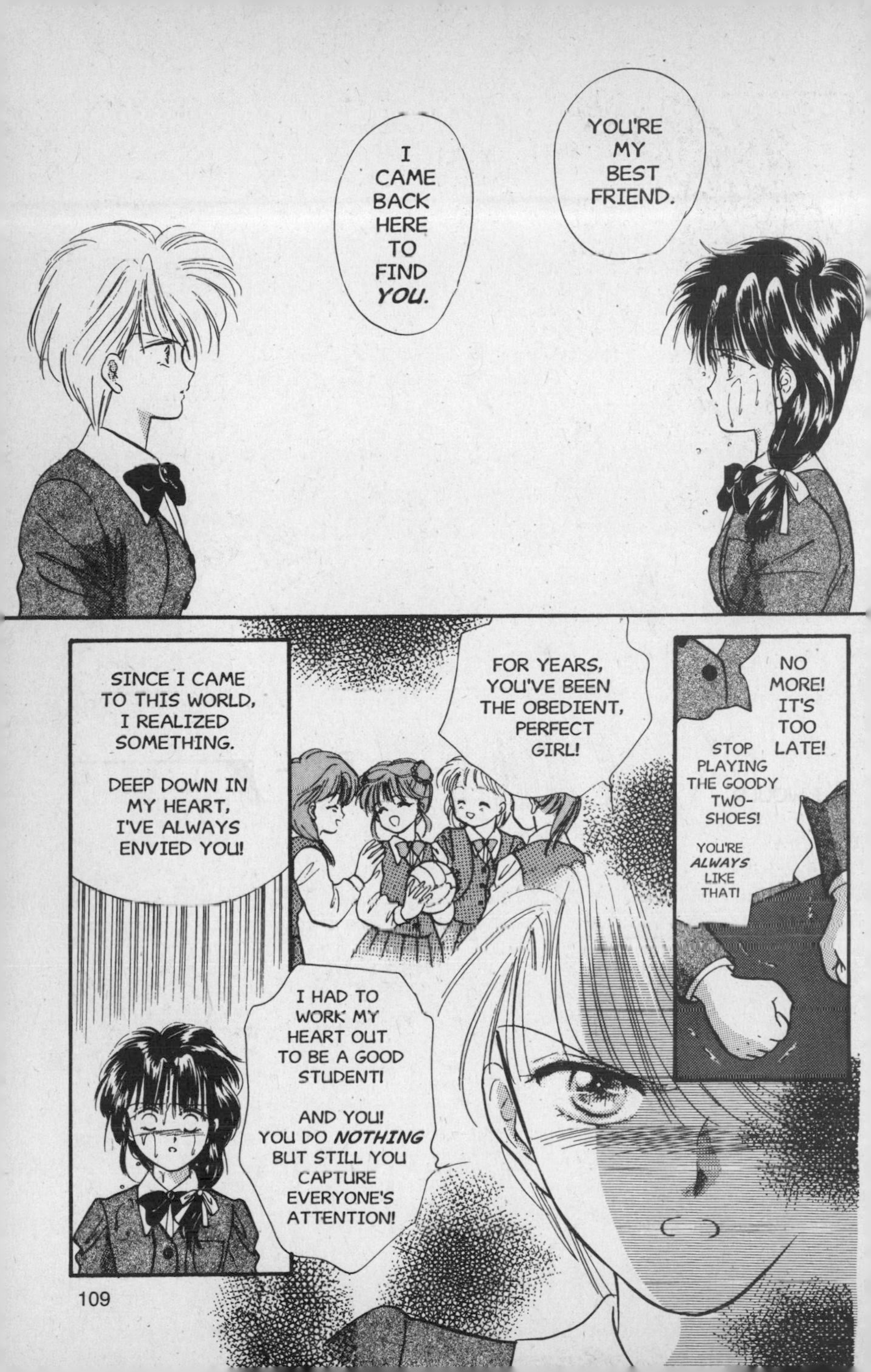
YOU'RE MY BEST FRIEND.
I CAME BACK HERE TO FIND *YOU.*
NO MORE! IT'S TOO LATE!
STOP PLAYING THE GOODY TWO-SHOES!
YOU'RE *ALWAYS* LIKE THAT!
FOR YEARS, YOU'VE BEEN THE OBEDIENT, PERFECT GIRL!
SINCE I CAME TO THIS WORLD, I REALIZED SOMETHING.
DEEP DOWN IN MY HEART, I'VE ALWAYS ENVIED YOU!
I HAD TO WORK MY HEART OUT TO BE A GOOD STUDENT!
AND YOU! YOU DO *NOTHING* BUT STILL YOU CAPTURE EVERYONE'S ATTENTION!

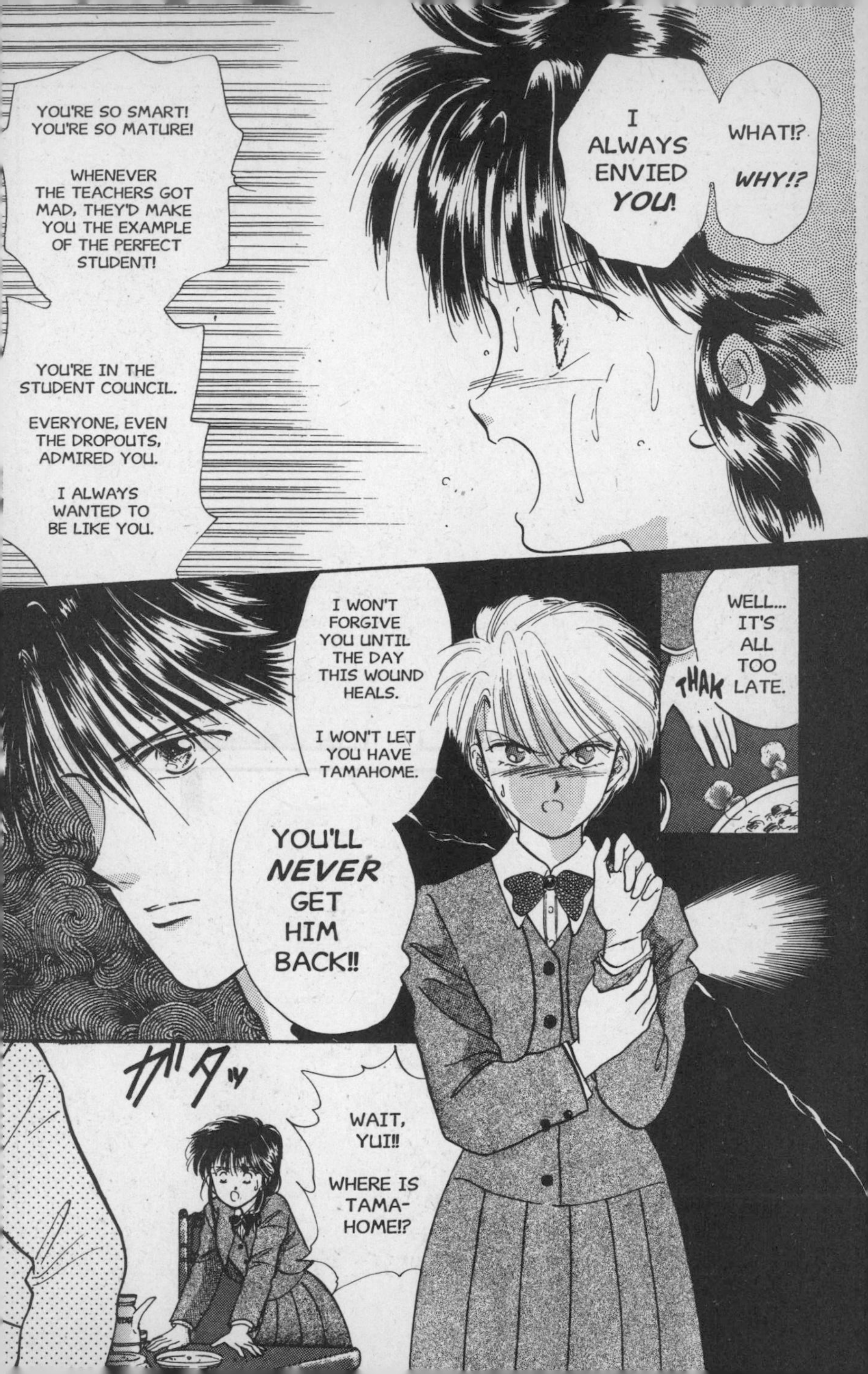

WHAT!? WHY!?
I ALWAYS ENVIED YOU!
YOU'RE SO SMART! YOU'RE SO MATURE!
WHENEVER THE TEACHERS GOT MAD, THEY'D MAKE YOU THE EXAMPLE OF THE PERFECT STUDENT!
YOU'RE IN THE STUDENT COUNCIL.
EVERYONE, EVEN THE DROPOUTS, ADMIRED YOU.
I ALWAYS WANTED TO BE LIKE YOU.
WELL... IT'S ALL TOO LATE.
THAK
I WON'T FORGIVE YOU UNTIL THE DAY THIS WOUND HEALS.
I WON'T LET YOU HAVE TAMAHOME.
YOU'LL NEVER GET HIM BACK!!
ガタッ
WAIT, YUI!!
WHERE IS TAMA-HOME!?

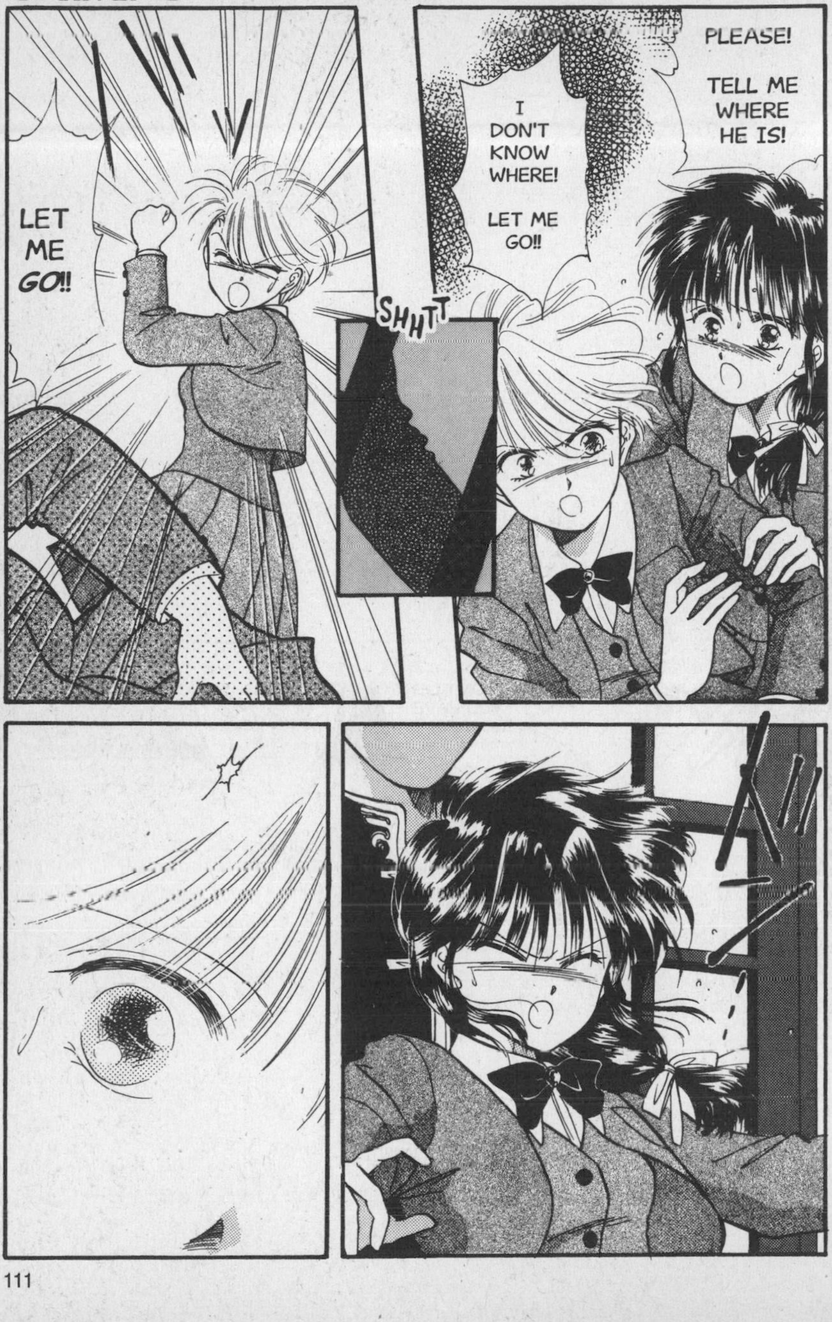
PLEASE!
TELL ME WHERE HE IS!
I DON'T KNOW WHERE!
LET ME GO!!
SHHTT
LET ME GO!!

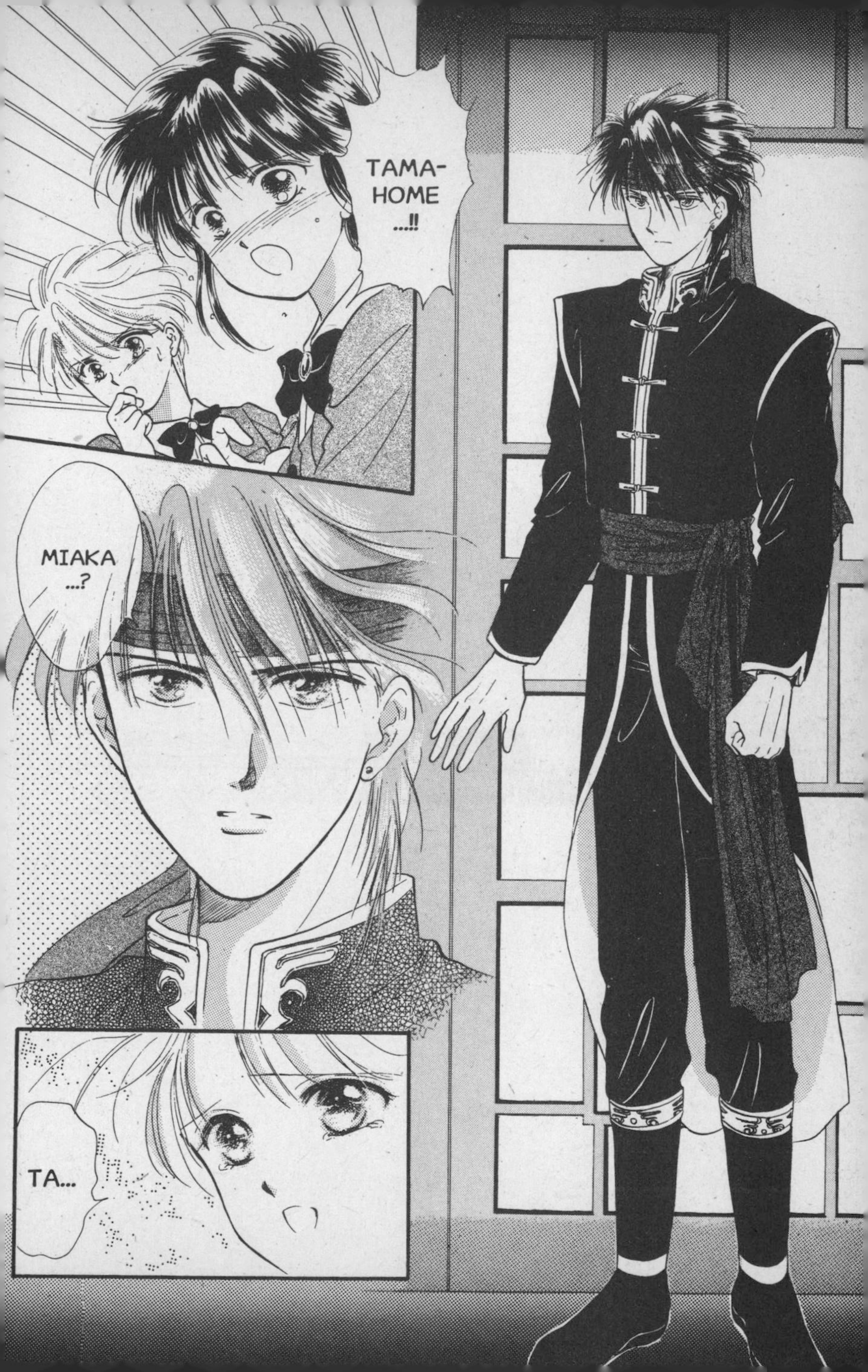
TAMA-HOME ...!!
MIAKA ...?
TA...

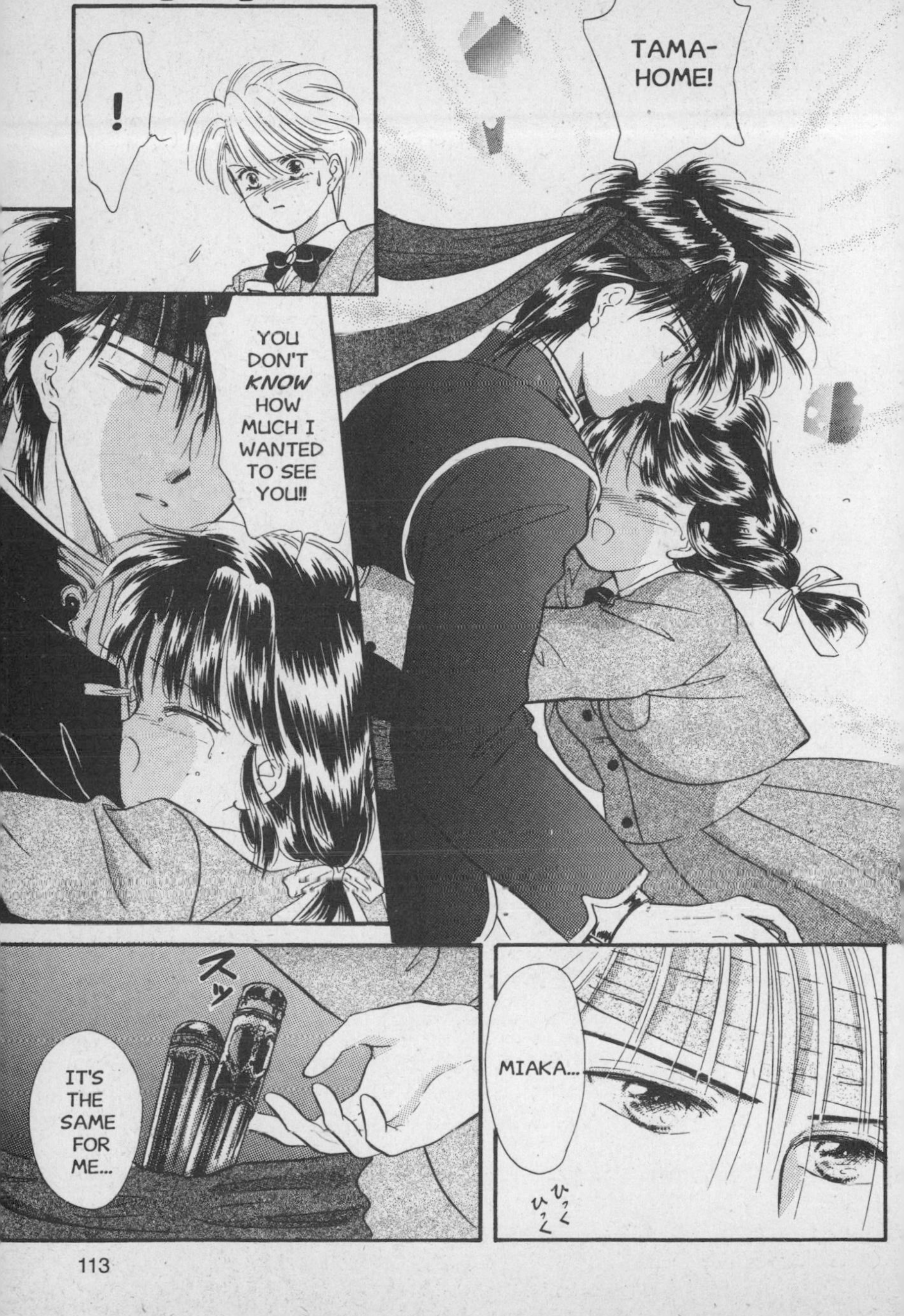
TAMA-HOME!
!
YOU DON'T *KNOW* HOW MUCH I WANTED TO SEE YOU!!
MIAKA...
ひっく ひっく
スッ
IT'S THE SAME FOR ME...

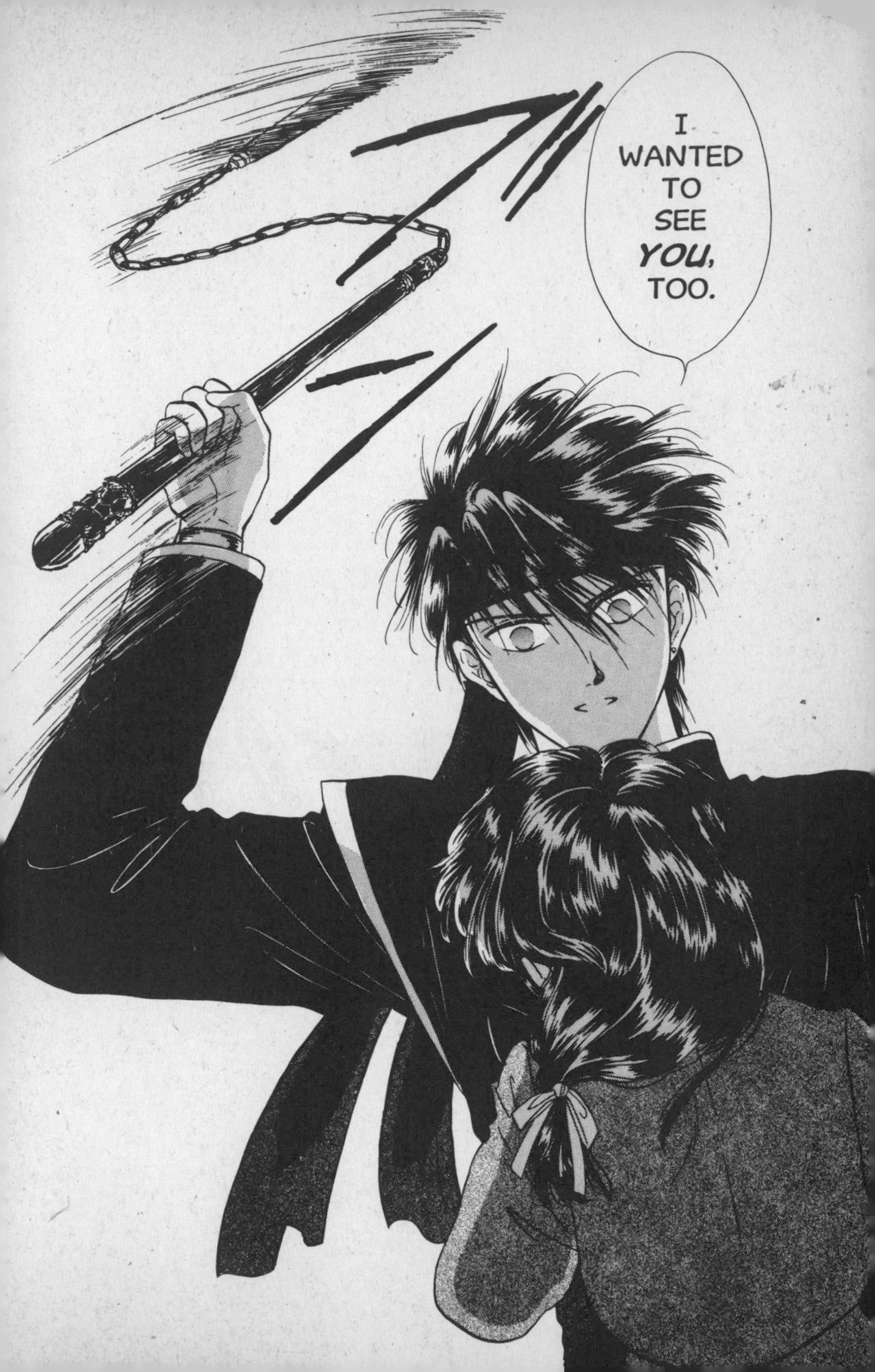
I WANTED TO SEE *YOU*, TOO.

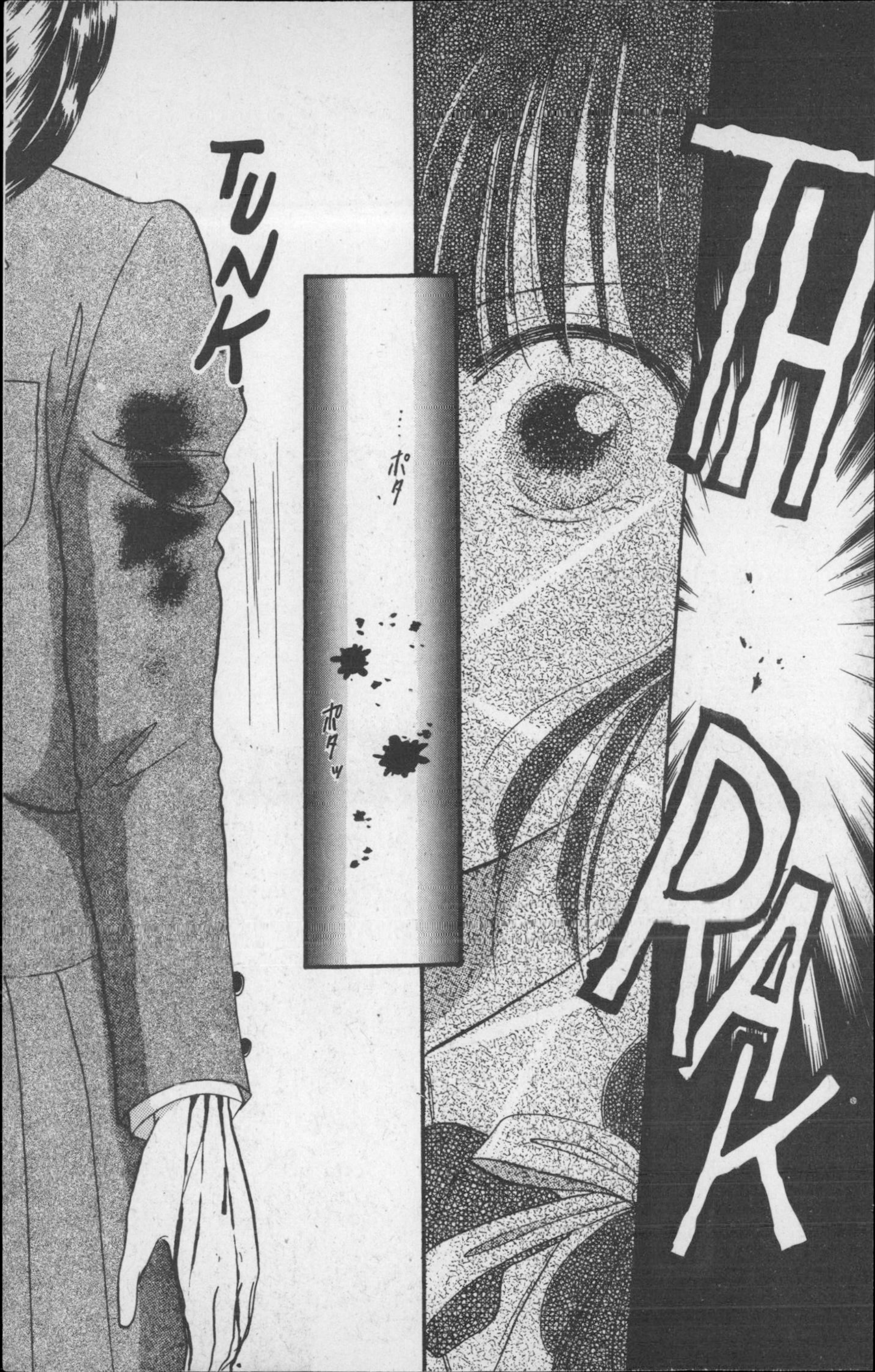
TH
DAK
ポタ
ポタッ
TUNK

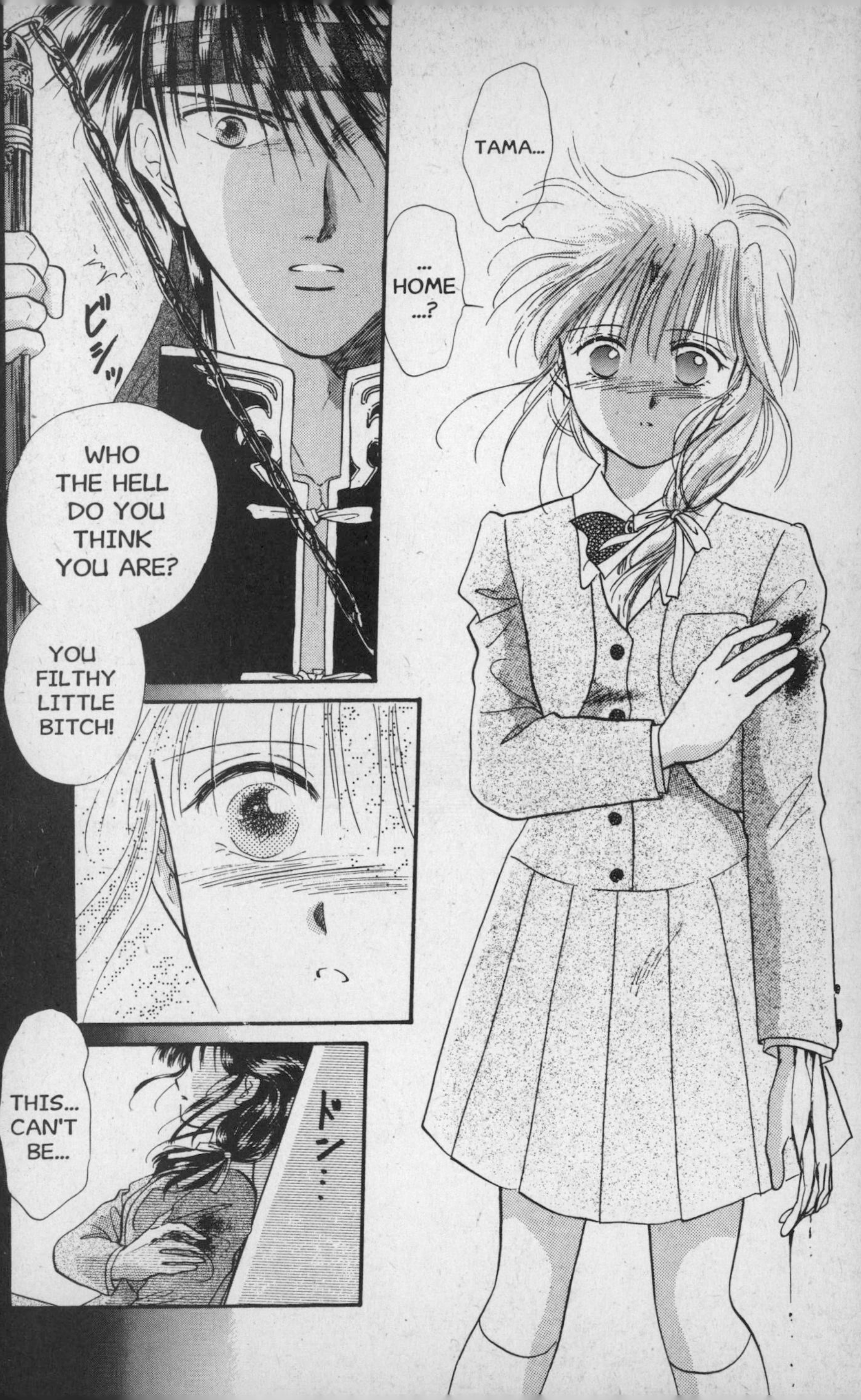
TAMA...
...HOME...?
ビシッ
WHO THE HELL DO YOU THINK YOU ARE?
YOU FILTHY LITTLE BITCH!
THIS... CAN'T BE...
ドン…

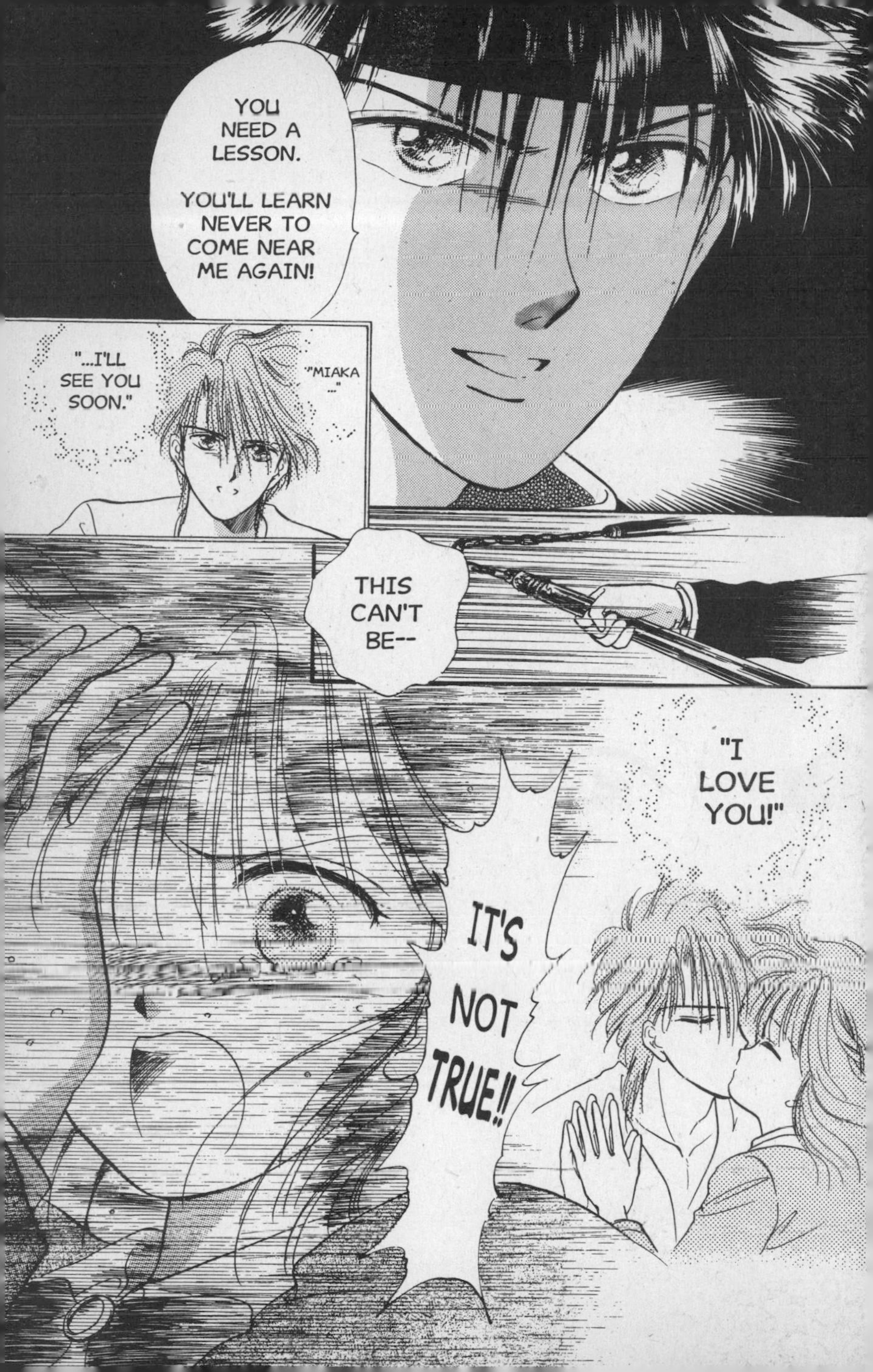
YOU NEED A LESSON.
YOU'LL LEARN NEVER TO COME NEAR ME AGAIN!
"MIAKA ..."
"...I'LL SEE YOU SOON."
THIS CAN'T BE--
"I LOVE YOU!"
IT'S NOT TRUE!!

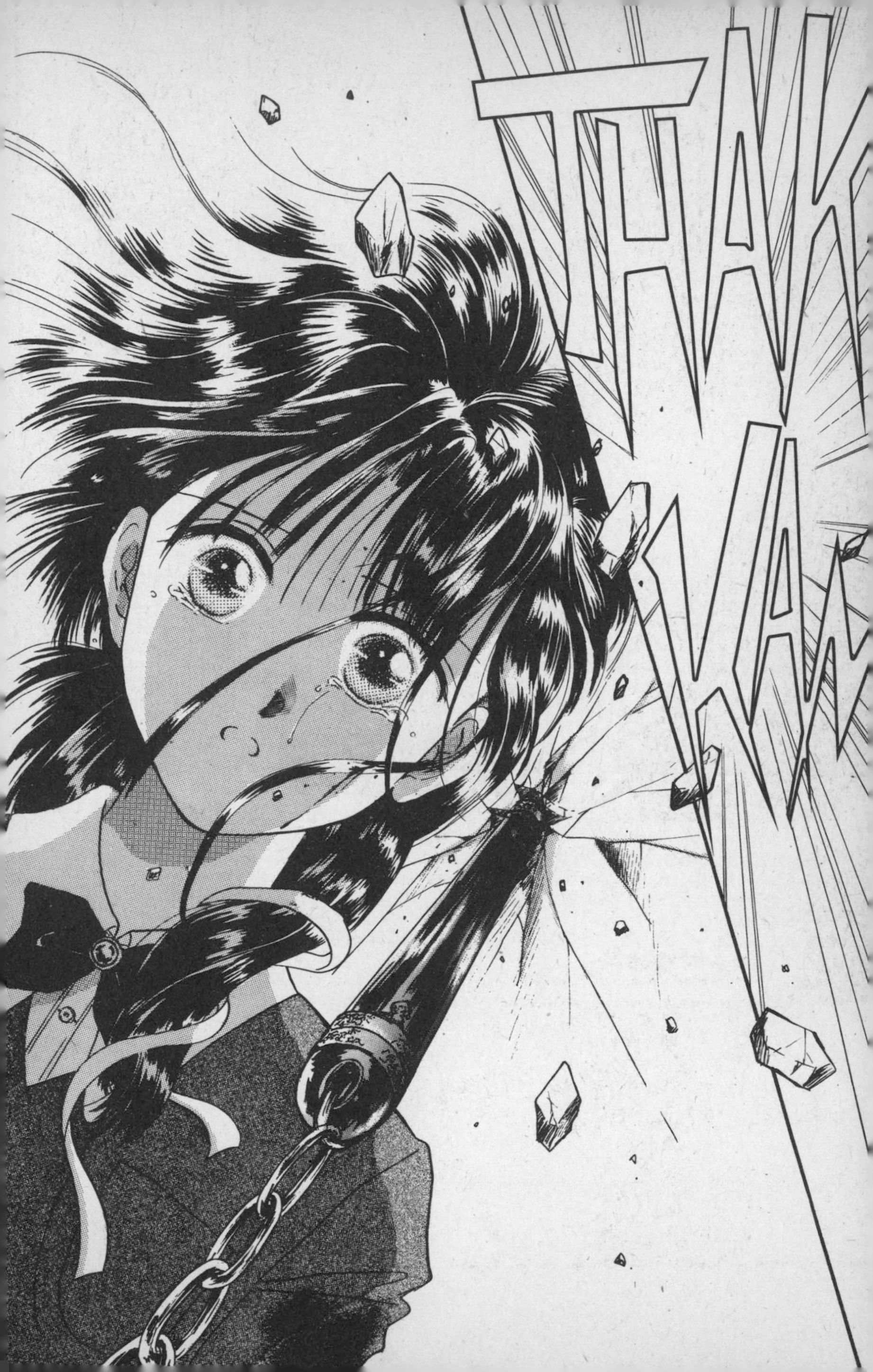
THAK
WAK

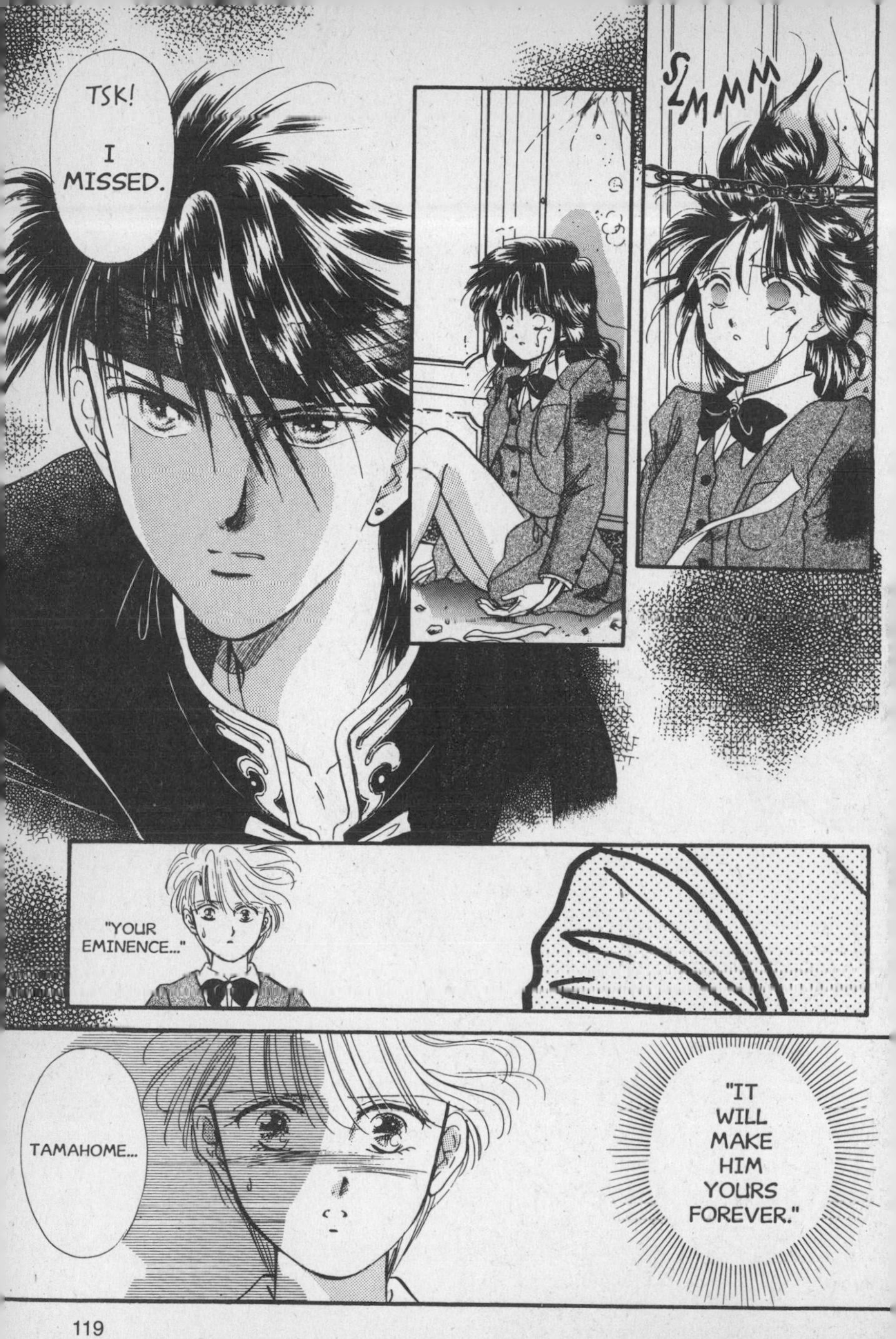
SLMMM
TSK!
I MISSED.
"YOUR EMINENCE..."
"IT WILL MAKE HIM YOURS FOREVER."
TAMAHOME...

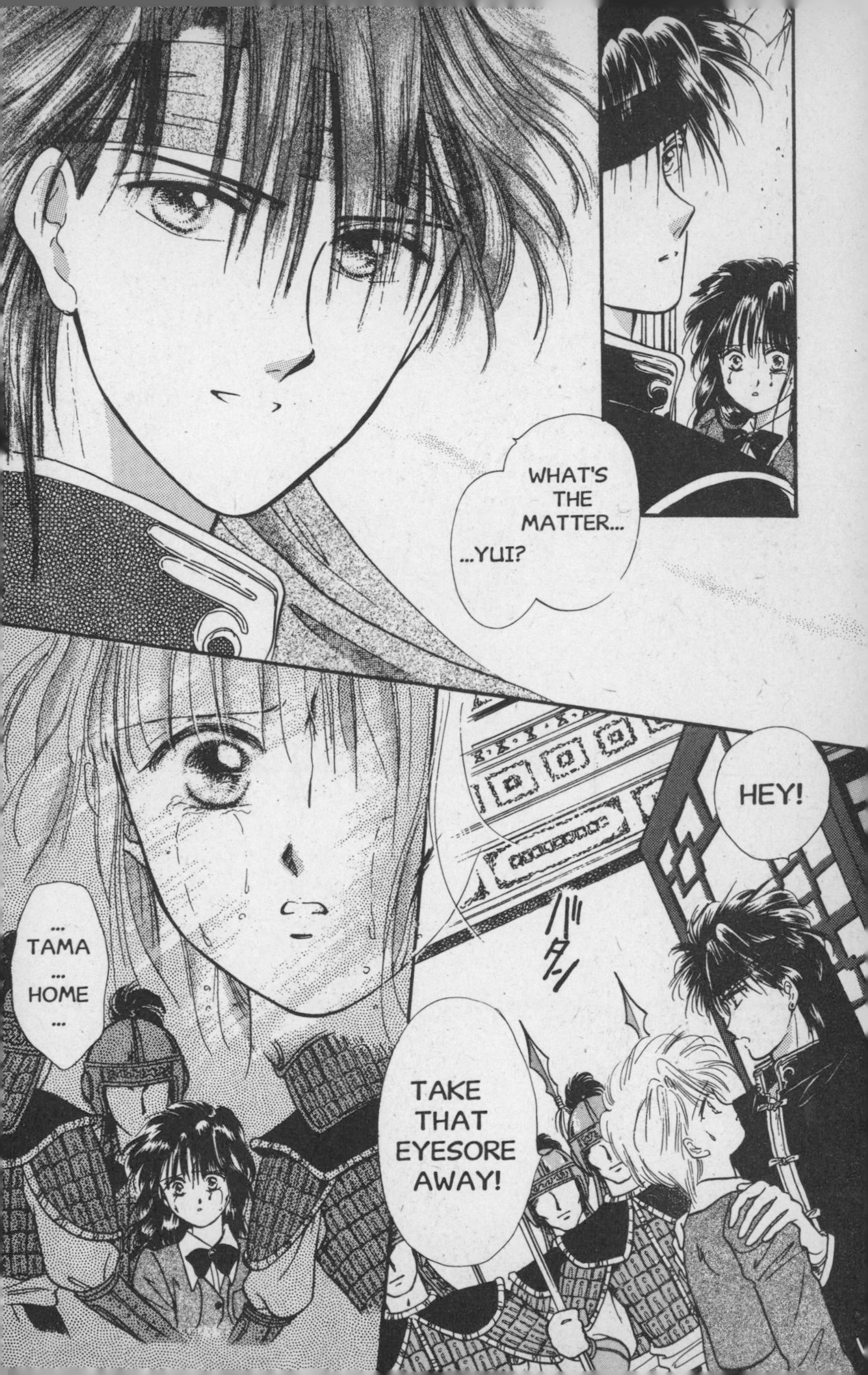
WHAT'S THE MATTER... ...YUI?
HEY!
バタン
TAKE THAT EYESORE AWAY!
... TAMA ... HOME ...

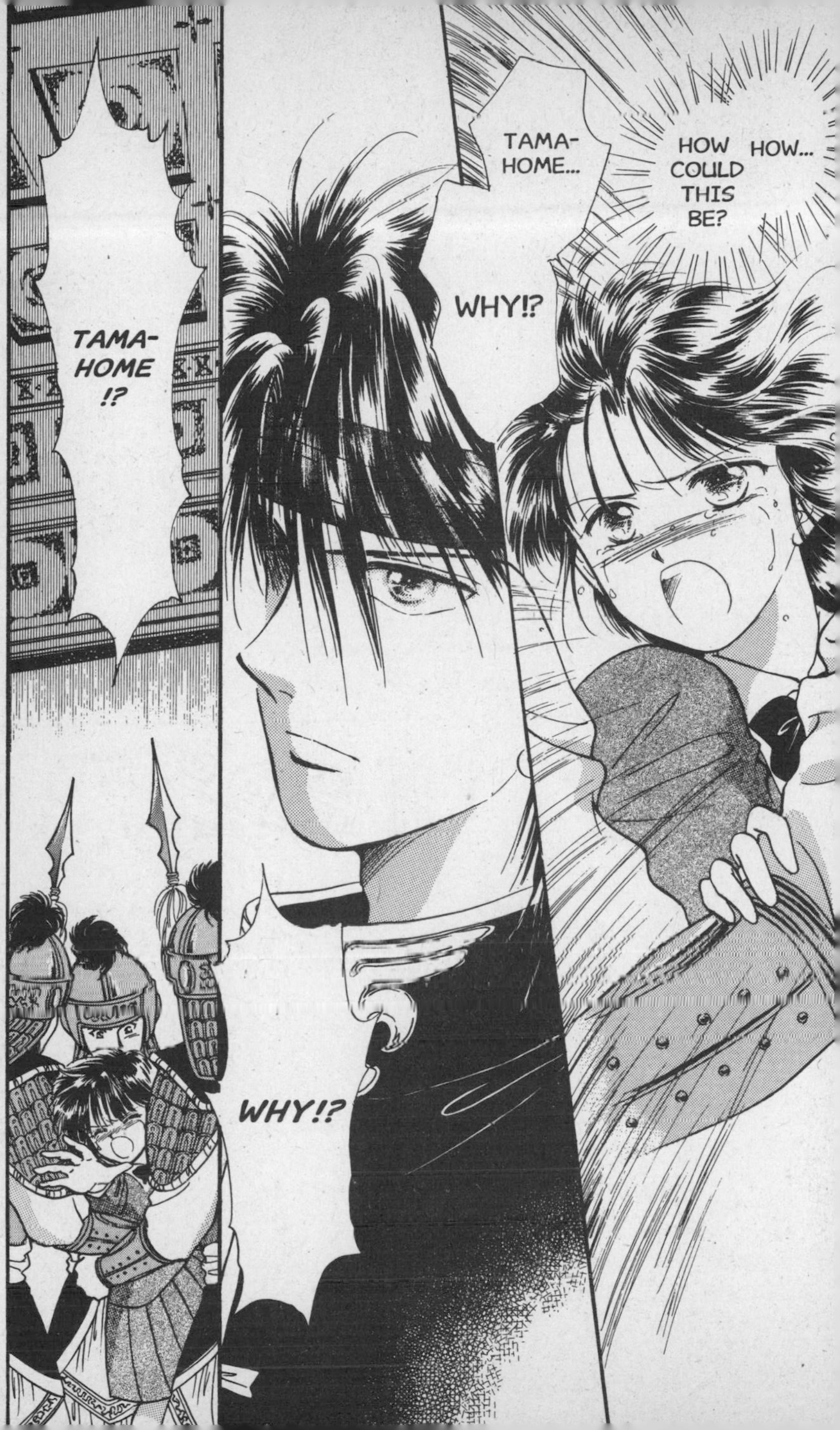
HOW... HOW COULD THIS BE?
TAMA-HOME...
WHY!?
WHY!?
TAMA-HOME!?

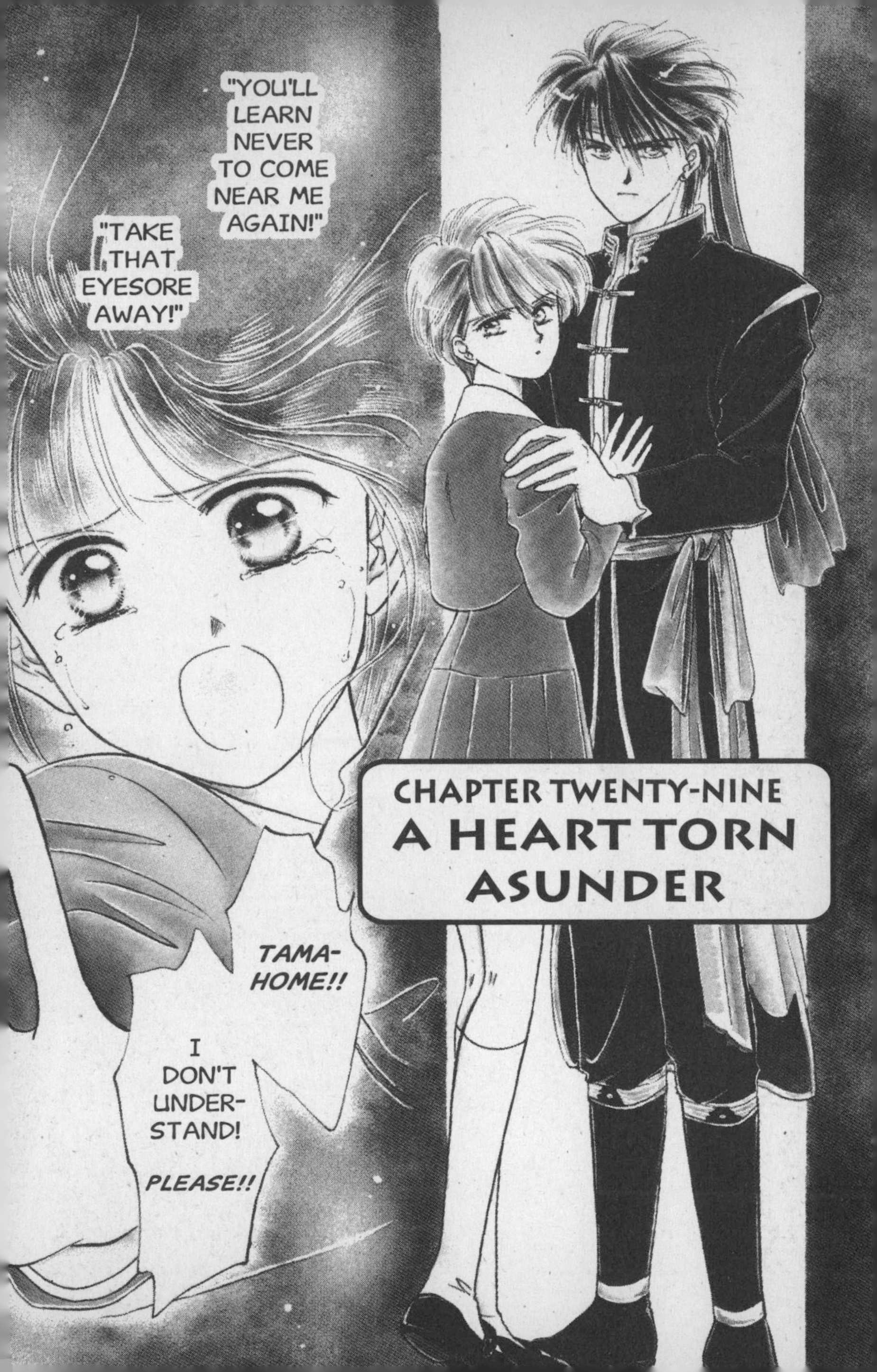
"YOU'LL LEARN NEVER TO COME NEAR ME AGAIN!"
"TAKE THAT EYESORE AWAY!"
CHAPTER TWENTY-NINE
A HEART TORN ASUNDER
TAMA-HOME!!
I DON'T UNDER-STAND!
PLEASE!!

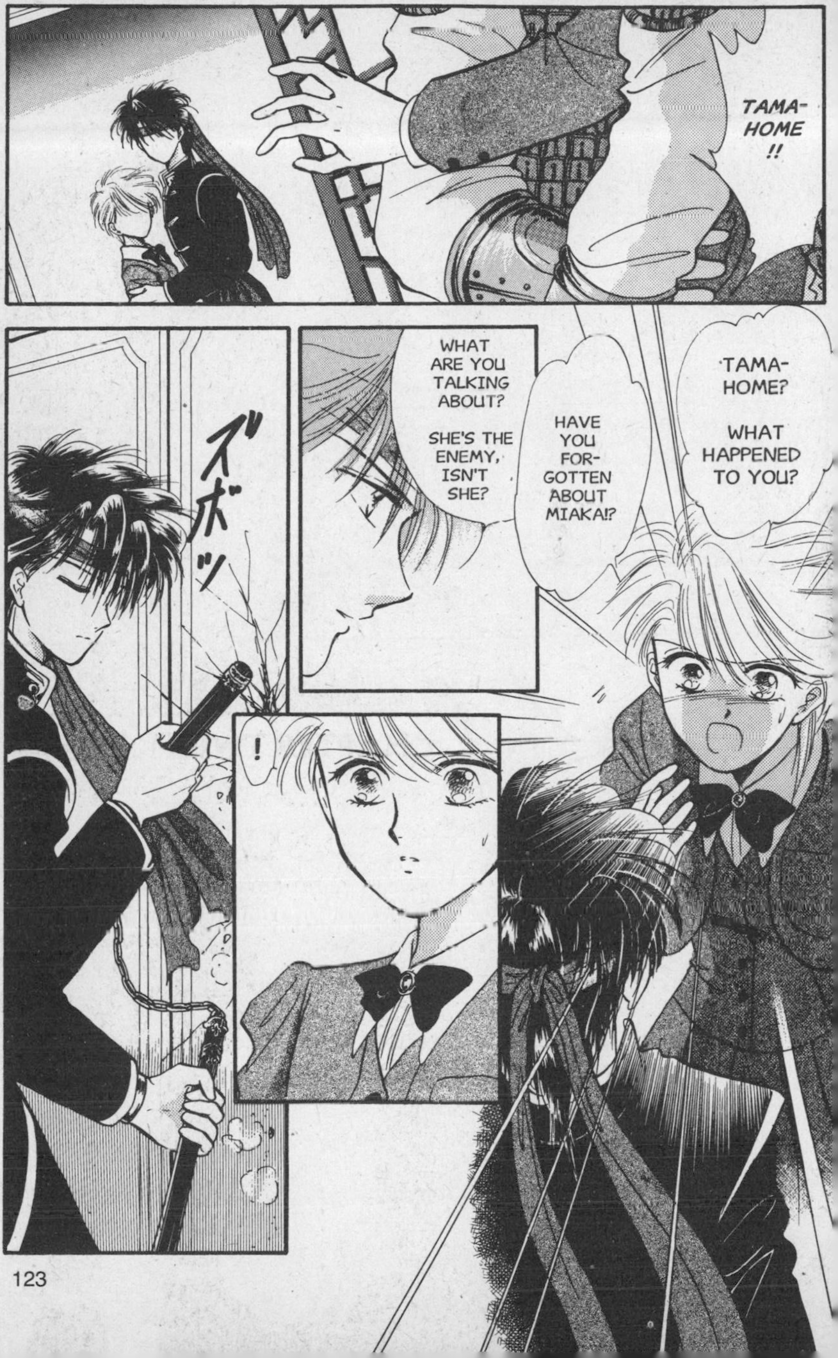
TAMA-HOME!!
TAMA-HOME? WHAT HAPPENED TO YOU?
HAVE YOU FOR-GOTTEN ABOUT MIAKA!?
WHAT ARE YOU TALKING ABOUT? SHE'S THE ENEMY, ISN'T SHE?
!
ズボッ

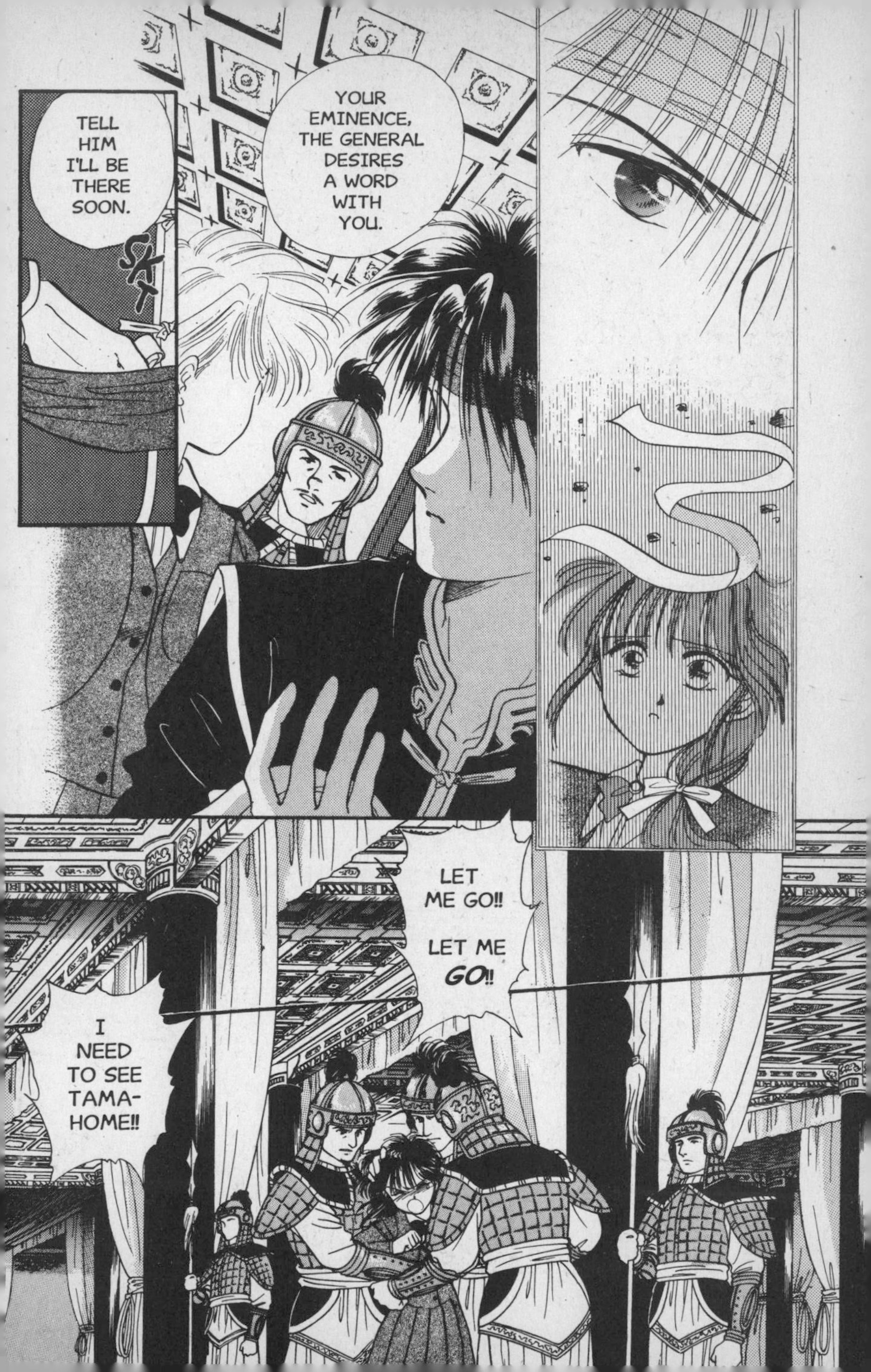
YOUR EMINENCE, THE GENERAL DESIRES A WORD WITH YOU.
TELL HIM I'LL BE THERE SOON.
SKT
LET ME GO!!
LET ME GO!!
I NEED TO SEE TAMA-HOME!!

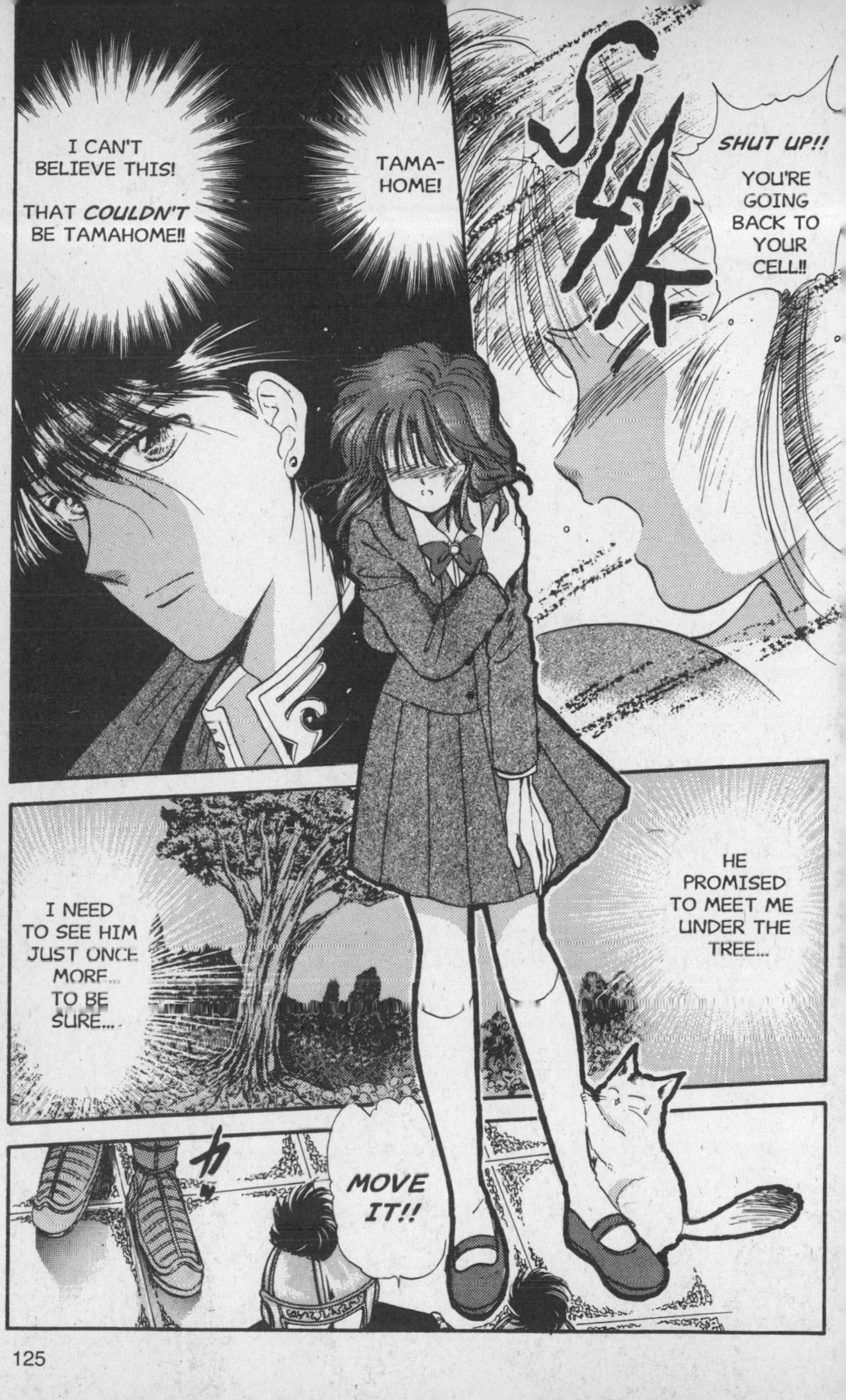
SHUT UP!!
YOU'RE GOING BACK TO YOUR CELL!!
TAMA-HOME!
I CAN'T BELIEVE THIS!
THAT COULDN'T BE TAMAHOME!!
HE PROMISED TO MEET ME UNDER THE TREE...
I NEED TO SEE HIM JUST ONCE MORE... TO BE SURE...
MOVE IT!!

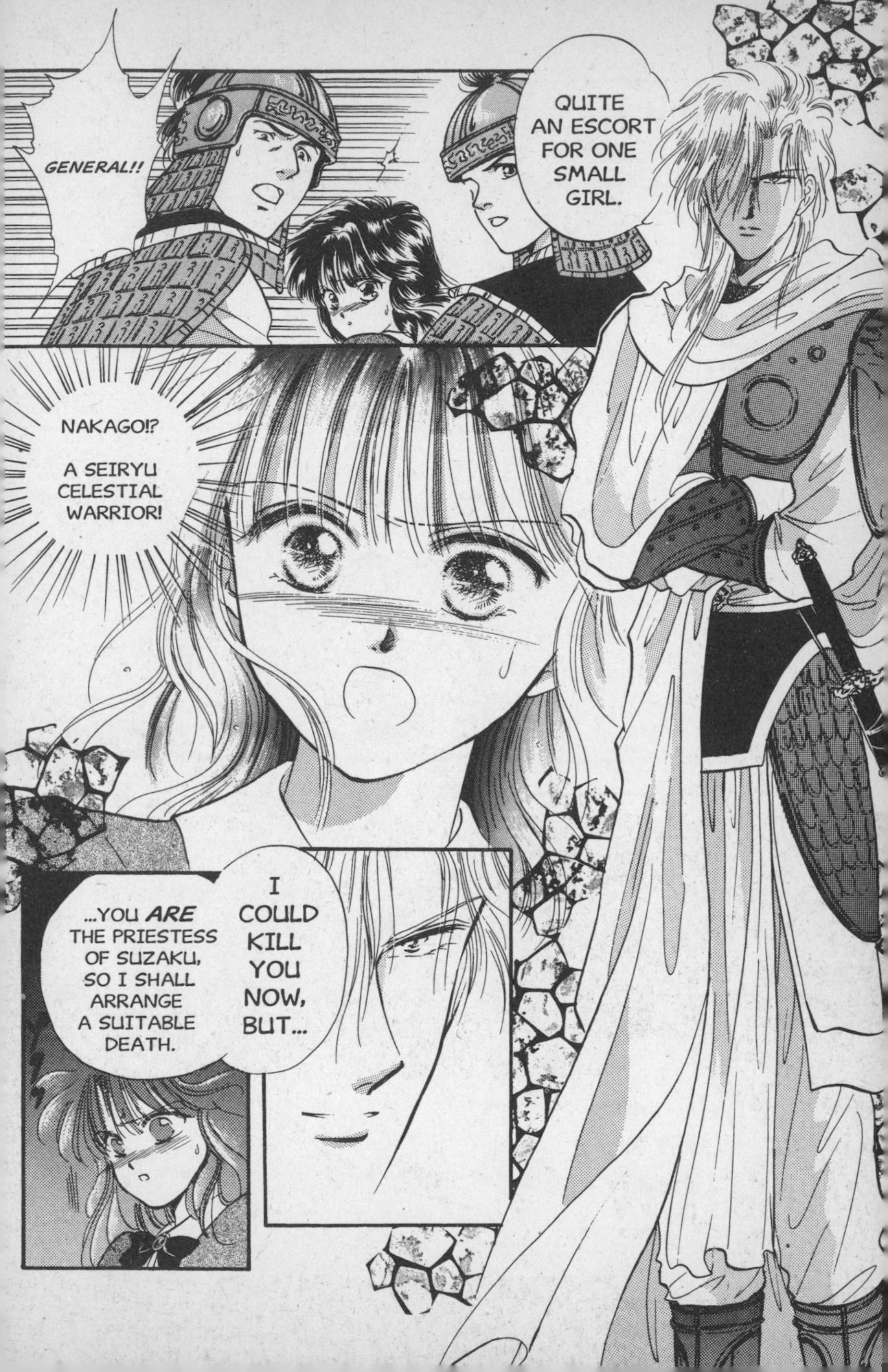
QUITE AN ESCORT FOR ONE SMALL GIRL.
GENERAL!!
NAKAGO!?
A SEIRYU CELESTIAL WARRIOR!
I COULD KILL YOU NOW, BUT...
...YOU **ARE** THE PRIESTESS OF SUZAKU, SO I SHALL ARRANGE A SUITABLE DEATH.

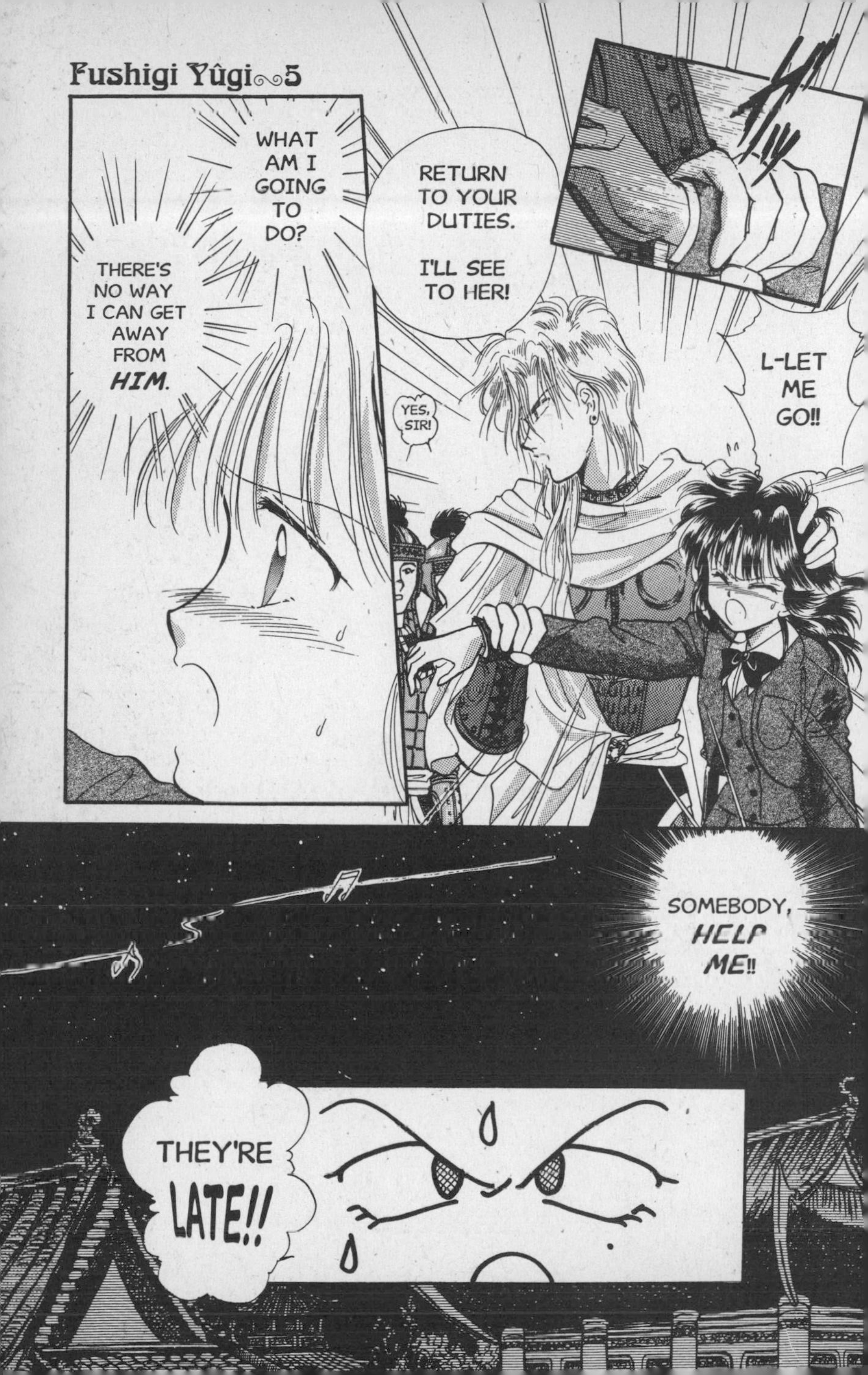
L-LET ME GO!!
RETURN TO YOUR DUTIES.
I'LL SEE TO HER!
YES, SIR!
WHAT AM I GOING TO DO?
THERE'S NO WAY I CAN GET AWAY FROM *HIM*.
SOMEBODY, *HELP ME*!!
THEY'RE LATE!!

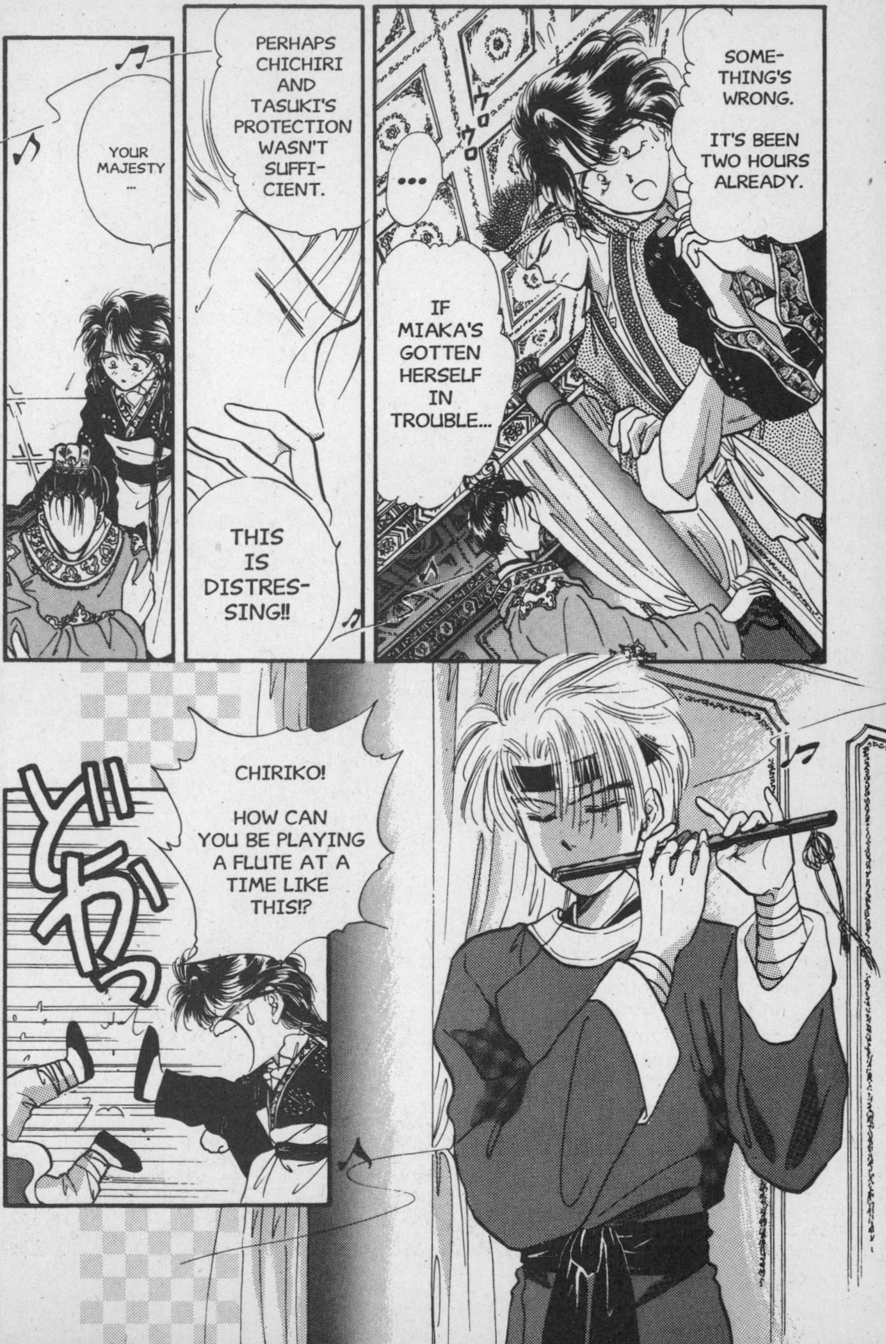
SOME-THING'S WRONG.
IT'S BEEN TWO HOURS ALREADY.
ウロウロ
...
IF MIAKA'S GOTTEN HERSELF IN TROUBLE...
PERHAPS CHICHIRI AND TASUKI'S PROTECTION WASN'T SUFFI-CIENT.
THIS IS DISTRES-SING!!
YOUR MAJESTY ...
CHIRIKO!
HOW CAN YOU BE PLAYING A FLUTE AT A TIME LIKE THIS!?

Rival

So, aside from checking out a bunch of game centers, I went with a different friend to see a "Caramel Box" performance. My editor had taken me to one of their performances before, and I liked it so much that later I took my friend Ms. N. She became totally obsessed with them. She invited me to go again just recently. I love fantasy that takes place in the real world. It's got comedy, scenes that make you cry, and interesting characters. No matter how many times I've seen it, I still get something new and interesting out of it. I highly recommend it, so go check it out. Even if you're still in junior high, I'm sure you'll love it! I have a birthday card from "Caramel Box" right in front of me. It's March 1, so in four days it'll be my birthday. My editor sends me a bouquet of flowers (I love the beautiful flowers!), which is nice, but for the past two years, they've arrived 10 days late. I wonder why. Will they be late again this year? It's not a big deal, though. My background music right now is the soundtrack to "Final Fantasy V, IV."
Thank you! I wanted this so badly.
Thank you for the chocolate on Valentine's Day. It's so interesting to see how popular each Celestial Warrior is. You all sent chocolate to Tamahome, Mitsukake (that really surprised me. That's one stylin' fan!), Chiriko, etc. But Tamahome's biggest competition is pretty much limited to Tasuki and Chichiri. But, hey! Who knows when the rankings will change?

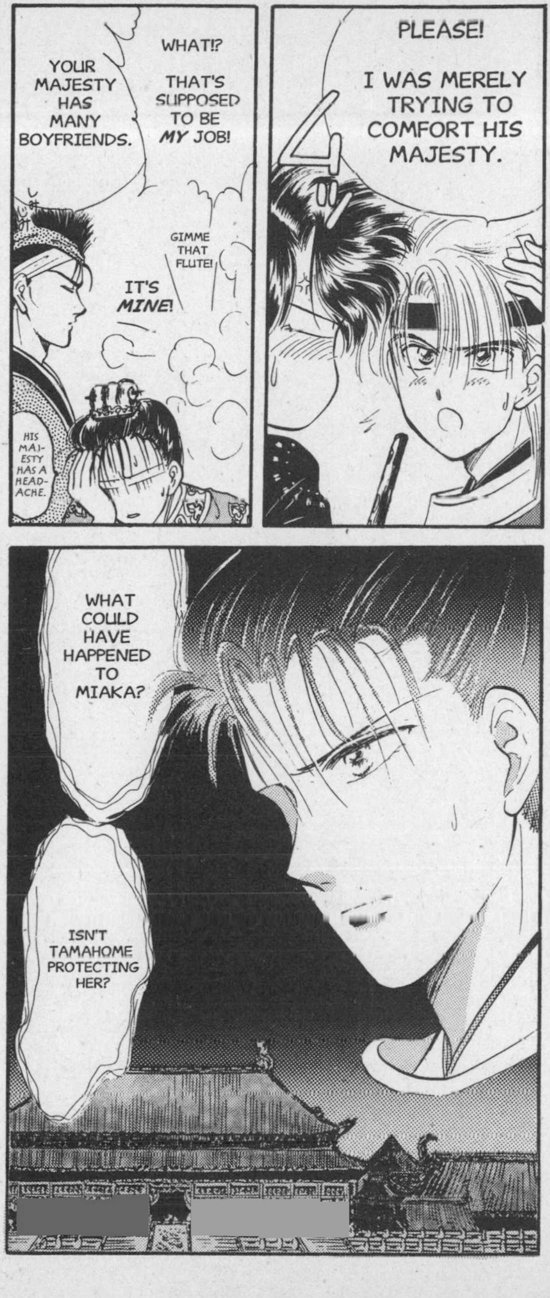
PLEASE!
I WAS MERELY TRYING TO COMFORT HIS MAJESTY.
WHAT!? THAT'S SUPPOSED TO BE *MY* JOB!
YOUR MAJESTY HAS MANY BOYFRIENDS.
GIMME THAT FLUTE!
IT'S *MINE*!
HIS MAJESTY HAS A HEADACHE.
WHAT COULD HAVE HAPPENED TO MIAKA?
ISN'T TAMAHOME PROTECTING HER?

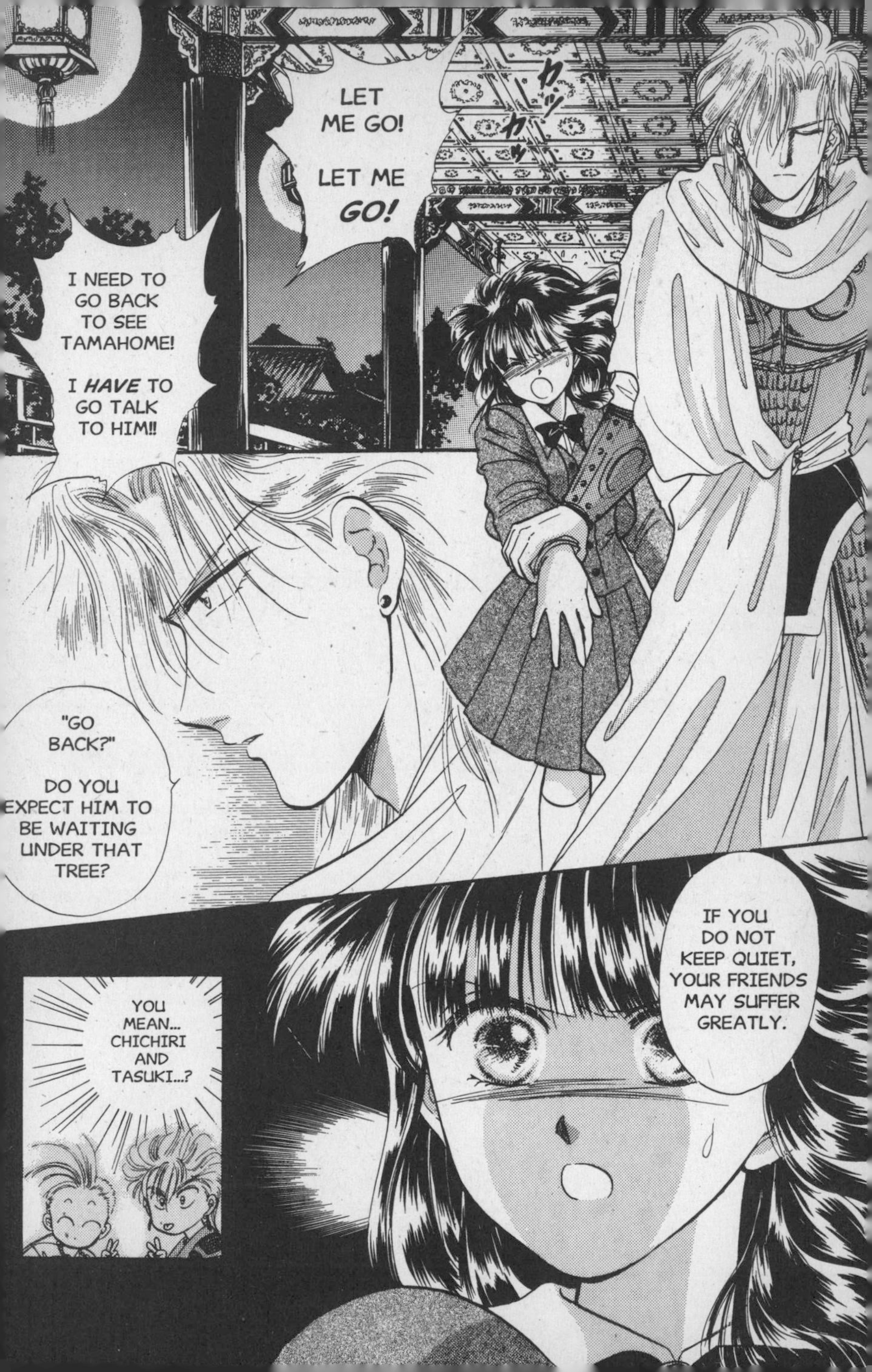
LET ME GO!
LET ME GO!
I NEED TO GO BACK TO SEE TAMAHOME!
I *HAVE* TO GO TALK TO HIM!!
"GO BACK?"
DO YOU EXPECT HIM TO BE WAITING UNDER THAT TREE?
IF YOU DO NOT KEEP QUIET, YOUR FRIENDS MAY SUFFER GREATLY.
YOU MEAN... CHICHIRI AND TASUKI...?

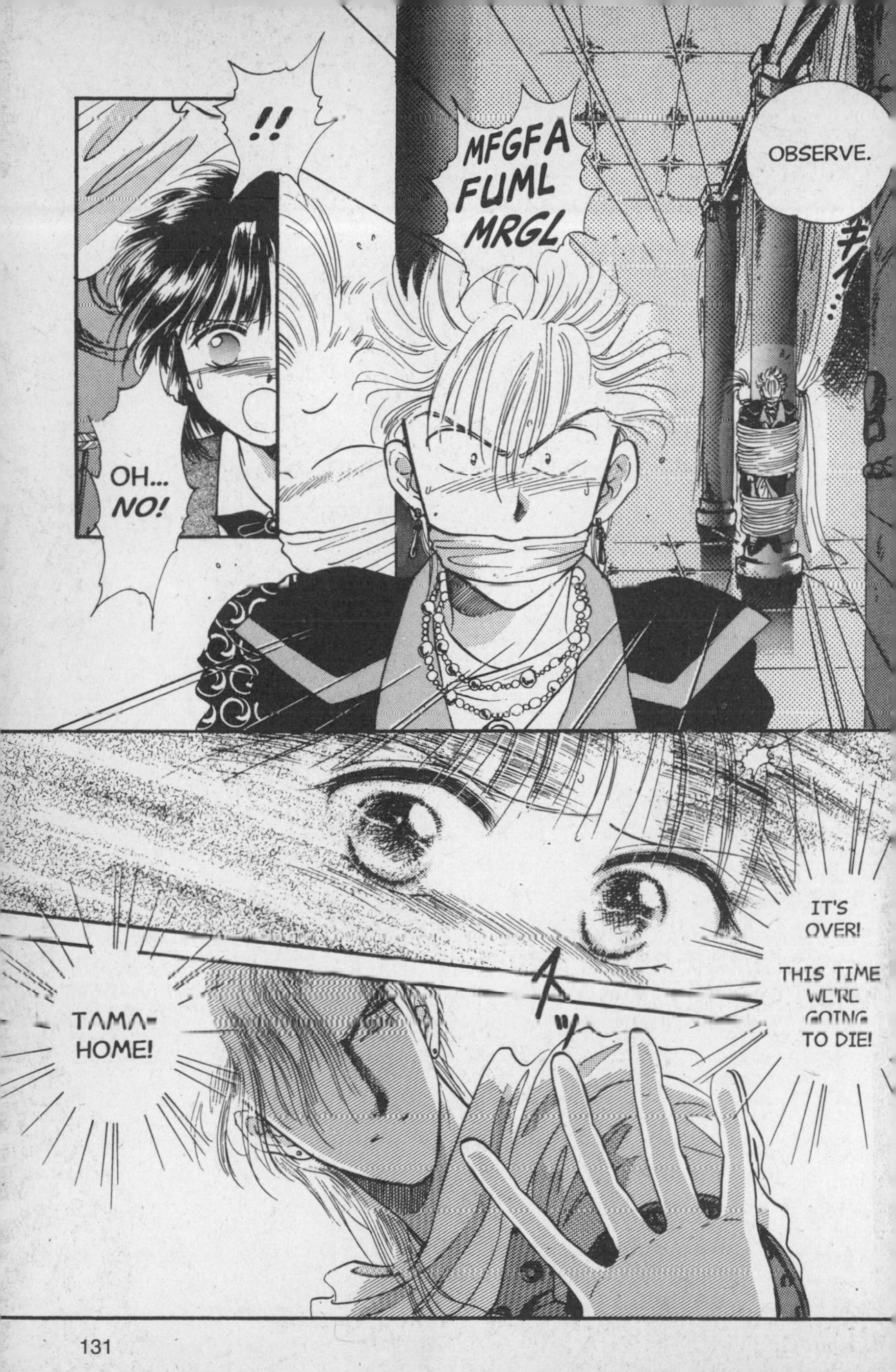
OBSERVE.
MFGFA FUML MRGL
!!
OH... NO!
IT'S OVER!
THIS TIME WE'RE GOING TO DIE!
TAMA-HOME!

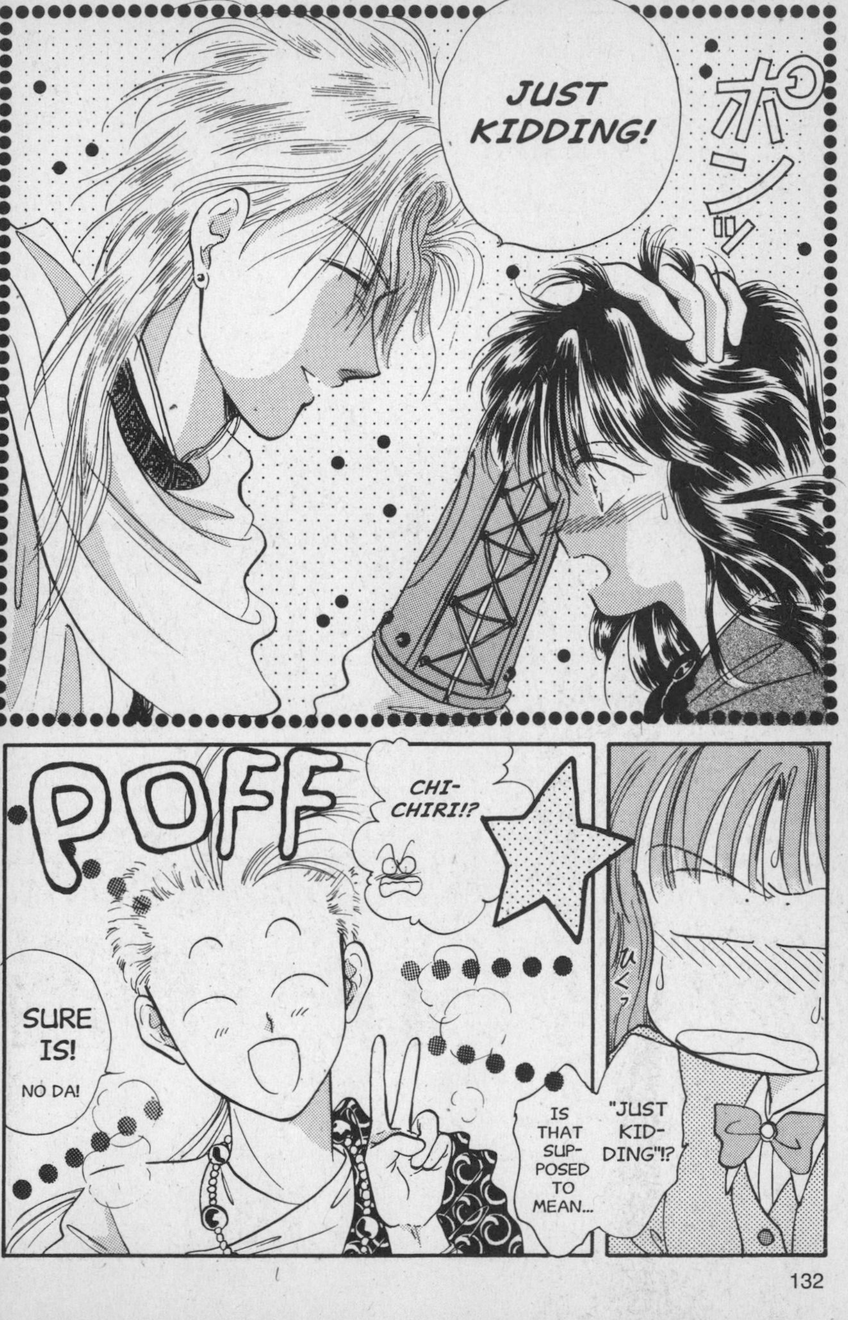
JUST KIDDING!
ポンッ
ひくっ
"JUST KID-DING"!?
IS THAT SUP-POSED TO MEAN...
CHI-CHIRI!?
POFF
SURE IS!
NO DA!

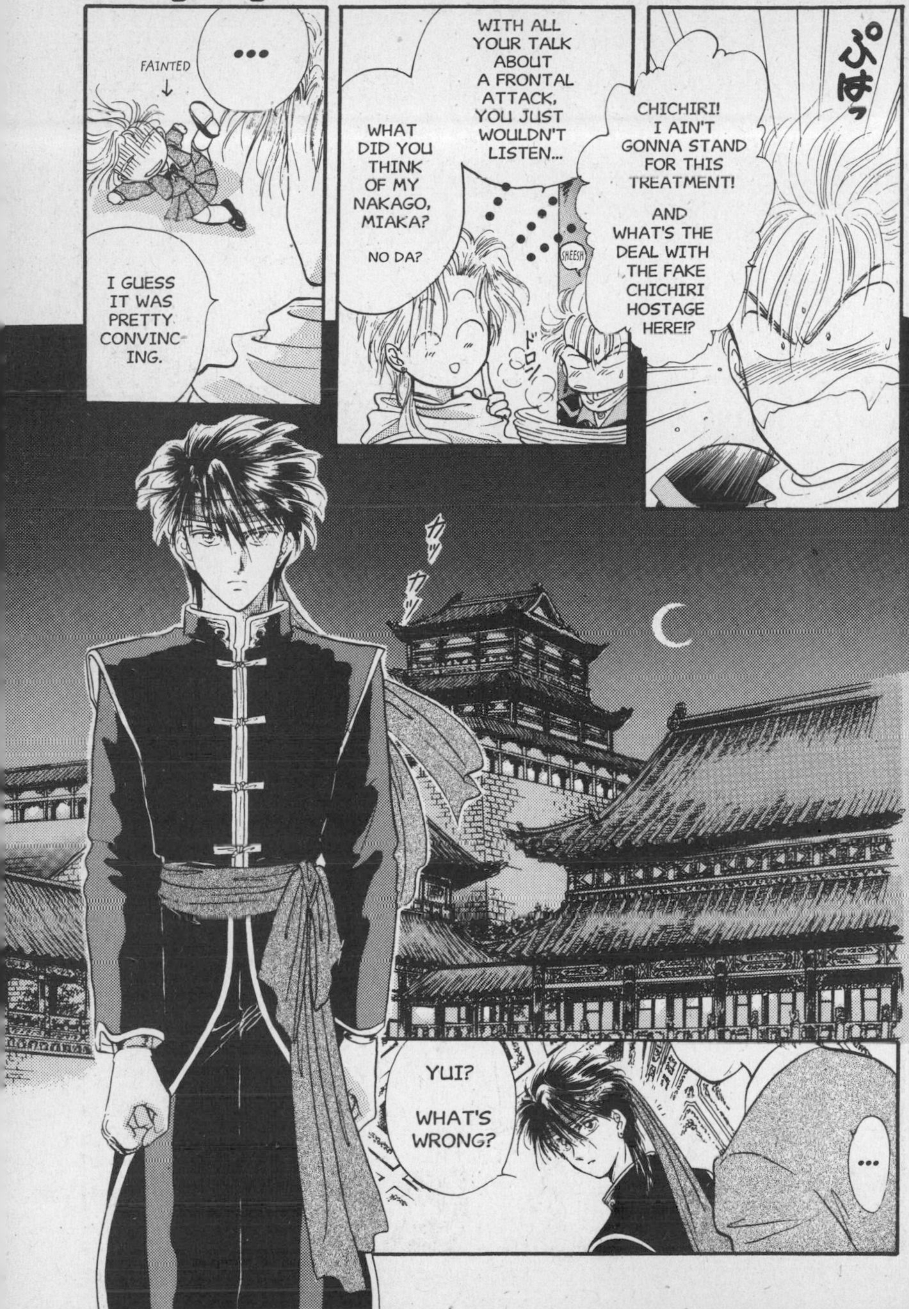
ぷはっ
CHICHIRI! I AIN'T GONNA STAND FOR THIS TREATMENT!
AND WHAT'S THE DEAL WITH THE FAKE CHICHIRI HOSTAGE HERE!?
WITH ALL YOUR TALK ABOUT A FRONTAL ATTACK, YOU JUST WOULDN'T LISTEN...
WHAT DID YOU THINK OF MY NAKAGO, MIAKA?
NO DA?
SHEESH
ドロン
...
FAINTED
I GUESS IT WAS PRETTY CONVINC-ING.
カッ
カッ
...
YUI?
WHAT'S WRONG?

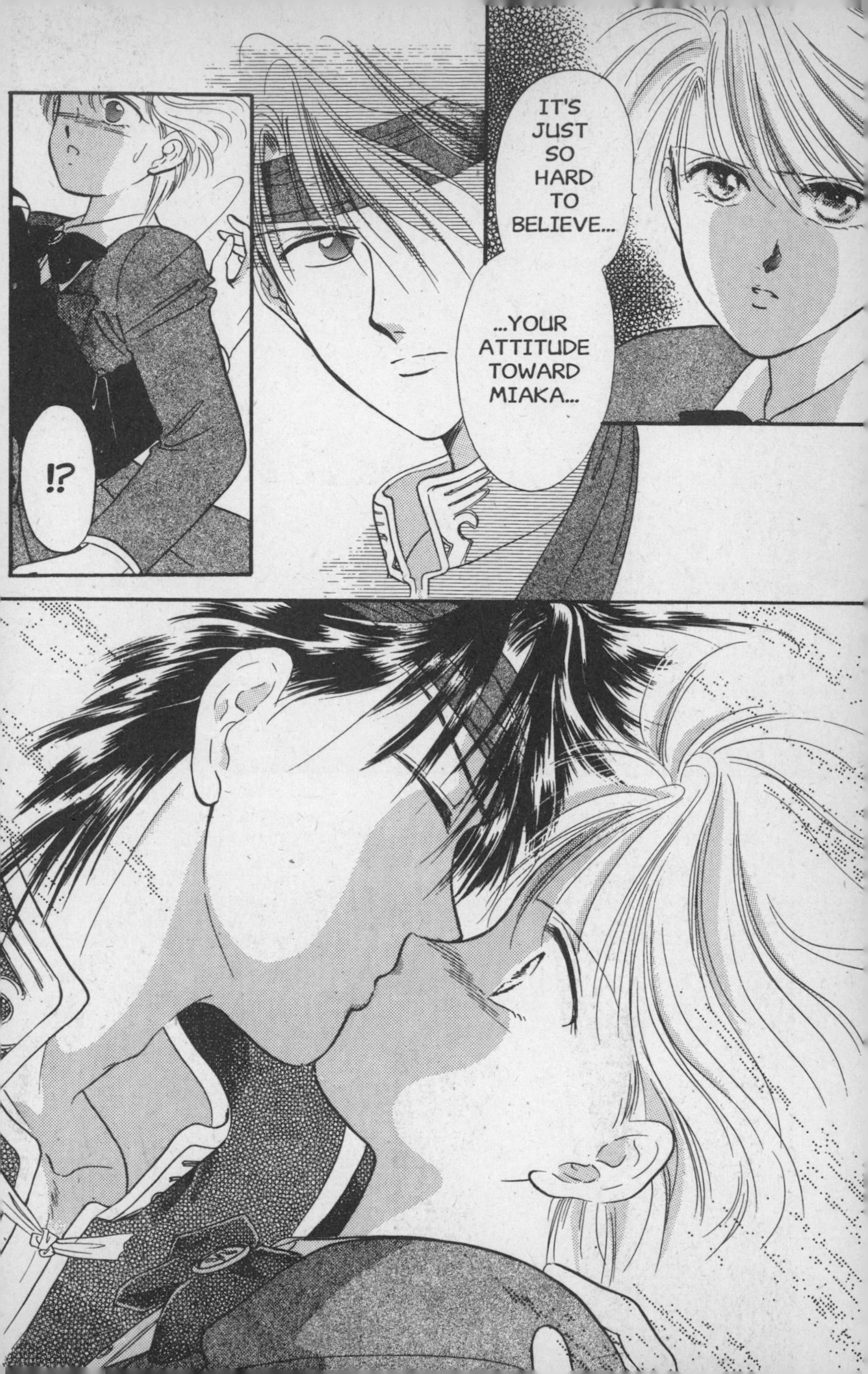
IT'S JUST SO HARD TO BELIEVE...
...YOUR ATTITUDE TOWARD MIAKA...
!?

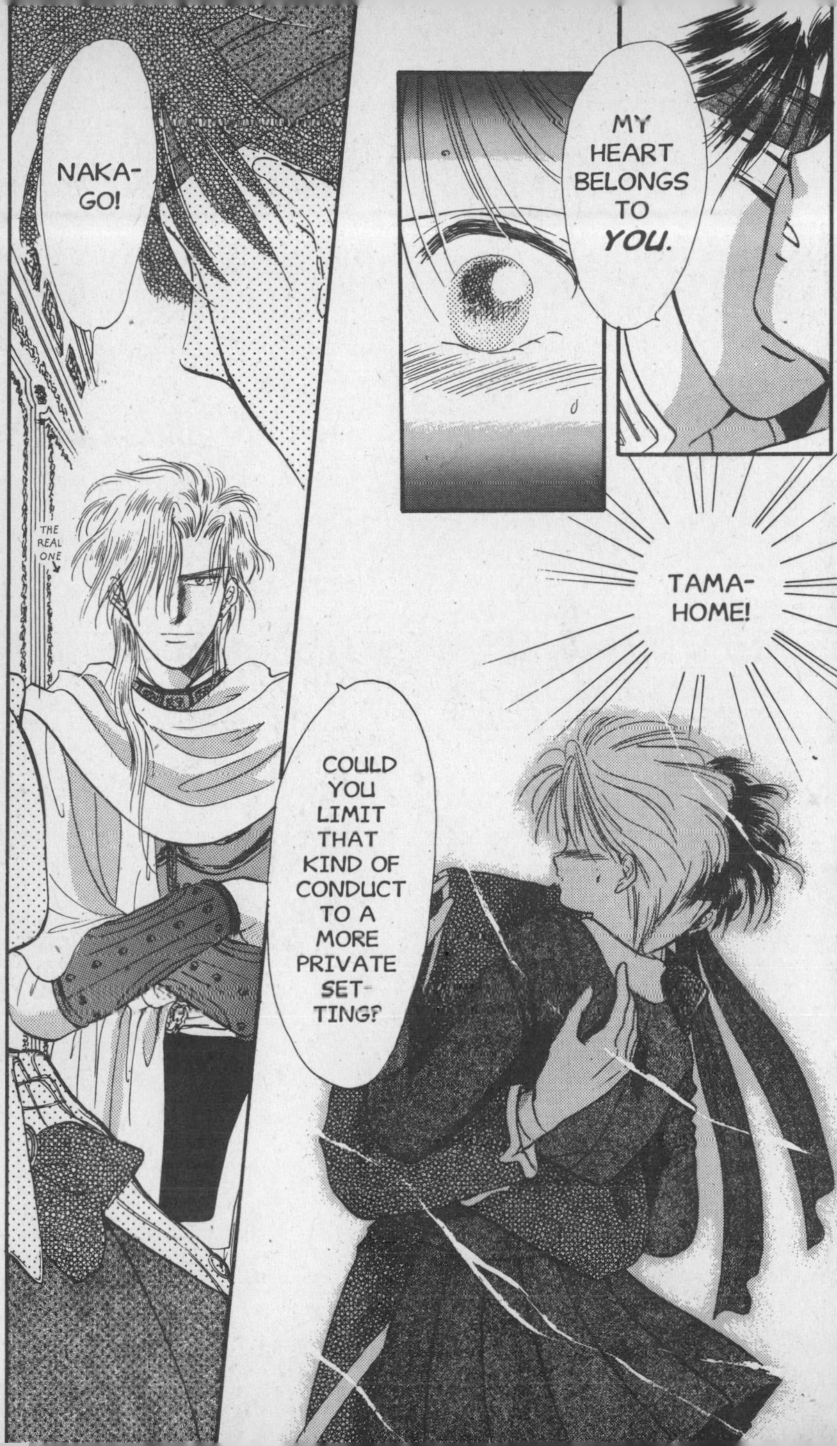
MY HEART BELONGS TO *YOU*.
TAMA-HOME!
COULD YOU LIMIT THAT KIND OF CONDUCT TO A MORE PRIVATE SET-TING?
NAKA-GO!
THE REAL ONE

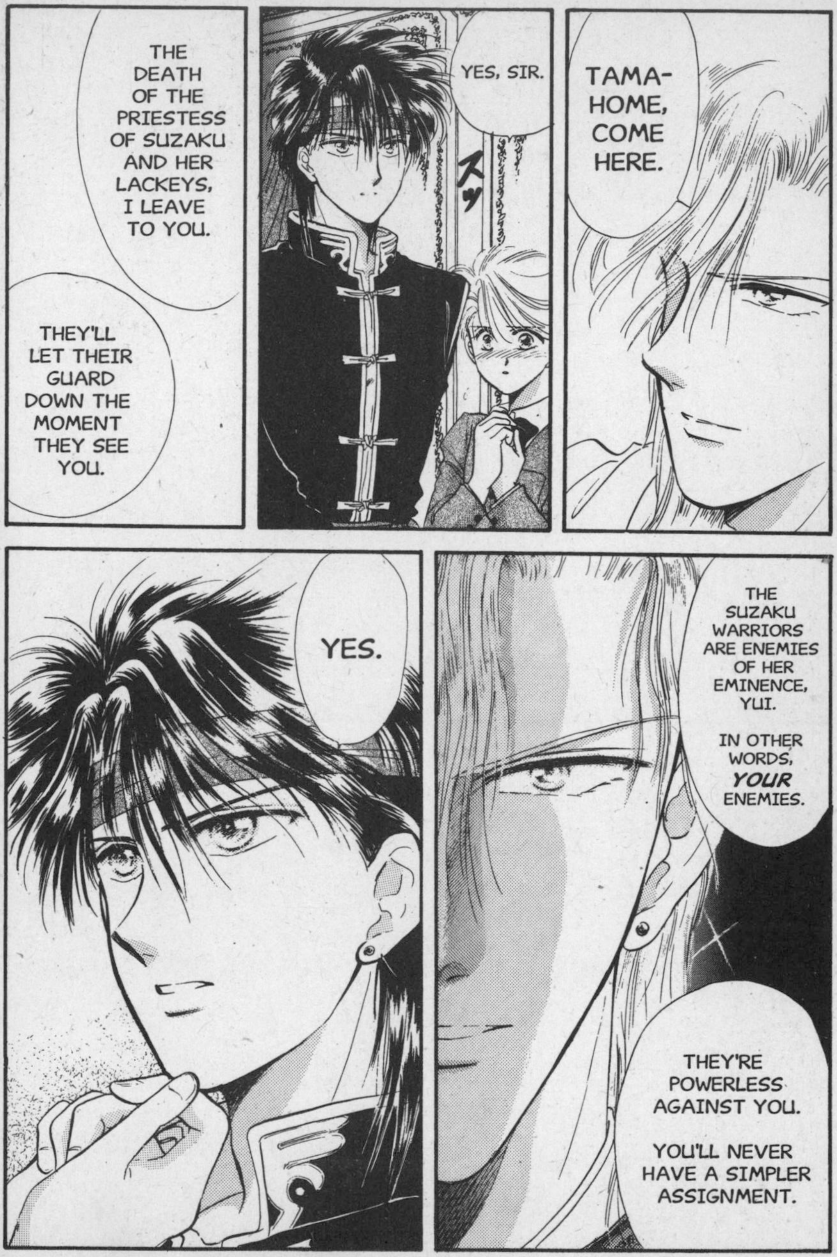
TAMA-HOME, COME HERE.
YES, SIR.
スッ
THE DEATH OF THE PRIESTESS OF SUZAKU AND HER LACKEYS, I LEAVE TO YOU.
THEY'LL LET THEIR GUARD DOWN THE MOMENT THEY SEE YOU.
THE SUZAKU WARRIORS ARE ENEMIES OF HER EMINENCE, YUI.
IN OTHER WORDS, ***YOUR*** ENEMIES.
THEY'RE POWERLESS AGAINST YOU.
YOU'LL NEVER HAVE A SIMPLER ASSIGNMENT.
YES.

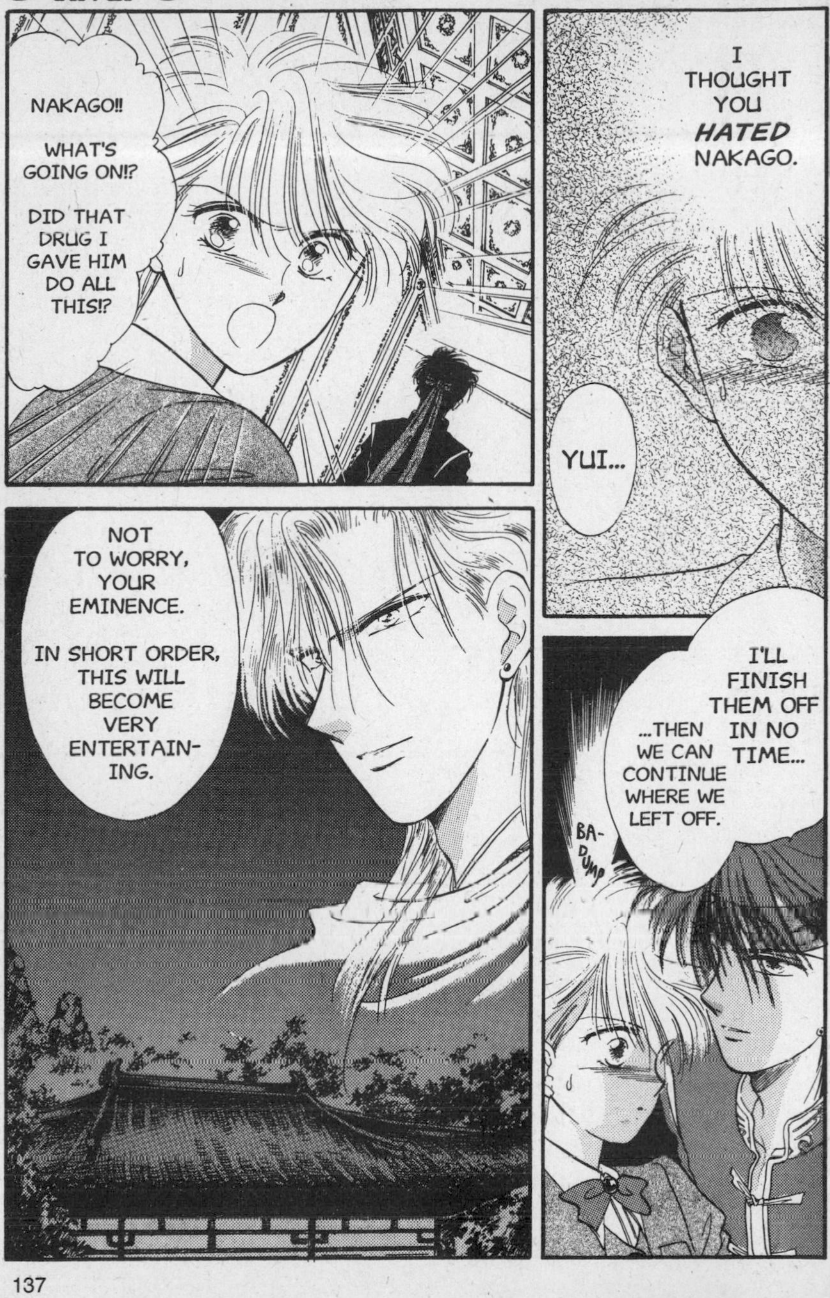
I THOUGHT YOU ***HATED*** NAKAGO.
YUI...
NAKAGO!!
WHAT'S GOING ON!?
DID THAT DRUG I GAVE HIM DO ALL THIS!?
NOT TO WORRY, YOUR EMINENCE.
IN SHORT ORDER, THIS WILL BECOME VERY ENTERTAIN-ING.
I'LL FINISH THEM OFF IN NO TIME...
...THEN WE CAN CONTINUE WHERE WE LEFT OFF.
BA-DUMP

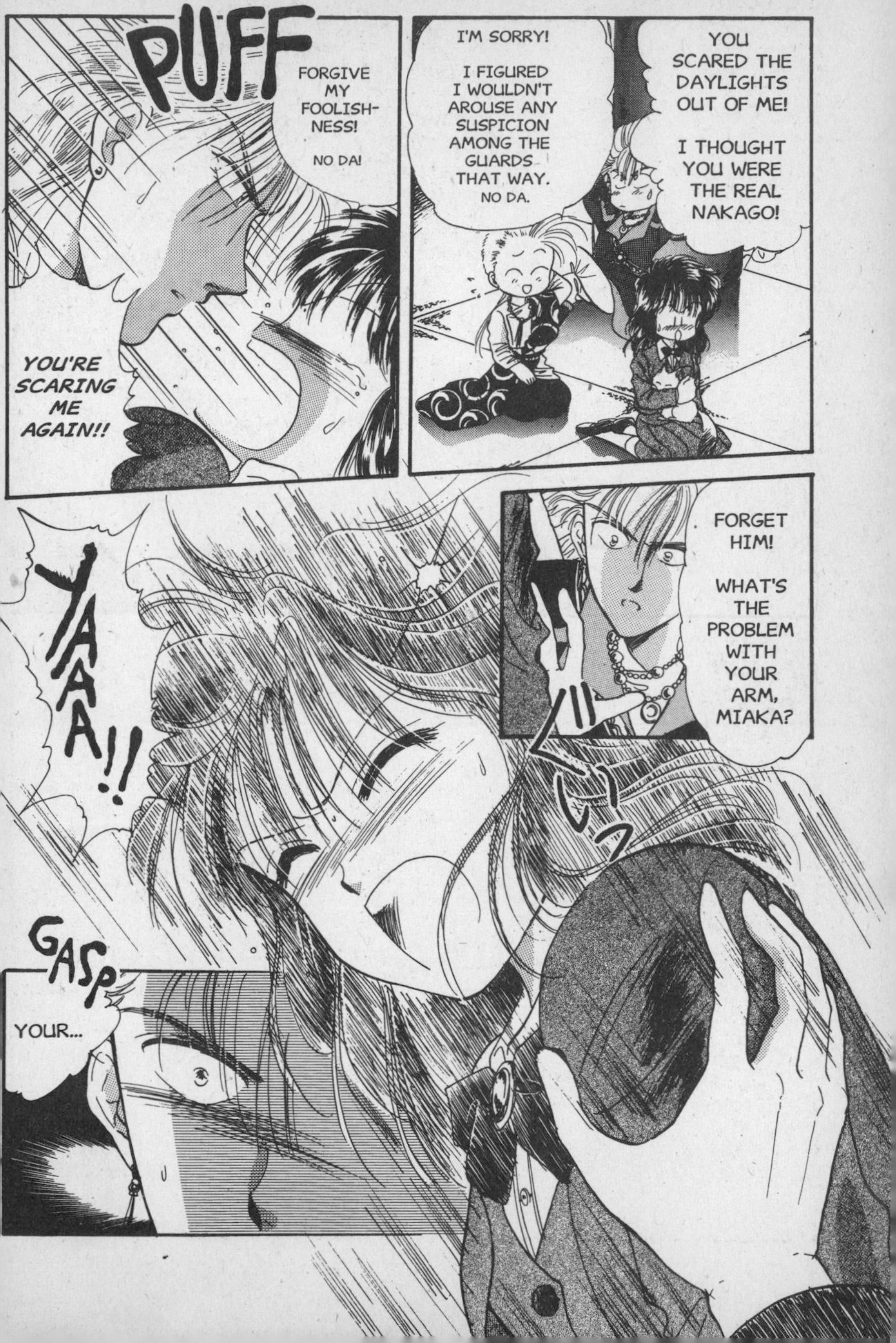
YOU SCARED THE DAYLIGHTS OUT OF ME!
I THOUGHT YOU WERE THE REAL NAKAGO!
I'M SORRY!
I FIGURED I WOULDN'T AROUSE ANY SUSPICION AMONG THE GUARDS THAT WAY. NO DA.
FORGIVE MY FOOLISH-NESS!
NO DA!
PUFF
YOU'RE SCARING ME AGAIN!!
FORGET HIM!
WHAT'S THE PROBLEM WITH YOUR ARM, MIAKA?
YAAAA!!
GASP
YOUR...

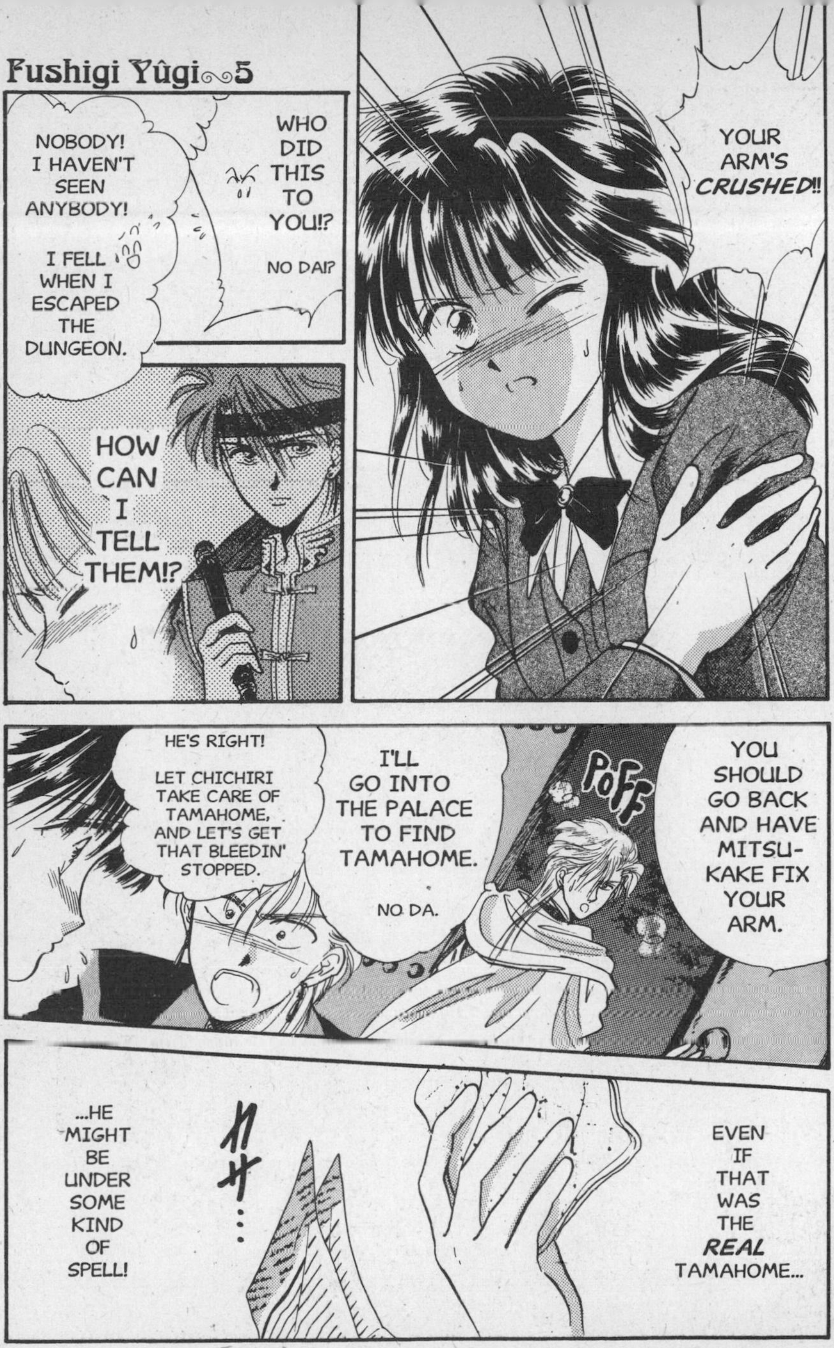
YOUR ARM'S *CRUSHED*!!
WHO DID THIS TO YOU!?
NO DA!?
NOBODY! I HAVEN'T SEEN ANYBODY!
I FELL WHEN I ESCAPED THE DUNGEON.
HOW CAN I TELL THEM!?
YOU SHOULD GO BACK AND HAVE MITSU-KAKE FIX YOUR ARM.
POFF
I'LL GO INTO THE PALACE TO FIND TAMAHOME.
NO DA.
HE'S RIGHT!
LET CHICHIRI TAKE CARE OF TAMAHOME, AND LET'S GET THAT BLEEDIN' STOPPED.
EVEN IF THAT WAS THE *REAL* TAMAHOME...
...HE MIGHT BE UNDER SOME KIND OF SPELL!

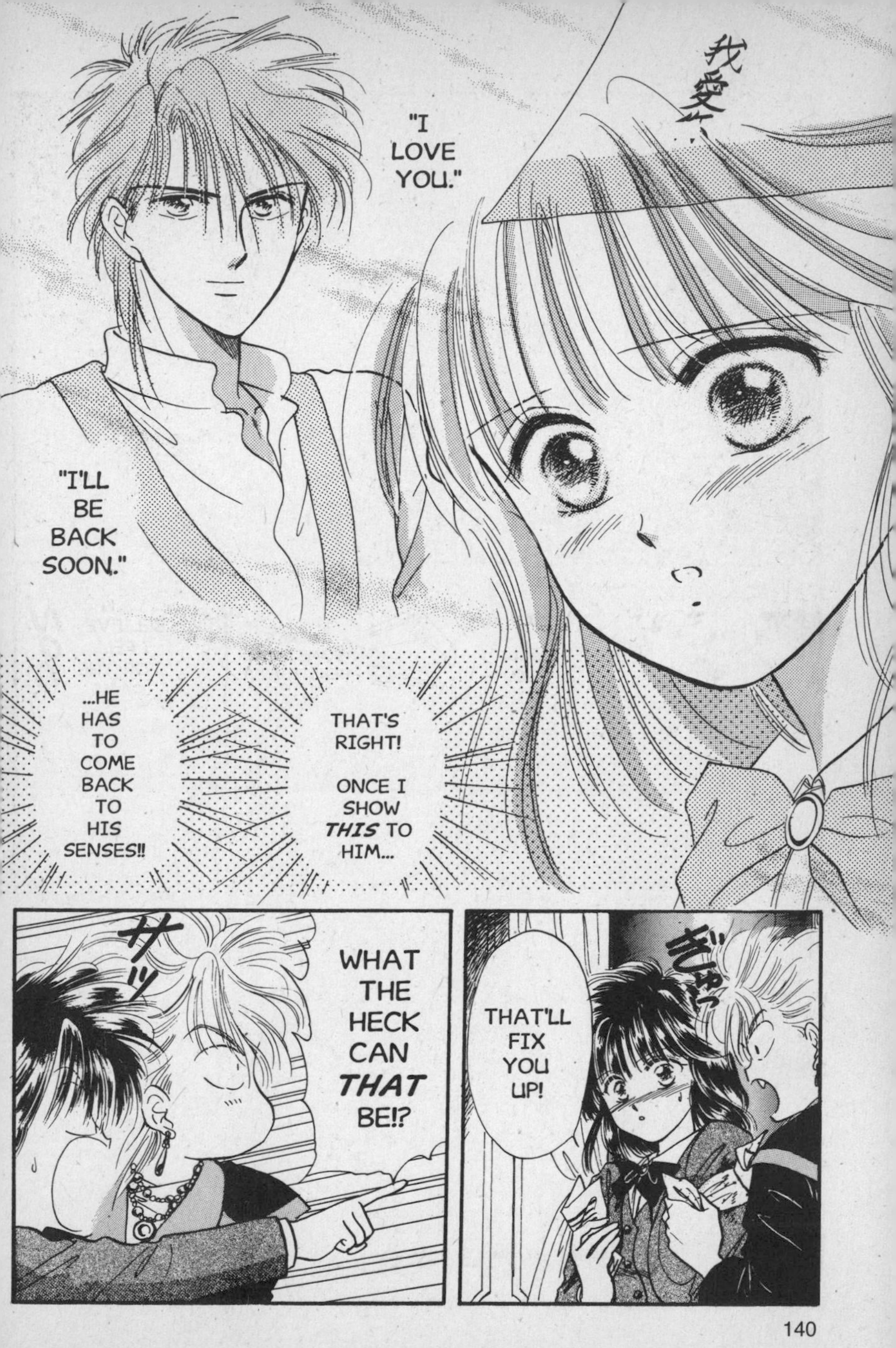
我愛
"I LOVE YOU."
"I'LL BE BACK SOON."
THAT'S RIGHT!
ONCE I SHOW *THIS* TO HIM...
...HE HAS TO COME BACK TO HIS SENSES!!
ぎゅっ
THAT'LL FIX YOU UP!
サッ
WHAT THE HECK CAN *THAT* BE!?

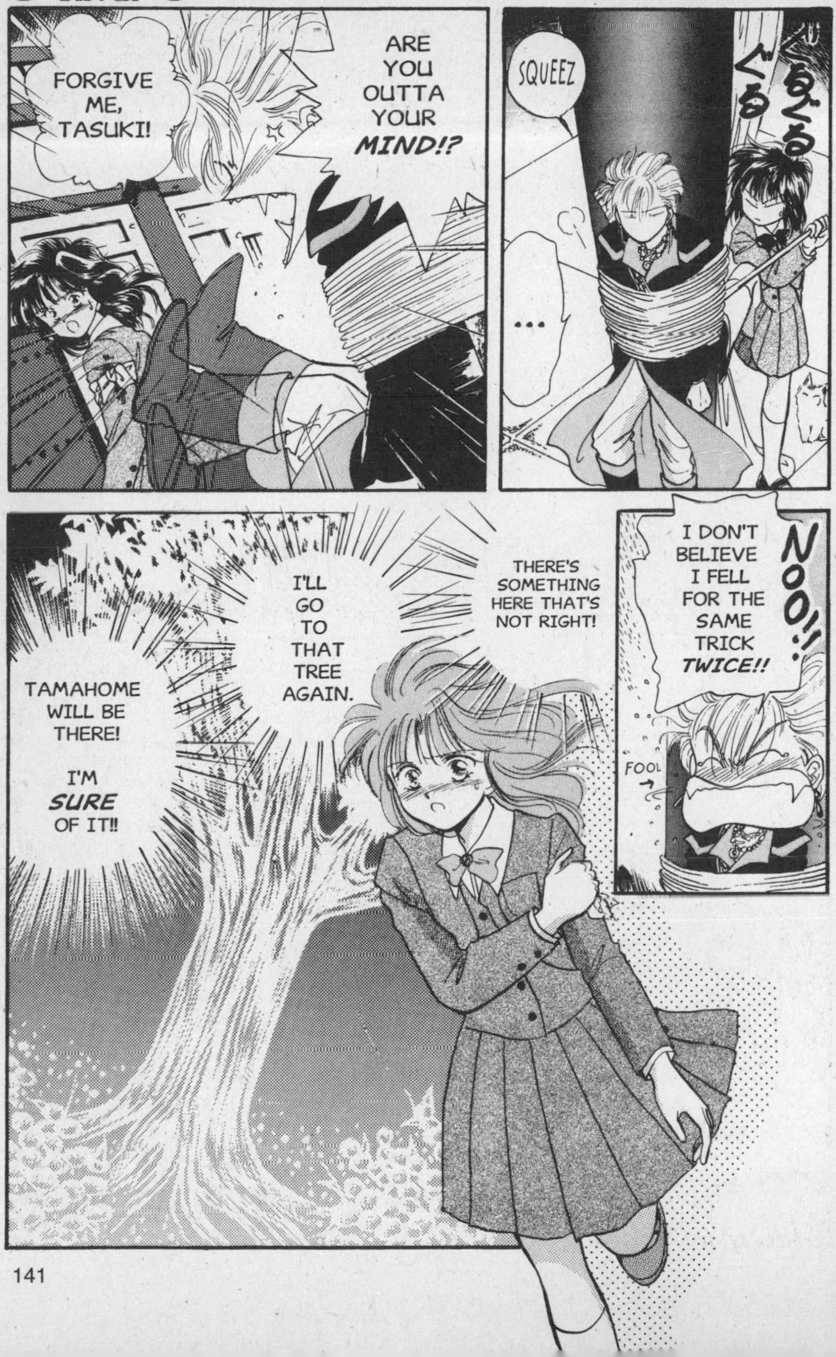
SQUEEZ
ぐるぐる
ぐる
...
ARE YOU OUTTA YOUR *MIND!?*
FORGIVE ME, TASUKI!
NOOO!!
I DON'T BELIEVE I FELL FOR THE SAME TRICK *TWICE!!*
FOOL
THERE'S SOMETHING HERE THAT'S NOT RIGHT!
I'LL GO TO THAT TREE AGAIN.
TAMAHOME WILL BE THERE!
I'M *SURE* OF IT!!

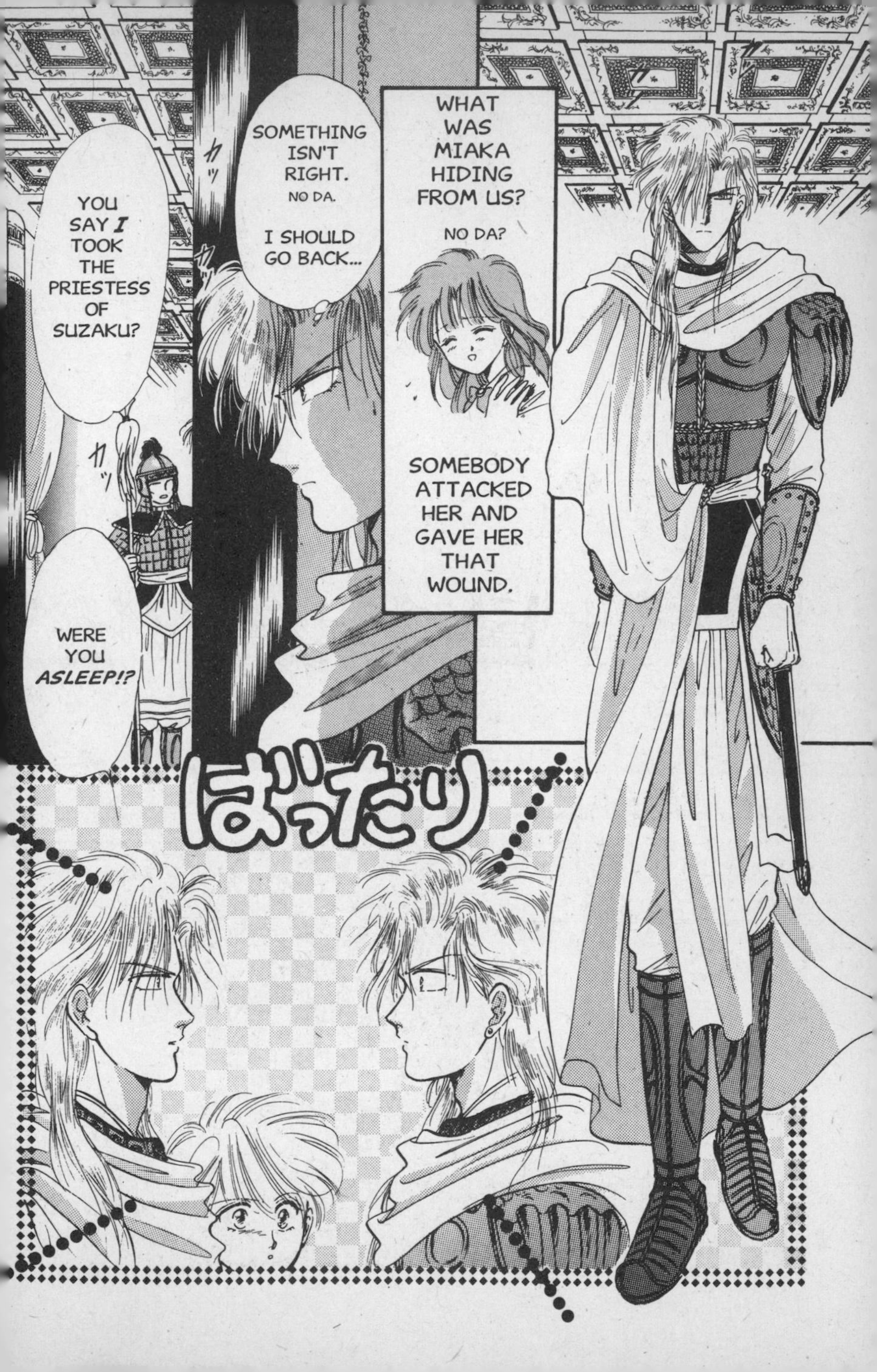
WHAT WAS MIAKA HIDING FROM US?
NO DA?
SOMEBODY ATTACKED HER AND GAVE HER THAT WOUND.
SOMETHING ISN'T RIGHT. NO DA.
I SHOULD GO BACK...
YOU SAY *I* TOOK THE PRIESTESS OF SUZAKU?
WERE YOU *ASLEEP!?*
ばったり

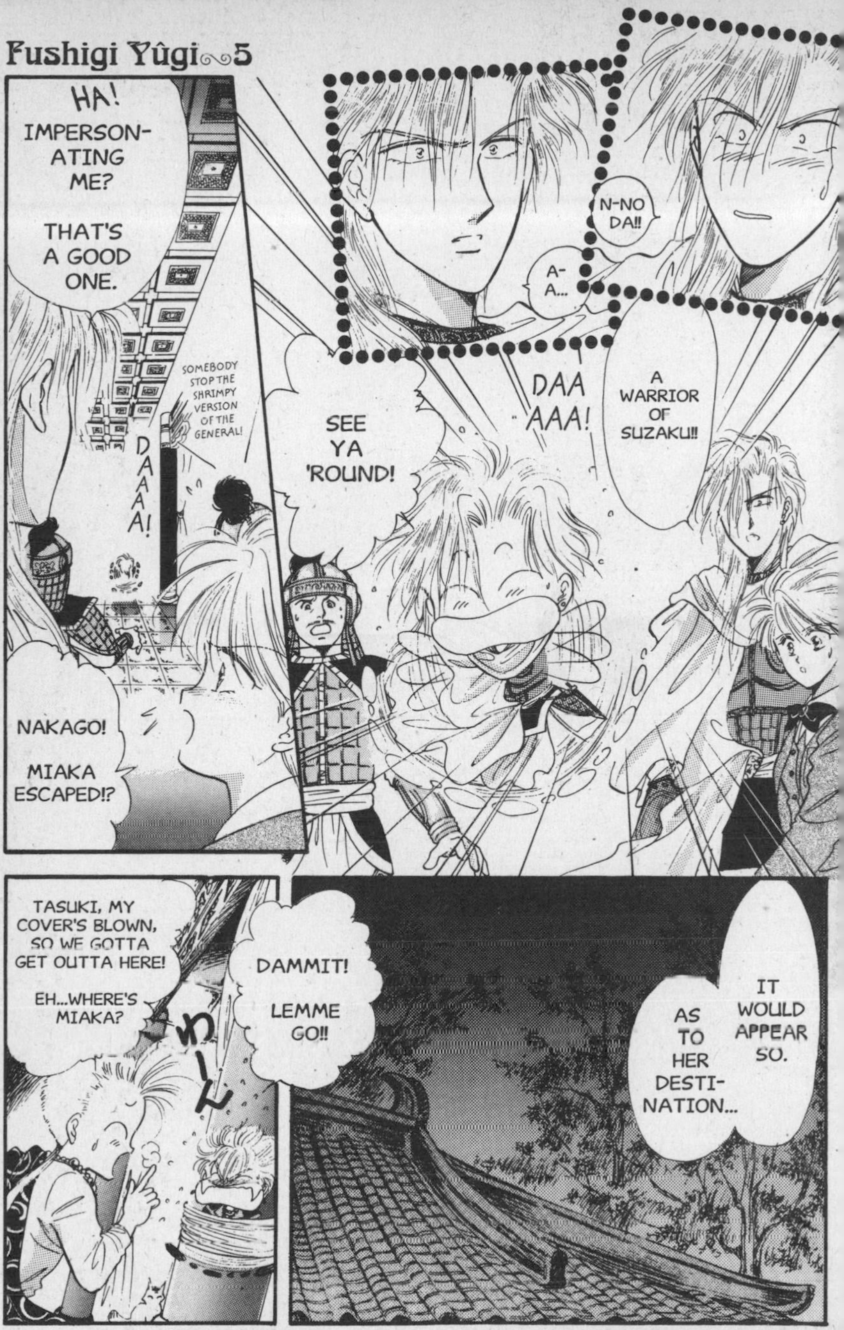
N-NO DA!!
A-A...
A WARRIOR OF SUZAKU!!
DAA AAA!
SEE YA 'ROUND!
HA! IMPERSONATING ME?
THAT'S A GOOD ONE.
SOMEBODY STOP THE SHRIMPY VERSION OF THE GENERAL!
DAAAAA!
NAKAGO!
MIAKA ESCAPED!?
IT WOULD APPEAR SO.
AS TO HER DESTINATION...
DAMMIT!
LEMME GO!!
TASUKI, MY COVER'S BLOWN, SO WE GOTTA GET OUTTA HERE!
EH...WHERE'S MIAKA?
わーん

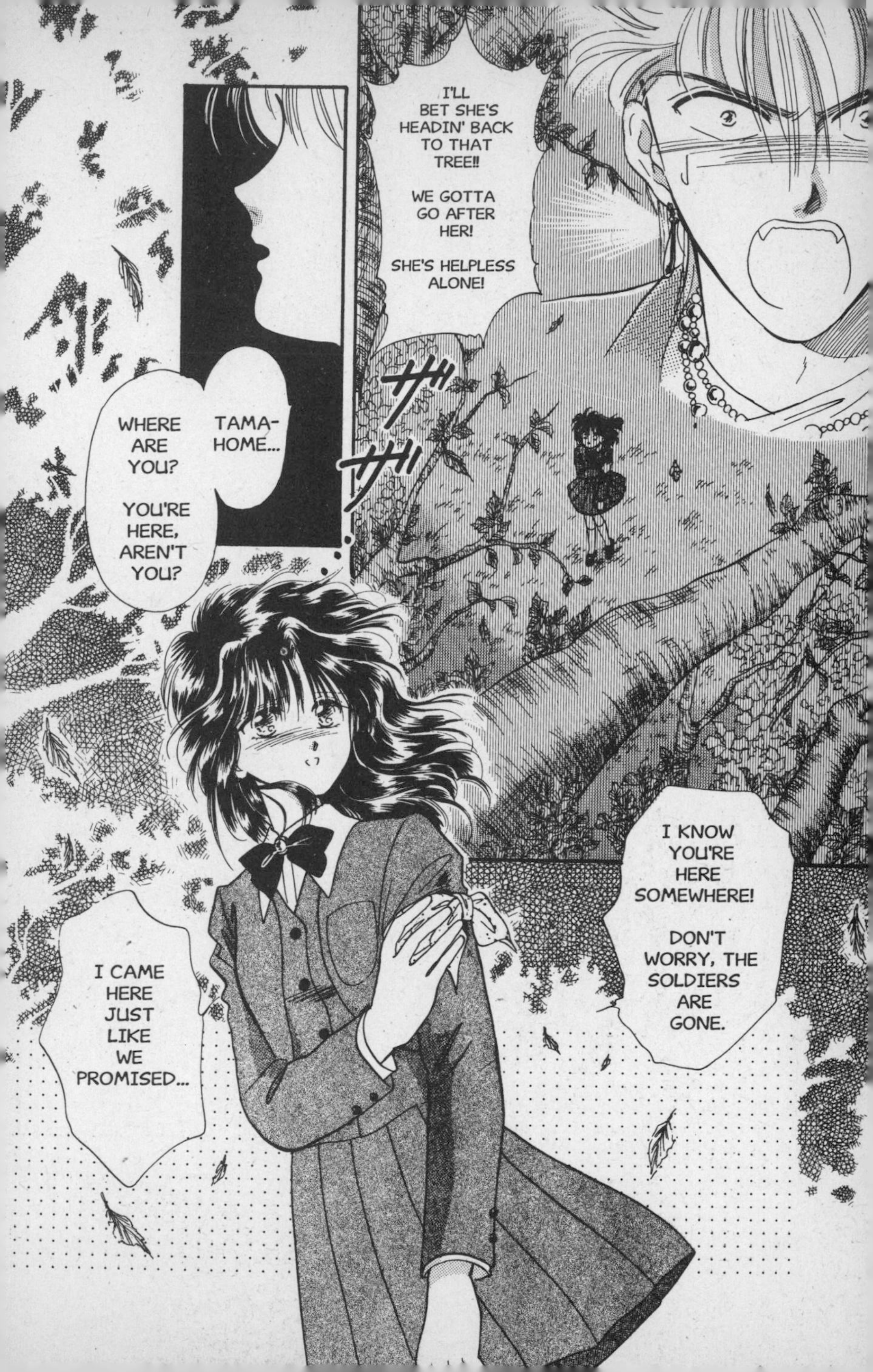
I'LL BET SHE'S HEADIN' BACK TO THAT TREE!!
WE GOTTA GO AFTER HER!
SHE'S HELPLESS ALONE!
ザザ
TAMA-HOME...
WHERE ARE YOU?
YOU'RE HERE, AREN'T YOU?
I KNOW YOU'RE HERE SOMEWHERE!
DON'T WORRY, THE SOLDIERS ARE GONE.
I CAME HERE JUST LIKE WE PROMISED...

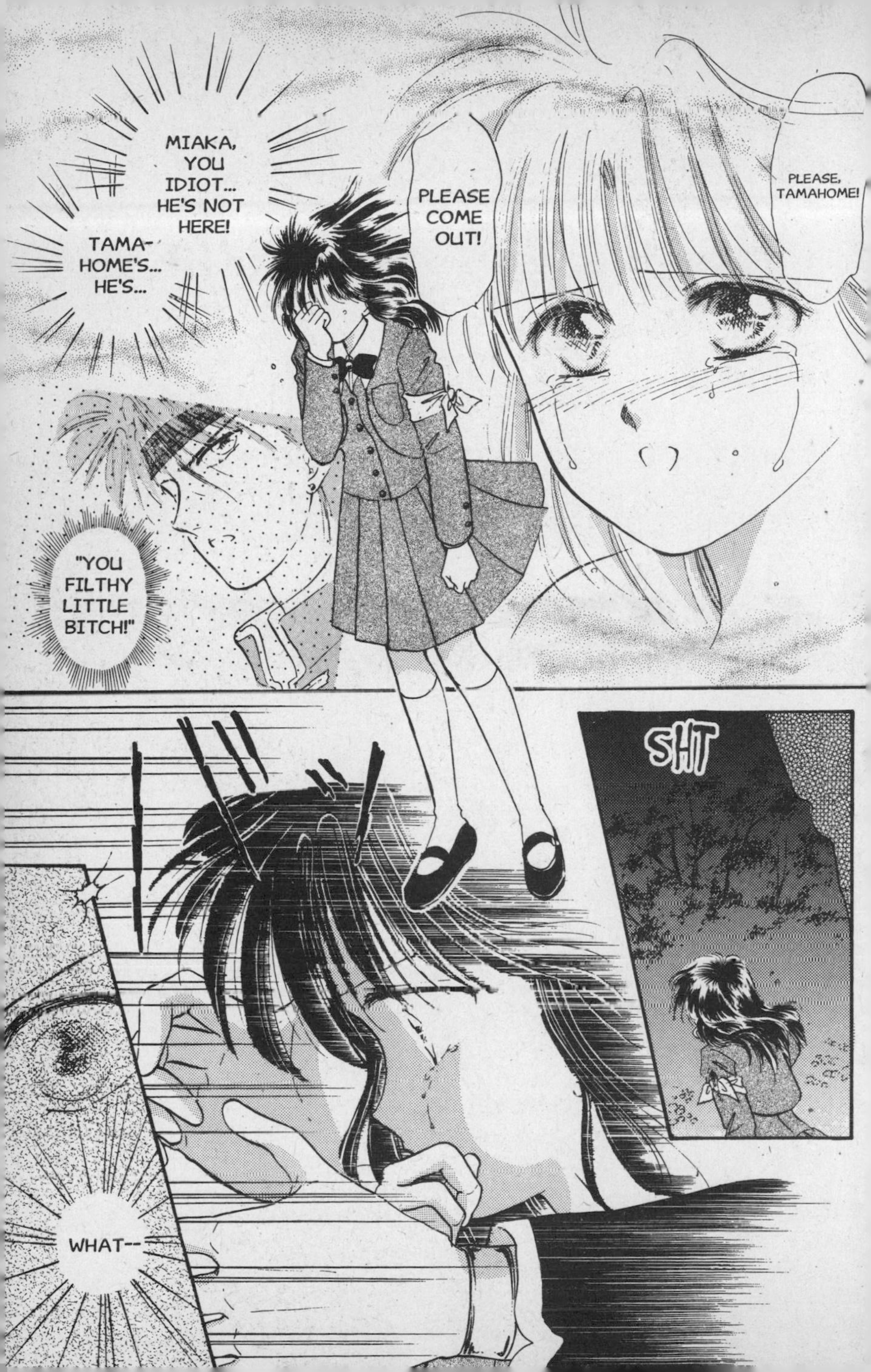
PLEASE, TAMAHOME!
PLEASE COME OUT!
MIAKA, YOU IDIOT... HE'S NOT HERE!
TAMA-HOME'S... HE'S...
"YOU FILTHY LITTLE BITCH!"
SHT
WHAT--

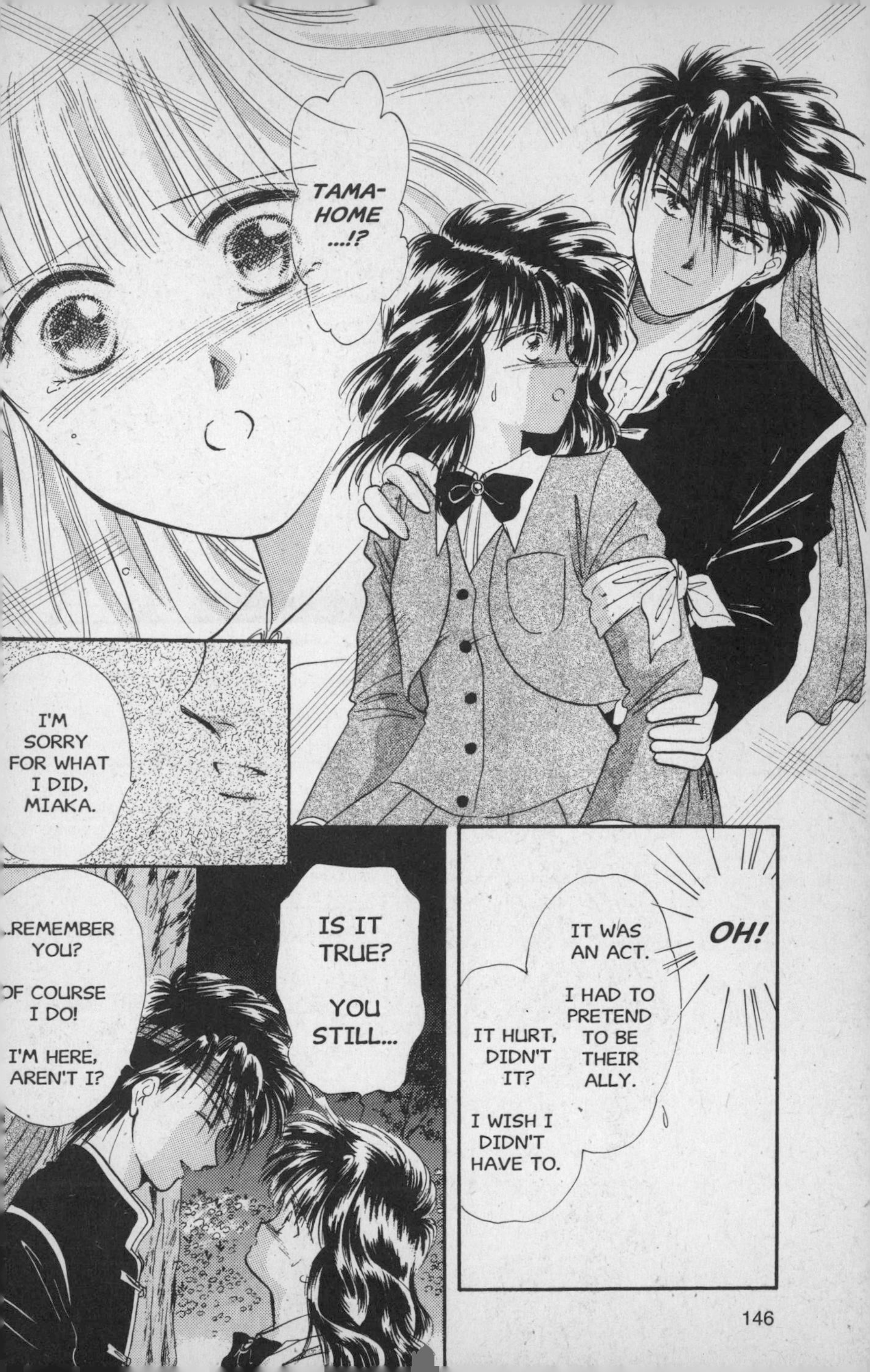
TAMA-HOME ...!?
I'M SORRY FOR WHAT I DID, MIAKA.
OH!
IT WAS AN ACT. I HAD TO PRETEND TO BE THEIR ALLY.
IT HURT, DIDN'T IT? I WISH I DIDN'T HAVE TO.
IS IT TRUE? YOU STILL...
..REMEMBER YOU? OF COURSE I DO! I'M HERE, AREN'T I?

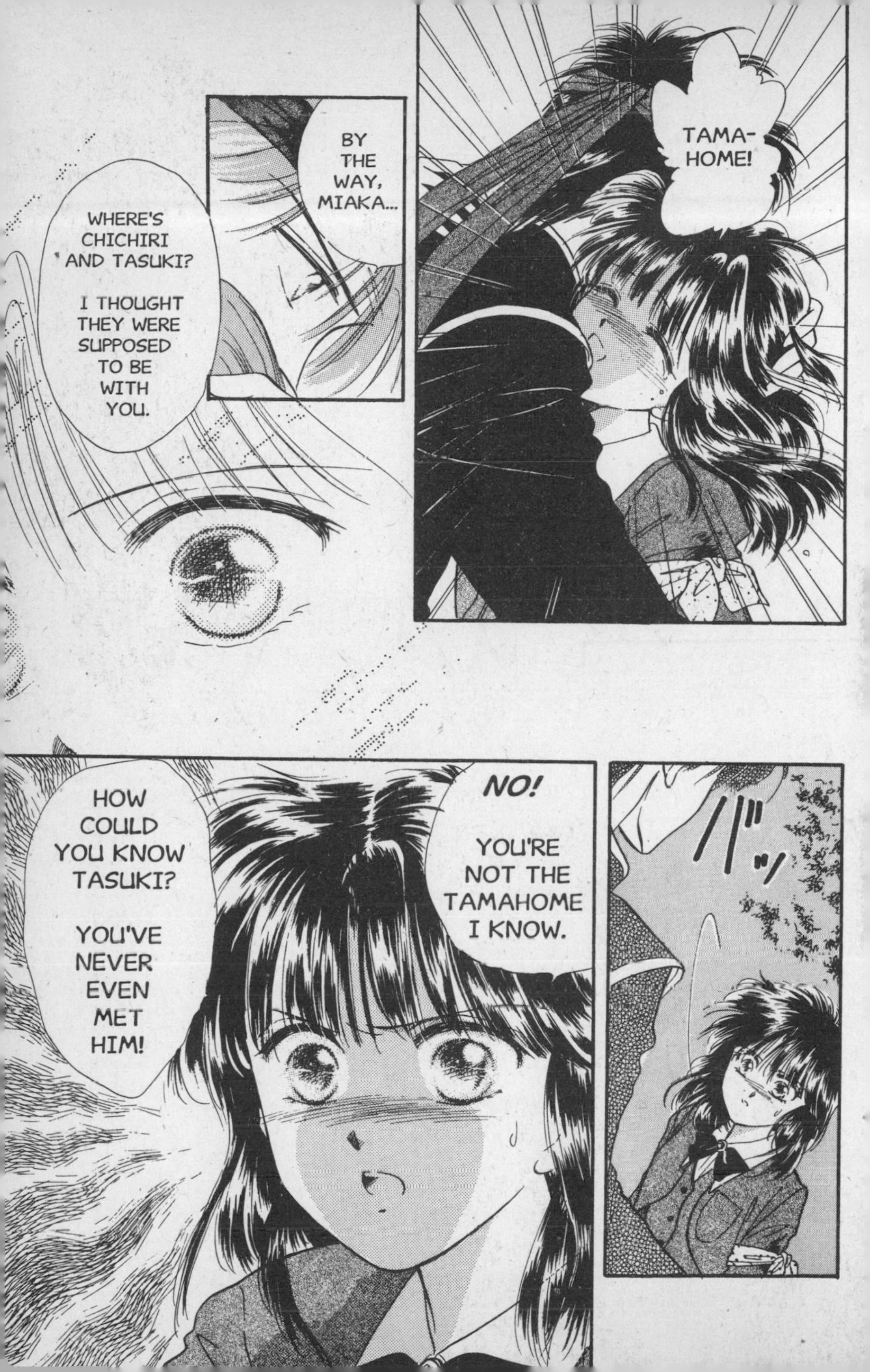
TAMA-HOME!
BY THE WAY, MIAKA...
WHERE'S CHICHIRI AND TASUKI?
I THOUGHT THEY WERE SUPPOSED TO BE WITH YOU.
バッ
NO!
YOU'RE NOT THE TAMAHOME I KNOW.
HOW COULD YOU KNOW TASUKI?
YOU'VE NEVER EVEN MET HIM!

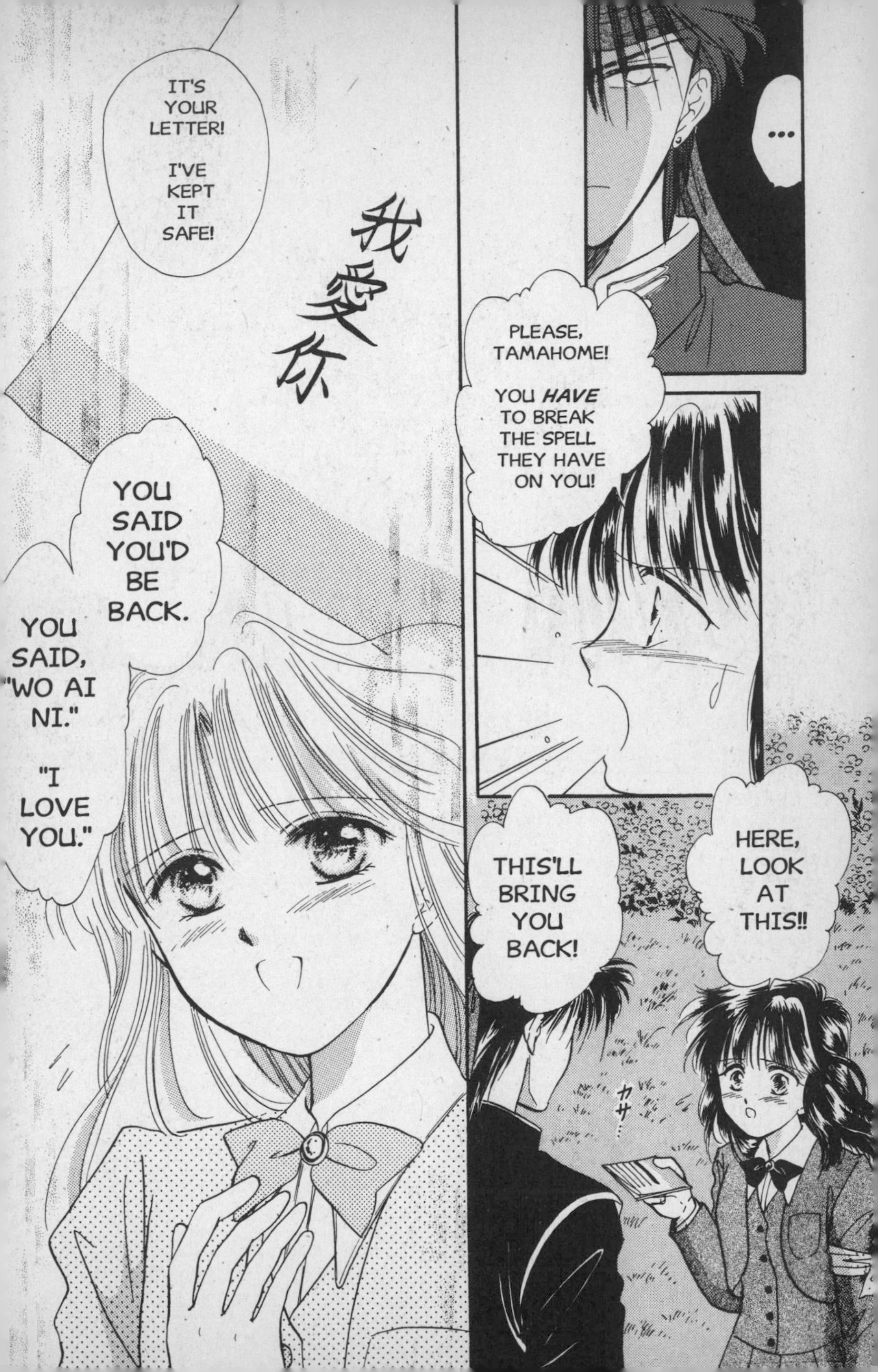
...
PLEASE, TAMAHOME! YOU *HAVE* TO BREAK THE SPELL THEY HAVE ON YOU!
HERE, LOOK AT THIS!!
THIS'LL BRING YOU BACK!
カサ
IT'S YOUR LETTER! I'VE KEPT IT SAFE!
我愛你
YOU SAID YOU'D BE BACK.
YOU SAID, "WO AI NI." "I LOVE YOU."

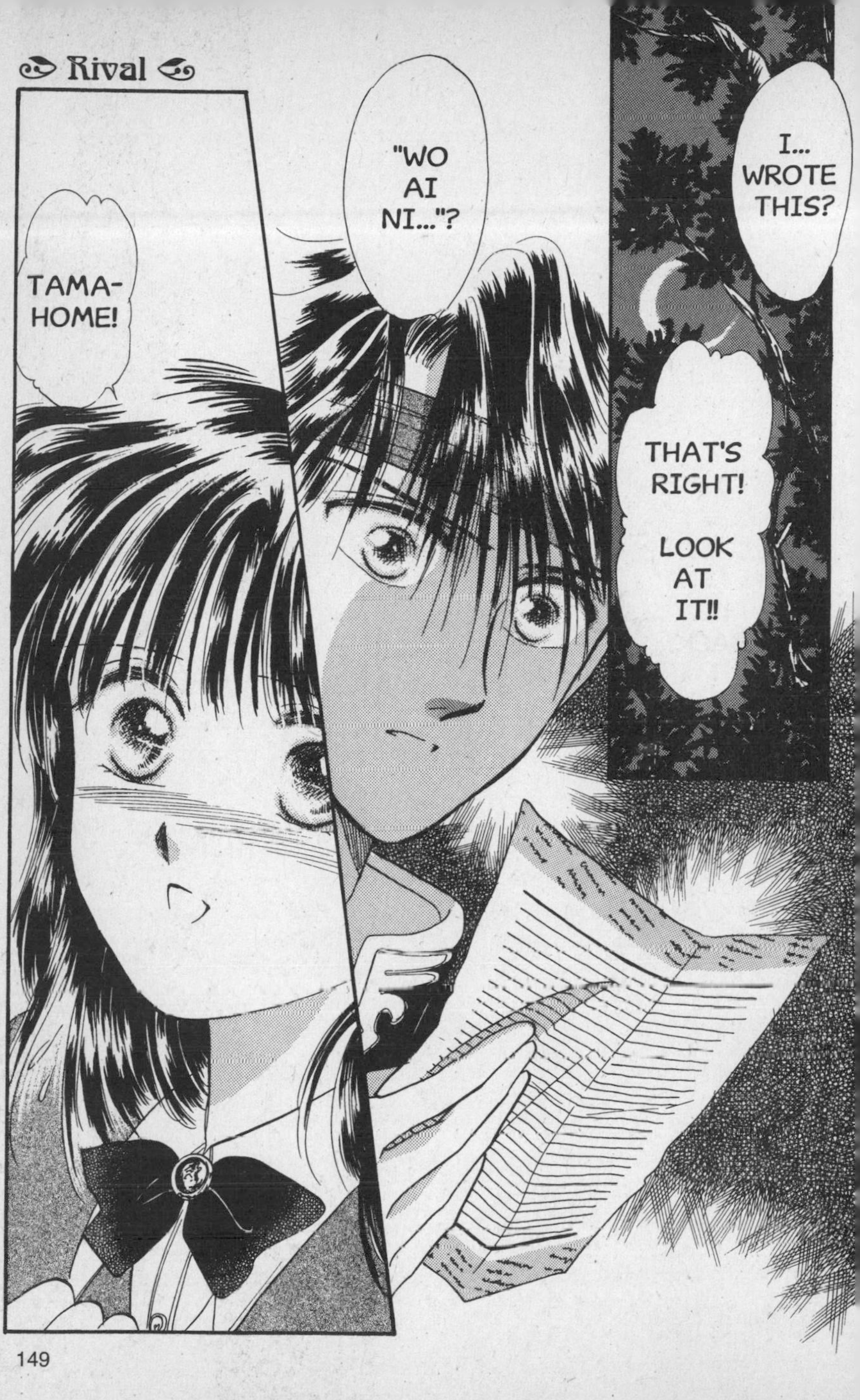
I... WROTE THIS?
THAT'S RIGHT! LOOK AT IT!!
"WO AI NI..."?
TAMA-HOME!

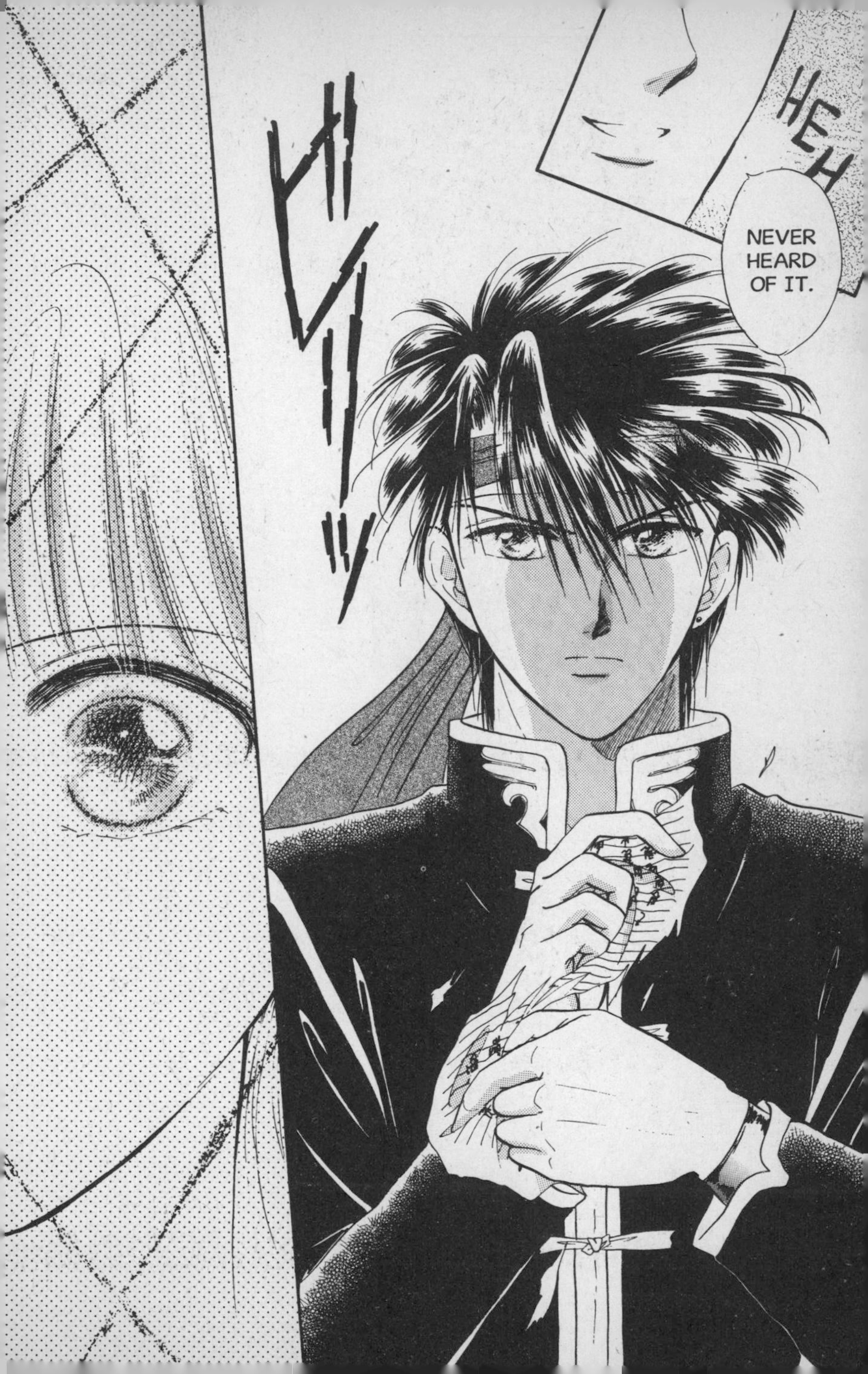
HEH
NEVER HEARD OF IT.

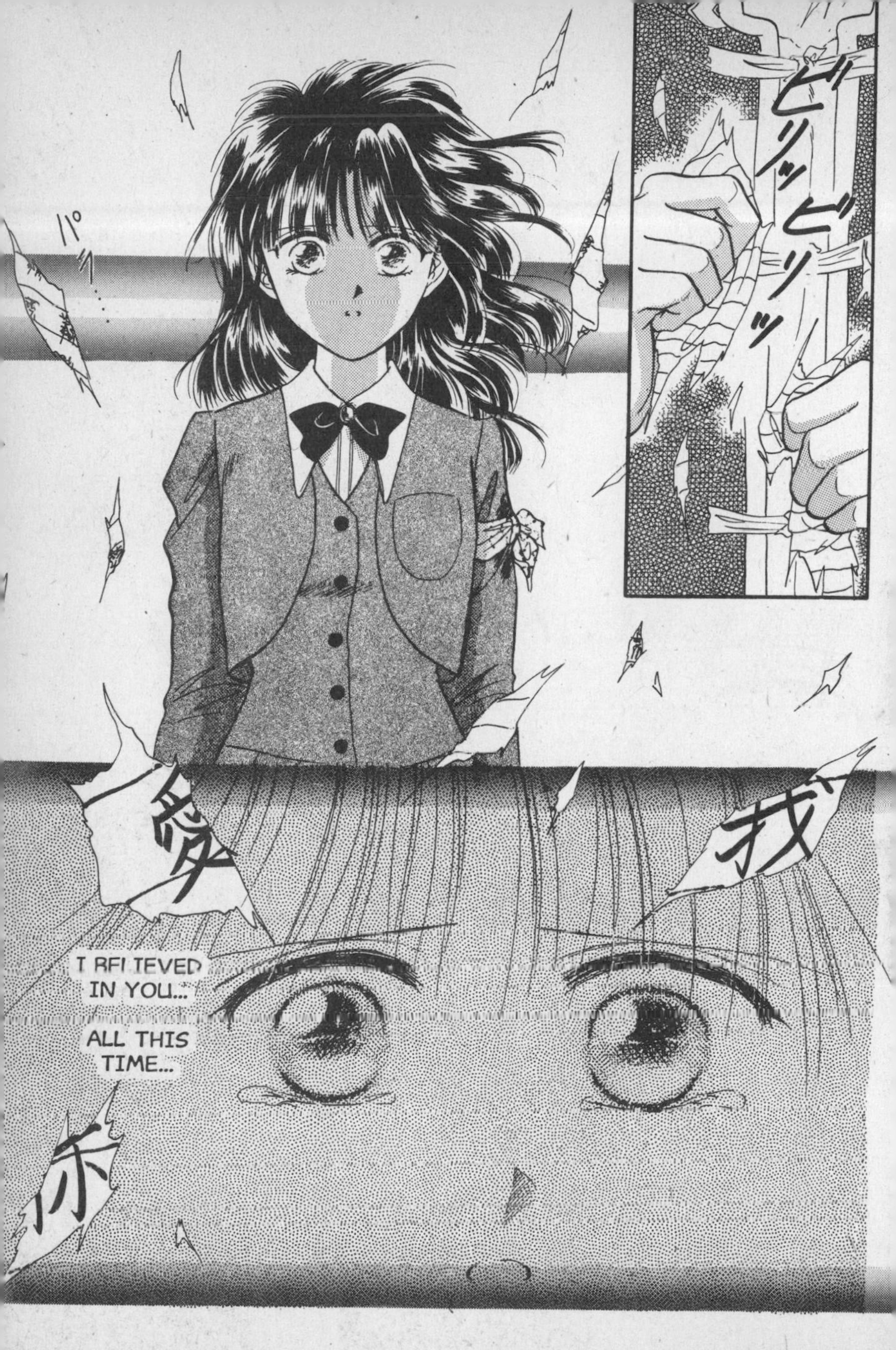
ビリッビリッ
パリ
我
愛
I BELIEVED IN YOU...
ALL THIS TIME...
你

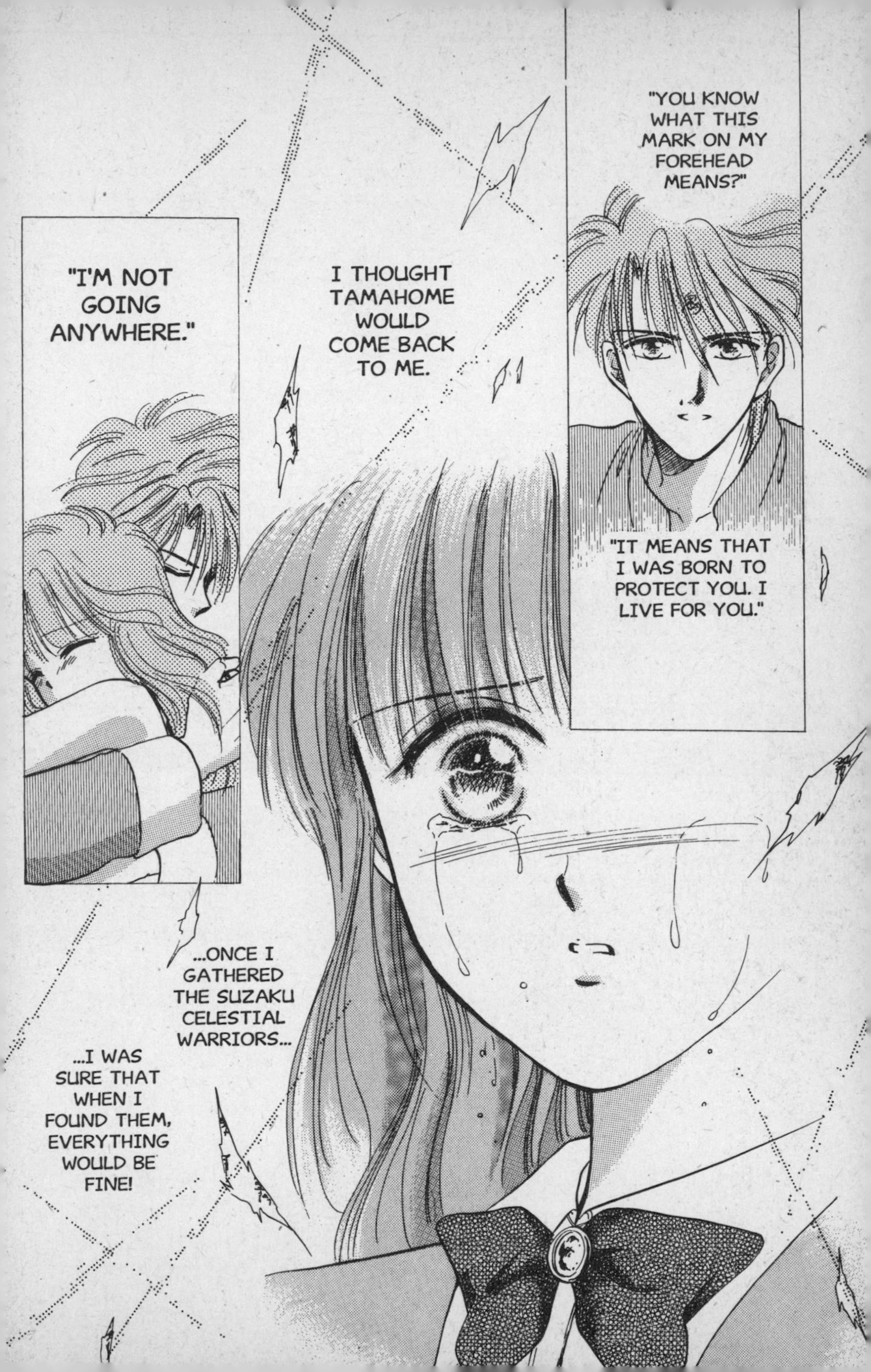
"YOU KNOW WHAT THIS MARK ON MY FOREHEAD MEANS?"
"IT MEANS THAT I WAS BORN TO PROTECT YOU. I LIVE FOR YOU."
I THOUGHT TAMAHOME WOULD COME BACK TO ME.
"I'M NOT GOING ANYWHERE."
...ONCE I GATHERED THE SUZAKU CELESTIAL WARRIORS...
...I WAS SURE THAT WHEN I FOUND THEM, EVERYTHING WOULD BE FINE!

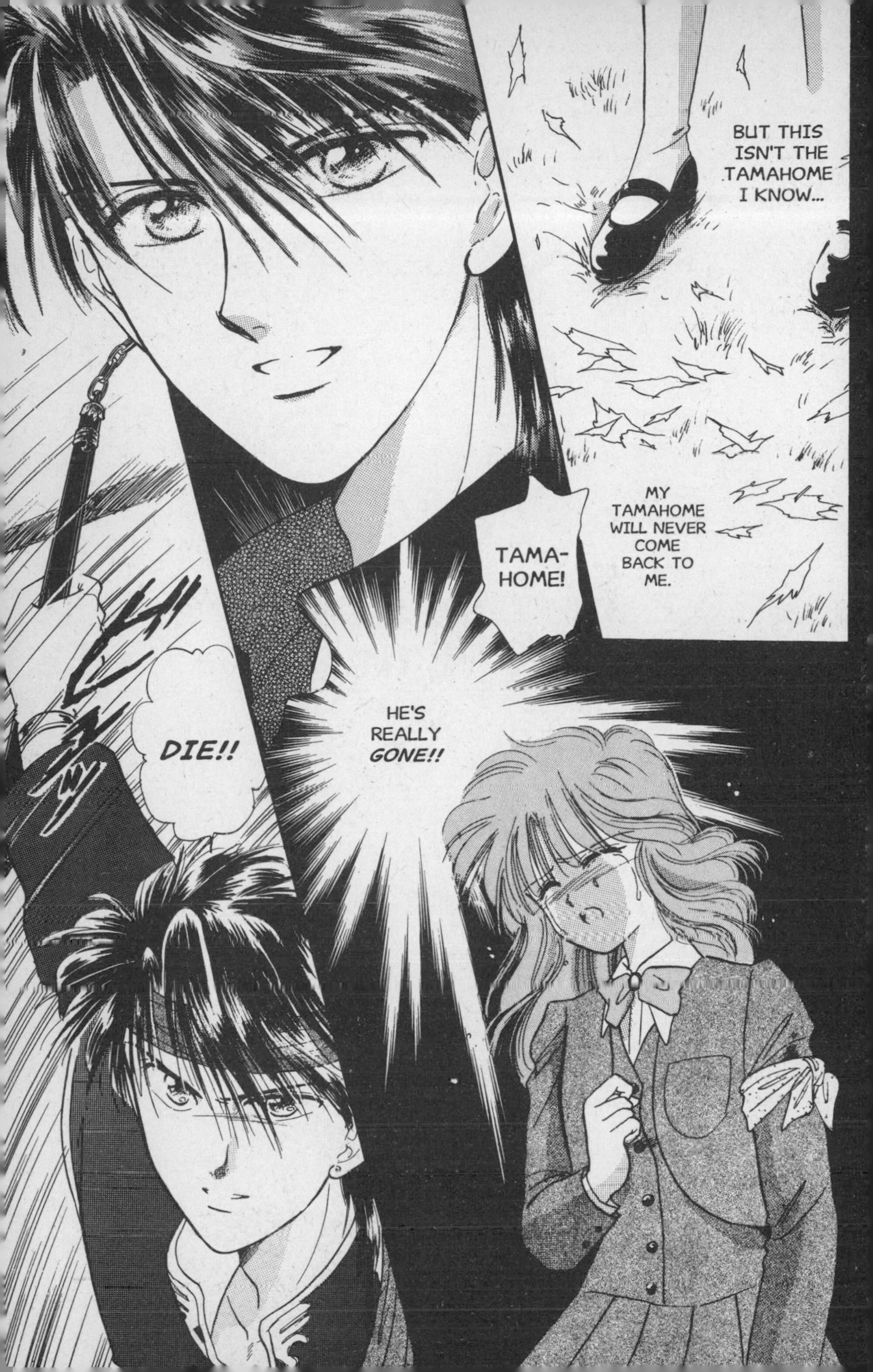
BUT THIS ISN'T THE TAMAHOME I KNOW...
MY TAMAHOME WILL NEVER COME BACK TO ME.
TAMA-HOME!
HE'S REALLY *GONE!!*
DIE!!

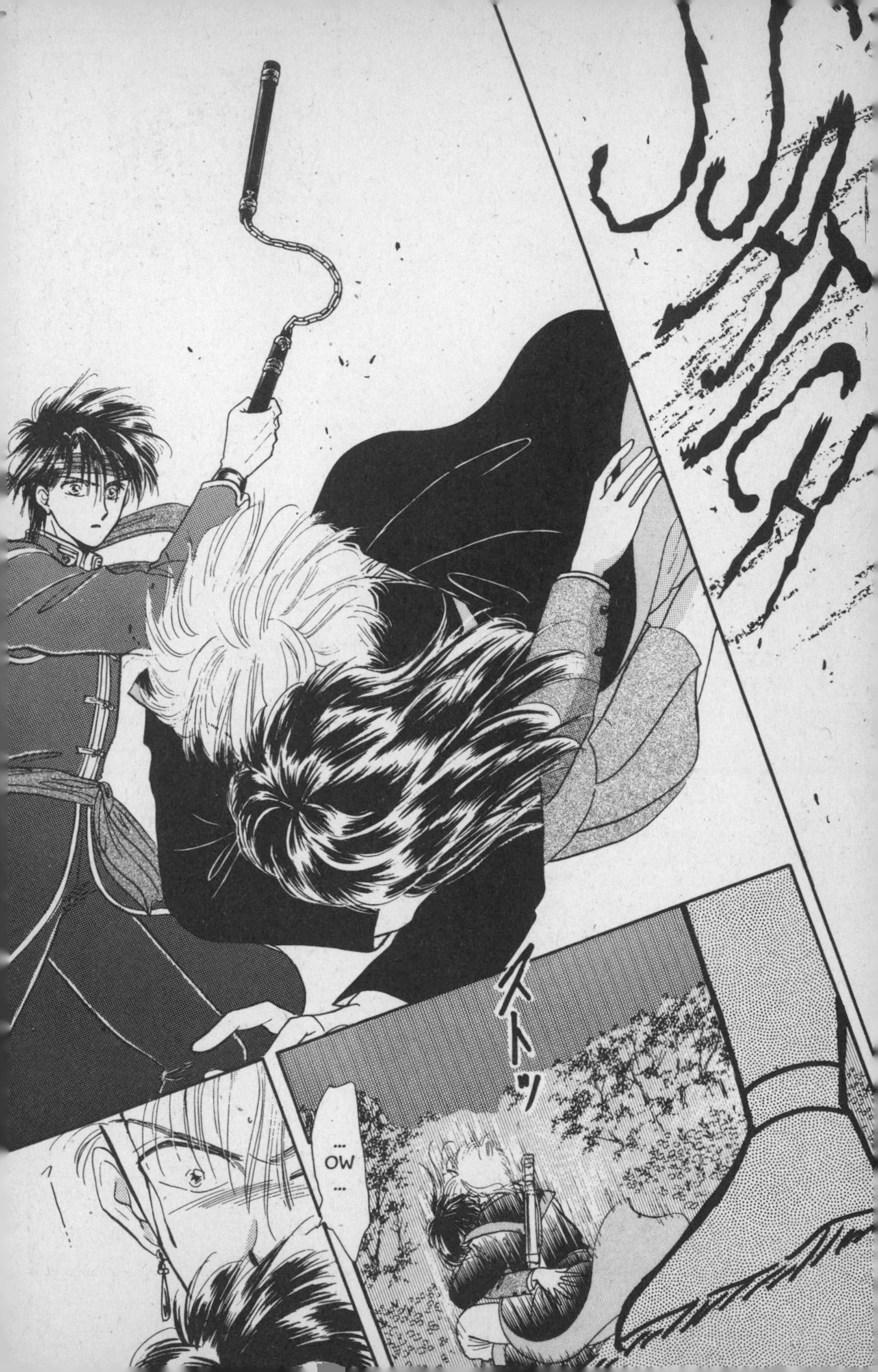
ストッ
... OW ...

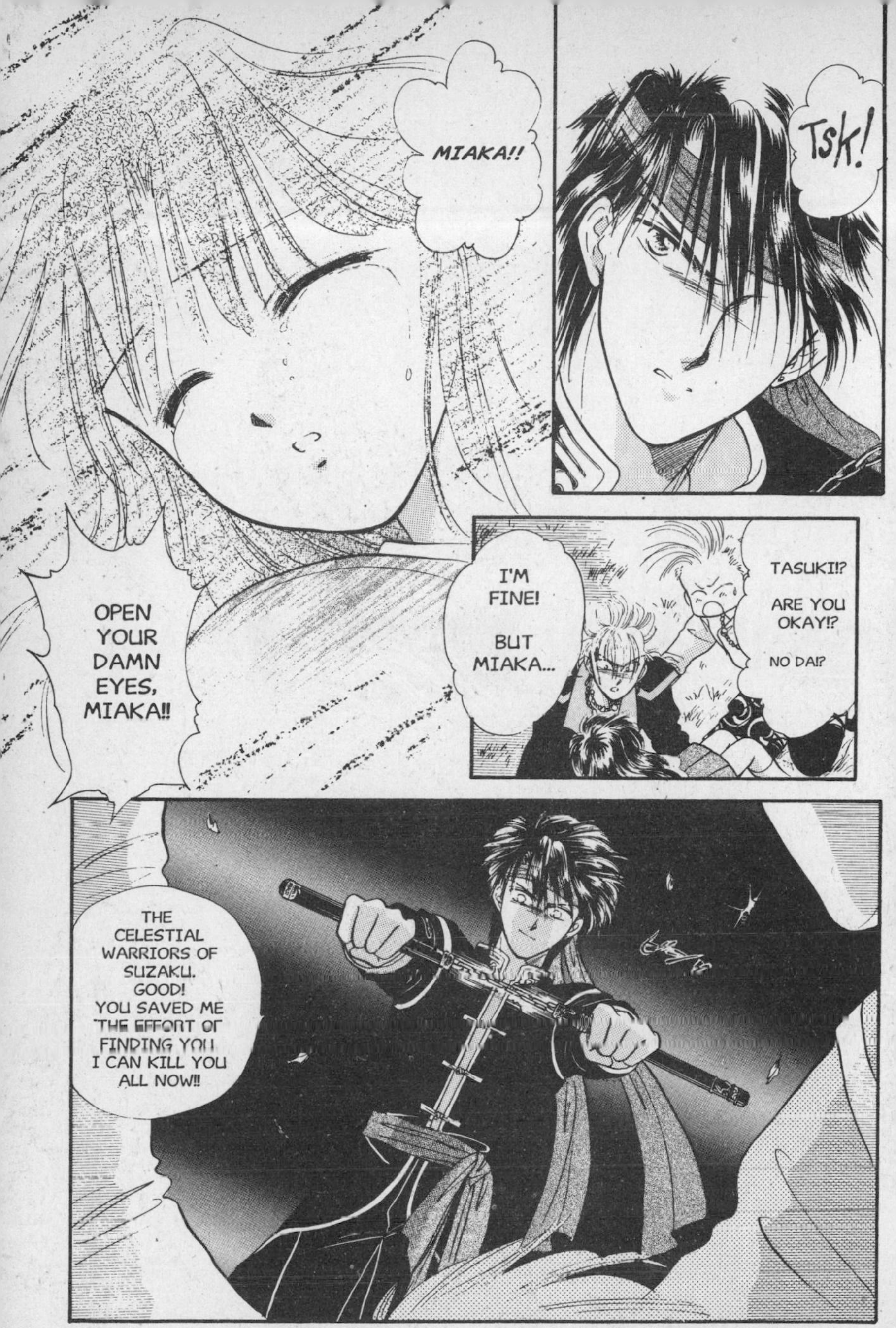
TSK!
TASUKI!? ARE YOU OKAY!? NO DA!?
I'M FINE! BUT MIAKA...
MIAKA!!
OPEN YOUR DAMN EYES, MIAKA!!
THE CELESTIAL WARRIORS OF SUZAKU. GOOD! YOU SAVED ME THE EFFORT OF FINDING YOU. I CAN KILL YOU ALL NOW!!

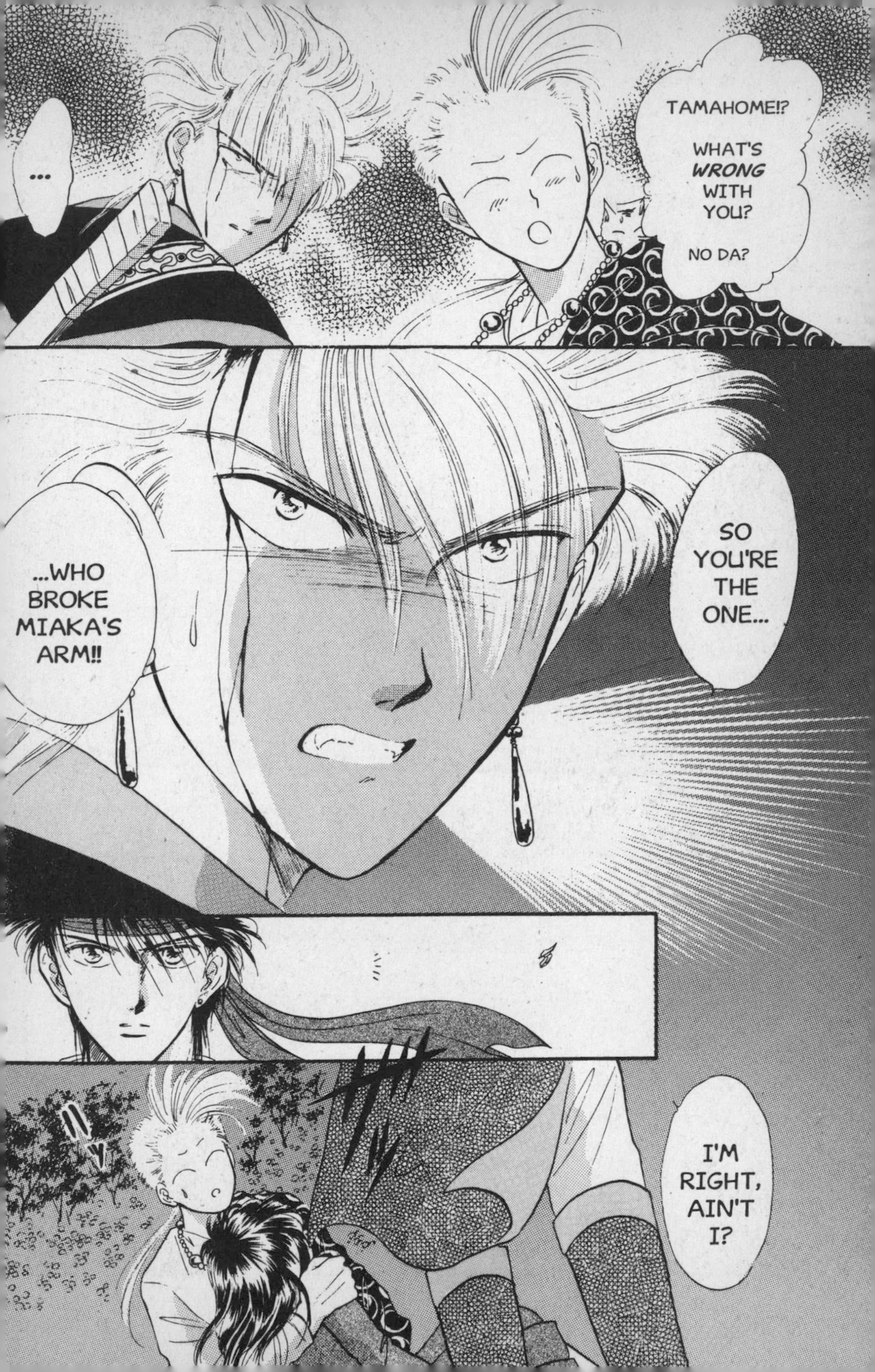
TAMAHOME!? WHAT'S WRONG WITH YOU?
NO DA?
...
SO YOU'RE THE ONE...
...WHO BROKE MIAKA'S ARM!!
I'M RIGHT, AIN'T I?

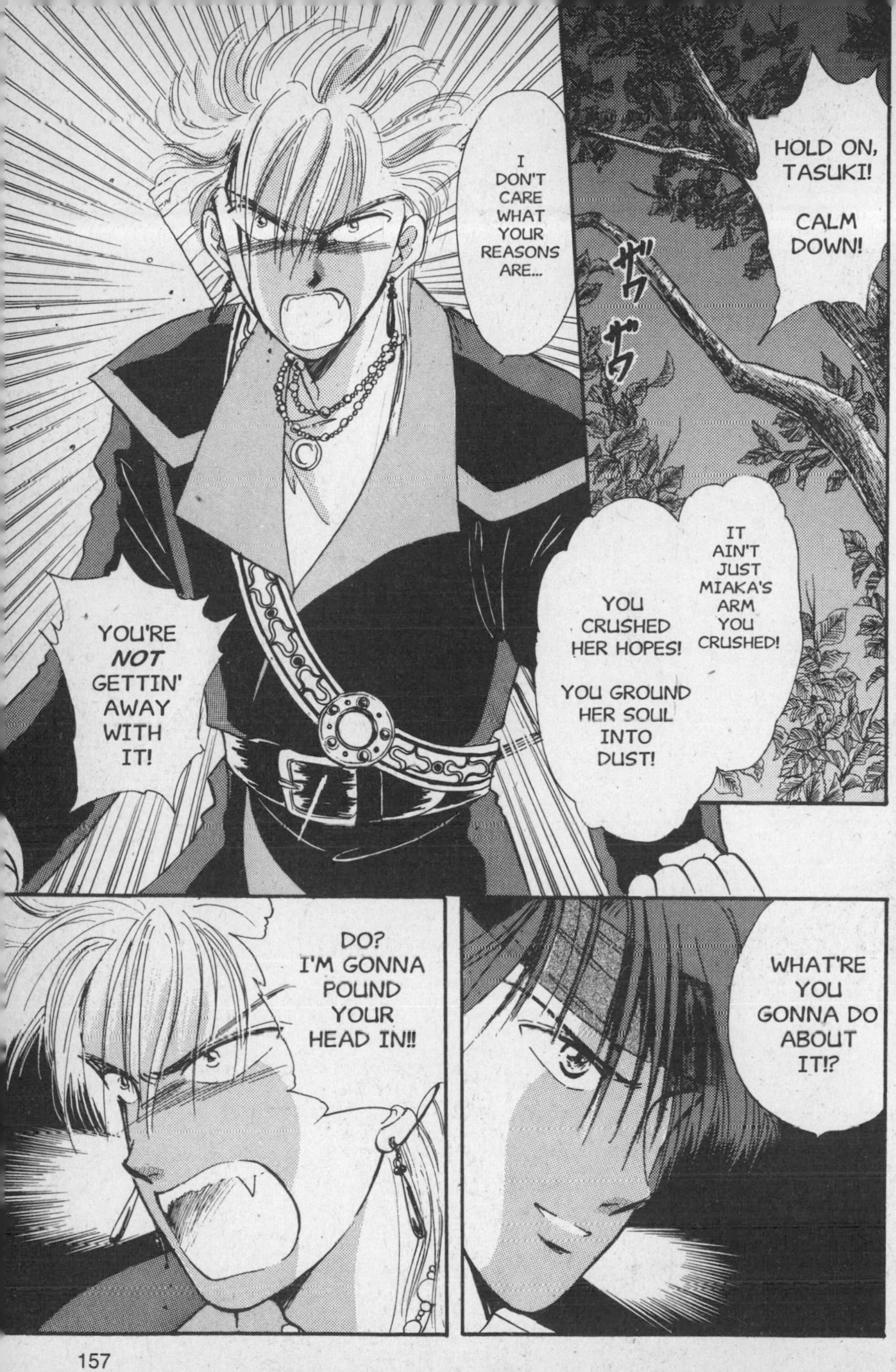
HOLD ON, TASUKI!
CALM DOWN!
I DON'T CARE WHAT YOUR REASONS ARE...
IT AIN'T JUST MIAKA'S ARM YOU CRUSHED!
YOU CRUSHED HER HOPES!
YOU GROUND HER SOUL INTO DUST!
YOU'RE ***NOT*** GETTIN' AWAY WITH IT!
WHAT'RE YOU GONNA DO ABOUT IT!?
DO? I'M GONNA POUND YOUR HEAD IN!!

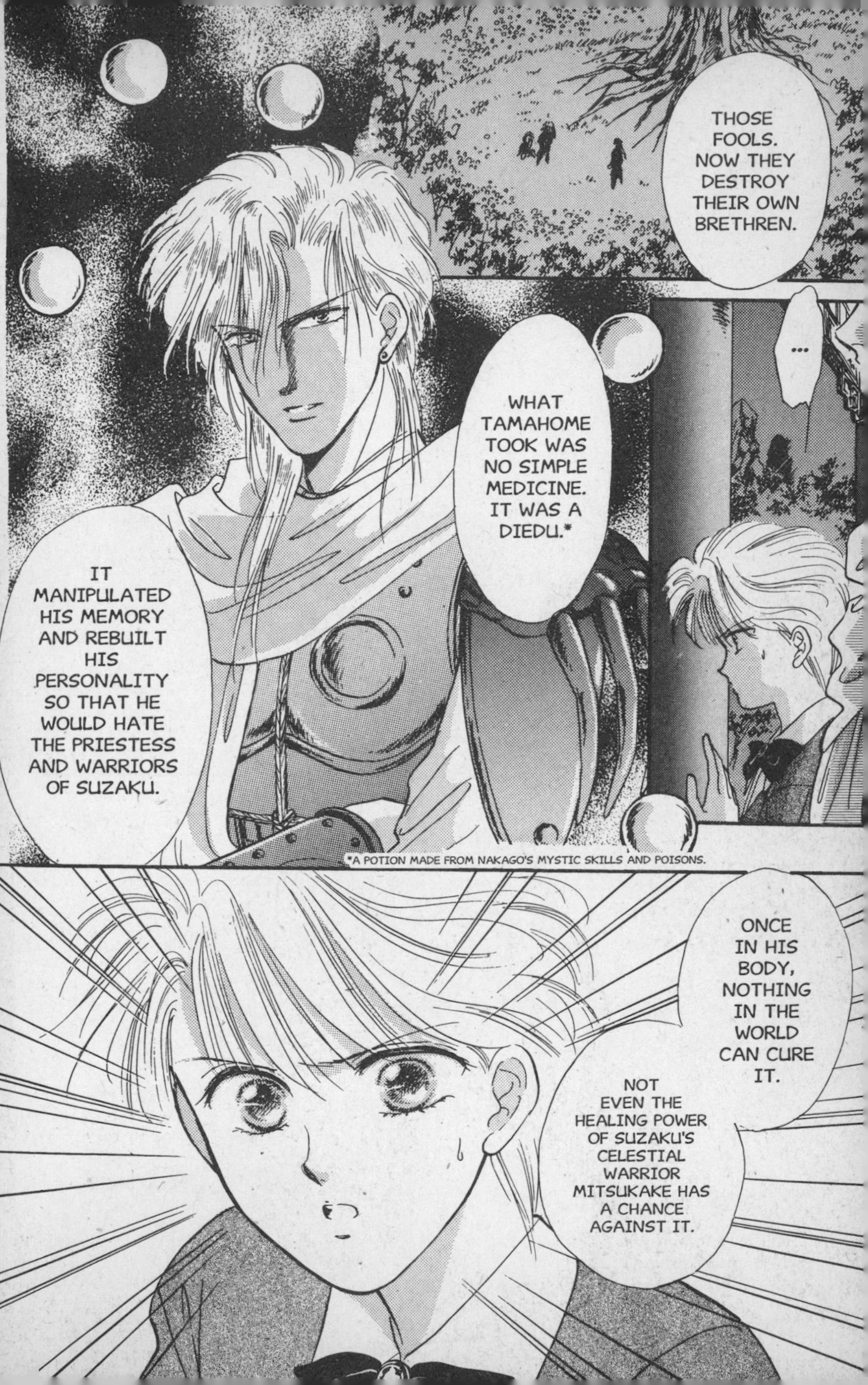
THOSE FOOLS. NOW THEY DESTROY THEIR OWN BRETHREN.
...
WHAT TAMAHOME TOOK WAS NO SIMPLE MEDICINE. IT WAS A DIEDU.*
IT MANIPULATED HIS MEMORY AND REBUILT HIS PERSONALITY SO THAT HE WOULD HATE THE PRIESTESS AND WARRIORS OF SUZAKU.
ONCE IN HIS BODY, NOTHING IN THE WORLD CAN CURE IT.
NOT EVEN THE HEALING POWER OF SUZAKU'S CELESTIAL WARRIOR MITSUKAKE HAS A CHANCE AGAINST IT.

*A POTION MADE FROM NAKAGO'S MYSTIC SKILLS AND POISONS.

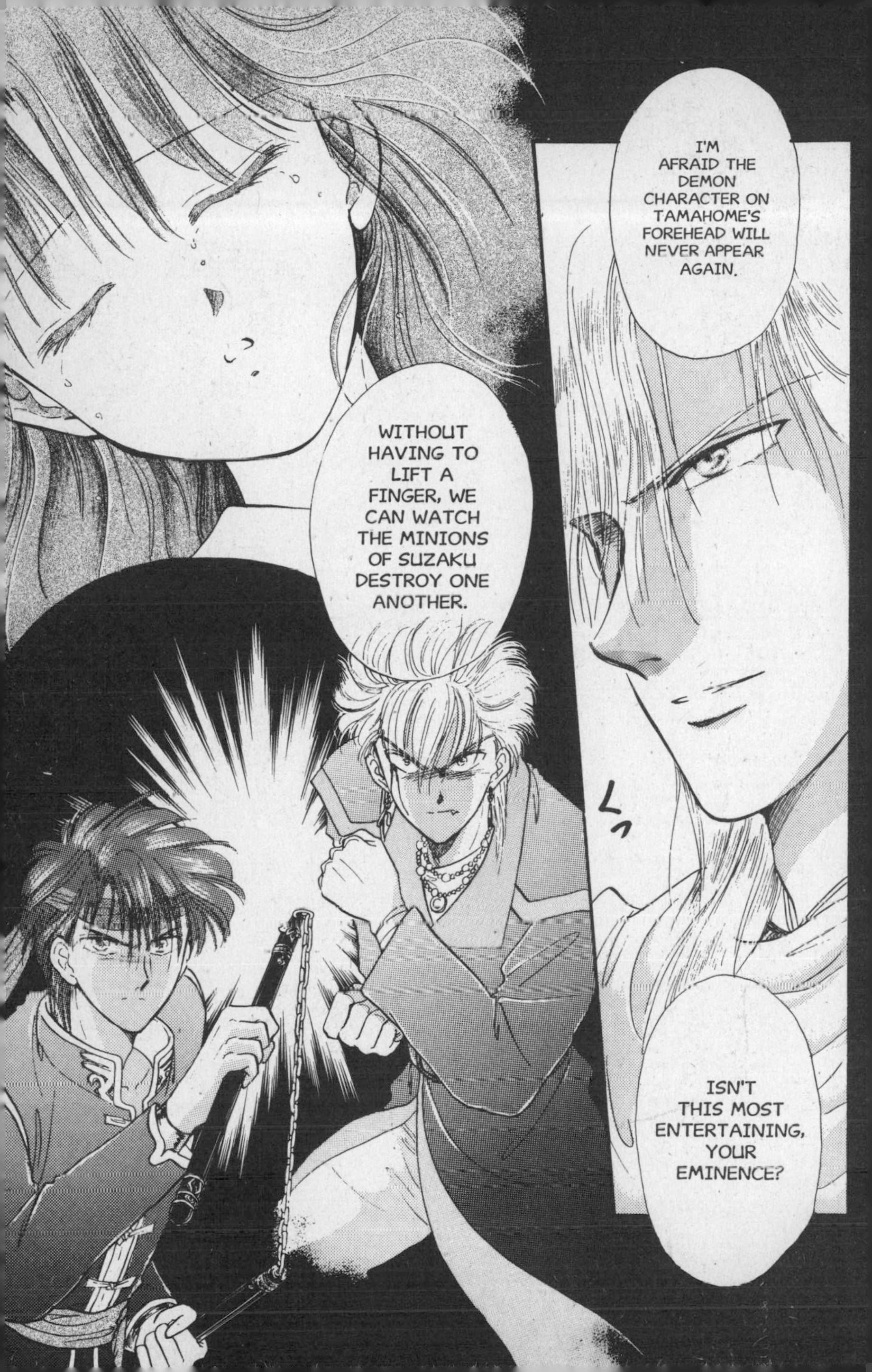
I'M AFRAID THE DEMON CHARACTER ON TAMAHOME'S FOREHEAD WILL NEVER APPEAR AGAIN.
WITHOUT HAVING TO LIFT A FINGER, WE CAN WATCH THE MINIONS OF SUZAKU DESTROY ONE ANOTHER.
ISN'T THIS MOST ENTERTAINING, YOUR EMINENCE?

Tiao 迢 Liu 柳 Chuan 娟

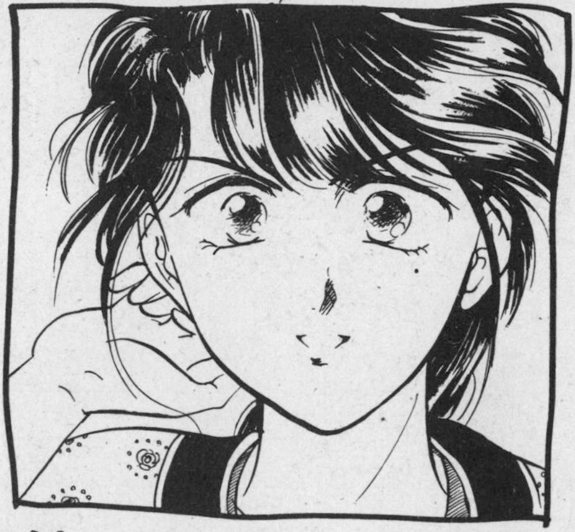

Hydra

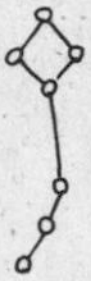

NURIKO

- The second son of a shopkeeper in the Hsien-Wu district of Hong-Nan's capital city of Rong-Yang.
- Age: Presently 18 years old.
- Family: Parents and an older brother.
  Kang-Lin was the name of his deceased sister. (Name from vol. 1)
- Talents: Enormous strength, come-hither eyes What's that supposed to mean?
- Hobby: Cross-dressing
- Height: 5 feet, 5 inches
- Blood type: B (I think)

- Nuriko is biologically a man, but judging by his looks, tone of voice, and all other factors, Nuriko seems like a woman, and as a woman, is infatuated with Hotohori. The uninitiated may simply see a homosexual, but as Nuriko puts it, "I have a man's body but a woman's heart." When not angry or being calculating, Nuriko can be a pretty cool person. The jealous type, but also a worrier. Nuriko seems to worry most about Miaka and Tamahome's relationship. Miaka looks to Nuriko as an older sister (?), but there is a part that remains very manly.

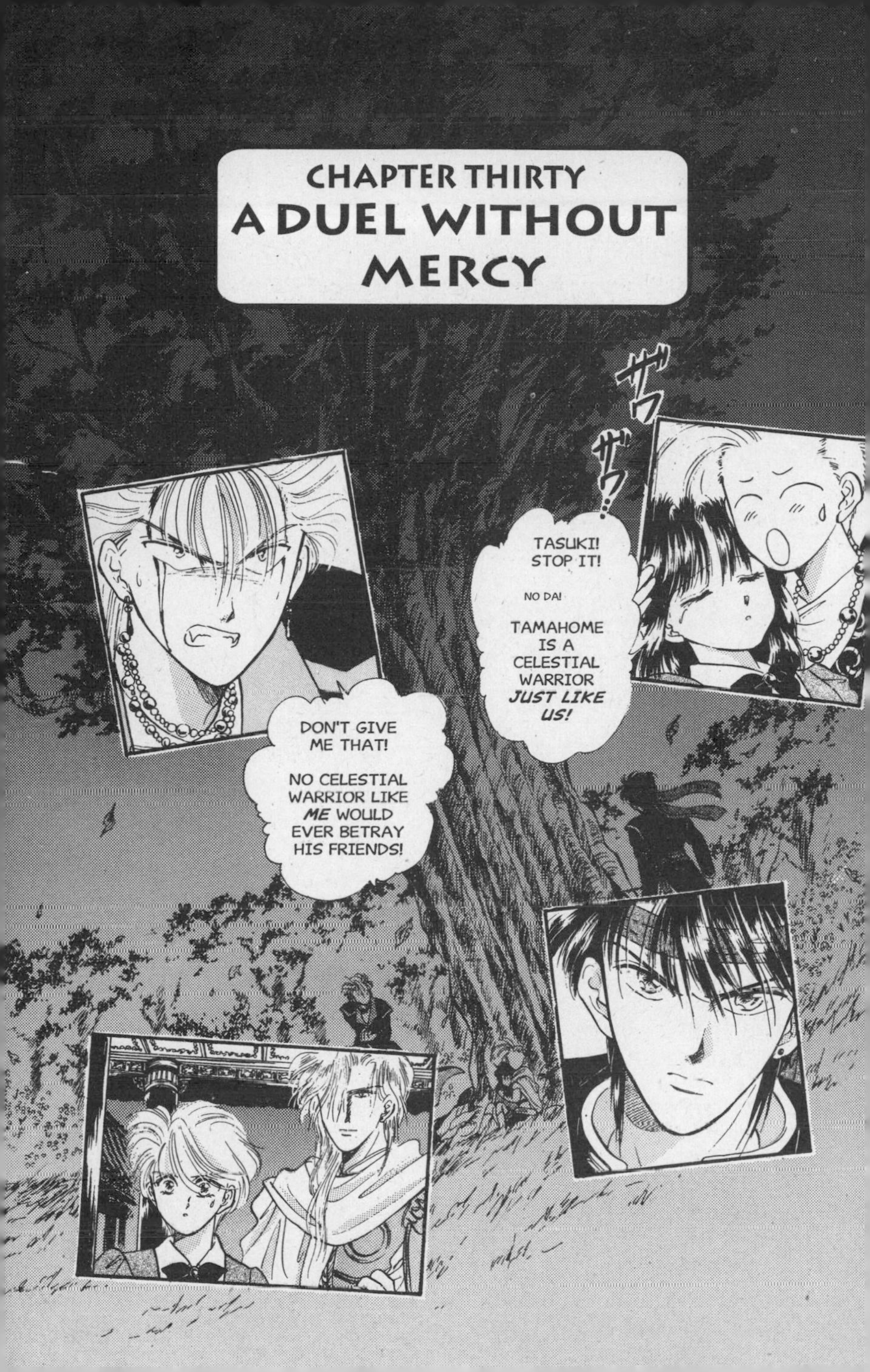
CHAPTER THIRTY
A DUEL WITHOUT MERCY
ザワ
ザワ
TASUKI! STOP IT!
NO DA!
TAMAHOME IS A CELESTIAL WARRIOR *JUST LIKE US!*
DON'T GIVE ME THAT!
NO CELESTIAL WARRIOR LIKE *ME* WOULD EVER BETRAY HIS FRIENDS!

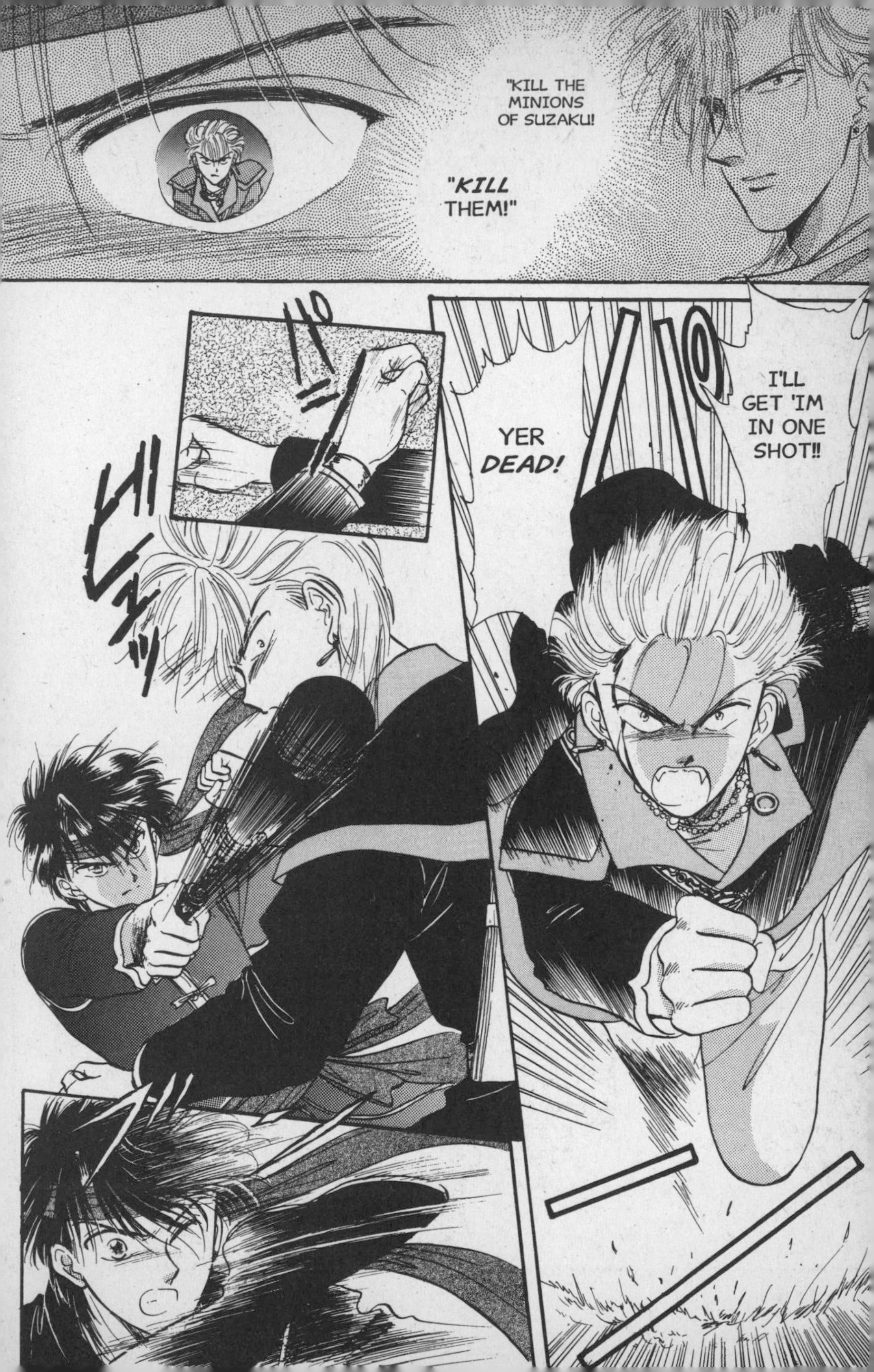
"KILL THE MINIONS OF SUZAKU!
"KILL THEM!"
I'LL GET 'IM IN ONE SHOT!!
YER DEAD!

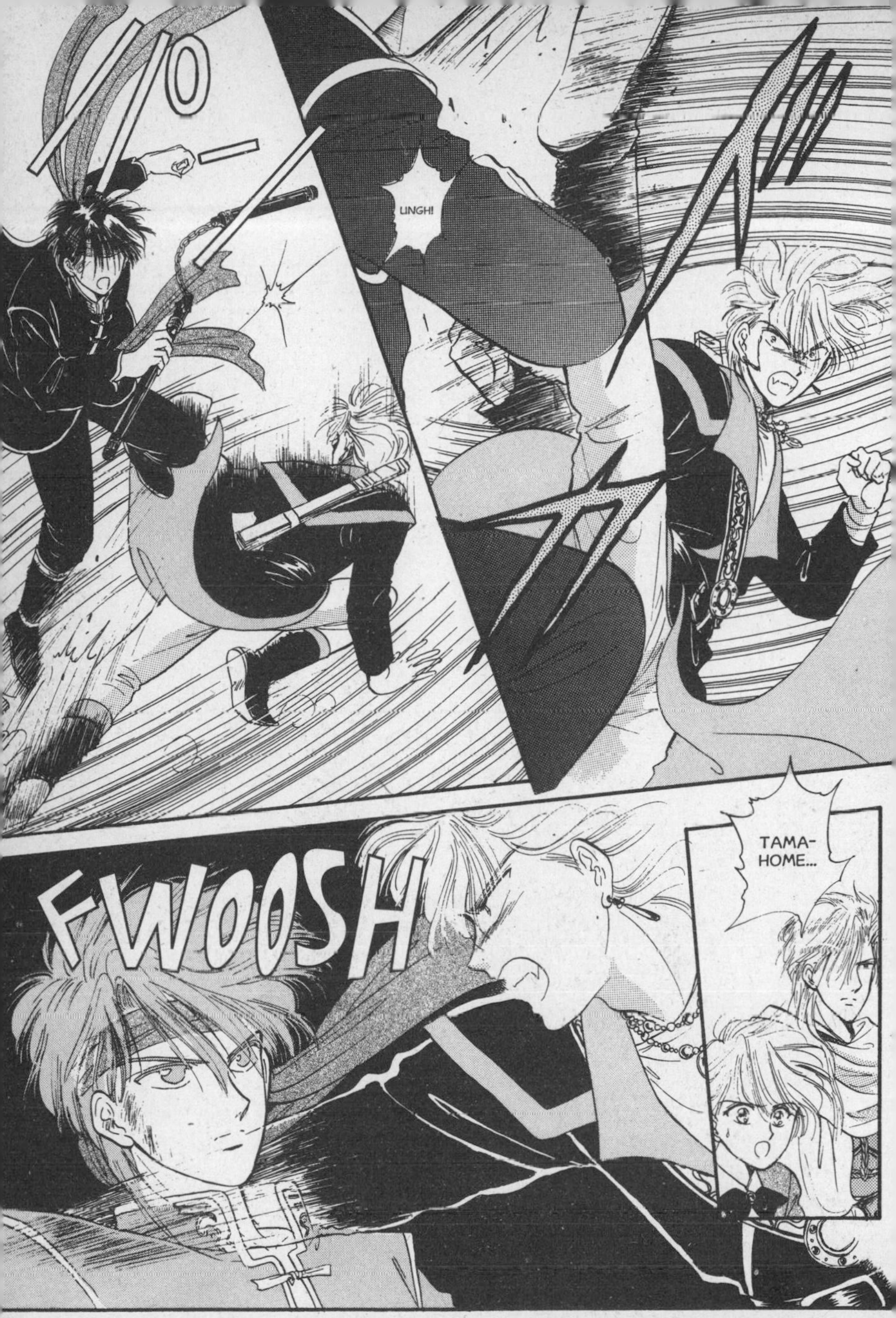
UNGH!
TAMA-
HOME...
FWOOSH

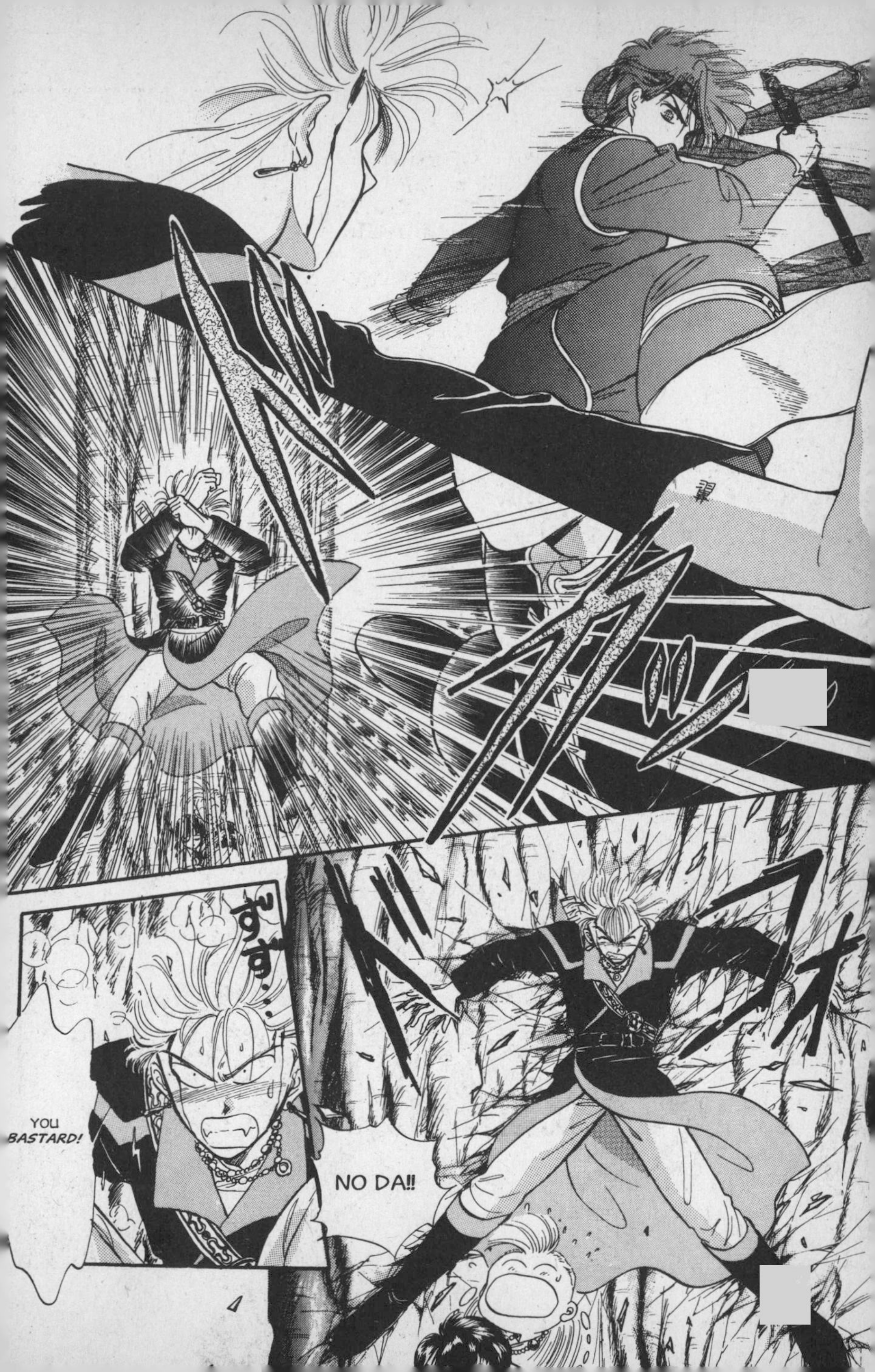
NO DA!!
ずず…
YOU BASTARD!

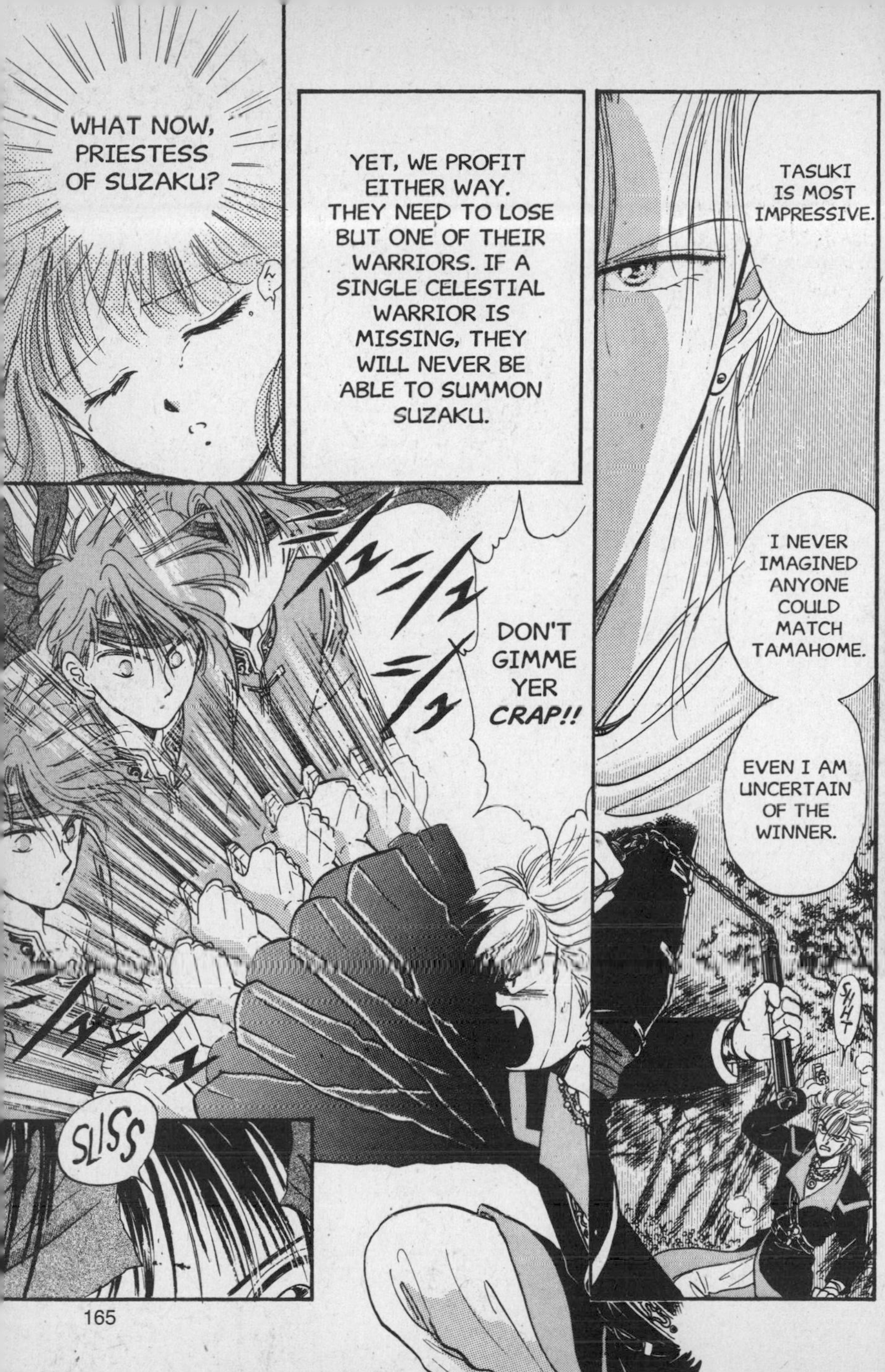
TASUKI IS MOST IMPRESSIVE.
I NEVER IMAGINED ANYONE COULD MATCH TAMAHOME.
EVEN I AM UNCERTAIN OF THE WINNER.
YET, WE PROFIT EITHER WAY. THEY NEED TO LOSE BUT ONE OF THEIR WARRIORS. IF A SINGLE CELESTIAL WARRIOR IS MISSING, THEY WILL NEVER BE ABLE TO SUMMON SUZAKU.
WHAT NOW, PRIESTESS OF SUZAKU?
DON'T GIMME YER *CRAP!!*
SHHT
SLISS

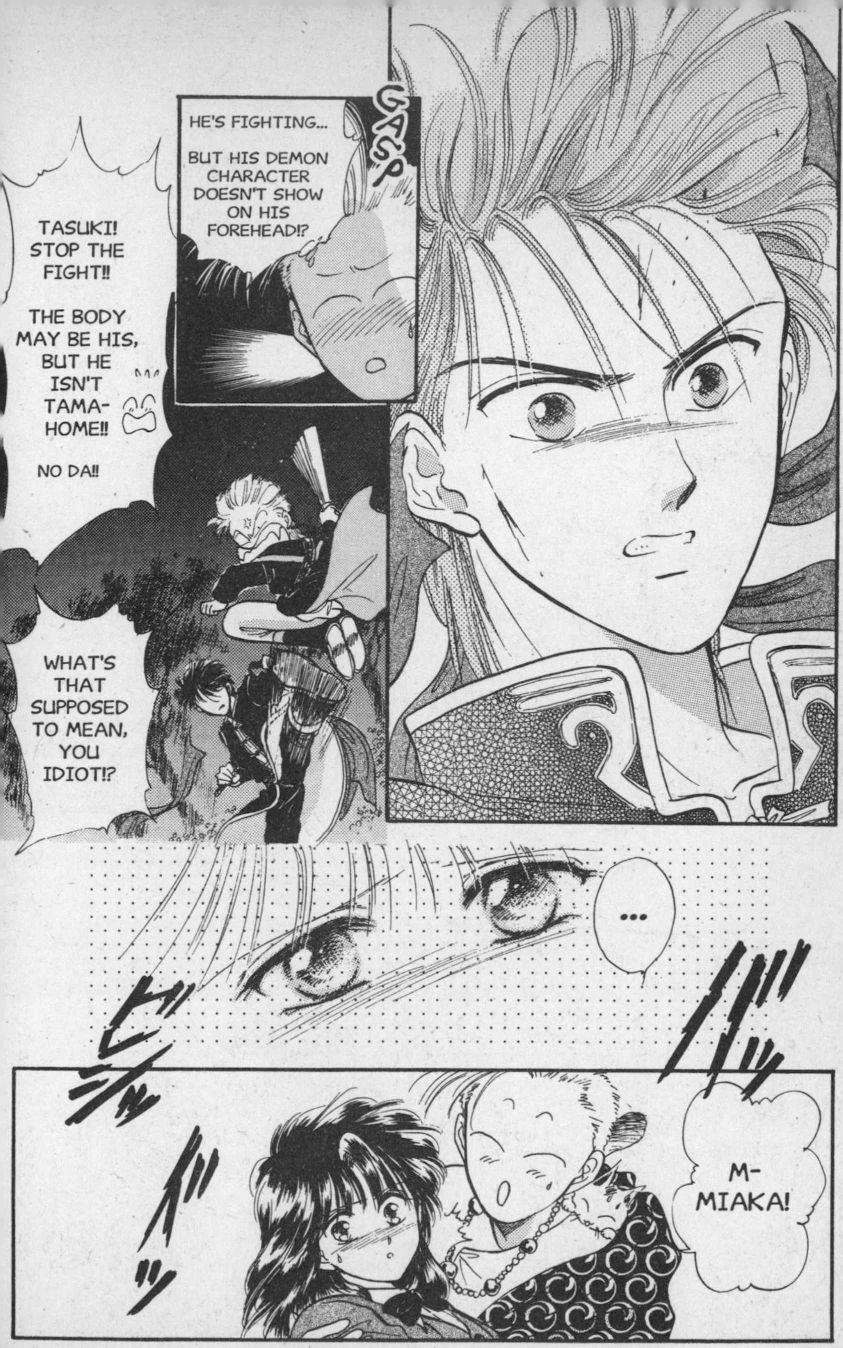
GASP
HE'S FIGHTING... BUT HIS DEMON CHARACTER DOESN'T SHOW ON HIS FOREHEAD!?
TASUKI! STOP THE FIGHT!! THE BODY MAY BE HIS, BUT HE ISN'T TAMA-HOME!! NO DA!!
WHAT'S THAT SUPPOSED TO MEAN, YOU IDIOT!?
...
M-MIAKA!

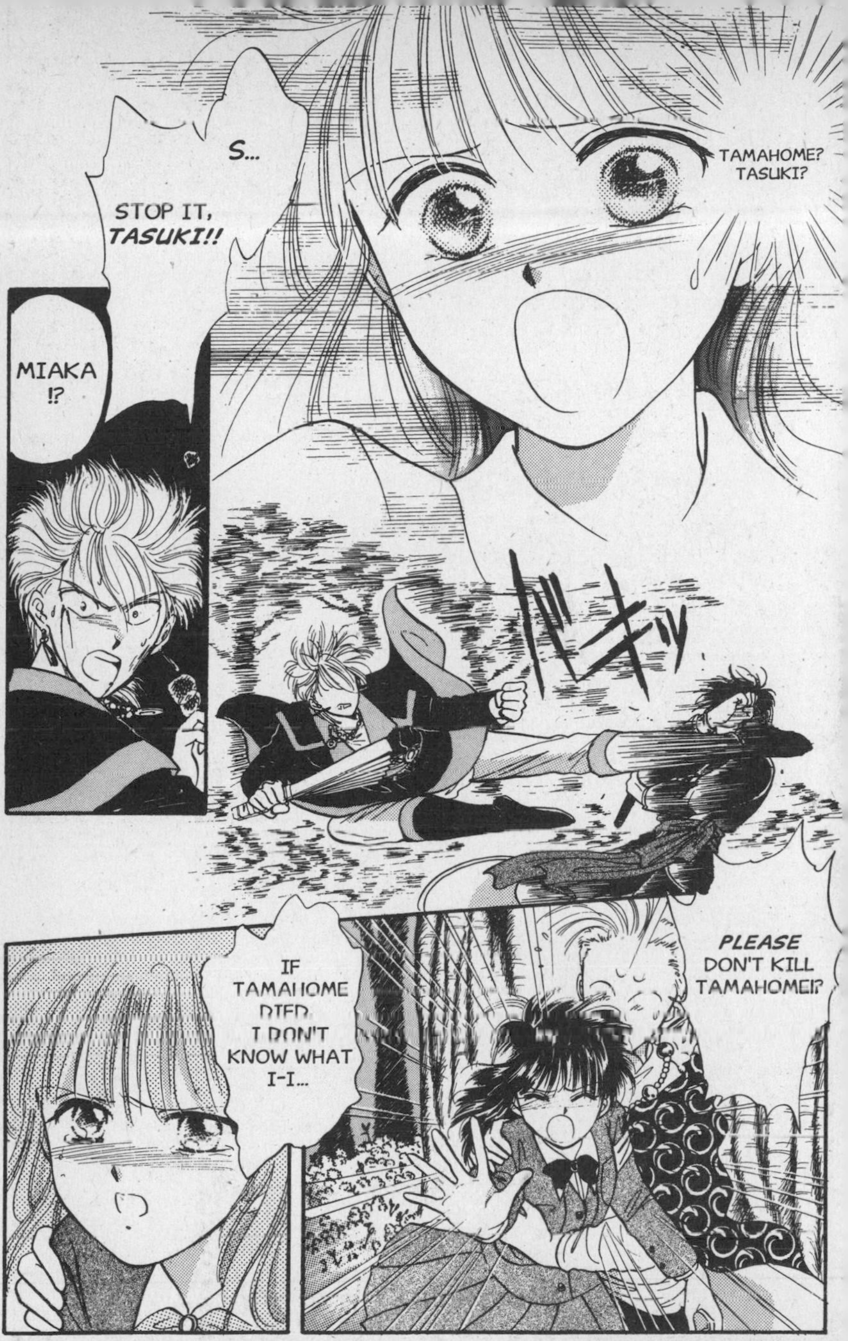
TAMAHOME? TASUKI?
S... STOP IT, TASUKI!!
MIAKA !?
ガキッ
PLEASE DON'T KILL TAMAHOME!?
IF TAMAHOME DIED, I DON'T KNOW WHAT I-I...

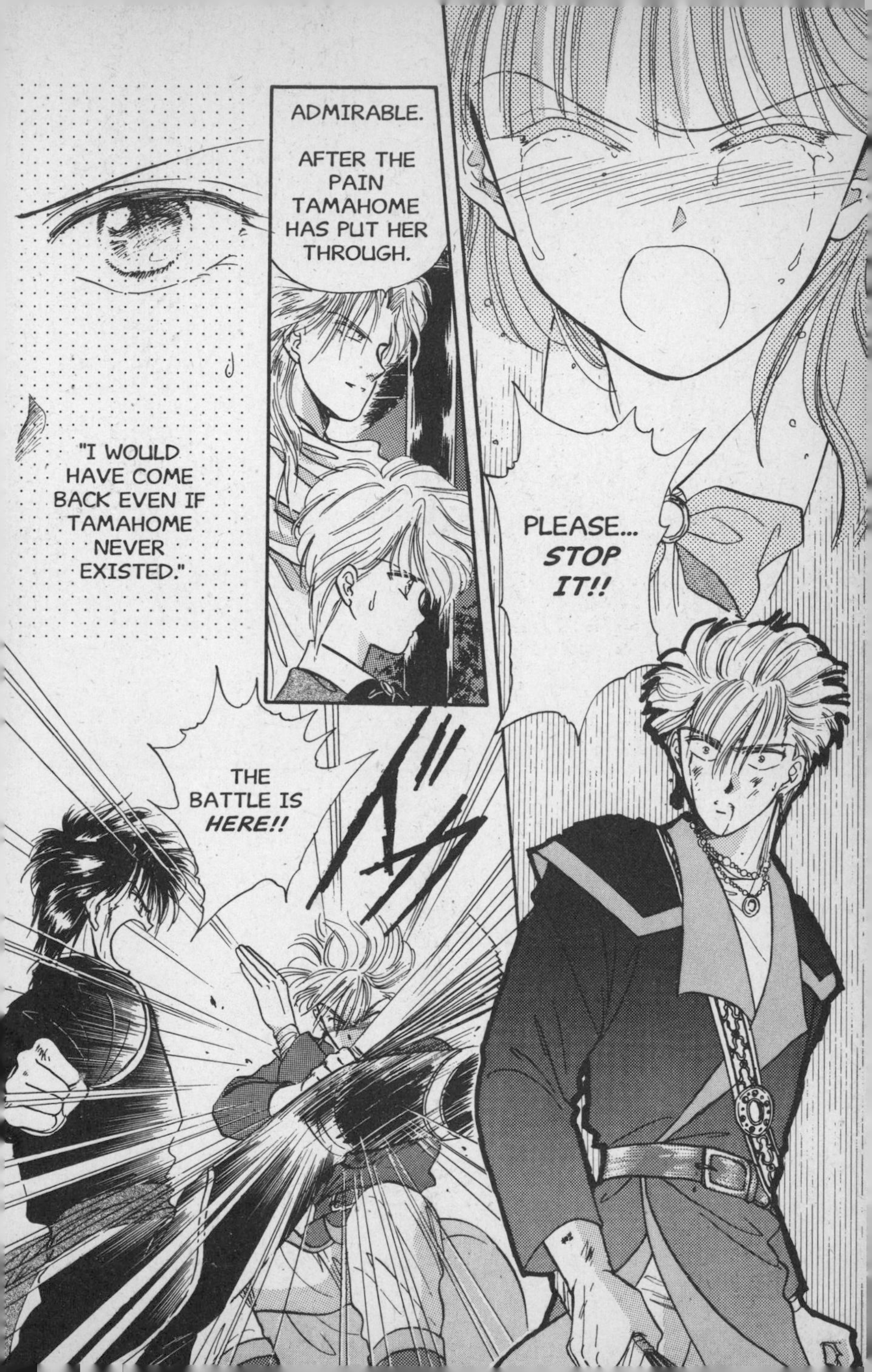
PLEASE... *STOP IT!!*
ADMIRABLE.
AFTER THE PAIN TAMAHOME HAS PUT HER THROUGH.
"I WOULD HAVE COME BACK EVEN IF TAMAHOME NEVER EXISTED."
THE BATTLE IS *HERE!!*

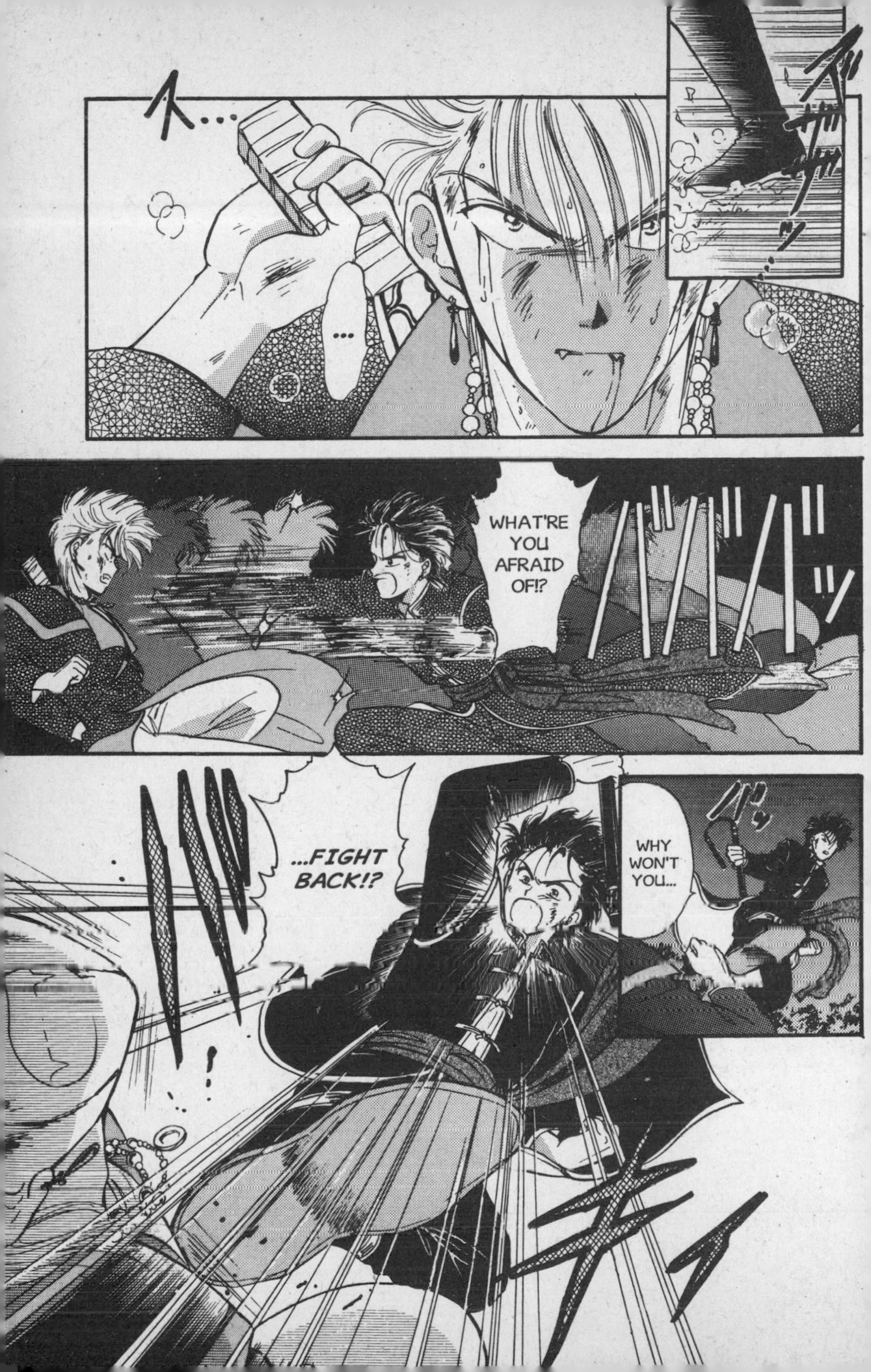
...
WHAT'RE YOU AFRAID OF!?
WHY WON'T YOU...
...FIGHT BACK!?

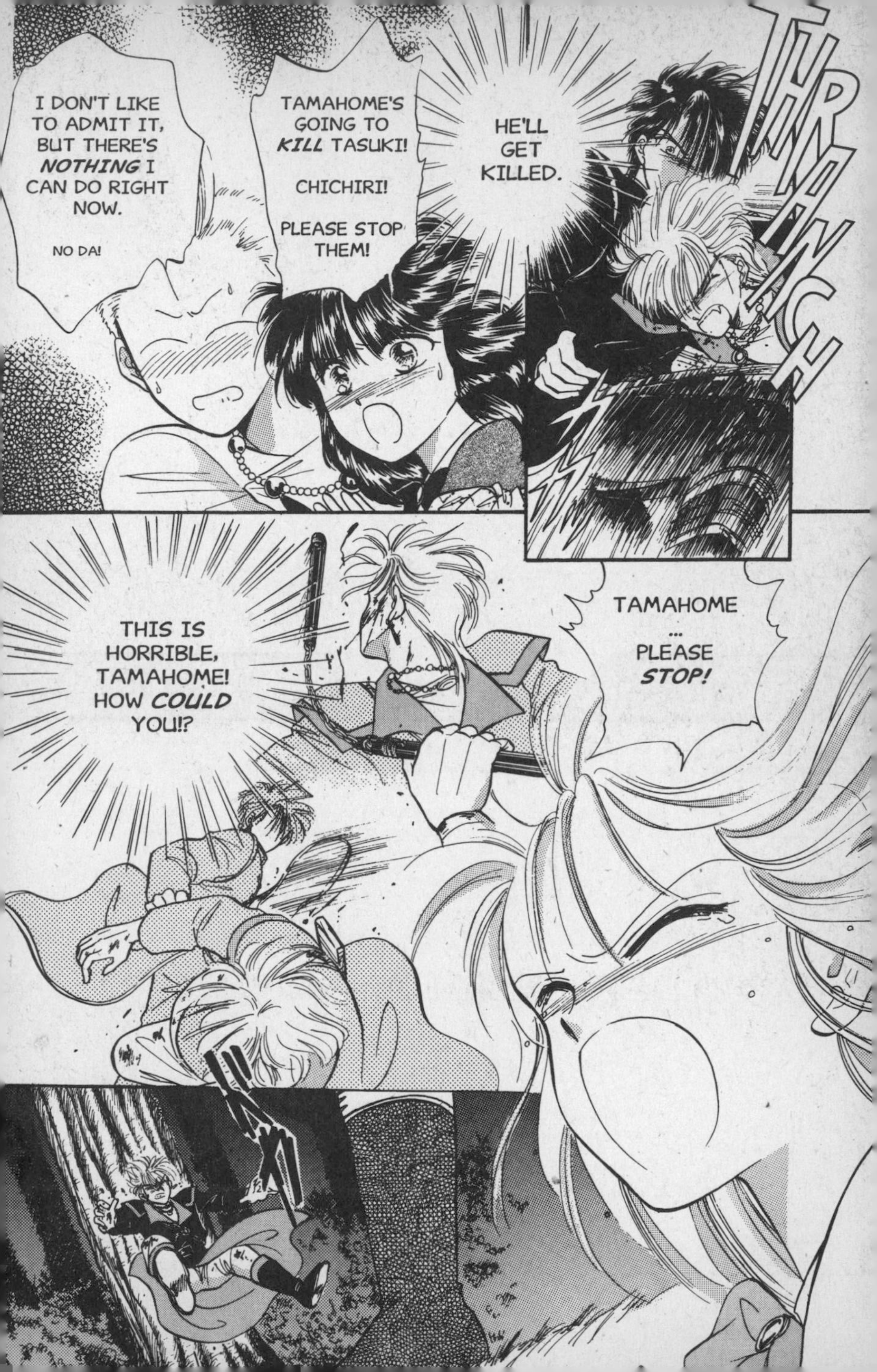
THRANCH
HE'LL GET KILLED.
TAMAHOME'S GOING TO KILL TASUKI!
CHICHIRI!
PLEASE STOP THEM!
I DON'T LIKE TO ADMIT IT, BUT THERE'S NOTHING I CAN DO RIGHT NOW.
NO DA!
TAMAHOME ... PLEASE STOP!
THIS IS HORRIBLE, TAMAHOME! HOW COULD YOU!?

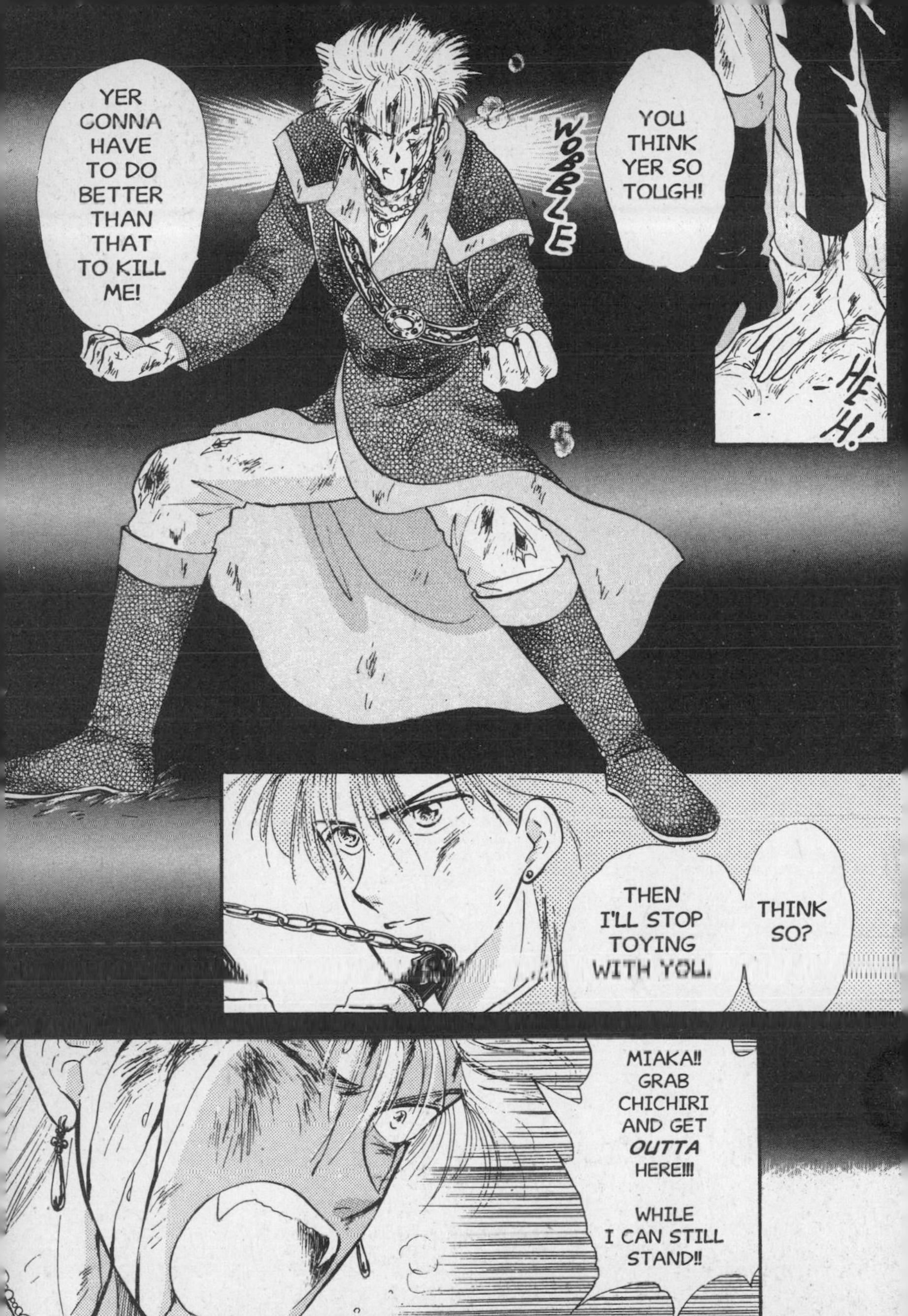
HEH!
YOU THINK YER SO TOUGH!
WOBBLE
YER GONNA HAVE TO DO BETTER THAN THAT TO KILL ME!
THINK SO?
THEN I'LL STOP TOYING WITH YOU.
MIAKA!! GRAB CHICHIRI AND GET *OUTTA* HERE!!!
WHILE I CAN STILL STAND!!

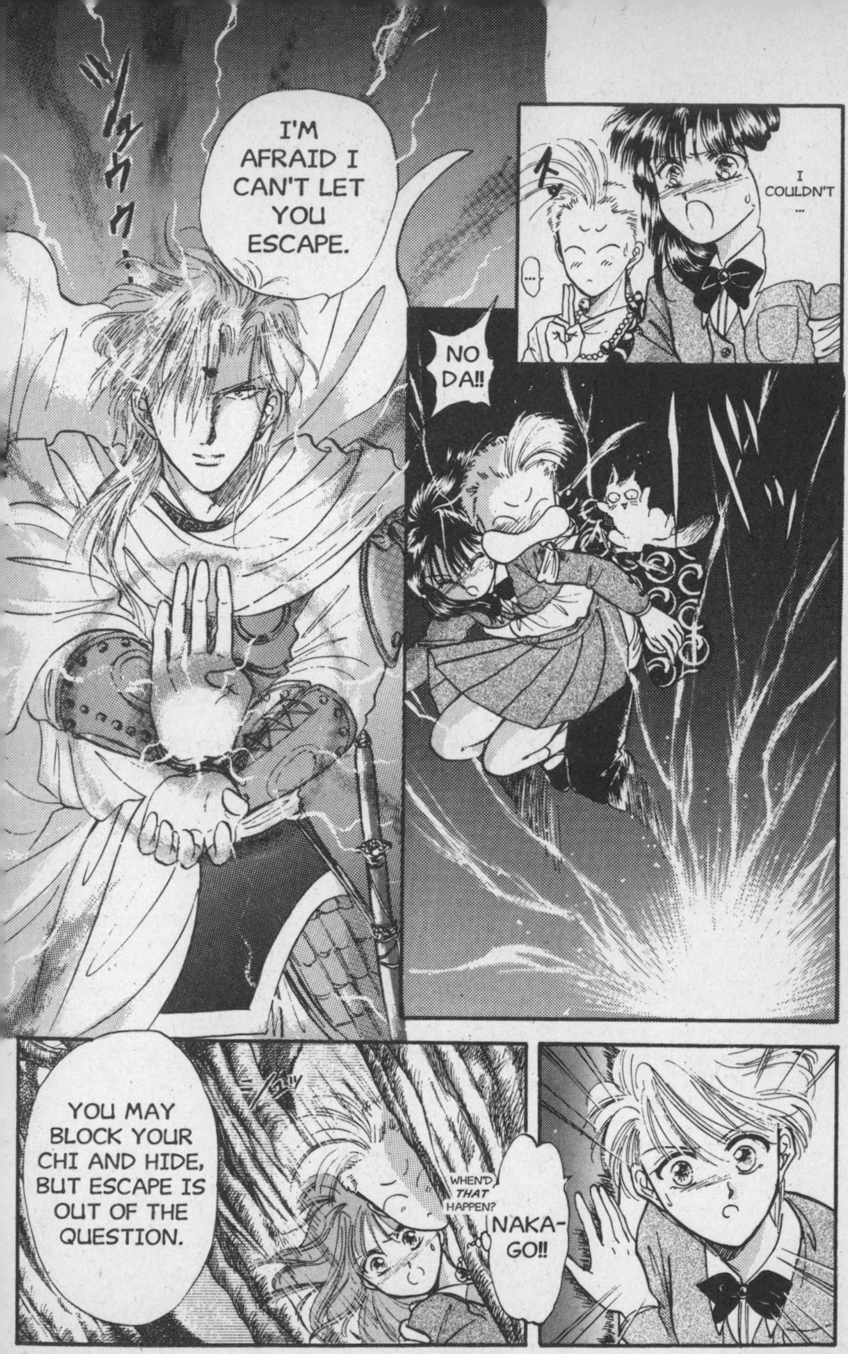
I COULDN'T ...
...
NO DA!!
I'M AFRAID I CAN'T LET YOU ESCAPE.
WHEN'D *THAT* HAPPEN?
NAKA-GO!!
YOU MAY BLOCK YOUR CHI AND HIDE, BUT ESCAPE IS OUT OF THE QUESTION.

Now that Tamahome's become an enemy, I've been getting mad mail and sad mail. But it's not Tamahome's fault!! Diedu isn't your work-a-day potion! Even Hotohori or Chichiri would have ended up the same if they took it. Bwa ha ha! Perhaps Watase enjoys putting her characters through hell! But if I do, it's out of love. Really! So when I get mail from people who say they hate Tamahome or Miaka, it makes me sad. (Honestly!) And when people say they like all my characters, it makes me happiest of all. (There's been a lot of those recently! ♥) I want to hug those readers. Right now everybody's against Nakago, but I love him! He's so fun to draw. I love Yui, too. Sometimes I hear from readers who have dreams with characters like Miaka in them, but I'd never had one. I had mine for the first time recently, but the character was Nakago!! He was wearing sunglasses and a uniform. I also get occasional mail from male readers who say they're embarrassed about reading "Fushigi Yûgi." Don't get so stressed! I have a lot of male readers: late grade school students, guys in junior high, high school students, college students, and business men! So don't worry. Guys' opinions tend to be more level-headed and less emotional than those of my female readers, so I love those letters. Although right now I'm busy with "Fushigi Yûgi" and the special "Prepubescence" story, for the past year I've been getting ideas for short stories. (I haven't had enough material to compile into a graphic novel.) So now I'm all jazzed up to put out a short story graphic novel! A CD book should be out this summer so look for it. A drama disk is also in the works. Oh! My hot bath is getting cold waiting for me. I'll see you all in volume 6.

Farewell!

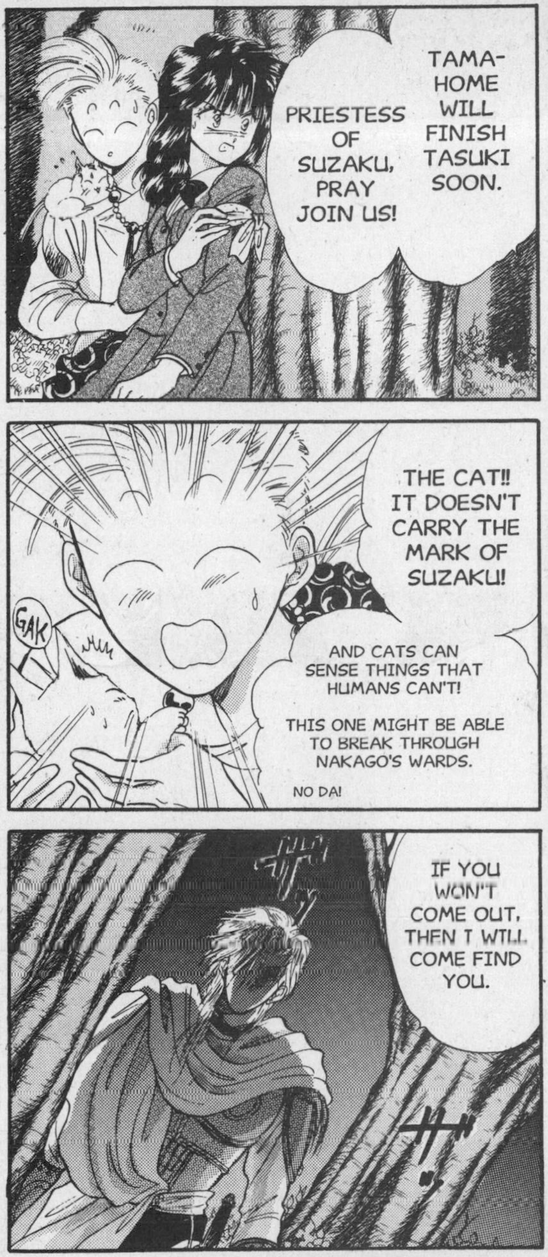
TAMA-HOME WILL FINISH TASUKI SOON.
PRIESTESS OF SUZAKU, PRAY JOIN US!
THE CAT!! IT DOESN'T CARRY THE MARK OF SUZAKU!
GAK
AND CATS CAN SENSE THINGS THAT HUMANS CAN'T!
THIS ONE MIGHT BE ABLE TO BREAK THROUGH NAKAGO'S WARDS.
NO DA!
IF YOU WON'T COME OUT, THEN I WILL COME FIND YOU.

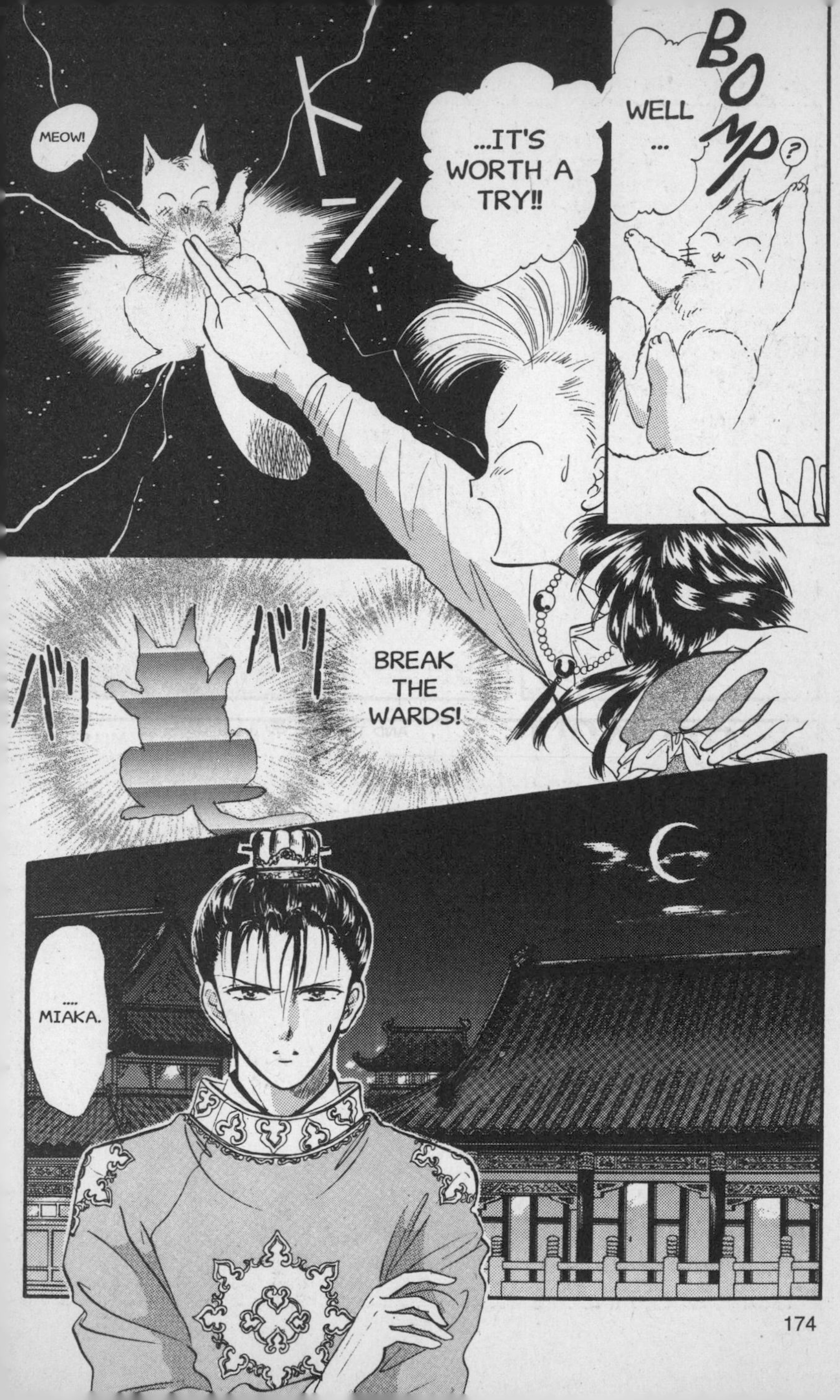
WELL ...
BOMP
?
...IT'S WORTH A TRY!!
MEOW!
BREAK THE WARDS!
バリ
バリ
.... MIAKA.

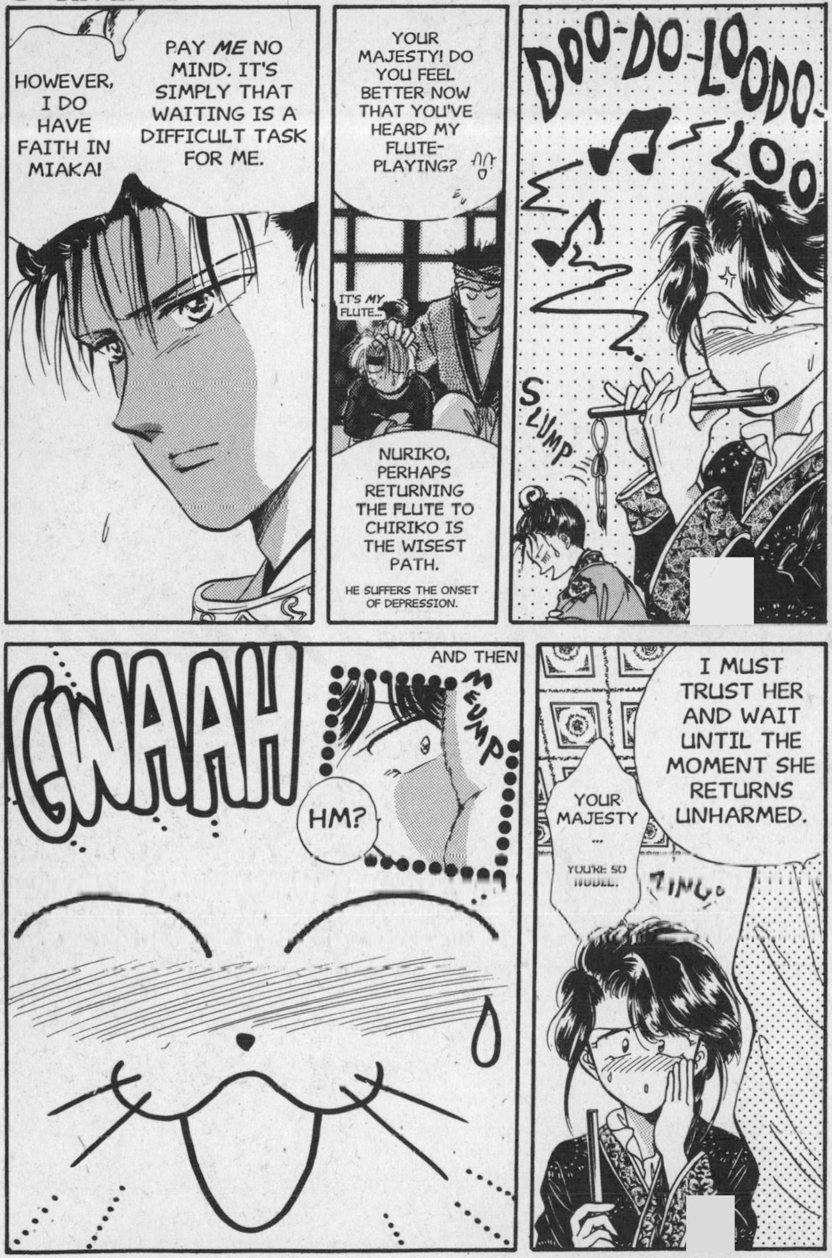
DOO-DO-LOODO-LOO
SLUMP
YOUR MAJESTY! DO YOU FEEL BETTER NOW THAT YOU'VE HEARD MY FLUTE-PLAYING?
IT'S MY FLUTE...
NURIKO, PERHAPS RETURNING THE FLUTE TO CHIRIKO IS THE WISEST PATH.
HE SUFFERS THE ONSET OF DEPRESSION.
PAY *ME* NO MIND. IT'S SIMPLY THAT WAITING IS A DIFFICULT TASK FOR ME.
HOWEVER, I DO HAVE FAITH IN MIAKA!
I MUST TRUST HER AND WAIT UNTIL THE MOMENT SHE RETURNS UNHARMED.
YOUR MAJESTY ...
YOU'RE SO NOBLE.
AND THEN
MEUMP
HM?
GNAAH

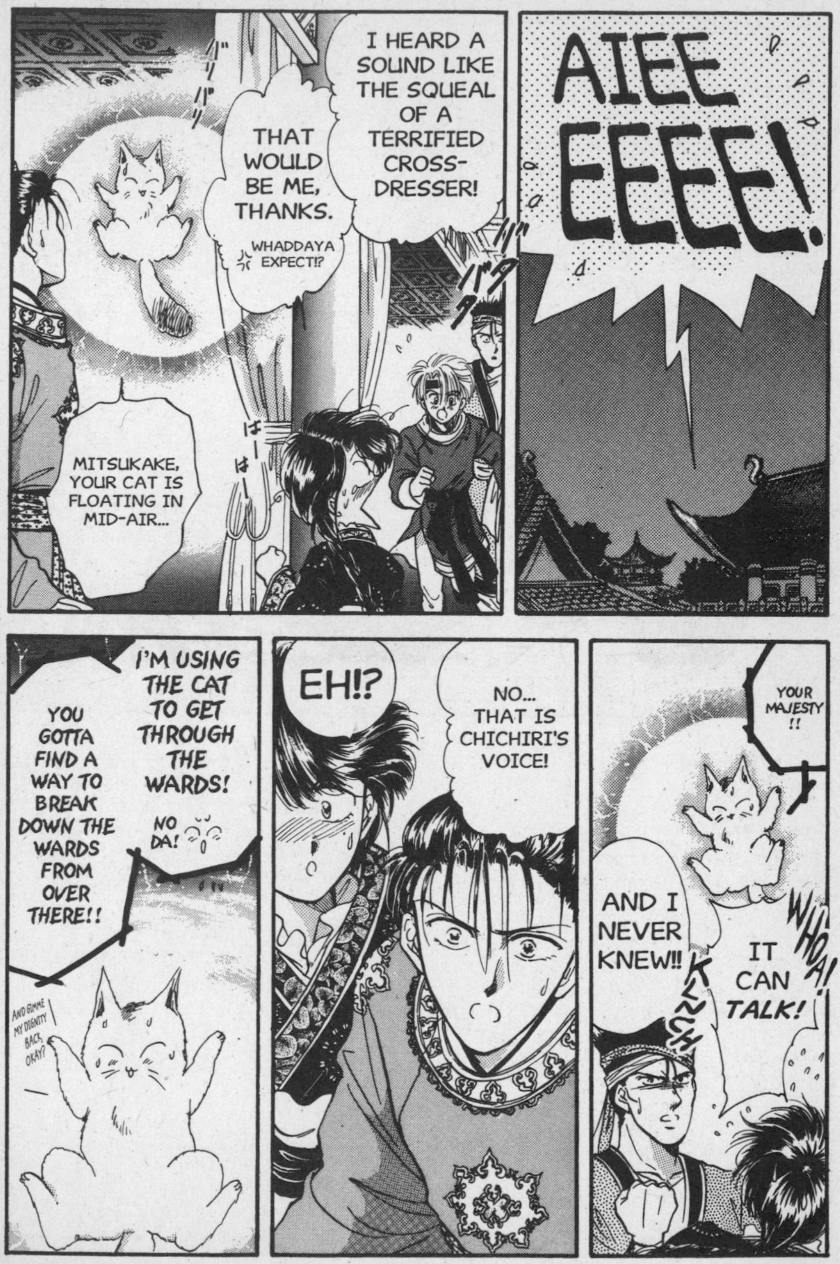
AIEE EEEEE!
I HEARD A SOUND LIKE THE SQUEAL OF A TERRIFIED CROSS-DRESSER!
THAT WOULD BE ME, THANKS.
WHADDAYA EXPECT!?
MITSUKAKE, YOUR CAT IS FLOATING IN MID-AIR...
YOUR MAJESTY!!
WHOA!
IT CAN TALK!
AND I NEVER KNEW!!
KLUNCH
NO... THAT IS CHICHIRI'S VOICE!
EH!?
I'M USING THE CAT TO GET THROUGH THE WARDS!
YOU GOTTA FIND A WAY TO BREAK DOWN THE WARDS FROM OVER THERE!!
NO DA!
AND GIMME MY DIGNITY BACK, OKAY?

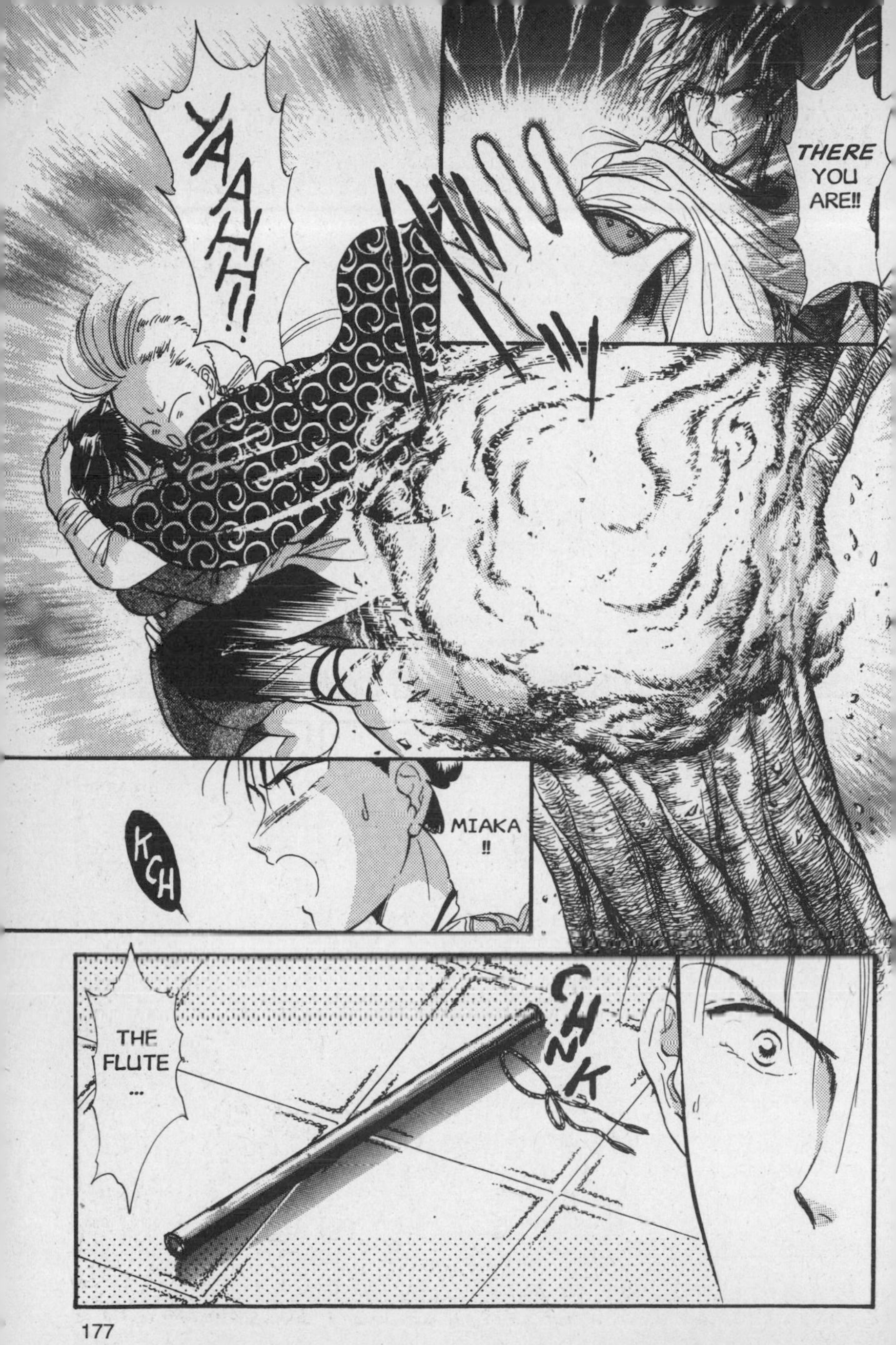
THERE YOU ARE!!
YAAHH!!
MIAKA !!
KCH
CHNK
THE FLUTE ...

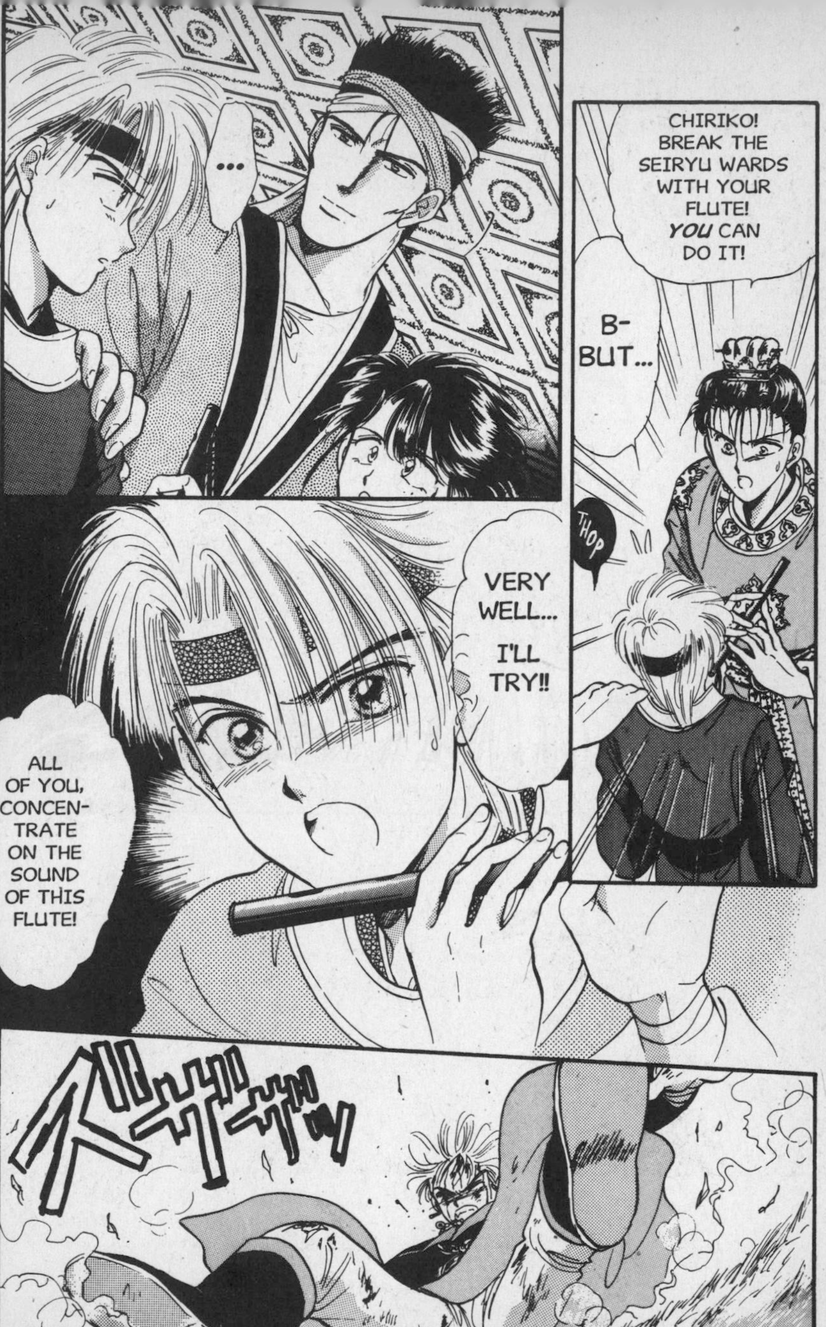
CHIRIKO! BREAK THE SEIRYU WARDS WITH YOUR FLUTE! *YOU* CAN DO IT!
B- BUT...
THOP
...
VERY WELL...
I'LL TRY!!
ALL OF YOU, CONCENTRATE ON THE SOUND OF THIS FLUTE!

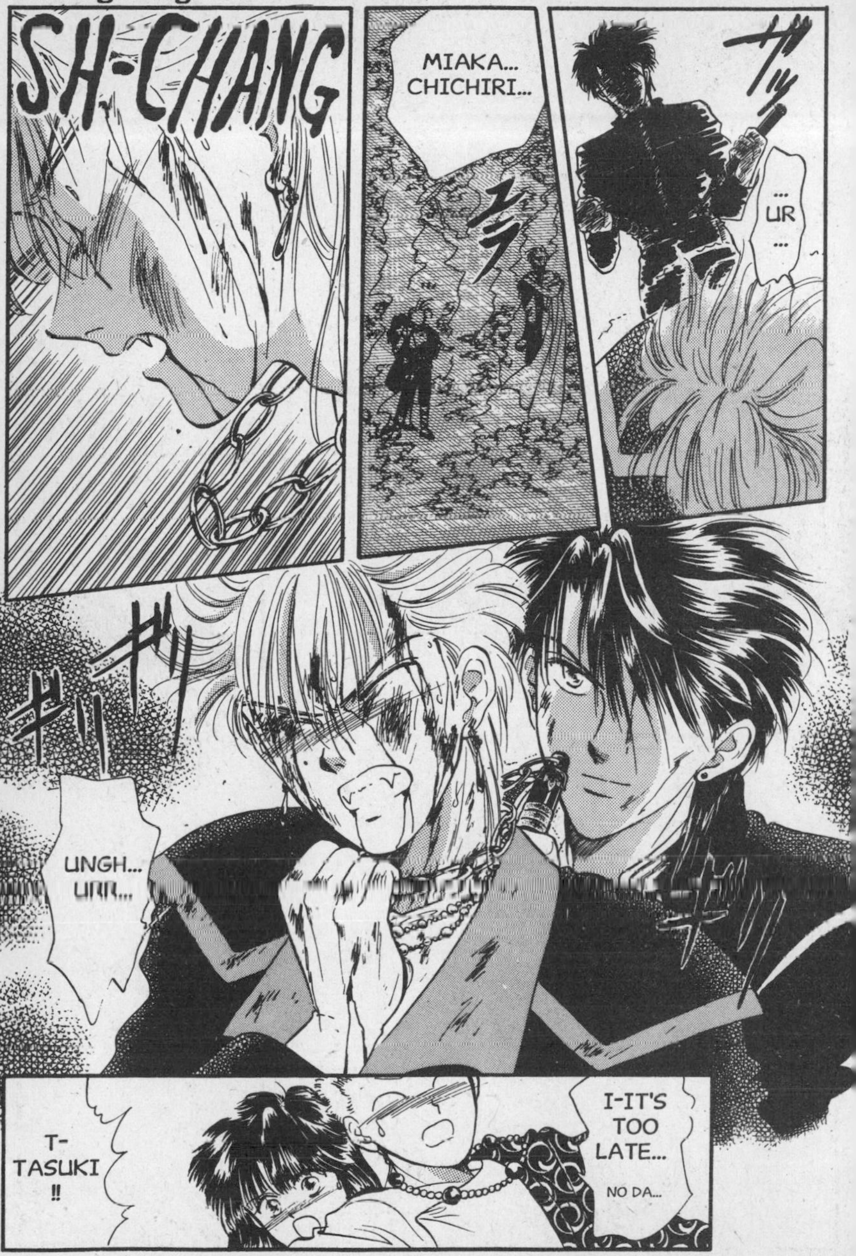
...UR...
MIAKA... CHICHIRI...
SH-CHANG
UNGH... URR...
I-IT'S TOO LATE...
NO DA...
T-TASUKI!!

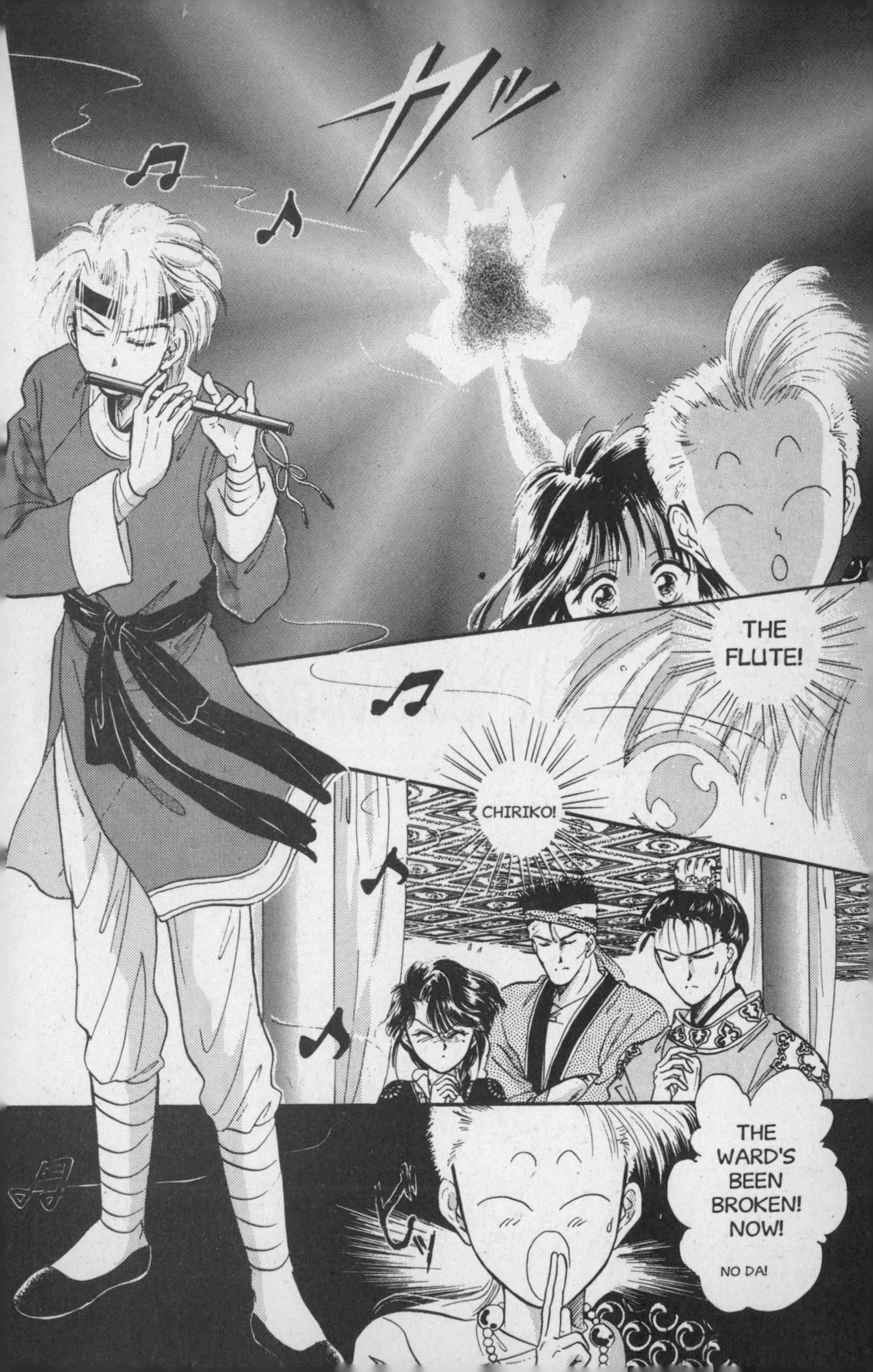
THE FLUTE!
CHIRIKO!
THE WARD'S BEEN BROKEN! NOW!
NO DA!

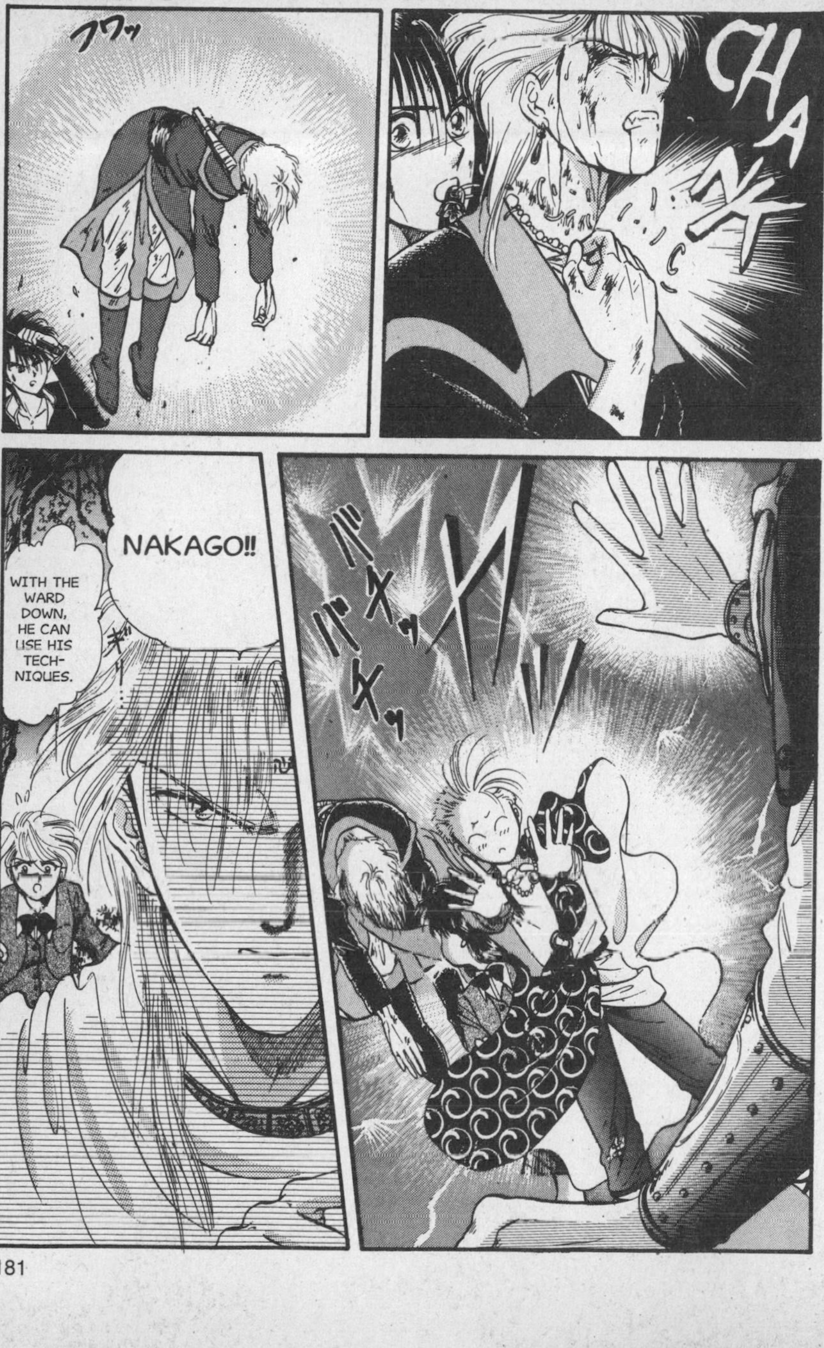
CHANK
フワッ
バタッ
バタッ
NAKAGO!!
WITH THE WARD DOWN, HE CAN USE HIS TECHNIQUES.

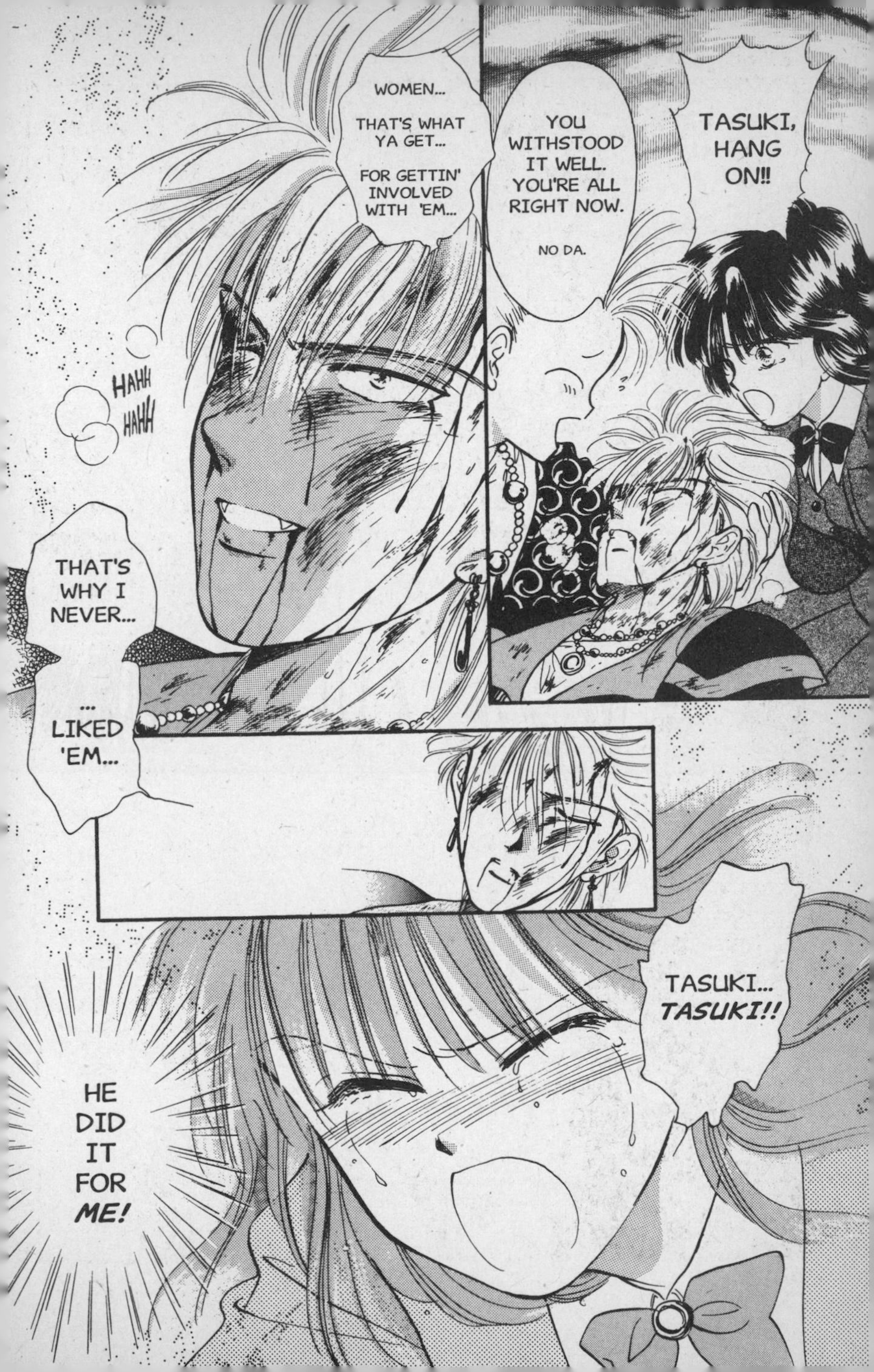
TASUKI, HANG ON!!
YOU WITHSTOOD IT WELL. YOU'RE ALL RIGHT NOW. NO DA.
WOMEN... THAT'S WHAT YA GET... FOR GETTIN' INVOLVED WITH 'EM...
HAHH HAHH
THAT'S WHY I NEVER...
... LIKED 'EM...
TASUKI... *TASUKI!!*
HE DID IT FOR *ME!*

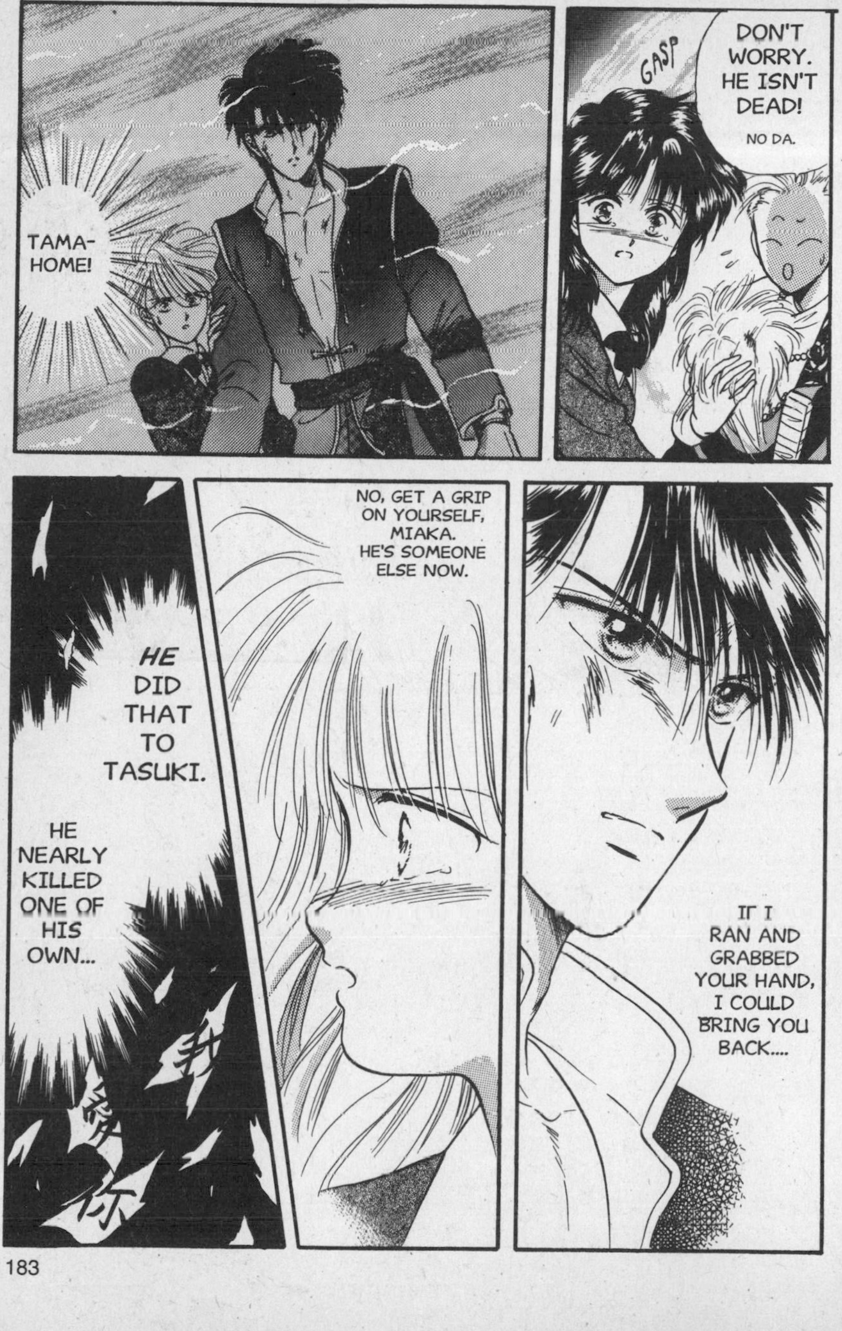
GASP
DON'T WORRY. HE ISN'T DEAD!
NO DA.
TAMA-HOME!
IF I RAN AND GRABBED YOUR HAND, I COULD BRING YOU BACK....
NO, GET A GRIP ON YOURSELF, MIAKA. HE'S SOMEONE ELSE NOW.
HE DID THAT TO TASUKI.
HE NEARLY KILLED ONE OF HIS OWN...

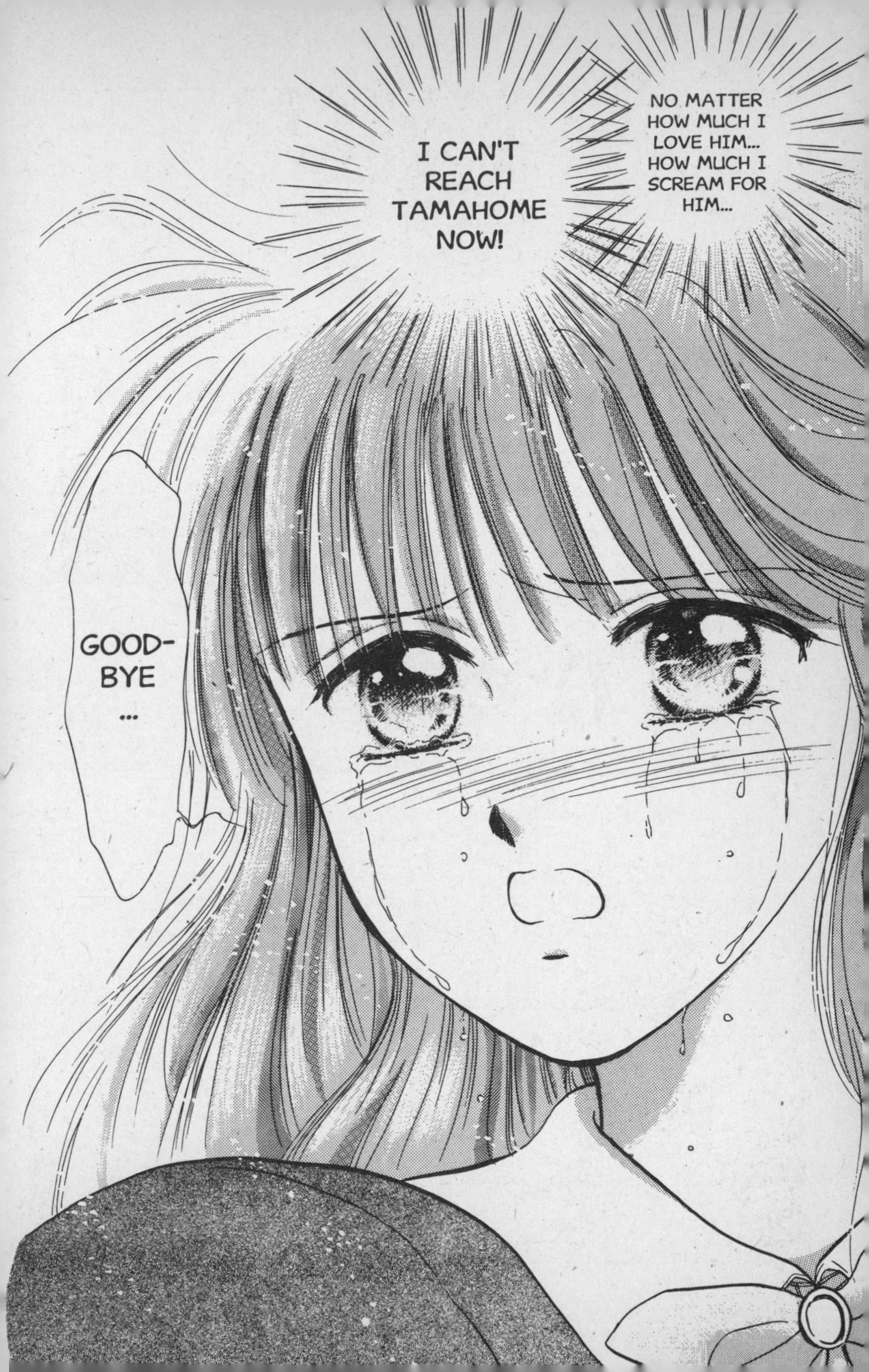
NO MATTER HOW MUCH I LOVE HIM... HOW MUCH I SCREAM FOR HIM...
I CAN'T REACH TAMAHOME NOW!
GOOD-BYE ...

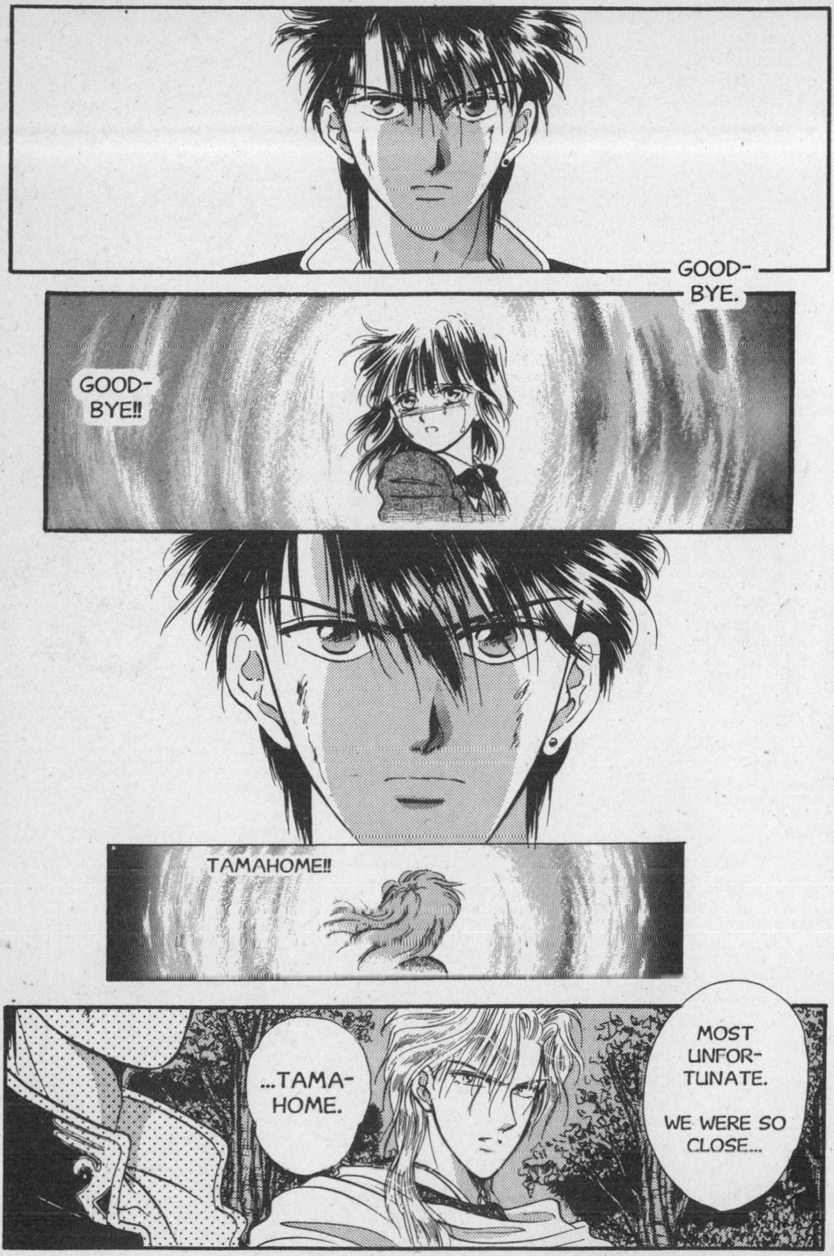
GOOD-BYE.
GOOD-BYE!!
TAMAHOME!!
MOST UNFOR-TUNATE.
WE WERE SO CLOSE...
...TAMA-HOME.

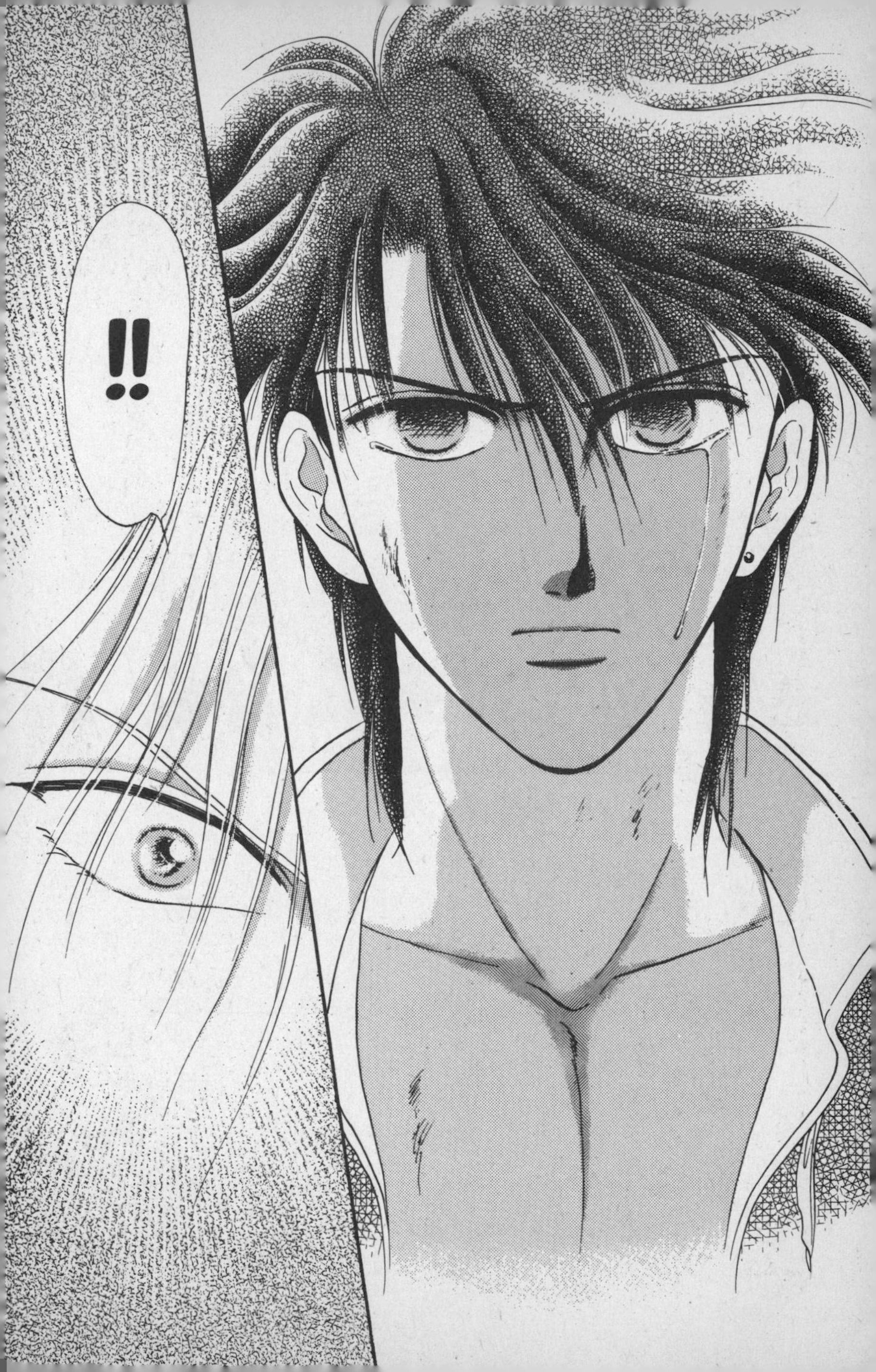
!!

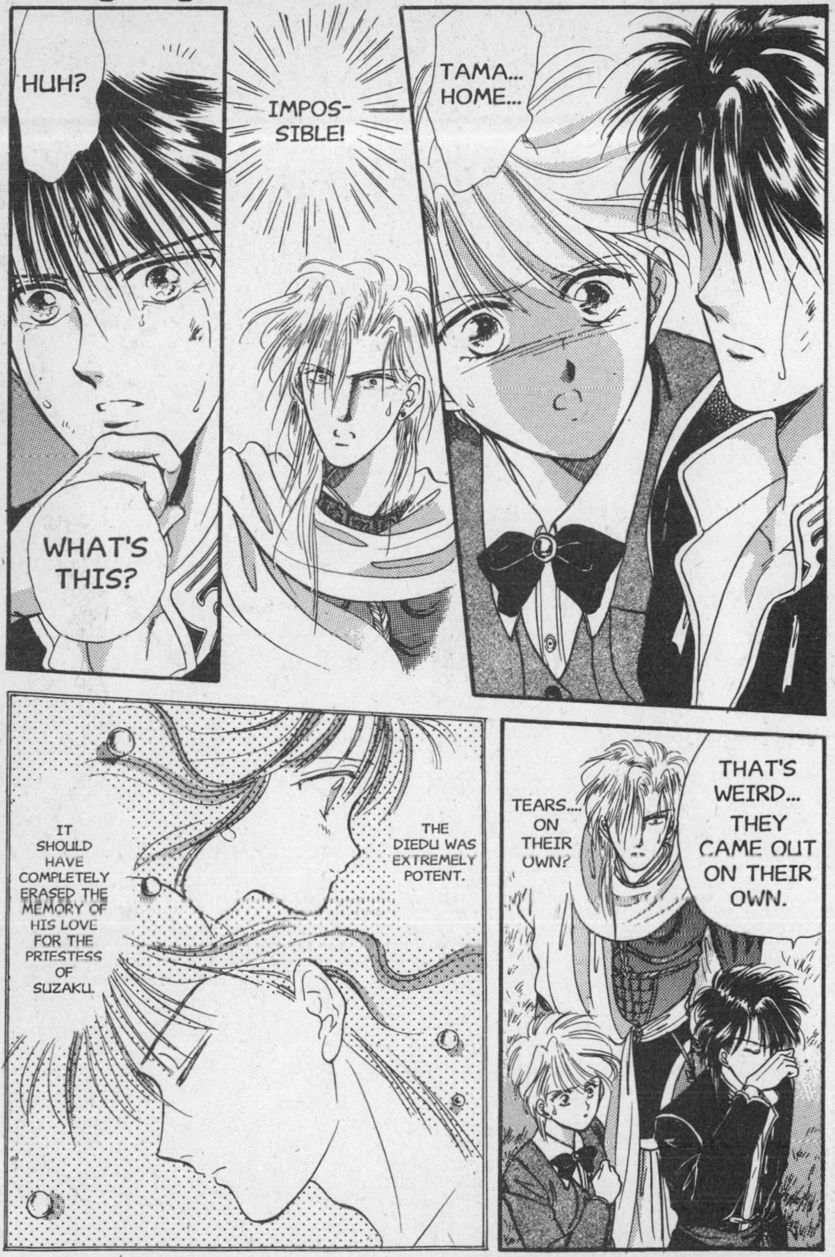
TAMA... HOME...
IMPOSSIBLE!
HUH?
WHAT'S THIS?
THAT'S WEIRD... THEY CAME OUT ON THEIR OWN.
TEARS.... ON THEIR OWN?
THE DIEDU WAS EXTREMELY POTENT.
IT SHOULD HAVE COMPLETELY ERASED THE MEMORY OF HIS LOVE FOR THE PRIESTESS OF SUZAKU.

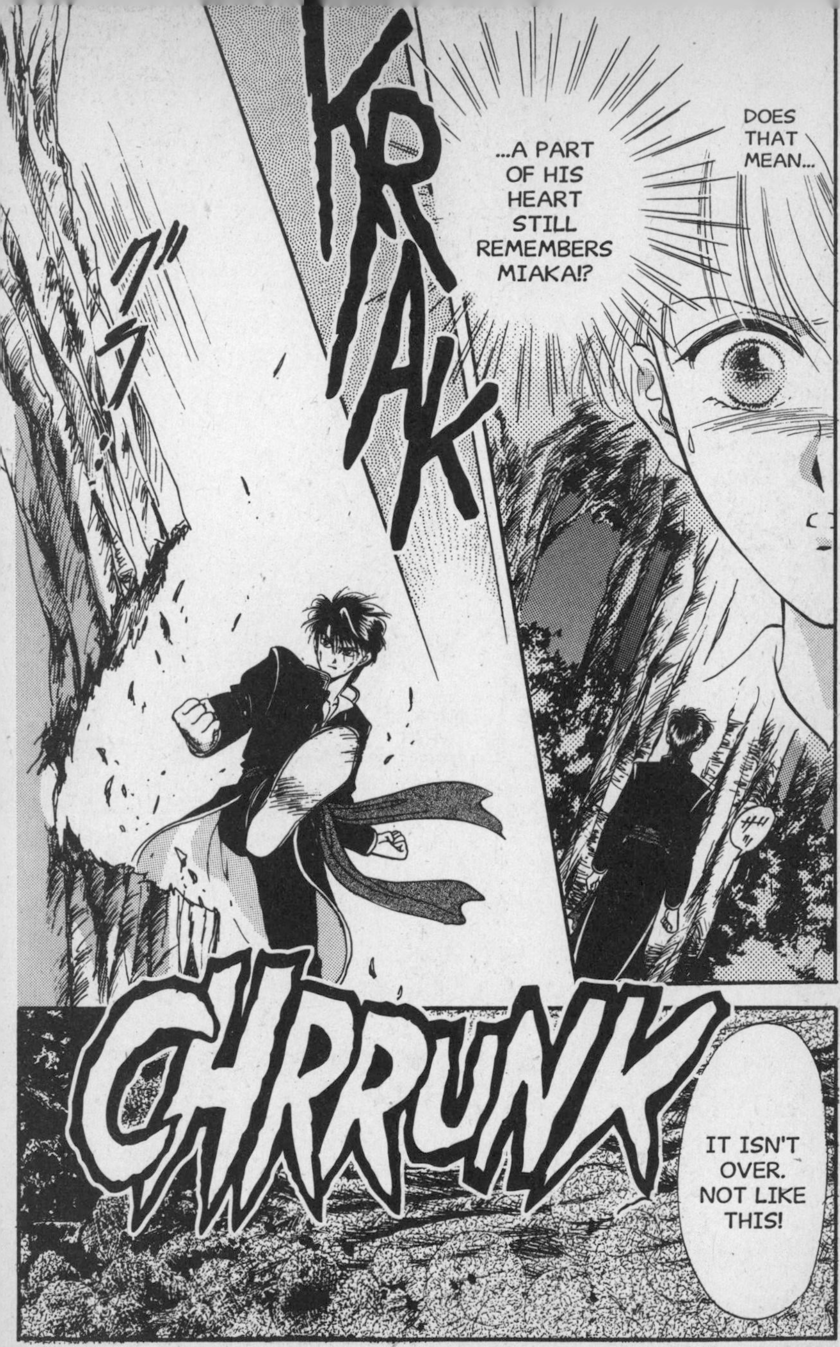
DOES THAT MEAN...
...A PART OF HIS HEART STILL REMEMBERS MIAKA!?
KRAK
CHRRUNK
IT ISN'T OVER. NOT LIKE THIS!

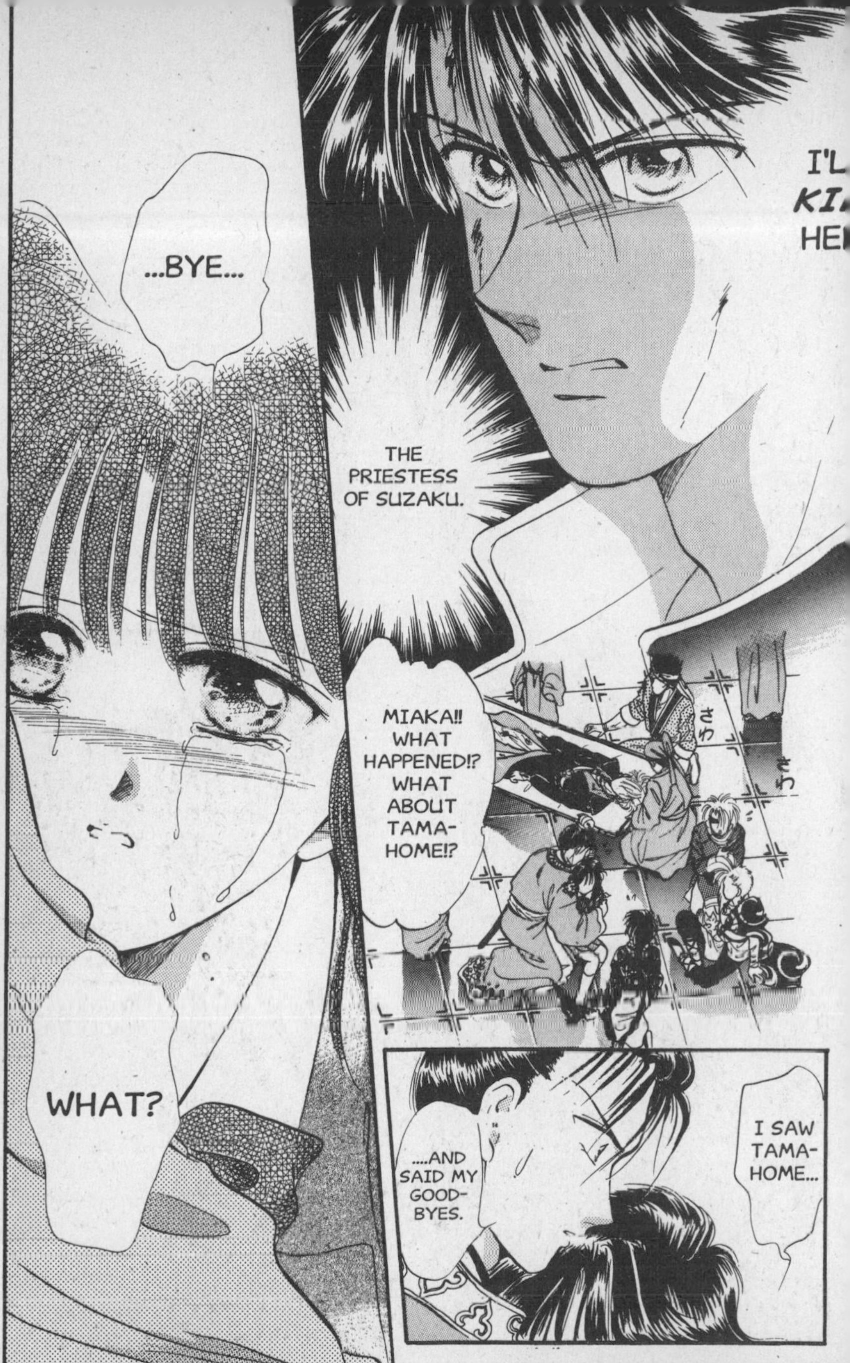
THE PRIESTESS OF SUZAKU.
MIAKA!! WHAT HAPPENED!? WHAT ABOUT TAMA-HOME!?
さわ
さわ
I SAW TAMA-HOME...
....AND SAID MY GOOD-BYES.
...BYE...
WHAT?

TO BE CONTINUED IN VOLUME 6: SUMMONER

ABOUT THE AUTHOR

Yuu Watase was born on March 5 in a town near Osaka,
Japan, and she was raised there before moving to Tokyo
to follow her dream of creating manga. In the decade
since her debut short story, *PAJAMA DE OJAMA* ("An
Intrusion in Pajamas"), she has produced more than 50
compiled volumes of short stories and continuing series.
Her latest series, *ZETTAI KARESHI* ("Absolute Boyfriend"), is
currently running in the anthology magazine *SHŌJO COMIC*
and *SHOJO BEAT magazine*. Watase's long-running
horror/romance story *CERES: CELESTIAL LEGEND* and her most
recent completed series, *ALICE 19TH*, are now available in
North America published by VIZ Media. She loves science
fiction, fantasy and comedy.

The Fushigi Yûgi Guide to Sound Effects

Most of the sound effects in FUSHIGI YÜGI are the way Yû Watase created them, in their original Japanese.

We created this glossary for a page-by-page, panel-by-panel explanation of the action and background noises. By using this guide, you may even learn some Japanese.

The glossary lists page and panel number. For example, page 1, panel 3, would be listed as 1.3.

28.2 FX:Pita (frozen in mid-air)
28.5 FX:Bashi bashi (thwack thwack)

30.2 FX:Putsu... (snap...)
30.4 FX:Yura (wobble)

31.2 FX:Za... (rustle...)
31.4 FX:Niko (grin)

32.1 FX:Fu... (faint...)

35.2 FX:Basa basa (flutter flutter)
35.3 FX:Gusha (crush)

CHAPTER TWENTY-SIX

37.1 FX:Gyu (hug)

38.2 FX:Fu... (getting drowsy)

40.2 FX:Kili (snap)

41.3 FX:Nyu (suddenly appearing)

42.1 FX:Kachi kochi (stiff)

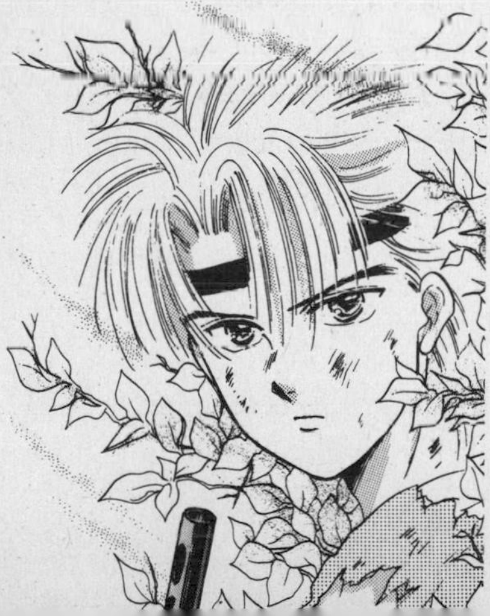

CHAPTER TWENTY-FIVE

8.3 FX:Da (dash)

10.3 FX:Ha ha (huff huff)
10.5 FX:Suu... (word appearing)
10.6 FX:Pou... (glow...)

11.1 FX:Suu... (word disappearing)
11.3 FX:Muku (getting up quickly)

13.2 FX:Jiii (stare)
13.4 FX:Ku (hm)
13.5 FX:Tata (dash)

14.1 FX:Dokin (heart stopping)

16.1 FX:Ku ku (ha ha)
16.3 FX:Zawa zawa... (rustle rustle...)
16.4 FX:Byuuu... (whoosh...)

20.5 FX:Ba (jerk)

21.1 FX:Bata bata... (running)
21.3 FX:Shako shako (brush brush)

22.1 FX:Gara gara (gargle gargle)
22.2 FX:Golon (rolling over)

24.1 FX:Basa basa (flap flap)

25.1 FX:Ga (pounce)
25.3 FX:Bata bata bata (rushed footsteps)
25.4 FX:Da (dash)

26.2 FX:Dota (thud)
26.3 FX:Ba ba (sword moving through air)
26.5 FX:Goooo (roar)

27.1 FX:Byuuuu (whoosh)
27.3 FX:Basa basa basa (flap flap)

45.3 FX:Hiku hiku (twitch twitch)
45.5 FX:Katshuun katshuun (walking)

49.3 FX:Tan (slap)
49.5 FX:Suuu… (vision becoming hazy)

51.2 FX:Hiku hiku (twitch twitch)
51.3 FX:Zuzuzu… (slink…)

53.2 FX:Doki… (jolt…)

55.2 FX:Golon (tumble)
55.4 FX:Muku (getting up)

58.2 FX:Ba (grasp)

61.3 FX:Bata bata (stomp stomp)

CHAPTER TWENTY-SEVEN

64.2 FX:Sawa sawa (hustle bustle)

65.3 FX:Goshi goshi goshi (rub rub)

66.3 FX:Ha ha (huff huff)
66.4 FX:Muku (getting up)

68.5 FX:Pan (crack)

69.1 FX:Kalan… (ka-chink…)

70.1 FX:Kacha kacha (clatter clatter)

71.6 FX:Pata pata… (pitter patter…)

72.1 FX:Gari gari (scratch scratch)
72.5 FX:Ki… (creak…)

75.2 FX:Shan (clink)

76.5 FX:Basa (flap)
76.6 FX:Ka (tonk)
76.6 FX:Suuu (swoosh)

77.1 FX:Su (slither)
77.3 FX:Suuu (swoosh)

78.2 FX:Odango (smashed together like an odango – a glutinous dessert ball)
78.6 FX:Nade nade (stroke stroke)

79.4 FX:Suta suta (stomp stomp)

80.4 FX:Gyu (squeeze)

86.5 FX:Su (standing up)

89.1 FX:Kusu kusu kusu… (giggle giggle…)
89.1 FX:Zawa zawa… (rustle rustle…)

CHAPTER TWENTY-EIGHT

92.1 FX:Zawa zawa… (chitter chatter…)
92.4 FX:Su (approaching quietly)

93.1 FX:Ba (flinging arm up)
93.3 FX:Fu (hmph)
93.4 FX:Su (raising hand)

94.6 FX:Gu (grip)

95.2 FX:Fu (fwoosh)

97.2 FX:Don (wham)

98.1 FX:Peta… (plop)

99.3 FX:Gaku (slump)

100.3 FX:Sa (rush)
100.4 FX:Ki (glare)

101.1 FX:Ha (gasp)
101.2 FX:Ba (pounce)

103.4 FX:Ha ha (pant pant)

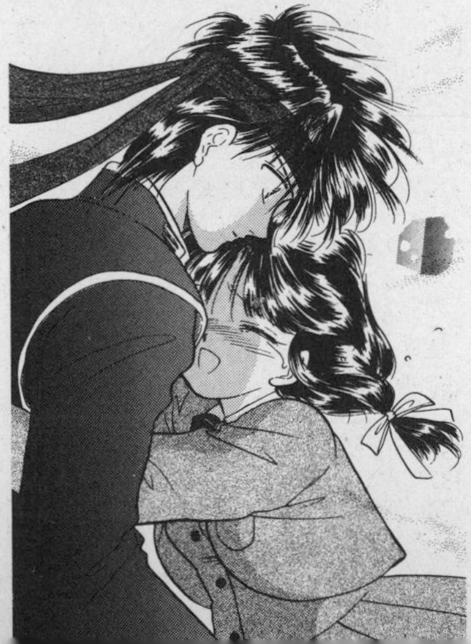

136.2 FX:Su (walking)

138.4 FX:Gui (grip)

139.5 FX:Kasa… (rustle…)

140.3 FX:Gyu (clutch)
140.4 FX:Sa (pointing suddenly)

141.1 FX:Guru guru guru (tying)

142.1 FX:Ka ka (click clack)
142.2 FX:Ka ka (click clack)
142.3 FX:Ka (click)
142.4 FX:Battari (wham)

143.6 FX:Waaan (waah)

144.1 FX:Zaza (rustle rustle)

145.3 FX:Ba (grabbing suddenly)

147.4 FX:Ba (flinch)

148.3 FX:Kasa… (holding paper out)

150.1 FX:Ku (ha)
150.2 FX:Bili (rip)

151.1 FX:Bili bili (rip rip)
151.2 FX:Pala… (flutter…)

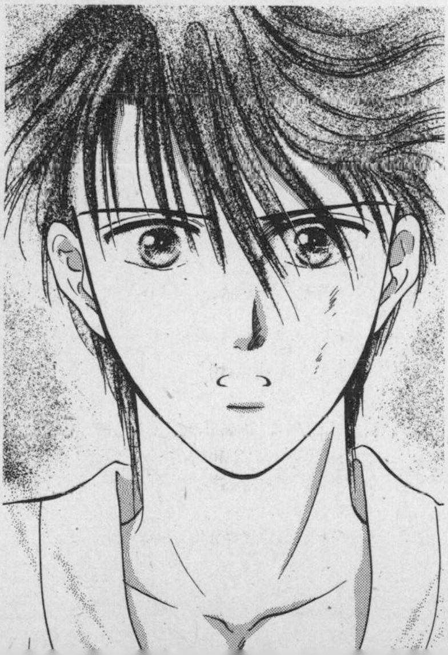

104.4 FX:Kii (creak)

105.1 FX:Patan… (door closing quietly)

106.1 FX:Katan… (sitting down)

110.4 FX:Gata (rising from chair suddenly)

111.3 FX:Ba (yank)
111.4 FX:Don… (thud)

113.4 FX:Hiiku hiiku (hiccuping)
113.5 FX:Su (moving hand)

114.1 FX:Bun (whoosh)

115.3 FX:…Pota pota (…plip plop)

116.2 FX:Bishi (ka-chink)
116.4 FX:Don… (thud…)

119.2 FX:Heta… (sitting up)

120.3 FX:Batan (bam)

CHAPTER TWENTY-NINE

123.5 FX:Zubo (pulling weapon from wall)

125.4 FX:Ka (step)

126.5 FX:Zoku (shiver)

127.1 FX:Ga (grab)

128.1 FX:Uro uro (flustered)
128.5 FX:Doka (kick)

129.1 FX:Mu (grrr)
129.2 FX:Shimi jimi (pondering)

130.1 FX:Ka ka (walking)

131.1 FX:Ki… (creak…)
131.4 FX:Su (raising hand quickly)

132.2 FX:Hiku (shock)

133.1 FX:Puha (gasp)
133.2 FX:Dolon (poof)
133.4 FX:Ka ka (click clack)

172.3 FX:Shuu… (energy ball building)
172.5 FX:Shu (hiding)

173.3 FX:Za za (walking)

174.2 FX:Don (tap)
174.3 FX:Bali bali (crackle crackle)

176.2 FX:Bata bata (stomp stomp)
176.2 FX:Bari bari (crackle crackle)
176.2 FX:Haa haa (huff huff)

177.1 FX:Ba (unleashing energy ball)
177.4 FX:Ha (gasp)

178.4 FX:Zuzaza (skid)

179.1 FX:Za (standing firm)
179.2 FX:Yura (vision blurring)
179.4 FX:Giri giri giri (tug)

180.1 FX:Ka (flash)
180.4 FX:Bi (striking a pose)

181.3 FX:Ka (flash)
181.3 FX:Bachi bachi (crackle crackle)
181.4 FX:Giri… (gnashing of teeth)

185.4 FX:Suuu (disappearing)

188.1 FX:Za (walking)

189.1 FX:Zawa zawa (shuffle shuffle)

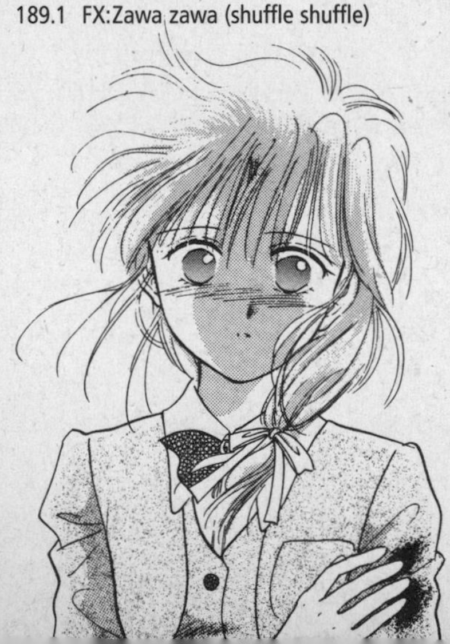

153.3 FX:Byu (whoosh)

154.3 FX:Suto (thud)
154.4 FX:Tsuu… (drip…)

155.4 FX:Bin (snap)

156.4 FX:Za (step)
156.4 FX:Ha (gasp)

157.1 FX:Zawa zawa (rustle rustle)

159.1 FX:Ku (hmph)

CHAPTER THIRTY

161.1 FX:Zawa zawa (rustle rustle)

162.2 FX:Pan (pounce)
162.3 FX:Pashi (tonk)
162.4 FX:Byu (whoosh)
162.5 FX:Bun (swoosh)

163.1 FX:Doka (whack)
163.2 FX:Pan (thwak)

164.2 FX:Doka (bam)
164.3 FX:Dokoo (wham)
164.4 FX:Zuzu… (slide)

165.1 FX:Su (swish)
165.4 FX:Shu shu shu shu shu (slish slash)
165.5 FX:Bi (rip)

166.5 FX:Ba bishi do (biff bang boom)

167.1 FX:Baki (thwack)

168.4 FX:Doka (kick)

169.1 FX:Zuzaza… (digging feet into ground)
169.2 FX:Su… (swish)
169.3 FX:Bababa (punch)
169.4 FX:Ba (pounce)
169.5 FX:Bakii (bam)

170.4 FX:Doka (thud)

171.1 FX:Zulu… (drag)

172.1 FX:Su (raising arm)
172.2 FX:Ba (energy ball strike)

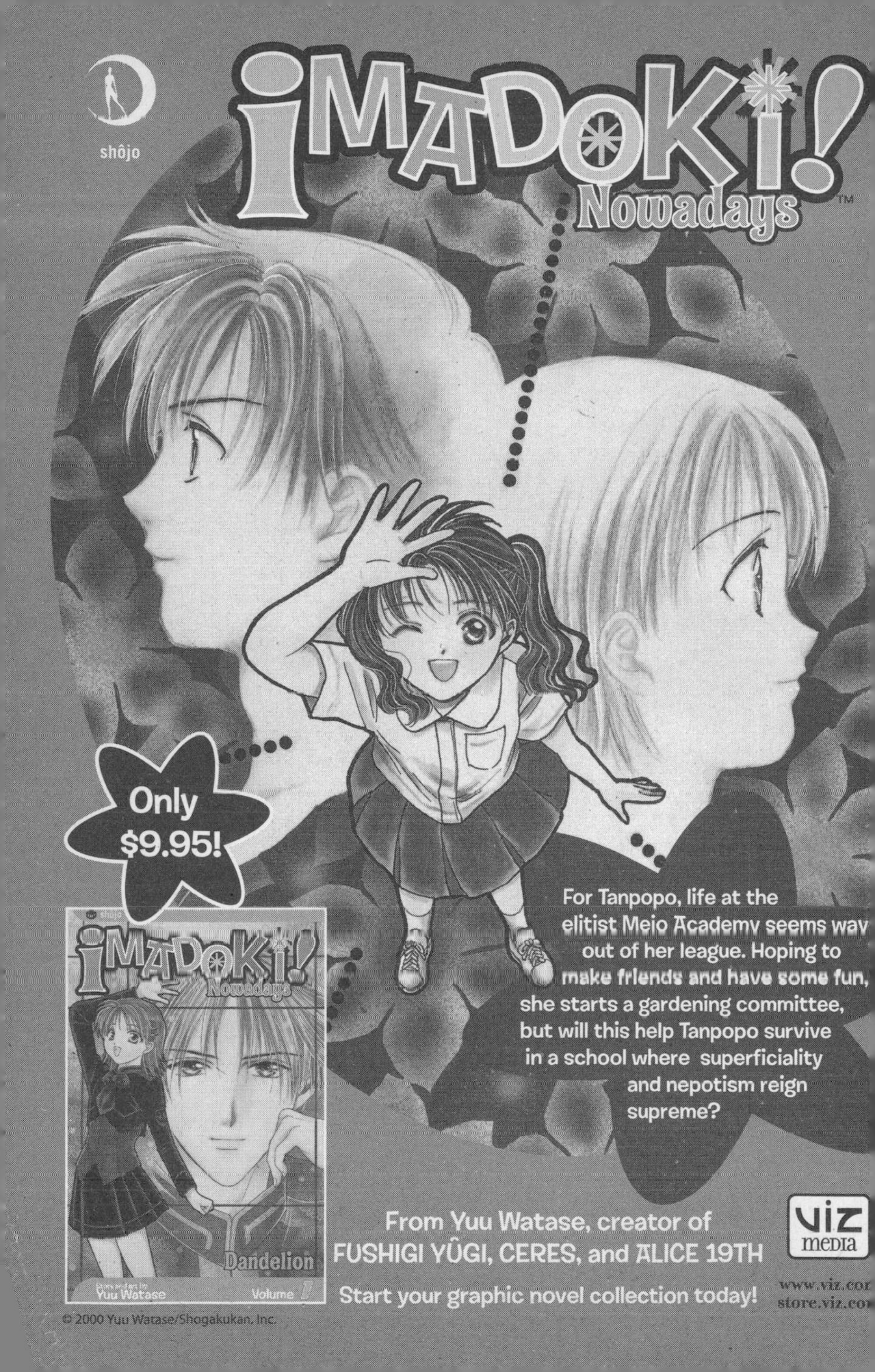
shôjo
iMADOKi!
Nowadays™
Only $9.95!
For Tanpopo, life at the elitist Meio Academy seems way out of her league. Hoping to make friends and have some fun, she starts a gardening committee, but will this help Tanpopo survive in a school where superficiality and nepotism reign supreme?
From Yuu Watase, creator of FUSHIGI YŪGI, CERES, and ALICE 19TH
Start your graphic novel collection today!
viz media
www.viz.com
store.viz.com
© 2000 Yuu Watase/Shogakukan, Inc.

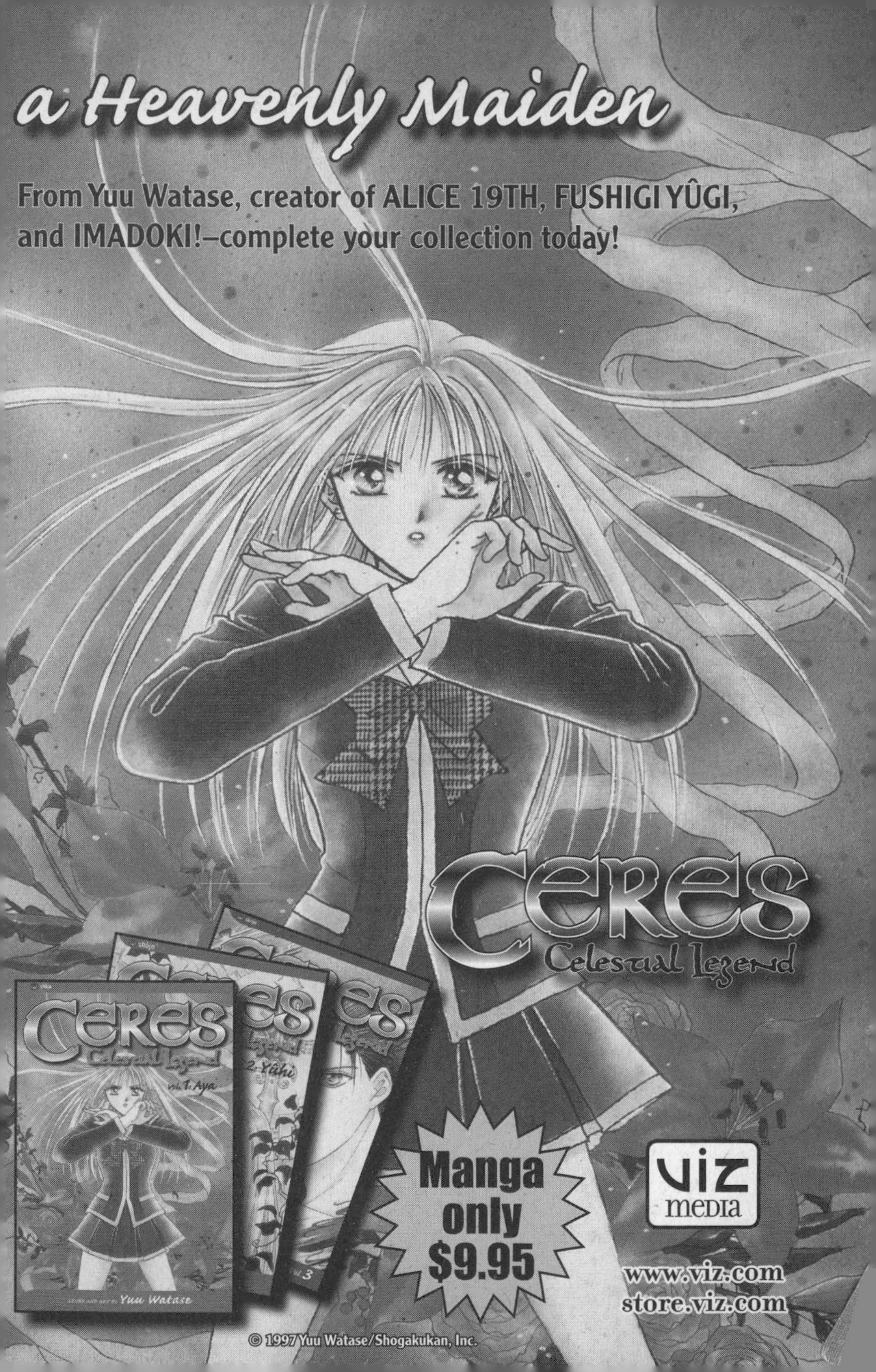
a Heavenly Maiden
From Yuu Watase, creator of ALICE 19TH, FUSHIGI YÛGI, and IMADOKI!—complete your collection today!
Ceres
Celestial Legend
Ceres
Celestial Legend
Yuu Watase
Manga only $9.95
viz media
www.viz.com
store.viz.com
© 1997 Yuu Watase/Shogakukan, Inc.

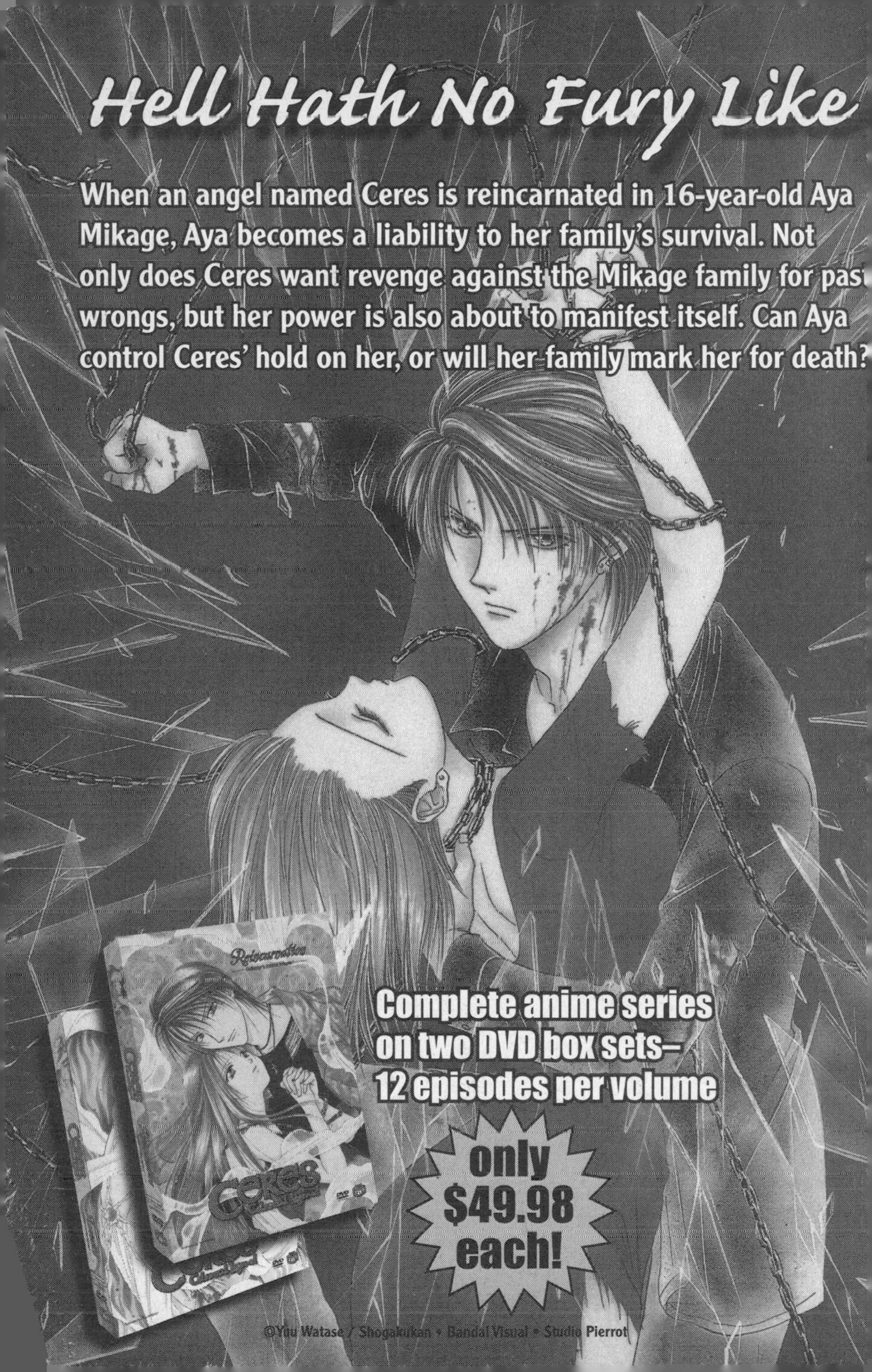
Hell Hath No Fury Like
When an angel named Ceres is reincarnated in 16-year-old Aya Mikage, Aya becomes a liability to her family's survival. Not only does Ceres want revenge against the Mikage family for past wrongs, but her power is also about to manifest itself. Can Aya control Ceres' hold on her, or will her family mark her for death?
Complete anime series on two DVD box sets– 12 episodes per volume
only $49.98 each!
©Yuu Watase / Shogakukan • Bandai Visual • Studio Pierrot

Sometimes Love is Just

Godai can barely pass his classes, hold a job, or keep a clean house. And when he falls in love with Kyoko, he's even more hopeless (some might say "clueless")! With romantic rivals, nosy neighbors, and hilarious misunderstandings, can Godai win the woman of his dreams?

Only $49.98 volume!

Collector's Edition DVD Box Sets

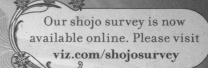